POCKET

WINE BUYER'S

GUIDE

DORLING KINDERSLEY
London•New York•Sydney•Moscow

A DORLING KINDERSLEY BOOK

First published in Great Britain in 1997
by Dorling Kindersley Limited,
9 Henrietta Street, London WC2E 8PS
Visit us on the World Wide Web at http://www.dk.com

A CIP catalogue second for this book is available
from the British Library.

ISBN 0 7513 0459 X

Printed and bound in Great Britain
by Bath Press Colourbooks, Glasgow.

CONTENTS

INTRODUCTION 5

THE INTERNATIONAL WINE CHALLENGE 6

WINES OF THE YEAR 10

THE TROPHIES 12

HOW TO USE THIS BOOK 18

THE WINES

Australia 19 • Austria 72

Eastern Europe 80 • England 86 • France 89

Germany 145 • Italy 48 • New Zealand 165

North America 182 • Portugal 204

South Africa 221 • South America 231

Spain 249 • Other Countries 266

WINES UNDER £5 & SPARKLING UNDER £10 271

STOCKISTS 280

TROPHY WINNERS AT A GLANCE 294

INDEX 296

INTRODUCTION

Buying wine today can be a terrifyingly confusing experience. Britain's biggest supermarkets, for example, each offer around 100 different wines made solely or partly from Chardonnay. Some come from reassuringly well-known regions or producers; others, however, may fail to ring even the faintest bell of recognition.

Besides, as most of us have discovered, when their corks are pulled, many of those well-known wines prove to be quite unworthy of their reputation.

– SORTING THE SHEEP FROM THE GOATS –

So, what's the answer? How can one improve the odds of getting a wine that tastes good and interesting and warrants its price tag? One solution would be to convene a group of experienced palates and get them to taste their way "blind" through the wines that are on offer. Why not, however, allow someone else to hold that tasting for you - in the shape of the annual International Wine Challenge.

Since its launch in 1983, WINE magazine's International WINE Challenge has become the world's leading, and most influential, wine competition. This year, it brought together some 6,700 wines and over 300 finely-tuned palates. The results of those tasters' efforts appear on the following pages in the form of the 1,700 winners, descriptions of how they taste, where to buy them and how much they should cost. All of which should help you to find your way around all those Chardonnays - and every other variety you care to mention!

THE CHALLENGE

The International WINE Challenge was created in 1984 by Robert Joseph, WINE's publishing editor, and Charles Metcalfe, associate editor, as the basis of an article which examined how English winemakers were doing compared to their counterparts in other countries. Neither had any idea at that stage that the Challenge would transform itself into the world's most international, most comprehensive and, increasingly, most respected wine competition. During the

Wine into words

past 13 years, the number of wines entered into the Challenge has grown from 38 to 6,700. The number of judges has risen from 20 to 350, and now includes many international wine makers who fly in specially for the event.

– GLOBAL COMPETITION –

Broken down to a basic level, the Challenge's success lies in two essential factors. The first is the support it receives from both the wine trade in this country and the wine producers elsewhere in the world; the second is the ruthless impartiality and organisation with which it is run.

During the past ten years, wines appearing in this country have become increasingly diverse, due mainly to wine retailers looking to attract the consumer. Wines from the former Soviet republic of Moldova now sit alongside Australian Chardonnay and German Gewürztraminer.

– THE LEVEL PLAYING FIELD –

However, the difficulty for retailers is that diversity is not enough; quality and value for money are the real selling points, especially to discerning British consumers. The same is true within the wine trade itself, where restaurateurs buying from importers are justly looking to make money from the wines they put on their lists. Consequently, both retail and wholesale merchants quickly recognised the need for a fair method of evaluating the wines on the market and, more importantly, for an effective mechanism of putting the results across to the wine drinker.

– ALL WINES ARE BORN EQUAL –

Thus their support for the International WINE Challenge began, and so it continues. Companies ranging from such retail giants as Safeway, Tesco and Marks & Spencer, retail chains such as Thresher, Wine Cellar and Victoria Wine, to specialist merchants such as Justerini & Brooks and Morris & Verdin all submit wines to compete on level terms.

Equally important is the support of such companies in the evaluation of Challenge wines, for it is their representatives who judge each and every wine. Buyers from these companies, renowned for their experience and accuracy,

The judges needed the odd diversion from time to time

together with winemakers from all over the world and Britain's most respected wine writers make up the tasting team which works so hard for the two weeks of the Challenge. It is their involvement that generates the unique trust in the results, and reinforces the care with which every entrant to the Challenge is examined.

– THE MACHINE STIRS TO LIFE –

The process begins in January, when entry kits are distributed to thousands of companies worldwide, inviting them to submit their wines. Within a few weeks, the replies start pouring in, detailing information on every wine to be tasted, such as the principle grape varieties used and the regions in which the grapes were grown.

Once this information is logged in, the entire Challenge team descends to the venue to begin receiving the wines themselves. Some are delivered by local companies; others are New World samples brought in specially by courier. During the following two weeks, 28,000 individual bottles are unpacked, labelled and coded.

– FLIGHTS OF FANCY –

Next comes the 'flighting': placing entries into groups of 12-18 wines. All wines within a group are similar in origin, variety and retail price so that they can be evaluated fairly

Wines are individually numbered and stored

among equals. This process normally takes the team of 24 Challenge helpers several days. Bottles are then inserted into special 'co-extruded' wine bags, tagged with tamper-proof seals, and boxed, ready for tasting. Sparkling wines are chilled, vintage ports decanted and wines with distinctive bottles transferred.

A team in action

– ALL WINES ARE BORN EQUAL –

It is now that the tasters arrive in droves, only to be split into tasting teams of five or six to tackle the wines. Flights are tasted, removed and recorded. Corked bottles are replaced within four minutes, and corks pulled at an alarming rate. Over 1,500 wines are tasted each day.

Lurking beneath is the less glamorous process of control. All results are double-checked; discarded wines are tasted once again by a 'Super Juror', an experienced and respected trade member or Master of Wine whose task it is to ensure no worthy wine slips the net. Tasting sheets proceed to the computer 'nerve-centre', where every result is recorded and double-checked. This information is used to create the flights for the second-round, where medals are awarded by a separate panel of judges. Attention to detail is meticulous: even the chlorine was removed from a nearby fountain to reduce the risk of contaminating smells!

– THE SPOILS –

After two weeks of frenetic activity, the medals are decided. This year, only 149 Gold Medals were awarded, indicating how harshly some of the best palates in the world judge some of the best wines in the world.

All of which helps to explain why, when you buy the winners listed in this book, you'll be drinking some of the tastiest, most interesting and best-value wines in the world.

WINES OF THE YEAR

The Wines of the Year are either Gold or Silver Medal wines which fit two crucial criteria: price (under £6 and £8 for table wines and under £12 for sparkling) and widespread availability.

– THE WHITES –

This year, the winners all shared the same grape variety. The tropically fruity Chilean **Trio Chardonnay 1996** from **Concha y Toro** was produced by superstar winemaker Ignacio Recabarren. The **Montana Reserve Chardonnay 1996** is a lovely example of new-wave New Zealand wine with real complexity. The Old World was represented too - The **Vigneti di Carama 1996** is richly oaky, and perfect for people who find New World Chardonnays a little too raucous.

– THE REDS –

There were four winners this year, representing a quartet of different styles and countries.

The Rhône was represented by the peppery **Domaine de Grande Bellane Côtes du Rhône Villages 1996**, while an even spicier wine - the **Maglieri McLaren Vale Shiraz 1995** – was a great example of what Australia can do with the Rhône's other red grape, the Syrah.

Alongside these, there were two exceptional wines from the Iberian Peninsula. The **Cosme Palacio y Hermanos Rioja Tinto 1995** owes much of its quality to the efforts of Bordeaux guru Michel Rolland, while the pair of award-winning plummy, oaky **Quinta do Crasto Douro 1995** and **1996** were made by Portuguese-based David Baverstock.

– THE FIZZ –

The fact that the rich, creamy **Brown Brothers Pinot Noir & Chardonnay** came from Australia was hardly surprising - the Aussies have, after all, produced several previous winners. Spain's Cavas have improved immeasurably in recent years too, as we discovered when we uncovered the smooth and refreshing **Segura Viudas Heredad Brut Reserva**. Happy drinking!

THE TROPHIES

Having tasted the wines and chosen the Gold Medal winners, the next task was to select supreme champions in each category.

The judges in this year's trophy tasting were, for the most part, the Super-Jurors who had toiled so hard during the Challenge. Among them were Paul Bastard of CWS Retail, Martin Everet MW, Justin Howard-Sneyd of Safeway, Jane Hunt MW, Keith Isaac MW, Tony Keys of the Australian Wine Bureau, Tony Laithwaite of Bordeaux Direct, Peter McCombie MW, Patrick McGrath MW, David Peppercorn MW, Liz Robertson MW, Derek Smedley MW and wine writers Joanna Simon, Tom Stevenson and Simon Woods.

Unlike other events, the judges were not constrained by the obligation to award a single Trophy in every category. From the outset, they were told to make awards only where they thought they were deserved.

The first trophy to be awarded in the white wine section was for CHARDONNAY, which brought recognition for a wine from New Zealand in the shape of the **Morton Estate Black Label Reserve 1995**. Combining ripe fruit with some of the subtlety usually associated with Europe, this outpointed top wines from both the New and Old World to win the prize

The New Zealanders were given further cause for celebration when the creamy gooseberryish **Villa Maria Wairau Valley Reserve 1996** walked off with the SAUVIGNON BLANC TROPHY, once again proving the Kiwis' mastery of this variety.

The AROMATIC TROPHY brought a surprise when it was discovered that the delicious lychheeish wine came, not from Alsace as the tasters had imagined, but from - yes, you guessed, New Zealand. When it was unveiled, the label revealed it to be the **Stonecroft Gewürztraminer 1996**.

The Old World fought back, however, with **Grans Fassian**'s

brilliant and unusual **Piesporter Goldtröpfchen Riesling 1992** which won the GERMAN WHITE & RIESLING TROPHY, and the **Domaine Zind-Humbrecht** which maintained its extraordinary prize-winning record at the Challenge by carrying off the DESSERT WINE TROPHY with the **Pinot d'Alsace 1995.**

When it came to the reds, the New World really showed its mettle. First off was the BORDEAUX & CABERNET/MERLOT TROPHY which, as last year, went to an Australian. The winner this time was the rich, ripe **Jacaranda Ridge Cabernet 1991**. Following on, the BURGUNDY & PINOT NOIR TROPHY travelled in the same direction, going to the delightful raspberyish **Tarrawarra Estate Pinot Noir 1995**. The Aussie hat-trick came with the RHONE & SHIRAZ/GRENACHE TROPHY which was won by the gloriously spicy **Maglieri Mclaren Vale Shiraz 1995**.

A lovely example of South Africa's "own" Pinotage grape – the **Jacana Pinotage Reserve 1995**, made in Stellenbosch by British-born Hugh Ryman –

won the SPICY RED TROPHY and the judges were sufficiently impressed by the **Château de Pibarnon 1993**, from Bandol to give it a FRENCH REGIONAL RED TROPHY.

There were no trophies for Spanish or Portuguese reds this year, but a stunning berryish Vino da Tavola from Italy, the **Umani Ronchi Pelago 1994** from the Marches was the unanimous winner of the ITALIAN RED TROPHY.

Another category confronted the judges with a dilemma: they found it almost impossible to choose between two sparkling wines that were equally highly marked.. Ultimately, justice was done by giving both wines prizes - the **Champagne le Brun de Neuville Non Vintage Rosé** winning a specially created ROSE CHAMPAGNE & SPARKLING WINE TROPHY, while the **Blanc des Millenaires 1985** from **Champagne Charles Heidsieck** took the overall SPARKLING WINE TROPHY

The fortified wines as usual yielded a fascinating set of wines, including the intense **McWilliam's Liqueur Muscat Show Series** which claimed the FORTIFIED MUSCAT TROPHY,

and followed the same producer's success with this award last year.

The PORT TROPHY went to an extraordinary wine, **the Quinta do Noval Colheita 1937**, a wonderfully marmaladey Tawny that shows how well port can mature in wood rather than bottle. The SHERRY TROPHY was won by another wood-aged wine with lovely rich, fresh nutty flavours, **Sandeman's Royal Coregidor Rare Rich Oloroso** which was fine enough to be awarded the overall FORTIFIED TROPHY.

Finally, the judges had to decide which trophy winners would receive the overall white and red wine trophies. The WHITE WINE TROPHY went to **the Grans Fassian Piesporter Riesling 1992**, while the RED WINE TROPHY was claimed by the **Umani Ronchi Pelago 1994.**

So, an almost perfect spilt in honours between the New and Old Worlds. Champagne still dominates the sparkling section, distinctive regional wines continue to impress and stand out from the crowd and the new-comers futher impose on the established order.

THE
WINES

HOW TO USE THIS BOOK

Every wine in this guide has been awarded a medal at the **1997 International Wine Challenge**. The winning wines are listed by country and region, with up to seven wine headings: red, white, sweet white, rosé, sparkling, sparkling rosé and fortified.

Under each heading the wines are listed in price order, from the least to the most expensive. Each wine carries the same range of information: the wine name (and vintage where applicable), the tasting note, the average retail price, the code for stockists (*see* page 280), and the medal the wine was awarded. Below is an example of how wines are listed.

			The Medal:
The wine name, vintage and region	*The average retail price*		*G Gold, S Silver, or B Bronze*
CHATEAU REYNELLA SHIRAZ 1995, BRL HARDY WINE CO. South Australia	*A concentrated, complex wine demonstrating wonderful black olive and mocha characteristics.*	£9.10	DBY W VLW IVY NEI VDV A	(G)

The tasting note provided by Challenge tasters.   *Codes for stockists (see page 242)*

The following colours are used in the book to highlight gold and silver medal winners and the Wines of the Year:

Gold medal winners are shaded gold.	*Silver medal winners are shaded silver.*	*This colour denotes a Wine of the Year.*

AUSTRALIA

From the cool climate vineyards of Tasmania, to the baked valleys of the Hunter, Australia produces an increasing diversity of red, white, sparkling and dessert wines which are steadily becoming models for wine producers the world over. Subtle styles are becoming part of the wine-makers' ethos, resulting in increasing regional variations. This means Australian wines will go from strength to strength.

AUSTRALIA • CABERNET SAUVIGNON

KANARIE CREEK CABERNET SHIRAZ NV, ANGOVES PTY. LTD. South Australia	*Elegant, blackcurrant aromas precede juicy fruits on the palate, with fresh acidity on the lengthy finish.*	**£4.00**	WRT	(B)
CO-OP AUSTRALIAN CABERNET SAUVIGNON 1995, ANGOVES PTY. LTD. South Australia	*Prominent 'ribena' aromas lead to a lengthy, smooth, black-currant palate with a spicy, warm finish.*	**£4.50**	CWS	(B)
STOCKMANS BRIDGE CABERNET SHIRAZ 1995, SOUTHCORP WINES South Australia	*Rich, succulent, spicy fruit nose, with lots of chocolate and well-rounded berry fruit on the palate.*	**£5.00**	U	(S)
YALUMBA OXFORD LANDING CABERNET SHIRAZ 1996, YALUMBA WINERY South Australia	*A fruity nose of cherry and plum with a softly balanced palate of rich, succulent fruit.*	**£5.20**	Widely Available	(B)
ANGOVE'S CLASSIC RESERVE CABERNET SAUVIGNON 1995, ANGOVE'S PTY LTD. South Australia	*Showing some age, this wine displayed jammy blackcurrant aromas with a spicy fruit palate.*	**£5.20**	MWW CHF HOU	(B)

SAFEWAY AUSTRALIAN OAKED CABERNET SAUVIGNON 1996, BRL HARDY South Australia	*Intense nose of summer fruits with vanilla notes. A light palate with fine, balanced tannins.*	**£5.30**	SAF	**B**
KINGSTON ESTATE CABERNET SAUVIGNON 1994, KINGSTON ESTATE South Australia	*Spicy, herbal nose with eucalypt, oak and chocolate notes. A huge mouthful of sweet, juicy cassis fruit.*	**£6.00**	NEI WWI VNO GLY	**S**
TESCO COONAWARRA CABERNET SAUVIGNON, RYMILL COONAWARRA WINES South Australia	*Intense, spicy nose with vegetal, cigar box and oak notes. Complex, concentrated, fruit flavours with integrated oak.*	**£6.00**	TO	**S**
IRONSTONE CABERNET SHIRAZ 1995, IRONSTONE VINEYARDS Western Australia	*The palate explodes with lingering, well-balanced flavours and displays impressive integrated oak and tannin.*	**£6.20**	Widely Available	**G**
MARIENBERG CABERNET SAUVIGNON 1993, MARIENBERG WINE CO South Australia	*A rich Christmas cake nose with tobacco notes; rounded, ripe and herbal with soft fruits on the lingering palate.*	**£6.70**	CPW TMW CMI	**S**
TATACHILLA PARTNERS CABERNET SAUVIGNON SHIRAZ 1996, TATACHILLA WINERY South Australia	*The oaky tannins are smooth and show complexity up to a long, lingering finish displaying excellent fruit.*	**£6.80**	BD	**G**
MONTROSE CABERNET SAUVIGNON 1994, ORLANDO WYNDHAM GROUP New South Wales	*Warm, spicy nose with rich, berry fruit and cedar notes. Intense, complex, lingering, palate of black fruits.*	**£6.90**	DBY AMW DIO JCK WTR PEA SEL	**S**
DEEN DE BORTOLI VAT 9 CABERNET SAUVIGNON 1995, DE BORTOLI WINES Victoria	*Intense aromas of black-currants with herbal, eucalypt and spice notes carried over onto a concentrated palate.*	**£7.00**	IVY OWL LEA SCK	**B**

PENFOLDS CLARE VALLEY CABERNET SHIRAZ 1995, PENFOLDS South Australia	*A rich, balanced wine with well-structured tannin, that shows a good maturing potential.*	£7.10	Widely Available	(B)
ROSEMOUNT ESTATE CABERNET SAUVIGNON 1995, ROSEMOUNT ESTATES New South Wales	*Concentrated ripe, herbaceous, cassis fruit on the nose and a palate of intense, structured and complex fruit.*	£7.20	Widely Available	(S)
D'ARENBERG THE HIGH TRELLIS CABERNET 1995, D'ARENBERG WINES South Australia	*Intensely concentrated colour and dense, fruity, spice aromas. Big tannins on the palate show promise.*	£7.40	CHF VDV	(S)
MAGLIERI MCLAREN VALE CABERNET MERLOT 1993, MAGLIERI WINES South Australia	*Berry fruit aromas with rich, new oak carries over to a sweet, creamy berry palate.*	£7.50	TO BWG U	(B)
TATACHILLA CABERNET SAUVIGNON 1995, TATACHILLA WINERY South Australia	*Intense aroma of ripe plums. Cigar box and spice characters are mirrored on the smooth, concentrated palate.*	£7.50	W	(S)
CHÂTEAU TAHBILK CABERNET SAUVIGNON 1992, TAHBILK WINES Victoria	*Summer fruits and mint on the nose followed by a suave, well-structured palate.*	£7.70	DBY CRS VDV	(B)
PETER LEHMANN CABERNET SAUVIGNON 1995, PETER LEHMANN WINES South Australia	*Ripe fruit nose with oaky, eucalypt nuances. Concentrated black fruit-gum flavour, with creamy blueberry hints.*	£7.70	Widely Available	(S)
LEASINGHAM DOMAINE CABERNET MALBEC 1995, BRL HARDY South Australia	*Fresh, clean fruit with green herbaceous characters and cherries. A balanced palate.*	£7.80	Widely Available	(B)

TIM KNAPPSTEIN CABERNET MERLOT 1995, TIM KNAPPSTEIN WINES South Australia	*Powerful, soft spearmint and fruit nose followed by big ripe, herbal fruit flavours with a wonderfully warm finish.*	£7.90	TP VDV WCS	**B**
MAGLIERI CABERNET SAUVIGNON 1995, MAGLIERI WINES South Australia	*Lots of powerful new oak and spicy fruit on this wine's nose and balanced palate.*	£7.90	U PLB	**B**
TIM KNAPPSTEIN CABERNET MERLOT 1994, TIM KNAPPSTEIN WINES South Australia	*Ripe fruit aromas with berry and herbal hints carrying over onto an intense, smoky palate.*	£7.90	MM TP WMK VDV WCS	**S**
BENDIGO CABERNET SAUVIGNON 1995, WATER WHEEL VINEYARDS Victoria	*Rich, concentrated cassis aromas on the nose follow through to the firm, structured palate.*	£8.00	AUC SOM RD	**B**
MORRIS CABERNET SAUVIGNON 1994, ORLANDO WYNDHAM GROUP Victoria	*Strawberries and berry fruits on the nose lead to a mouth-filling, jammy palate with a minty, fresh finish.*	£8.00	AMW VDV CEN DIO JCK WTR PEA	**S**
KRONDORF SHOW RESERVE CABERNET SAUVIGNON 1994, KRONDORF WINERY South Australia	*Deep colour; concentrated fruit and integrated oak aromas. Opulent strawberry flavours and eucalypt notes.*	£8.40	DIR HW SV GS GRO	**B**
GOUNDREY CABERNET MERLOT 1995, GOUNDREY WINES Western Australia	*Intense, berried nose with oak hints and sweet, ripe currant fruits. Vanilla hints on the lingering palate.*	£8.50	PAV BOO HW TP GRT IVY ALL SWS	**B**
YALUMBA "THE MENZIES" 1993, YALUMBA WINERY South Australia	*Strong redcurrant and bramble aromas on a large nose. Long palate of ripe fruits.*	£8.70	DBY JN VDV GRA FRT	**S**

Wine	Description	Price	Stockists	
RYMILL CABERNET SAUVIGNON 1994, RYMILL COONAWARRA WINES South Australia	*Intense mint and cassis aromas with eucalyptus highlights and vibrant berry flavours. A smoky, earthy complexity.*	£8.70	PLB VDV HVW WBE	G
ST. HALLETT CABERNET MERLOT 1995, ST. HALLETT WINES South Australia	*Ripe, concentrated fruit aromas lead onto a balanced palate of cassis with creamy new oak.*	£8.80	JS DBY CWI AUC HVW RD HN ADN	B
PENFOLDS BIN 407 CABERNET SAUVIGNON 1994, PENFOLDS South Australia	*Minty, mulberry nose. Hints of chocolate with a concentrated palate of well-structured fruit and dense tannins.*	£8.80	Widely Available	S
GRANT BURGE CABERNET SAUVIGNON 1995, GRANT BURGE WINES South Australia	*A rich blackcurrant and vanilla nose leads into juicy black fruits and firm, balanced tannins.*	£8.80	DBY CNL GGW VLW FUL GNW	S
THISTLE HILL CABERNET SAUVIGNON 1992, THISTLE HILL VINEYARDS New South Wales	*Powerful gamey, savoury notes lead through to a figgy bouquet. A dense palate of ripe black fruits and cedar.*	£8.80	VR	S
CHÂTEAU REYNELLA CABERNET SAUVIGNON MERLOT 1995, BRL HARDY South Australia	*Rich cedar and berry nose with fruits-of-the-forest flavours on a smoky, spicy palate.*	£8.90	DBY VLW TO A CWS VDV SAF JS	B
YALDARA 'JULIANS' CABERNET MERLOT 1995, YALDARA WINES South Australia	*Deep plum, sweet oak and eucalypt aromas on a palate with creamy, jammy flavours.*	£9.00	SWS	B
BUXTON CABERNET MERLOT 1993, HILLSTOWE WINERY South Australia	*Distinctive eucalypt and black fruit nose. A medium-bodied palate with deep fruit and sandalwood flavours.*	£9.00	MK TW MYS	S

TIM KNAPPSTEIN CABERNET SAUVIGNON 1994, TIM KNAPPSTEIN WINES South Australia	*Intense colour and spicy 'ribena' nose has sweet berry and vanilla flavours with cinnamon .*	**£9.00**	OD	(S)
BRANDS LAIRA CABERNET MERLOT 1994, McWILLIAMS WINES South Australia	*Intense aromas of tobacco, pine and plum fruit followed by soft, spicy blackcurrant and vanilla.*	**£9.00**	CDT	(G)
ROUGE HOMME CABERNET SAUVIGNON 1993, ROUGE HOMME WINERY South Australia	*Rich blackberry aromas, fresh redcurrant flavours and hints of cedary leather on a lingering, warm palate.*	**£9.10**	Widely Available	(B)
VASSE FELIX CABERNET MERLOT 1995, VASSE FELIX WINES Western Australia	*Dense plum nose and minty oak notes followed by complex fruit flavours and fresh tannins.*	**£9.10**	TAN RBS CPW VDV BEN	(B)
HARDY'S COONAWARRA CABERNET SAUVIGNON 1994, BRL HARDY South Australia	*Light, jammy, mint and chocolate aromas lead to a fruit-driven palate with a sweet finish.*	**£9.10**	DBY VLW FUL IVY CWS WMK VDV SAF	(B)
BEST'S GREAT WESTERN CABERNET SAUVIGNON 1993, BEST'S WINES Victoria	*The aromas of capsicums and juicy plums are reflected in this real mouthful of a wine.*	**£9.20**	Widely Available	(B)
INGLEWOOD SHOW RESERVE CABERNET SAUVIGNON 1995, INGLEWOOD VINEYARDS New South Wales	*Intense blackcurranty, coconut nose. Integrated palate of concentrated cassis, sandalwood and eucalypt. A serious wine.*	**£9.30**	HW SV	(G)
MIRANDA GREY SERIES CABERNET SAUVIGNON 1994, MIRANDA WINES South Australia	*The fruity vanilla nose is followed by a balanced palate of oak and ripe, stewed plums.*	**£9.40**	BD	(B)

AUSTRALIA • RED • CABERNET SAUVIGNON

STONIERS CABERNET SAUVIGNON 1994, STONIERS WINERY Victoria	*Pungent eucalyptus fruit and pepper aromas lead to a sweet cherry, menthol and vanilla palate of great warmth.*	£9.50	DIR WAW CRM GNW PV HOL	**B**
BARWANG CABERNET SAUVIGNON 1994, McWILLIAM'S WINES New South Wales	*The delicate spicy nose is followed by ripe fruit and sweet oak on the medium-weight palate.*	£9.50	SWI	**B**
YALUMBA "THE SIGNATURE" 1993, YALUMBA WINERY South Australia	*Deep ruby with ripe fruits, marzipan and eucalypt notes. Concentrated mulberry flavours go on and on!*	£9.70	DBY JN VDV OD GRA FRT	**S**
BEST'S GREAT WESTERN CABERNET SAUVIGNON 1994, BEST'S WINES Victoria	*Intense, jammy fruit nose with concentrated flavours of ripe, red fruits and eucalypt. Soft tannins.*	£9.80	DBY BOO TP GRT IVY U COK SWS	**B**
CHAPEL HILL CABERNET SAUVIGNON 1993, CHAPEL HILL WINES South Australia	*Aromatic black fruit and oak on the nose with good balance and firm tannins on the palate.*	£9.80	TH DBY TO AUC NRW	**B**
CABERNET SAUVIGNON 1994, WYNNS COONAWARRA ESTATE South Australia	*Ripe, dark fruit and light oak aromas with concentrated black cherry flavours on a smooth, balanced palate.*	£9.90	Widely Available	**B**
MOUNT HELEN CABERNET MERLOT 1995, TISDALL WINES Victoria	*Sweet, berry fruit; almost raisiny aromas with intense black fruits on a persistent palate.*	£10.00	HW	**B**
CHÂTEAU REYNELLA CABERNET SAUVIGNON 1995, BRL HARDY South Australia	*Strong aromas of ripe, dark fruits are followed by concentrated rich, cassis fruit flavours.*	£10.00	IVY VDV SAF JMC	**B**

CHÂTEAU REYNELLA CABERNET SAUVIGNON 1994, BRL HARDY South Australia	*Perfumed aromas of mint, oak, eucalypt and liquorice lead into a ripe loganberry palate.*	£10.00	IVY WMK VDV SAF JMC	(S)
ROSEMOUNT SHOW RESERVE CABERNET SAUVIGNON 1994, ROSEMOUNT ESTATES New South Wales	*Intense, ripe blackcurrant, cigar box aromas and powerful flavours of cedar, summer fruits and fresh cream.*	£10.10	DBY LNR HOU TO	(S)
VICTORIA RESERVE CABERNET SAUVIGNON 1994, MITCHELTON VINTNERS Victoria	*Intense ruby red colour, rich, minty, eucalypt nose; concentrated palate of black fruits.*	£10.20	SHG BC BOO W WMK WCS MTL ROD	(S)
MIRANDA GREY SERIES CABERNETS 1995, MIRANDA ROVALLEY South Australia	*Attractive mint and mulberry nose with oak highlights leading to creamy, summer fruit pudding flavours.*	£10.30	BD	(S)
WOLF BLASS PRESIDENT'S SELECTION CABERNET SAUVIGNON 1994, MILDARA BLASS South Australia	*Up-front blueberry fruit on the nose with a powerful, elongated, oak and fruit palate.*	£10.40	Widely Available	(B)
PLANTAGENET CABERNET SAUVIGNON 1994, PLANTAGENET WINES Western Australia	*Deep, dark, sweet plummy fruit on the nose and palate with lashings of blackcurrant flavours.*	£11.00	GI NAD BBR WSO	(B)
DE BORTOLI CABERNET MERLOT 1992, DE BORTOLI WINES Victoria	*Intense, deep colour with complex fruit nose; herbaceous, with eucalypt reflected in the lingering palate.*	£11.00	DBY IVY HVW SCK	(S)

Pinpoint who sells the wine you wish to buy by turning to the stockist codes. If you know the name of the wine you want to buy, use the alphabetical index. If the price is your motivation, refer to the invaluable price guide index; red and white wines under £5, sparkling wines under £10 and champagne under £15. Happy hunting!

COLDSTREAM HILLS CABERNET SAUVIGNON 1994, COLDSTREAM HILLS Victoria	*Solid fruit aromas with hints of minty eucalypt carried over onto the full-bodied palate.*	**£11.40**	DBY VDV OD	(B)
KATNOOK ESTATE COONAWARRA CABERNET SAUVIGNON 1995, WINGARA WINES South Australia	*Dark fruit aromas with nuances of marzipan and cedar. Intense flavours of mulberries, cherries and plums.*	**£11.50**	BI WIN VW	(B)
SKILLOGALEE 'THE CABERNETS' 1994, SKILLOGALEE WINES South Australia	*Concentrated aromas of forest fruits, new oak, cedar and eucalypt. A mouthful of ripe, minty, blackcurrants.*	**£11.70**	DIR NY ENO	(G)
CHAPEL HILL 'THE VICAR' 1994, CHAPEL HILL WINES South Australia	*Vanilla and plum aromas front this excellent big, oaky wine with huge, juicy fruit.*	**£12.00**	TH AUC WR BU	(G)
ROSEMOUNT ESTATE ORANGE CABERNET SAUVIGNON 1993, ROSEMOUNT ESTATES New South Wales	*A delicious wine with mature, herbal, blackcurrant, vanilla and cedar aromas and flavours. Good balance.*	**£12.20**	LNR HOU M&S FTH BWC	(B)
STONIER'S RESERVE CABERNET SAUVIGNON 1993, STONIERS WINERY Victoria	*Intense, spicy, herbaceous, fruit aromas. Oaky violet notes carry over onto a powerful fruit-packed palate of some length.*	**£12.20**	DIR WAW PV	(S)
LINDEMANS ST GEROGE CABERNET SAUVIGNON 1993, LINDEMANS WINES South Australia	*Ripe, fruit aromas with hints of tar and mint. Blackcurrants and oak on a lengthy palate.*	**£12.60**	Widely Available	(B)
VASSE FELIX CABERNET SAUVIGNON 1995, VASSE FELIX WINES Western Australia	*Up-front flavours of concentrated black fruits follow a sweet nougat and baked-fruit nose.*	**£12.90**	RBS CPW VDV BEN TAN	(B)

McGuigan Brothers Personal Reserve Cabernet Sauvignon 1995 South Australia	*Jammy, herbaceous nose with clean, concentrated plummy, black fruit flavours on the palate.*	£13.00	IVY VNO GLY P&R JAG	B
Petaluma Coonawarra 1994, Petaluma Wines South Australia	*Mossy, earthy nose with hints of eucalypt, oak and cedar; develops delicious fruit flavours on a balanced palate.*	£13.40	TP BEN	S
Xanadu Cabernet Sauvignon 1995, Château Xanadu Western Australia	*Deep colour and minty, blackcurrant, oak nose; fruit impressed, as did the long cedary flavours.*	£13.50	DIR	S
Keyneton Estate 1994, Henschke Cellars South Australia	*A very intense, classy wine with a leathery nose, fine tannins and good length.*	£14.00	Widely Available	S
Leasingham Classic Clare Cabernet Sauvignon 1994, BRL Hardy South Australia	*Blackcurrant and herbaceous notes on the nose. Impressive palate of oak and concentrated cassis flavours.*	£14.00	VWC DBY VLW VDV VW JHL	S
Leasingham Classic Clare Cabernet Sauvignon 1995, BRL Hardy South Australia	*Mint, vanilla and berry fruit on the nose. Concentrated flavours on the long, complex, balanced palate.*	£15.30	VWC VLW VDV VW JHL	S
Penley Estate Cabernet Sauvignon 1993, Penley Estate South Australia	*Big, black colour with dense fruit and oak flavours on the nose and long palate.*	£15.80	DBY L&W NY AUC VDV	B
Mountadam "The Red" 1994, Mountadam Vineyards South Australia	*A spicy, herbal nose with overt oak developing a mature and excellently integrated palate.*	£16.10	NY CWI P TO HVW	B

Wine	Tasting Notes	Price	Stockists	
THOMAS HARDY CABERNET SAUVIGNON 1993, BRL HARDY South Australia	*Aromas of chocolate, ripe blackcurrants, mint and capsicum were reflected in huge, intense flavours.*	£16.30	DBY VLW VDV TO MAK	G
PENLEY ESTATE CABERNET SAUVIGNON 1994, PENLEY ESTATE South Australia	*Delicate fruit and violets on the nose; cedar notes, silky-soft palate with good balance.*	£17.70	DIR MFS VDV	S
JACARANDA RIDGE CABERNET SAUVIGNON 1989, ORLANDO WYNDHAM GROUP South Australia	*Oak, vanilla and black fruit bouquet leading to sweet, dried flavours on the palate.*	£18.20	Widely Available	B
JACARANDA RIDGE CABERNET SAUVIGNON 1991, ORLANDO WYNDHAM GROUP South Australia	*Nose packed with luscious fruit and minty eucalypt; masses of elegant, spicy fruit on the long palate.*	£18.20	Widely Available	G
SHADNACH CABERNET SAUVIGNON 1993, GRANT BURGE WINES South Australia	*This dark ruby-purple wine has earthy, vegetal aromas, followed by a blackcurrant palate.*	£19.50	Widely Available	B
PIERRO CABERNETS 1994, PIERRO VINEYARDS Western Australia	*A powerful wine with liquorice and fruit aromas, soft berries and creamy mint on the lingering palate.*	£20.00	BBR	G
RAVENSWOOD CABERNET SAUVIGNON 1993, HOLLICK WINES South Australia	*Minty, eucalypt aromas with hints of oak. Concentrated blackcurrant flavours and a clean, fresh finish.*	£20.60	L&W NY JN VDV HVW	S
CYRIL HENSCHKE CABERNET SAUVIGNON 1993, HENSCHKE CELLARS South Australia	*A sweet, jammy blackcurrant aroma with peppery, black fruits on the soft, round palate.*	£24.40	DBY DIR L&W NY JN COK VDV	B

PENFOLDS BIN 707 CABERNET SAUVIGNON 1994, PENFOLDS South Australia	*Inky-black colour, rich nose of spices, tobacco and intense black-currants. Tannins show great potential.*	£29.50	Widely Available	(S)
JOHN RIDDOCH CABERNET SAUVIGNON 1994, WYNNS COONAWARRA ESTATE South Australia	*Amazing purple, with a fantastic concentration of fruit on nose and palate. Will age exceptionally well.*	£30.00	Widely Available	(S)

AUSTRALIA • SHIRAZ

KINGSTON PRINT SHIRAZ MATARO 1996, KINGSTON ESTATE South Australia	*Deceptively full and ripe on the nose. Quite a lean wine with some powerful flavours.*	£4.00	IVY CWS WWI VNO H+W BTH	(B)
TESCO AUSTRALIAN SHIRAZ CABERNET, South Australia	*A very old-world style wine of medium body with a nice, sweet finish.*	£4.30	TO	(B)
KINGSTON ESTATE JARRAH RIDGE SHIRAZ MATARO 1995, KINGSTON ESTATE South Australia	*A lighter style of wine; fresh and uncomplicated with hints of oak on the juicy palate.*	£4.80	Widely Available	(B)
DEAKIN ESTATE SHIRAZ 1996, WINGARA WINES Victoria	*An easy-drinking, oaky style of wine low in tannins with spicy, peppery, plummy fruit.*	£5.20	VWC BI GGW CHF VW	(B)
CRANSWICK ESTATE SHIRAZ 1995, CRANSWICK ESTATES New South Wales	*A relatively light Shiraz style displaying balanced aromas of ripe peppers and soft berry fruits.*	£6.00	VWC	(B)

SALTRAM CLASSIC SHIRAZ 1996, SALTRAM WINE ESTATES South Australia	*A ripe, round, spicy and fragrant wine, very warm and soft. Firm on the palate and very appealing.*	**£6.10**	DBY GRT IVY COK PMA NRW LLV	(B)
MARIENBERG SHIRAZ 1993, MARIENBERG WINE CO South Australia	*A slightly red-brown wine; classy and complex, soft and rich, with a cedar nose.*	**£6.40**	CPW CMI	(B)
PENFOLDS KOONUNGA HILL SHIRAZ CABERNET 1995, PENFOLDS South Australia	*An easy drinking wine with peppery hints on the nose and blackcherry fruit on the palate.*	**£6.50**	Widely Available	(B)
HARDY'S BANKSIDE SHIRAZ 1995, BRL HARDY South Australia	*Deep purple in colour, this is a peppery wine which is relatively easy on the palate.*	**£6.50**	Widely Available	(B)
PETER LEHMANN SHIRAZ 1995, PETER LEHMANN WINES South Australia	*A firm, well-balanced Shiraz showing well-integrated wood and sweet fruit flavours.*	**£6.60**	DBY W BOO CR GDS CHF VDV OD G&M	(S)
YALDARA RESERVE SHIRAZ 1996, YALDARA WINES South Australia	*Rich tobacco aromas lead on to a warm, strong palate with strong mint and fruit flavours.*	**£6.70**	Widely Available	(B)
HAMILTON RIDGE SHIRAZ 1995, PETER LEHMANN WINES South Australia	*A purple, oaky and rich wine, quite delicate with a spicy, lifted nose. A fine, fruity finish.*	**£6.80**	BD	(S)
WYNNS COONAWARRA ESTATE SHIRAZ 1995, WYNNS COONAWARRA ESTATE South Australia	*A chocolatey, concentrated red wine with a spicy nose and a very good finish. A good New World example.*	**£6.90**	Widely Available	(B)

MOCULTA SHIRAZ 1995, BRL HARDY South Australia	*A fruity, peppery nose precedes a palate of sweet oak and rich, creamy vanilla flavours.*	£6.90	DBY VLW FUL TO BRP JMC	**G**
TESCO SHIRAZ 1995, MAGLIERI WINES South Australia	*A light, spicy wine offering a soft finish to a peppered, ripe fruit on the palate with a full finish.*	£7.00	TO	**B**
RIDDOCH SHIRAZ 1995, WINGARA WINES South Australia	*Tarry and spicy, a lighter style of wine with good juicy cherry and lush plum fruit.*	£7.20	TH BI GGW CHF VDV NRW	**B**
D'ARENBERG THE OLD VINE SHIRAZ 1995, D'ARENBERG WINES South Australia	*A dark, slightly rustic wine with spicy, dusty fruit, good acid and firm tannins.*	£7.20	CHF POR VDV	**B**
STONYFELL METALA SHIRAZ CABERNET 1994, SALTRAM WINE ESTATES South Australia	*The eucalyptus and minty fruit on the nose is backed up with good weighty concentration.*	£7.40	Widely Available	**B**
BRIDGEWATER MILL SHIRAZ 1994, PETALUMA WINES South Australia	*A modern style of wine with minty aromas and rich, spicy flavours dominating the palate.*	£7.40	CLA WMK	**B**
THE WILLOWS SHIRAZ 1994, WILLOWS VINEYARD South Australia	*Lovely, spicy fruits can be found in abundance on a complex and firm palate following through.*	£7.50	TH MTL AUC WR BU	**G**
BEST'S VICTORIA SHIRAZ 1996, BEST'S WINES Victoria	*A full, rich-structured, complex wine with some fresh, ripe fruit and considerable length.*	£7.60	Widely Available	**B**

ST. HALLETT BAROSSA SHIRAZ 1994, ST. HALLETT WINES South Australia	*A rich, spicy wine with a lovely, warm nose and a moderately complex palate and a good finish.*	£7.80	TH AUC HVW BU WR	(B)
LEASINGHAM DOMAINE SHIRAZ 1995, BRL HARDY South Australia	*A massive wine with a new oak nose that is packed with fruit and tannins. Wonderfully smooth on the palate.*	£7.90	Widely Available	(S)
WATER WHEEL VINEYARDS SHIRAZ 1995, WATER WHEEL VINEYARDS Victoria	*Rich and ripe - a wine with nice, spicy, peppery fruit and grippy tannins. Firm and fruity.*	£8.00	AUC SOM RD	(B)
MOUNT HURTLE SHIRAZ 1994, MOUNT HURTLE South Australia	*An attractive damson nose follows onto this wine's medium-weight but balanced palate.*	£8.00	WMK SAF	(B)
BASEDOW SHIRAZ 1995, BASEDOW WINES South Australia	*A complex, well-integrated wine with a long finish showing rich, juicy fruit and oak.*	£8.00	Widely Available	(S)
MOUNT HURTLE SHIRAZ 1994, MOUNT HURTLE South Australia	*A delicious medium-weight wine with spicy fruit and oaky overtones on the palate.*	£8.00	SAF	(S)
ST. HALLETT FAITH SHIRAZ 1995, ST. HALLETT WINES South Australia	*This fabulously coloured, rich, minty Shiraz shows excellent complex, intense and persistent fruit flavours.*	£8.00	TO AUC	(G)
MAGLIERI MCLAREN VALE SHIRAZ 1994, MAGLIERI WINES South Australia	*A peppery, fruity wine with a complex, meaty nose and good tannins and balancing acidity.*	£8.10	RAE TO PLB BWG U	(B)

MAGLIERI MCLAREN VALE SHIRAZ 1995, MAGLIERI WINES South Australia	*An ebullient wine with a very New World, intense, minty nose, sweet fruit and good length*	£8.10	RAE TO U PLB	**G** WINE OF THE YEAR
STONYFELL METALA SHIRAZ CABERNET 1995, SALTRAM WINE ESTATES South Australia	*A pleasant, deep garnet wine that mixes juicy fruit with firm acidity and gentle tannins.*	£8.30	DBY W COK NRW SAF MFS	**B**
SEPPELT CHALAMBAR SHIRAZ 1994, SEPPELT South Australia	*A young, deeply-coloured, oaked wine with a fragrant nose and intense ripe fruit.*	£8.30	DBY WSG BOO POR VDV OD	**S**
BOTOBOLAR SHIRAZ 1994, BOTOBOLAR VINEYARDS New South Wales	*A concentrated wine with a lovely ripe, oaky nose, fleshy cherry fruit flavours and big tannins.*	£8.40	VR VDV	**B**
DENNIS SHIRAZ 1994, PETER DENNIS South Australia	*A heady, vibrant, well-balanced wine with solid big flavours and a great finish.*	£8.50	THP	**B**
WARBURN ESTATE SHOW RESERVE SHIRAZ 1996, COOPER COUNTY WINES New South Wales	*An outstanding wine demonstrating very complex and wonderfully chocolatey, spicy, rich, ripe fruit characters.*	£8.70	BD	**G**
PENFOLDS BIN 28 KALIMNA SHIRAZ 1994, PENFOLDS South Australia	*A deeply coloured wine with a baked fruit nose and a chewy character with plenty of elegance.*	£8.90	Widely Available	**B**
CHAPEL HILL SHIRAZ 1995, CHAPEL HILL WINES South Australia	*A long wine with good spicy, peppery fruit; quite heavily oaked but not overly so.*	£9.00	TH TO AUC	**B**

LITTLE'S SHIRAZ 1992, LITTLE'S WINERY New South Wales	*An intense, concentrated wine packed with peppered fruit, smoky bacon and ripe tannins.*	£9.00	CFN	(B)
BOBBIE BURNS RUTHERGLEN SHIRAZ 1995, CAMPBELLS Victoria	*Fresh and fruity, this young wine has good fruit and a tough long-lasting finish.*	£9.00	Widely Available	(S)
CAPEL VALE SHIRAZ 1995, CAPEL VALE WINES Western Australia	*A well-balanced complex wine showing soft fruit, some maturity and good use of oak.*	£9.00	MJW WRW	(S)
TIM ADAMS SHIRAZ 1995, TIM ADAMS WINES South Australia	*A cedary, concentrated, well-balanced Shiraz with a spicy, peppery nose and palate.*	£9.00	TO AUC	(S)
TISDALL MOUNT IDA SHIRAZ 1995, TISDALL Victoria	*An outstandingly well-made, deep ruby wine of excellent structure, weight and length.*	£9.10	PAV BNK HW OD	(G)
CHATEAU REYNELLA SHIRAZ 1995, BRL HARDY South Australia	*A concentrated, deeply flavoured, complex wine demonstrating wonderful black olive and mocha characteristics.*	£9.10	DBY W VLW IVY NEI VDV A	(G)
LINDEMANS HUNTER VALLEY SHIRAZ 1991, LINDEMANS South Australia	*A peppery wine with damson fruit and ripe black cherries on the palate.*	£9.20	MWW HOU WWI	(B)
PEPPER TREE SHIRAZ RESERVE 1996, PEPPER TREE WINES South Australia	*A deep and intense young wine with a great colour and a big oaky fruit palate.*	£9.20	CPW	(B)

CHÂTEAU REYNELLA BASKET PRESSED SHIRAZ 1994, BRL HARDY South Australia	*This concentrated, dark wine of moderate acidity has superb dusty fruit, tannins and long finish.*	£9.20	DBY W VLW CST A IVY WMK VDV	**G**
INGLEWOOD SHOW RESERVE SHIRAZ 1995, INGLEWOOD VINEYARDS New South Wales	*Rich, medicinal characters dominate a spicy nose and herbacous, fruit-cake palate with a softening finish.*	£9.50	HW AMW SV HVW	**B**
CHATSFIELD MOUNT BARKER SHIRAZ 1994, CHATSFIELD ESTATES Western Australia	*A spicy, lighter-weight wine with dry fruit and delicate greenish tannins on the palate.*	£9.50	DIR	**B**
HEYSEN SHIRAZ 1994, VERITAS WINES South Australia	*This is a young, concentrated wine with sweet fruit, supple tannins and a spicy finish.*	£9.50	L&W NY VDV	**S**
DAVID WYNN PATRIACH SHIRAZ 1994, MOUNTADAM VINEYARDS South Australia	*A prime example of cool climate Shiraz. Spicy undertones and even tannins on the palate.*	£9.60	ADN TO	**B**
BAILEYS 1920 BLOCK SHIRAZ 1994, BAILEYS OF GLENROWAN South Australia	*A very good Northern Rhône style wine with a smoky meaty nose and firm tannins.*	£9.80	Widely Available	**B**
WOLF BLASS PRESIDENT'S SELECTION SHIRAZ 1994, MILDARA BLASS South Australia	*A well-balanced and structured wine with a ripe fruit palate, good structure and finish.*	£9.90	Widely Available	**S**
BEST'S GREAT WESTERN SHIRAZ 1994, BEST'S WINES Victoria	*Subdued on the nose, this is an easy drinking wine with supple fruit and balanced tannins.*	£10.00	Widely Available	**B**

ST. HALLETT BLACKWELL SHIRAZ 1994, **ST. HALLETT WINES** South Australia	*A fairly delicate nose precedes a sweet fruit palate which lingers pleasantly on the finish.*	£10.00	TH AUC WR BU	(B)
ROTHBURY HUNTER VALLEY RESERVE SHIRAZ 1994, MILDARA BLASS New South Wales	*An old-fashioned style of wine with hot climate characteristics, but very classy none-the-less.*	£10.00	DIR VLW OD	(B)
YALDARA JULIANS SHIRAZ 1995, YALDARA WINES South Australia	*A smoky, black pepper nose gives way to an intense palate of cinnamon and herbs.*	£10.00	SWS	(S)
SANDALFORD WINERY SHIRAZ 1995, **SANDALFORD WINERY** Western Australia	*A tremendously deep and powerful wine with excellent, full fruit, balance and length.*	£10.00	U HBJ	(G)
GOUNDREY RESERVE SHIRAZ 1995, **GOUNDREY WINES** Western Australia	*This intense, rich wine with a classic Syrah nose has a good chewy structure that lasts and lasts.*	£10.30	TP COK ALL SWS	(S)
EBENEZER SHIRAZ 1994, BRL HARDY South Australia	*A wonderfully stylish wine, beautifully well-balanced with superb fruit, grip and wood.*	£10.40	DBY VLW VDV WCR	(G)
NORMAN'S CHAIS CLARENDON SHIRAZ 1995,NORMANS WINES LIMITED South Australia	*A rich and spicy red wine, full of ripe, berry fruit and vanilla oak characters. Delicious!*	£10.50	RAE PLB VDV OD	(G)
D'ARENBERG IRONSTONE PRESSINGS 1995, **D'ARENBERG WINES** South Australia	*Purple in colour, this is a powerful, jammy wine with a superb balancing tannins grip.*	£10.90	VDV	(S)

PENLEY ESTATE SHIRAZ CABERNET 1994, PENLEY ESTATE South Australia	*Given time the smoky, toasty fruit will develop to give a well-balanced, classy wine.*	£11.00	DBY DIR L&W AUC OD	(S)
McGUIGAN BROTHERS PERSONAL RESERVE SHIRAZ 1995, McGUIGAN BROTHERS South Australia	*An excellently put-together wine with a complex tarry, menthol, fruit nose.*	£11.00	DBY IVY COK VNO GLY P+R	(G)
SKILLOGALEE SHIRAZ 1995, SKILLOGALEE WINES South Australia	*A very New World-style juicy wine of excellent concentration, length and intensity.*	£11.10	DIR NY PHI ENO	(G)
BETHANY SHIRAZ 1995, BETHANY WINES South Australia	*Smoky on the nose this wine has a nicely-balanced palate and a firm finish.*	£11.60	DBY PO VDV WSC SOM BBO	(B)
PENFOLDS BIN 389 SHIRAZ CABERNET 1994, PENFOLDS South Australia	*An intensely coloured, Wine with peppery fruit and a youthful, minty nose. 'Grange' casks to the fore!*	£11.90	Widely Available	(S)
EBENEZER SHIRAZ 1993, BRL HARDY South Australia	*Showing some maturity, an intensely fruity, well-structured wine with a charred oak nose.*	£12.00	RAE VLW VDV WCR	(S)
ELDERTON SHIRAZ 1994, ELDERTON WINES South Australia	*A clean, ripe wine with lots of top-end complexity and a good palate. Intense, mouth-filling flavours with a lingering finish.*	£12.00	ALL BBR	(S)
ELDERTON SHIRAZ 1994, ELDERTON WINES South Australia	*A concentrated, generously-oaked wine. Rich and warm palate with medium tannins.*	£12.00	ALL	(S)

ST. HALLETT OLD BLOCK SHIRAZ 1993, ST. HALLETT WINES	*A big, complex wine with tarry, sweet fruit and well-integrated fruit on the palate.*	£12.10	Widely Available	(S)
YARRA VALLEY SHIRAZ 1994, DE BORTOLI WINES Victoria	*A good well-balanced wine with a big vanilla nose and concentrated, complex, jammy palate.*	£12.10	DBY GI IVY VDV PHI OWL SCK	(S)
MOUNT LANGI GHIRAN SHIRAZ 1995, MOUNT LANGI GHIRAN WINES Victoria	*Tarry mint, on a pronounced berry nose. Huge mouthful of black plumb tannins and juicy sweet fruits*	£12.20	DBY DIR NY CWI GGW VLW LIB	(S)
CHARLIE MELTON SHIRAZ 1995, CHARLES MELTON WINES Barossa	*An extremely elegant wine displaying mature, ripe, sweet blackcurrant fruit and a lingering, enticing finish.*	£12.60	Widely Available	(G)
JIM BARRY McCRAE WOOD SHIRAZ 1994, JIM BARRY WINES South Australia	*A very powerful, lovely, rich, herbal Shiraz showing well-integrated ripe, tarry fruit and oak.*	£12.70	TAN CPW VDV BEN TAM RBS OD	(S)
LINDEMANS LIMESTONE RIDGE SHIRAZ CABERNET 1993, LINDEMANS South Australia	*The intense, ripe fruit on the nose follows through to form rich, sweet berry flavours. A blockbuster!*	£12.90	Widely Available	(G)
LAWSON'S SHIRAZ 1992, ORLANDO WYNDHAM GROUP South Australia	*An intense, oak-dominated nose leads onto a palate packed with spicy vanilla fruit.*	£13.10	DBY VDV OD PEA CEN JCK WTR	(S)
LAWSON'S SHIRAZ 1993, ORLANDO WYNDHAM GROUP South Australia	*A black-red, wonderfully complex and remarkable wine of immense richness, intensity and concentration.*	£13.70	Widely Available	(G)

LEASINGHAM CLASSIC CLARE SHIRAZ 1994, BRL HARDY South Australia	*Intensely minty aromas, this thick, purple wine has sweet fruit and oak on the palate.*	**£13.80**	DBY VLW TO NI VDV JHL	S
D'ARENBERG 'THE DEAD ARM' 1995, D'ARENBERG WINES South Australia	*An extraordinarily good, big and alcoholic South Australian wine with huge chocolatey ripe berry fruit.*	**£14.20**	DBY CHF VDV	G
PENFOLDS ST HENRI 1993, SOUTHCORP WINES South Australia	*A pretty, deep, mature colour; a warm wine with masses of fruit and grippy tannins.*	**£15.00**	POR	B
TIM ADAMS 'THE ABERFELDY' 1995, TIM ADAMS WINES South Australia	*A very minty wine with good, rich fruit and some peppery, Shiraz spice.*	**£15.00**	AUC	S
LEASINGHAM CLASSIC CLARE SHIRAZ 1995, BRL HARDY South Australia	*A dark, big wine with a berry nose and rich palate that should reward keeping.*	**£15.30**	VLW TO VDV JHL	S
PETER LEHMANN STONEWELL SHIRAZ 1992, PETER LEHMANN WINES South Australia	*Being not overtly complex, a very quaffable wine showing sweet fruit on the nose and palate.*	**£15.40**	BOO BD FUL A WMK VDV	B
TYRRELL'S VAT 9 SHIRAZ RESERVE 1993, TYRRELL'S WINES New South Wales	*A well-balanced wine of medium length with ripe fruit and oak on the lengthy palate.*	**£16.60**	BNK VIL TP	B
YALUMBA 'THE OCTAVIUS' 1993, YALUMBA WINERY South Australia	*Elegant, fruit aromas and subtle, integrated, oak elements. An intense mouthful of soft ripe berry fruits.*	**£18.20**	JN VDV OD GRA FRT ZAK	G

AUSTRALIA • RED • SHIRAZ

GRANT BURGE MESHACH SHIRAZ 1993, GRANT BURGE WINES South Australia	*A beady wine with a warm nose, good, spicy fruit and comforting, warm, alcoholic structure.*	£18.50	Widely Available	(S)
EILEEN HARDY SHIRAZ 1994, BRL HARDY South Australia	*A full-flavoured, voluptuous wine, high in extract with soft, chewy fruit and ripe oak.*	£19.60	DBY IVY NI WMK VDV SAF MRS WCR	(S)
EILEEN HARDY SHIRAZ 1995, BRL HARDY South Australia	*An intensely coloured, deep red wine for keeping. Deliciously concentrated with big, chewy tannins.*	£20.00	VDV SAF WA	(S)
E&E BLACK PEPPER SHIRAZ 1994, BRL HARDY South Australia	*An outstanding, very hefty wine with a big, oaky nose and full, fleshy fruit. Mouthfilling!*	£20.60	Widely Available	(G)
MOUNT EDELSTONE SHIRAZ 1994, HENSCHKE CELLARS South Australia	*A wine with excellent, up-front fruit, a robust nose, firm acidity and superb structure.*	£22.10	Widely Available	(S)
ROSEMOUNT ESTATE BALMORAL SYRAH 1994, ROSEMOUNT ESTATES New South Wales	*A dark wine of good length, weight and concentration which shows delicious raspberry and oak characters.*	£23.40	DBY LNR TO CEB U WIN BTH BWC	(S)
JIM BARRY THE ARMAGH SHIRAZ 1994, JIM BARRY WINES South Australia	*An attractive New World nose fronts this un-usually balanced; spicy, ripe fruit dominate.*	£29.10	TAN RBS VDV BEN OD ETV	(S)
WYNNS MICHAEL SHIRAZ 1994, WYNNS COONAWARRA ESTATE South Australia	*Huge potential. Inky black colour, intense nose and a palate of concentrated fruit and structured tannins.*	£30.40	Widely Available	(S)

AUSTRALIA • OTHER RED

NANYA ESTATE MALBEC RUBY CABERNET 1996, ANGOVE'S PTY. LTD. South Australia	*Interesting chocolate and blackcurrant fruit aromas. Slightly spicy flavours leading up to the lingering finish.*	**£4.00**	TH SPR W	(S)
PETER LEHMANN BAROSSA VALLEY GRENACHE 1996, PETER LEHMANN WINES South Australia	*Rich and savoury aromas. A juicy wine with good fruit depth and tannins.*	**£5.60**	Widely Available	(S)
SALISBURY ESTATE GRENACHE 1996, ALAMBIE WINES South Australia	*An excellent, well put-together wine with warm, gutsy, juicy fruit dominating the palate.*	**£5.70**	VWC NY VLW ENO	(B)
STRATMER VINEYARDS WHO CARES RED 1995, MOUNT HURTLE VINTNERS South Australia	*A soft, easy-drinking, light wine with raspberry fruit and a deliciously mouthwatering finish.*	**£6.00**	SAF	(B)
THOMAS MITCHELL CABERNET SHIRAZ CABERNET FRANC 1995, MITCHELTON VINTNERS Victoria	*A youthful wine with rich peppery overtones and an intense, spicy Shiraz aroma.*	**£6.50**	WMK WCR	(S)
YALDARA OLD WHITMORE VINEYARD GRENACHE 1996, YALDARA WINES South Australia	*Simple, easy-drinking wine with up-lifting tannins. Well-rounded, fruity complexity on the palate. Easy drinking!*	**£6.70**	Widely Available	(B)
KEYSTONE GRENACHE SHIRAZ 1996, TATACHILLA WINERY South Australia	*A full-bodied, ruby-red wine with cigar box and leather characteristics. Good example of this un-usual blend.*	**£6.80**	BD	(S)

BUCKLEY'S WINES MALBEC 1996, BUCKLEYS WINES South Australia	*Deep red colour, showing intense aromas of stewed fruits carried over on to a lingering palate.*	**£7.00**	TO AUC	(B)
D'ARRY'S ORIGINAL 1995, D'ARENBERG WINES South Australia	*A good, ripe and spicy wine with impressive depth of rich fruit and grippy tannins.*	**£7.00**	WES VDV	(B)
BASEDOW BUSH VINE GRENACHE 1996, BASEDOW WINES South Australia	*Light in colour, this is a straight-forward wine with a youthful, sweet, juicy palate.*	**£7.10**	VWC BI GGW CHF VDV NRW VW	(B)
BETHANY PRESSINGS GRENACHE 1996, BETHANY WINES South Australia	*Ruby-red, this wine has an intense pepper nose and a rich, juicy fruit palate. Well-balanced.*	**£7.50**	DBY PO WSC	(B)
TATACHILLA MERLOT 1995, TATACHILLA WINERY South Australia	*Attractive colour with herbal and plum aromas. Jammy, fruit flavours on a soft, approachable palate.*	**£7.50**	W	(S)
TRENTHAM ESTATE MERLOT 1995, TRENTHAM ESTATE WINES New South Wales	*Ripe, summer-fruits nose with cedar notes leading to powerful fruit, vanilla and tobacco flavours.*	**£7.70**	L&W NY VDV HVW	(B)
TIM KNAPPSTEIN "THE FRANC" 1995, TIM KNAPPSTEIN WINES South Australia	*Deep purple wine with mint on the nose and spice on the palate. You don't get many better examples than this!*	**£7.70**	TP NEI CPW VDV	(S)
BETHANY PRESSINGS GRENACHE 1995, BETHANY WINES South Australia	*Spicy, fruit-cake aromas, backed up by sweet, blackcherry flavours on a rich palate.*	**£7.80**	DBY PO NI WSC SOM BBO	(B)

BEST'S GREAT WESTERN DOLCETTO 1994, BEST'S WINES Victoria	*A very New World, well-integrated, oaked wine. Intensely fruity with a minty finish.*	**£7.80**	FUL VDV SWS	(S)
PETER LEHMANN CLANCY'S RED 1995, PETER LEHMANN WINES South Australia	*Minty overtones combine with ripe berry flavours. An attractive wine with good fruit concentration.*	**£7.90**	Widely Available	(S)
JAMIESON'S RUN RED 1995, MILDARA BLASS South Australia	*Herbal, blackcurrant aromas lead to a youthful palate of cassis flavours with grippy, green tannins.*	**£8.00**	Widely Available	(B)
COLDSTREAM HILLS BRIASTON CABERNET MERLOT CABERNET FRANC 1995, COLDSTREAM HILLS Victoria	*A blackcurrant and mint nose with ripe fruits on the generous, well-balanced palate.*	**£8.50**	PEF	(B)
ST. HALLETT GRENACHE 1996, ST. HALLETT WINES South Australia	*A young, minty, ripe wine with great concentration. Slightly unusual but extremely tasty - try it!*	**£9.00**	TH AUC WR BU	(B)
CAPEL VALE MERLOT 1993, CAPEL VALE WINES Western Australia	*Ripe berries and oak on the nose with creamy, blackcurrant flavours on a lingering palate.*	**£9.00**	WRW K+B	(B)
TIM ADAMS 'THE FERGUS' 1996, TIM ADAMS WINES South Australia	*Mint and eucalyptus show on the nose, followed by a palate with elegant structure.*	**£9.00**	AUC WR BU	(B)
TUNNEL HILL PINOT NOIR 1995, TARRAWARRA ESTATE WINERY Victoria	*A deep-coloured wine offering rich aromas of red cherries and raspberries, with fresh, red fruit flavours.*	**£9.10**	DBY WNS LLV	(B)

COLDSTREAM HILLS GRENACHE SHIRAZ 1995, COLDSTREAM HILLS Victoria	*Soft and full-bodied. A deeply-coloured wine with a wonderful mixture of cigar box and fruit aromas.*	£9.30	DBY LNR VDV PHI	**B**
MORRIS DURIF 1994, ORLANDO WYNDHAM GROUP Victoria	*This inky, ruby wine has a distinctly sherbety quality, fresh acidity and firm tannins.*	£9.90	Widely Available	**B**
PENFOLDS BAROSSA VALLEY OLD VINE SHIRAZ GRENACHE MOURVEDRE 1994 South Australia	*Quite juicy with grippy tannins. This is a deeply coloured wine, warm with alcohol.*	£9.90	Widely Available	**B**
HOLLICK COONAWARRA 1993, HOLLICK WINES South Australia	*Deep ruby-garnet. Herbaceous and mulberry nose, with concentrated flavours of black fruits and oak.*	£9.90	L&W NY JN VDV BEN HVW	**S**
SHOTTESBROOKE CABERNET MERLOT MALBEC 1994, SHOTTESBROOKE VINEYARDS South Australia	*Minty, ripe fruit aromas lead into a palate reminiscent of blackcurrant jelly.*	£10.00	OD	**S**
STONIER'S PINOT NOIR 1996, STONIER'S WINERY Victoria	*Rich complexity of fruit coming through on the nose, with strawberry and vegetal notes combining on the palate.*	£10.30	WAW GNW PHI PV HOL DIR	**B**
HEGGIES VINEYARD MERLOT 1993, S SMITH & SON South Australia	*Concentrated mulberry and loganberry aromas. Nuances of oaky cedar and eucalypt on the lengthy palate.*	£10.30	VDV ADN GRA FRT	**S**
EBENEZER CABERNET MERLOT CABERNET FRANC 1993, BRL HARDY South Australia	*Brick-red wine. Complex aromas of plum and oak and a balanced palate of soft fruits.*	£11.30	VWC DBY VLW VDV VW JHL PTR	**S**

DE BORTOLI YARRA VALLEY PINOT NOIR 1995, DE BORTOLI WINES Victoria	*Very clean, ripe, jammy fruit with combined, soft tannins and bags of new oak. Good fruit!*	£11.30	Widely Available	(S)
COLDSTREAM HILLS PINOT NOIR 1996, COLDSTREAM HILLS Victoria	*This complex wine has heaps of green pepper fruit combined with some spicy, vegetal characteristics which emerge late.*	£11.40	DBY LNR CEB CPW VDV PHI	(S)
KATNOOK ESTATE MERLOT 1995, WINGARA WINE South Australia	*Intense plummy aromas with minty eucalypt notes and a soft palate with black cherry flavours.*	£11.50	BI WIN VW	(B)
GREEN POINT PINOT NOIR 1995, DOMAINE CHANDON Victoria	*Concentrated cherry aromas are reflected on a well-structured, ripe, lingering palate. Well-integrated oak.*	£11.50	DIR VLW	(B)
EBENEZER CABERNET MERLOT CABERNET FRANC 1994, BRL HARDY South Australia	*Mature, cedary nose and palate with some pepper notes and a lovely fruit and oak combination.*	£12.10	VWC VLW VDV VW JHL PTR	(B)
PIPERS BROOK PINOT NOIR 1995, PIPERS BROOK VINEYARDS Tasmania	*This has an attractively fragrant nose, while the palate shows a well-balanced, complexity.*	£12.40	Widely Available	(B)
LINDEMANS COONAWARRA PYRUS 1993, LINDEMANS WINES South Australia	*Fabulous depth of colour. Spicy, black fruit aromas and a deep palate of notable length.*	£12.70	Widely Available	(S)
NINE POPES 1995, CHARLES MELTON WINES Barossa	*Australia's answer to Châteauneuf-du-Pape. A myriad of grape varieties combine to produce a smoky, powerful wine.*	£14.00	Widely Available	(B)

PETER LEHMANN MENTOR 1991, **PETER LEHMANN WINES** South Australia	*Blackcurrant and toasty oak aromas reflected on a well-structured, creamy palate offering youthful tannins.*	**£14.10**	DBY FUL CHF VDV TMW PLE	(B)
STONIER'S RESERVE PINOT NOIR 1995, **STONIER'S WINERY** Victoria	*Green pepper fruit dominates this well-balanced wine. This follows through into an attractive finish.*	**£14.60**	DIR WAW HOL PV GNW	(B)
COLDSTREAM HILLS RESERVE PINOT NOIR 1996, **COLDSTREAM HILLS** Victoria	*The lovely, toasty oak is backed by an excellent concentration of fruit on the nose.*	**£14.60**	DBY COK VDV	(G)
TARRAWARRA ESTATE PINOT NOIR 1995, **TARRAWARRA ESTATE WINES** Victoria	*Strawberry fruit combines with vegetal notes, good acidity and firm tannins. A lovely complex wine.*	**£15.20**	DBY PHI	(G)
BEST'S GREAT WESTERN PINOT MEUNIER 1993, **BEST'S WINES** Victoria	*A good concentration of ripe, strawberry fruit; balanced by soft tannins and minty oak.*	**£15.40**	TP VDV SWS	(B)
YALDARA THE FARMS MERLOT CABERNET 1992, YALDARA WINES South Australia	*Rich, sweet evolved bouquet. Intense red-currant and American oak with concentrated blackberry flavours.*	**£15.70**	TP SWS SAF	(S)
YALDARA THE FARMS MERLOT 1996, YALDARA WINES South Australia	*A perfumed nose offering cinnamon and cedar aromas is backed by big tannins on the palate.*	**£16.00**	BD SWS	(S)

Pinpoint who sells the wine you wish to buy by turning to the stockist codes. If you know the name of the wine you want to buy, use the alphabetical index. If the price is your motivation, refer to the invaluable price guide index; red and white wines under £5, sparkling wines under £10 and champagne under £15. Happy hunting!

AUSTRALIA • CHARDONNAY

LINDEMANS CAWARRA UNOAKED CHARDONNAY 1996, LINDEMANS South Australia	*Delicate citrus and grapefruit peel aromas on this classic, refined and well-balanced wine.*	**£4.70**	Widely Available	B
LINDEMANS BIN 65 CHARDONNAY 1996, LINDEMANS South Australia	*Elegant, spicy nose with good weight in the mouth, leading to a lengthy finish.*	**£5.10**	Widely Available	B
CHANDLER'S HILL CHARDONNAY SEMILLON 1995, NORMAN'S WINES South Australia	*Lovely ripe, exotic tropical fruit and creamy toasty characteristics shine through on the palate.*	**£5.10**	CES PLB WBE	S
MOYSTON UNOAKED CHARDONNAY 1996, SEPPELT WINES Victoria	*Rich almond nose. Very full mouth. Quite citric and tangy with lots of ripe fruit.*	**£5.30**	Widely Available	S
OXFORD LANDING CHARDONNAY 1996, YALUMBA WINERY South Australia	*Buttery vanilla shines through on the nose. The fruity palate is balanced by crisp acidity.*	**£5.40**	Widely Available	S
GOSLING CREEK CHARDONNAY 1996, HIGHLAND HERITAGE ESTATE New South Wales	*Good intensity of almondy fruit in a clean, simple palate with reasonable length.*	**£6.00**	WF	B
KINGSTON ESTATE CHARDONNAY 1996, KINGSTON ESTATE South Australia	*Green, golden, ripe fruit is nicely balanced on a stylish nose and palate.*	**£6.00**	NEI WWI VNO GLY	S

SALTRAM CLASSIC CHARDONNAY 1996, SALTRAM WINE ESTATES South Australia	*Intense floral, fruity nose with a touch of buttery sweetness coming through on the palate.*	**£6.20**	DBY GRT IVY SHJ NRW JS LLV	**B**
MONTROSE CHARDONNAY 1995, ORLANDO WYNDHAM GROUP New South Wales	*A lightly-oaked wine offering hints of citrus fruit on a full, ripe, opulent palate.*	**£6.70**	DBY AMW EUR JCK WTR PEA CEN	**B**
TYRRELL'S OLD WINERY CHARDONNAY RESERVE 1996, TYRRELL'S WINES South Australia	*Youthful, straw green colour with light oak and good fruit. Balanced to perfection. Very drinkable!*	**£6.90**	VIL GNW CPW	**B**
WOLF BLASS BARREL-FERMENTED CHARDONNAY 1996, MILDARA BLASS South Australia	*A butterscotch, oak, ripe pineapple nose, with soft fruit on a lively well-balanced palate.*	**£7.00**	Widely Available	**B**
D'ARENBERG THE OLIVE GROVE CHARDONNAY 1996, D'ARENBERG WINES South Australia	*Restrained, elegant nose, with resinous oak and ripe fruit. Coats the mouth well and lasts.*	**£7.00**	DBY CHF POR WES VDV OD	**B**
RIDDOCH CHARDONNAY 1996, WINGARA WINES South Australia	*Skilfully-made wine with softly-oaked fruit on the palate, lingering to a well-held finish.*	**£7.00**	BI GGW TH	**S**
PREECE CHARDONNAY 1996, MITCHELTON VINTNERS Victoria	*Tangy lemon and well-integrated oak on the palate, rounded off by light, attractive acidity.*	**£7.10**	Widely Available	**S**
PENFOLDS THE VALLEYS CHARDONNAY 1996, PENFOLDS South Australia	*Attractive citrus flavours and uplifting oak. Rich and fat in the mouth; fruity and well-rounded.*	**£7.30**	Widely Available	**S**

WYNNS CHARDONNAY 1996, WYNNS COONAWARRA ESTATE South Australia	*The smooth palate shows hints of apple skin and butterscotch with a touch of fresh acidity.*	£7.30	Widely Available	**S**
WAKEFIELD ESTATE CHARDONNAY 1995, WAKEFIELD ESTATES South Australia	*Youthful wine with a varietal vanilla, citrus nose and creamy gentle oak finish.*	£7.40	DBY RAE SHG TP IVY SWS	**B**
McGUIGAN BROTHERS SHAREHOLDERS CHARDONNAY 1994, McGUIGAN BROTHERS South Australia	*Rich oak and herbal nose that follows through on a palate showing elegance and complexity.*	£7.40	DBY IVY VNO GLY EOR	**B**
ALLANDALE WINES CHARDONNAY 1996, ALLANDALE WINES New South Wales	*Fresh lime and bags of juicy fruit on a mouth-watering palate. A well-rounded wine.*	£7.50	AUC	**B**
CHÂTEAU TAHBILK CHARDONNAY 1995, TAHBILK WINES Victoria	*Sophisticated lemon; oaky aromas leading to a well-balanced palate. Good concentration and lovely length.*	£7.70	DBY VDV OD G&M	**B**
ST. HALLETT CHARDONNAY 1996, ST. HALLETT WINES South Australia	*Warm, toasted flavours with smoky, subtle fruit and fresh acidity. Well-worthy of a medal.*	£7.80	AUC HVW WR BU RD ADN	**B**
ST HILARY CHARDONNAY 1994, ORLANDO WYNDHAM GROUP South Australia	*An intense, vegetal aroma gives way to a dry palate filled with citrus fruit. Mouth-filling!*	£7.80	DBY WIN NRW JCK PEA CEN CDE CAP	**S**
HIGHLAND HERITAGE CHARDONNAY 1995, HIGHLAND HERITAGE ESTATES New South Wales	*Deep golden in colour with buttery citrus fruit and soft oak flavours lingering on the finish.*	£8.00	GRT	**B**

BROKE FORDWICH CHARDONNAY 1996, BROKE FORDWICH WINERY New South Wales	*Good weight of clean fresh fruit on the palate balanced by decently structured acidity.*	**£8.00**	RAE SWS	**B**
HILL SMITH ESTATE CHARDONNAY 1995, S SMITH & SON South Australia	*Creamy vanilla nose following through to a gentle, fruity palate with a lingering aftertaste.*	**£8.00**	JS WSO OD IRI GRA FRT	**B**
MOUNT HURTLE CHARDONNAY 1995, MOUNT HURTLE South Australia	*Creamy on the palate, with good bite and acidity. Marginally oaked, well-made and crisp on the finish.*	**£8.00**	WMK PLE	**B**
HILLSTOWE UDY'S HILL CHARDONNAY 1994, HILLSTOWE WINERY South Australia	*A pronounced oak, ripe, toasty, peachy nose, with rich tropical fruit on the lingering palate.*	**£8.00**	MK TW	**B**
CHAPEL HILL UNWOODED CHARDONNAY 1996, CHAPEL HILL WINERY South Australia	*Vibrant tropical fruit is balanced by lively acidity and a fresh, clean yeasty mid-palate.*	**£8.00**	TO AUC NRW	**S**
ST HILARY CHARDONNAY 1996, ORLANDO WYNDHAM GROUP South Australia	*Tropical limey flavours on the nose, with seductive fruit intensity, lead to a superb wine.*	**£8.00**	DBY NRW JCK PEA CEN CDE CAP	**G**
HARDY'S PADTHAWAY CHARDONNAY 1995, BRL HARDY South Australia	*Seductive creamy vanilla nose culminating in rich tropical fruit on a mouth-watering palate.*	**£8.10**	DBY MAK VLW WMK VDV JMC WCK	**B**
NINTH ISLAND CHARDONNAY 1996, PIPERS BROOK VINEYARDS Tasmania	*On the palate crisp acidity is balanced well by fresh apples and white peaches. Refreshing!*	**£8.10**	Widely Available	**S**

BROWN BROTHERS KING VALLEY CHARDONNAY 1995, BROWN BROTHERS Victoria	*A stylish Australian Chardonnay with velvety vanilla undertones o.• the rich melon and honey nose.*	**£8.30**	Widely Available	(B)
MITCHELTON VICTORIA RESERVE CHARDONNAY 1994, MITCHELTON VINTNERS Victoria	*Attractive sweet oak and lemon with complex buttery aromas leading into a mouthwatering, long finish.*	**£8.30**	Widely Available	(G)
BURGE CHARDONNAY BAROSSA RANGES 1996, GRANT BURGE WINES South Australia	*This wine shows youthfulness and toasty, tingly fruit flavours on an uplifting palate.*	**£8.40**	DBY VLW GNW FSW RBS	(B)
LINDEMANS PADTHAWAY CHARDONNAY 1996, LINDEMANS South Australia	*Generous aromas of pineapple and vanilla oak, followed by concentrated fruit and fresh acidity.*	**£8.40**	Widely Available	(S)
LEASINGHAM DOMAINE CHARDONNAY 1995, BRL HARDY South Australia	*Toasty vanilla oak aromas followed by hints of lemon on a well-balanced palate.*	**£8.50**	VLW WMK VDV SWS JHL BLS CWS SAF	(B)
DENNIS CHARDONNAY 1996, PETER DENNIS WINES South Australia	*Pineapple chunks on the nose are followed by biscuity flavours on a well-rounded palate.*	**£8.50**	THP	(B)
GOUNDREY UNWOODED CHARDONNAY 1995, GOUNDREY Western Australia	*Grassy, herbal characteristics fill this wine giving it a fresh, tangy feel in the mouth.*	**£8.60**	Widely Available	(B)
TIM KNAPPSTEIN CHARDONNAY 1995, TIM KNAPPSTEIN WINES South Australia	*Prominent sweet oak flavours leading to a buttery palate. Offers a smooth subtle finish.*	**£8.60**	MM CRM OD	(B)

CHAIS CLARENDON CHARDONNAY 1996, NORMAN'S WINES South Australia	*Soft well-rounded honey oak flavours on the middle palate leading to a slightly dry finish.*	£8.80	PLB OD	(B)
CAPEL VALE CHARDONNAY 1995, CAPEL VALE WINES Western Australia	*This wine is packed with intense grapey aromas, rich full-flavoured fruit and clean oak.*	£9.00	HUT LLT	(B)
LITTLE'S CHARDONNAY 1995, LITTLE'S WINERY New South Wales	*A ripe, buttery wine offering tropical fruit flavours and a long, delightfully rich finish.*	£9.00	CFN	(B)
ST HILARY CHARDONNAY 1995, ORLANDO WYNDHAM GROUP South Australia	*Up-front nose, with definate toasted oak aromas, showing good intensity of fruit and profound acidity.*	£9.00	NRW JCK PEA CEN CDE CAP	(S)
MADFISH BAY UNWOODED CHARDONNAY 1996, HOWARD PARK WINERY Western Australia	*This shows a very rich almond blossom nose which follows through onto the palate.*	£9.00	MFS NY JN PHI	(S)
CHÂTEAU REYNELLA CHARDONNAY 1995, BRL HARDY South Australia	*A lemony mouthful, with a seductive fruity nose and excellent integrated old oak on the finish.*	£9.00	Widely Available	(S)
BRANDS LAIRA CHARDONNAY 1995, MCWILLIAM'S WINES South Australia	*Straw-yellow colour with aromas of toasted oak and peaches. Great richness and firm acidity on the palate*	£9.00	CDT	(G)
JAMES HALLIDAY CHARDONNAY 1995, COLDSTREAM HILLS Victoria	*Beautifully presented apple nose followed by firm, rounded fruit on the lively palate.*	£9.20	LNR RBS	(B)

GREEN POINT CHARDONNAY 1995, DOMAINE CHANDON Victoria	*Buttery, well-oaked wine with a backbone of acidity that comes through on the finish.*	£9.20	Widely Available	Ⓑ
KRONDORF SHOW RESERVE CHARDONNAY 1996, KRONDORF WINERY South Australia	*Pleasant but slightly burnt oak on the nose, with good, underlying, integrated fruit aromas.*	£9.30	DIR HW AMW SV LLV	Ⓢ
INGLEWOOD SHOW RESERVE CHARDONNAY 1995, INGLEWOOD VINEYARDS New South Wales	*Hints of asparagus on the nose with a palate of medium-weight offering floral tones.*	£9.30	HW POR NI SV	Ⓢ
EBENEZER CHARDONNAY 1996, BRL HARDY South Australia	*Lemony, buttery aromas on the nose, that spread over nicely to the palate. Well-made all-round.*	£9.40	DBY VLW VDV SAF JMC	Ⓑ
MOUNT HELEN CHARDONNAY 1996, TISDALL WINES Victoria	*Soft and gentle, easy on the palate. Enhanced by ripe fruit and nicely balanced oak.*	£9.50	HW OD	Ⓑ
SHAW & SMITH UNOAKED CHARDONNAY 1996, SHAW & SMITH South Australia	*Fresh and light, this wine is perfectly balanced with citrus fruit and crisp, refreshing acidity.*	£9.60	Widely Available	Ⓑ
CHATEÂU REYNELLA CHARDONNAY 1996, BRL HARDY South Australia	*Wine shows a subtle feminine nose, with gentle, toasted oak and soft, creamy fruit.*	£9.60	VLW A IVY VDV SAF JHL	Ⓢ
ROSEMOUNT ESTATE SHOW RESERVE CHARDONNAY 1995, ROSEMOUNT ESTATES New South Wales	*Rich and smooth with a creamy apple aroma.This wine shows complexity and impressive balance.*	£9.70	Widely Available	Ⓑ

AUSTRALIA • WHITE • CHARDONNAY

EBENEZER CHARDONNAY 1994, BRL HARDY South Australia	*Superb balance of fruit and oak aromas on the palate, with distinctive apricot undertones.*	£9.70	W VLW VDV	(S)
STONIER'S CHARDONNAY 1995, STONIER'S WINERY Victoria	*Integrated wood with a mouthwatering buttery taste. Complemented by good acidity and length.*	£9.90	DIR MM WAW CRM CES GNW BBR HOL	(S)
WOLF BLASS PRESIDENT'S SELECTION CHARDONNAY 1996, MILDARA BLASS South Australia	*Delicate wine, made in a light aromatic style. Offering subtle oak and well-rounded fruit.*	£10.00	MTL DBY BNK VLW CEB PHI OD OD	(B)
BEST'S GREAT WESTERN CHARDONNAY 1996, BEST'S WINES Victoria	*A pungent nose of apples and a hint of earthiness, with intense fruit and well-rounded oak.*	£10.00	Widely Available	(G)
PLANTAGENET MOUNT BARKER CHARDONNAY 1996, PLANTAGENET WINES Western Australia	*Rich, ripe fruit is balanced by crisp acidity to give an extremely well-structured wine.*	£10.60	GI CRM NAD BBR WSO	(S)
GOUNDREY RESERVE CHARDONNAY 1995, GOUNDREY WINES Western Australia	*A lovely balance between fruit and oak with a creamy, flavoursome, smooth finish.*	£10.90	VLW TP GRT CPW ALL SWS	(S)
GEOFF MERRILL CHARDONNAY 1994, MOUNT HURTLE South Australia	*Nicely-balanced fruit, with lime undertones on a well-rounded palate, leading to a long, creamy finish.*	£11.00	WMK PLE SAF EOO	(S)
COLDSTREAM HILLS CHARDONNAY 1996, COLDSTREAM HILLS Victoria	*A beautiful, varietal nose with good structure and tropical fruit. Strong oak lasts through.*	£11.10	DBY CPW VDV PHI	(S)

BROWN BROTHERS FAMILY RESERVE CHARDONNAY 1994, BROWN BROTHERS Victoria	*Attractively light, tropical-style fruit on the palate. Beautifully made with rich acidity and elegant balance.*	**£11.10**	DBY VIL DIR TP U CPW PTR P&R	S
KATNOOK ESTATE CHARDONNAY 1995, WINGARA WINES South Australia	*Wonderful fruitiness on nose that follows through on a lively palate, with a long finish.*	**£11.50**	BI WIN	B
SHAW & SMITH RESERVE CHARDONNAY 1994, SHAW & SMITH South Australia	*A youngish wine with crisp acidity, that unfolds balanced fruitiness onto a long-lasting palate.*	**£11.60**	NY CWI GGW VLW JN LIB	S
PIPERS BROOK CHARDONNAY 1995, PIPERS BROOK VINEYARDS Tasmania	*Lovely melon and tropical aromas on the nose, combined with soft oaky fruitiness.*	**£12.30**	Widely Available	B
PETALUMA CHARDONNAY 1993, PETALUMA WINES South Australia	*Golden with a creamy, lemony nose. Oak dominant on the palate, with underlying fruit.*	**£12.40**	VDV	B
PETALUMA CHARDONNAY 1995, PETALUMA WINES South Australia	*This elegant wine is soft and delicate, but comes through to a long balanced, subtle oak finish.*	**£12.40**	Widely Available	G
TUNNEL HILL CHARDONNAY 1995, TARRAWARRA ESTATE Victoria	*Yellow in colour, with a lemony nose. Relatively high acidity backs up this fine wine.*	**£13.00**	WSO WNS	B
ROSEMOUNT ESTATE ORANGE CHARDONNAY 1995, ROSEMOUNT ESTATE New South Wales	*This young Australian Chardonnay is lightly oaked with some butteriness on the palate.*	**£13.10**	LNR HOU M&S FTH BWC	B

STONIER'S RESERVE CHARDONNAY 1994, STONIER'S WINERY Victoria	*This wine shows an attractive palate, with a smoky oak and tropical fruit nose.*	**£13.10**	DIR WAW PV HOL ODF	(S)
PETALUMA CHARDONNAY 1994, PETALUMA WINES South Australia	*Ripe melony flavours linger on the palate, backed up by long-lasting, gentle acidity.*	**£13.30**	Widely Available	(S)
EILEEN HARDY CHARDONNAY 1995, BRL HARDY South Australia	*Strong, tropical fruit flavours including ripe pineapple. A good balance of oak and fruit.*	**£13.40**	Widely Available	(S)
TARRAWARRA ESTATE CHARDONNAY 1995, TARRAWARRA ESTATE Victoria	*Oaky aromas that lead to a high intensity of fruit and rich concentration of wood.*	**£13.50**	DBY	(B)
XANADU CHARDONNAY 1996, CHATEÂU XANADU Western Australia	*Clean nose with hints of butterscotch, leading to a palate of oak and fresh, tropical fruit.*	**£13.50**	DIR	(S)
COLDSTREAM HILLS RESERVE CHARDONNAY 1996, COLDSTREAM HILLS Victoria	*Wholesome fruity flavours are well-defined with a slightly vanilla palate on the finnish.*	**£13.90**	DBY COK VDV OD	(G)
McGUIGAN BROTHERS PERSONAL RESERVE CHARDONNAY 1996, McGUIGAN BROTHERS South Australia	*This is a youthful, fresh well-balanced Chardonnay with a distinctive lemon and lime aroma.*	**£14.00**	IVY VNO GLY P&R	(B)
TYRRELL'S VAT 47 CHARDONNAY RESERVE 1996, TYRRELL'S WINES New South Wales	*Smooth, gentle peaches and cream flavours, with hints of oak on the smooth, long palate.*	**£15.20**	VIL TP U	(B)

D'ARENBERG THE OTHERSIDE CHARDONNAY 1996, D'ARENBERG WINES South Australia	*Slightly closed oak followed by a fruity nose that opens up on a well-rounded palate.*	£15.90	VDV	**B**

AUSTRALIA • RIESLING

PEWSEY VALE RIESLING 1996, S SMITH & SON South Australia	*Light and crisp with reasonable clean citrus and floral fruit. Overall an elegant wine.*	£6.20	TO VDV GRA FRT	**B**
WOLF BLASS SILVER LABEL REISLING 1995, MILDARA BLASS South Australia	*Lovely, fresh and clean nose with good lime character and some spicy perfumed fruit.*	£6.20	Widely Available	**B**
HEGGIES VINEYARD RIESLING 1992, S SMITH & SON South Australia	*Lovely petroly character on the nose with citrus fruit on the palate. Light and fresh.*	£6.40	JN ADN GRA FRT	**S**
WAKEFIELD ESTATES RIESLING 1992, WAKEFIELD ESTATES South Australia	*A well-balanced complex combination of lime and attractive acidity, finishes with lingering complexity.*	£6.50	RAE TP VDV SWS	**S**
ST. HALLETT RIESLING 1995, CHAPEL HILL WINES South Australia	*Intense lime and petrol aromas follow through on the nose to give great weight and depth.*	£7.00	AUC BU WR	**S**
BEST'S GREAT WESTERN RIESLING 1995, BEST'S WINES Victoria	*The herbal nuances to this wine lead on to honey and nuts on the palate. Very clean!*	£8.70	DBY L&W TP IVY HOU VDV SWS R	**B**

BROWN BROTHERS FAMILY RESERVE RIESLING 1994, BROWN BROTHERS Victoria	*Intense, rich, floral fruit with hints of spice combining to form a ripe, structured palate.*	**£9.10**	Widely Available	(S)
PETALUMA RIESLING 1996, PETALUMA WINES South Australia	*Spicy, floral nose leads to a good concentration of fresh, clean fruit on a well-balanced palate.*	**£9.50**	NY AUC VDV WCS PHI BEN	(S)
PETALUMA RIESLING 1995, PETALUMA WINES South Australia	*Subtle petrol flavours are showing along with good weight and length and a clean, rounded finish.*	**£9.60**	TAN AUC WIN VDV WCS PHI BEN	(B)
MOUNTADAM RIESLING 1995, MOUNTADAM VINEYARDS South Australia	*This well-made wine shows textured, spicy fruit flavours with fresh grapefruit and lime.*	**£10.00**	P TO	(S)
JULIUS RIESLING 1995, HENSCHKE CELLERS South Australia	*A well-made wine, with lingering fruit on the palate and lovely honey aromas on the nose.*	**£10.40**	DBY DIR L&W RBS GNW JN VDV PHI	(B)
GREEN'S HILL RIESLING 1995, HENSCHKE CELLERS South Australia	*Attractive flavours of apples and citrus on the nose. Ripe fruit and real power on the palate.*	**£11.00**	DIR L&W NY SEB JN VDV BEN	(B)

AUSTRALIA • SEMILLON

JACOB'S CREEK SEMILLON CHARDONNAY 1996, ORLANDO WYNDHAM GROUP South Australia	*Greenish gold in colour with an earthy nose and rich citrus fruit on the palate. Lovely, easy blend.*	**£4.70**	Widely Available	(B)

SACRED HILL SEMILLON CHARDONNAY 1996, DE BORTOLI WINES Victoria	*An attractive gentle, floral style, full of refreshingly appealing citrus fruit and pineapple flavours.*	**£4.80**	GI LNR HVW BWC NAD SKW SCK	**B**
WYNDHAM ESTATE BIN 777 SEMILLON CHARDONNAY 1996, ORLANDO WYNDHAM South Australia	*An earthy nose with hints of butter leads into a wine packed with juicy fruit flavours.*	**£5.60**	DBY BNK HOU EWA JCK A&A	**B**
PENFOLDS BAROSSA VALLEY SEMILLON CHARDONNAY 1996, PENFOLDS South Australia	*A wine offering delicate oak and honey aromas, with a hint of waxiness on the nose.*	**£5.80**	Widely Available	**S**
MARIENBERG SEMILLON CHARDONNAY 1994, MARIENBERG WINE CO South Australia	*Bright stuff, with a lemon and lime nose. A ripe, balanced, smoky, buttery palate.*	**£6.00**	TMW LAY	**B**
PENFOLDS BARREL FERMENTED SEMILLON 1994, PENFOLDS South Australia	*Golden colour wine, with a heavy oaky nose and a solid fruit structure.*	**£6.10**	W NY VDV ABY NRW	**B**
IRONSTONE SEMILLON CHARDONNAY 1996, IRONSTONE VINEYARDS Western Australia	*Citrus aromas are backed up by fresh, clean fruit with a light hint of oak.*	**£6.20**	Widely Available	**B**
ROSEMOUNT ESTATE SEMILLON CHARDONNAY 1996, ROSEMOUNT ESTATES New South Wales	*Delicate oak aromas on the nose. Good weight and fruit on a well-integrated palate.*	**£6.30**	Widely Available	**B**
MAGLIERI MCLAREN VALE SEMILLON 1995, MAGLIERI WINES South Australia	*Complex ,with a rich herbal nose. A wine of impressive weight and bags of style.*	**£7.20**	RAE U PLB	**B**

PENFOLDS BAROSSA VALLEY OLD VINE SEMILLON 1996, PENFOLDS South Australia	*Rich, tropical fruit aromas with powerful and strong oak vanilla tannins on the finish.*	**£7.20**	VWC DBY TO WWI VDV HVW OD	Ⓑ
BROWN BROTHERS SEMILLON 1995, BROWN BROTHERS Victoria	*Smoky oak on the nose, following through onto a palate with honey and caramel overtones.*	**£7.20**	Widely Available	Ⓑ
PETER LEHMANN CLANCY'S WHITE 1996, PETER LEHMANN WINES South Australia	*A lingering, fresh lemon aroma, backed by bags of fruit on the palate.*	**£7.60**	DBY SHG P FUL GDS VDV OD	Ⓑ
MOUNT PLEASANT ELIZABETH SEMILLON 1992, MCWILLIAM'S WINES Hunter Valley	*Strong, smoky oak elements on the nose with citrus and vanilla flavours to follow.*	**£7.90**	CDT	Ⓑ
CAPE MENTELLE SEMILLON SAUVIGNON 1996, CAPE MENTELLE VINEYARDS Western Australia	*A leafy, gooseberry nose precedes a full bodied palate of ripe citrus and tropical fruit.*	**£8.50**	Widely Available	Ⓑ
ELDERTON SEMILLON 1994, ELDERTON WINES South Australia	*Rich, fatty aromas of lanolin on the nose, backed by integrated fruit on the palate.*	**£9.80**	ALL	Ⓑ
TYRRELL'S VAT 1 SEMILLON RESERVE 1992, TYRRELL'S WINES New South Wales	*Golden green in colour with good acidity matched by pineapple fruit and a buttery finish.*	**£16.70**	VIL BEN	Ⓢ

Pinpoint who sells the wine you wish to buy by turning to the stockist codes. If you know the name of the wine you want to buy, use the alphabetical index. If the price is your motivation, refer to the invaluable price guide index; red and white wines under £5, sparkling wines under £10 and champagne under £15. Happy hunting!

AUSTRALIA • OTHER WHITE

MALT HOUSE VINTNERS SCENIC RIDGE AUSTRALIAN WHITE, REDELLO WINES New South Wales	*Delightful fruit precedes the palate, which shows good depth and length on the finish.*	**£3.70**	MHV	B
JARRAH RIDGE DRY WHITE 1996, KINGSTON ESTATE South Australia	*An attractive, grapey nose with lemon aromas is followed by a honeyed and buttery palate.*	**£3.90**	WES VNO TGW ABB BKT	B
DEAKIN ESTATE SAUVIGNON BLANC 1996, WINGARA WINES Victoria	*Delightful aromas of gooseberries on the nose leading to a fruity palate with good length.*	**£5.20**	VWC BI GGW NRW VW	B
TIM KNAPPSTEIN SAUVIGNON BLANC SEMILLON 1996, TIM KNAPPSTEIN WINES South Australia	*An aromatic wine with hints of asparagus, lemon and gooseberry on a lengthy palate.*	**£5.20**	CLA TP OD	S
ST. HALLETT POACHER'S BLEND 1996, ST. HALLETT WINES South Australia	*Intense citrus fruit aromas are followed by hefty fruit on the long-lasting palate.*	**£5.50**	TO AUC NRW RD K&B HN LEF	S
RICHMOND GROVE VERDELHO 1995, ORLANDO WYNDHAM GROUP South Australia	*Gentle almond aromas with lingering gooseberry fruit, leading to a well-structured palate.*	**£6.00**	AMW CWS TO WIN VDV DIO PEA WTR	B
HOUGHTON'S HWB 1996, HOUGHTON WINES Western Australia	*A big and heavy, aromatic wine with a spicy aftertaste that lingers on the palate.*	**£6.00**	Widely Available	B

THOMAS MITCHELL MARSANNE 1996, MITCHELTON VINTNERS Victoria	*Well-rounded, slightly toffee nose, with balanced fruit and oaky palate leading to a juicy finish.*	£6.10	BOO WMK WCR OD MRN	(B)
WAKEFIELD ESTATE CLARE CROUCHEN CHARDONNAY 1995, WAKEFIELD ESTATES South Australia	*Peardrop aromas are backed up by a palate of citrus flavours and tropical fruit.*	£6.50	TP U SWS BAL RAE	(B)
CHATEÂU TAHBILK MARSANNE 1995, TAHBILK WINES Victoria	*A stylish wine, made with complex fruit on a well-integrated palate. Good length on the finish.*	£6.70	DBY W TO CRS VDV	(B)
ROTHBURY HUNTER VALLEY VERDELHO 1995, MILDARA BLASS New South Wales	*Almond and spice on the nose is backed up superbly by a rounded, buttery palate on the finish.*	£6.80	DIR VLW PAR	(B)
RIDDOCH SAUVIGNON BLANC 1996, WINGARA WINES South Australia	*Pronounced grass and gooseberry aromas, precede the delicate palate, with a lovely freshness of acidity.*	£7.10	BI GGW VDV OD	(S)
PREECE SAUVIGNON BLANC 1996, MITCHELTON VINTNERS Victoria	*Rich gooseberry and grass aromas develop intense flavours on a balanced, atttractive a palate.*	£7.20	VIL NEI WMK OD COK VDV TMW POR	(B)
CHESTNUT GROVE VERDELHO 1996, CHESTNUT GROVE Western Australia	*Asparagus on the nose with big, juicy fruits on the palate creating a long finish.*	£7.50	D&D	(B)
HILL SMITH ESTATE SAUVIGNON BLANC 1996, S SMITH & SON South Australia	*This wine shows an exceptionally well-developed varietal nose with intense, fruity flavours.*	£7.80	DBY IRI GRA FRT OD	(B)

AUSTRALIA • WHITE • OTHER

VICTORIA RESERVE MARSANNE 1994, MITCHELTON VINTNERS Victoria	*Bright and clear with full, rich, toasty oak aromas and integrated fruit on the palate.*	£8.50	Widely Available	S
YALUMBA RESERVE VIOGNIER 1996, YALUMBA WINERY South Australia	*Youthful, sherbety nose. Lots of apple and pear aromas leading to a lengthy finish.*	£9.00	OD GRA FRT	B
VASSE FELIX SEMILLON SAUVIGNON BLANC CHARDONNAY 1996, VASSE FELIX WINES Western Australia	*A fresh, herbaceous nose leads into concentrated vanilla and citrus flavours on the palate.*	£9.00	TAN RBS CPW VDV BEN	B
CAPEL VALE SAUVIGNON BLANC SEMILLON 1996, CAPEL VALE WINES Western Australia	*An intense, tropical fruit nose, with hints of vanilla leading to a well-balanced palate.*	£9.00	LLT EWA	S
KATNOOK ESTATE SAUVIGNON BLANC 1996, WINGARA WINES South Australia	*Intense blackcurrant nose, with an oily structure, uplifting acidity and high alcohol on the finish.*	£9.30	TH BI FUL WIN W OD	B
SHAW & SMITH SAUVIGNON BLANC 1996, SHAW & SMITH South Australia	*The gooseberry nose opens up superbly on the palate, with a good weight of fruit.*	£9.90	Widely Available	S
HEGGIES VINEYARD VIOGNIER 1996, S SMITH & SON South Australia	*Elegant, slightly grapey nose, that opens up nicely on the palate. A clean, crisp finish.*	£11.40	JN VDV OD GRA FRT ODF	B

Pinpoint who sells the wine you wish to buy by turning to the stockist codes. If you know the name of the wine you want to buy, use the alphabetical index. If the price is your motivation, refer to the invaluable price guide index; red and white wines under £5, sparkling wines under £10 and champagne under £15. Happy hunting!

AUSTRALIA • SWEET WHITE

PIONEERS RAISINED MUSCAT BIN 168 1996, MIRANDA WINES South Australia	*Fresh grapey nose with honey notes; luscious palate of orange citrus flavours and cleansing acidity on the finish.*	£5.00	BD	**B**
TRENTHAM ESTATE NOBLE TAMINGA 1995, TRENTHAM ESTATE New South Wales	*A deep gold wine offering marmalade aromas and a creamy, toffee palate with balancing acidity.*	£6.10	L&W NY JN VDV	**S**
BROWN BROTHERS LATE HARVEST RIESLING 1995, BROWN BROTHERS Victoria	*Toffee-apple fruit on the nose precedes poached fresh apricots and oranges on the palate.*	£6.60	Widely Available	**S**
HEGGIES VINEYARD BOTRYTIS RIESLING 1996, S SMITH & SON South Australia	*Lovely combination of lemon and petrol on the nose and lasting richness on the weighty palate.*	£7.00	DBY MM JN OD GRA FRT	**S**
YALUMBA FAMILY RESERVE BOTRYTIS SEMILLON 1996, YALUMBA WINERY South Australia	*Ripe, tropical mango fruit aromas lead to lemon and lime marmalade flavours on a balanced, long-lasting palate.*	£7.10	JN MWW GRA FRT OD	**S**
D'ARENBERG NOBLE RIESLING 1996, D'ARENBERG WINES South Australia	*The soft velvety lime fruit character follows through to mouthfilling flavours on a honeyed palate.*	£10.00	POR WES VDV OD	**B**
CRANSWICK ESTATE AUTUMN GOLD BOTRYTIS SEMILLON 1994, CRANSWICK ESTATES New South Wales	*There is a subtle multi-layered quality to the nose with some lovely apricot and honey notes on a rich palate.*	£11.30	NY	**B**

CRANSWICK ESTATE BOTRYTIS SEMILLON 1995, CRANSWICK ESTATES New South Wales	*Rich, caramel toffee aromas with intense flavours of baked apples and a balancing citric acidity on the finish.*	**£11.50**	GNW CWS	(B)
DE BORTOLI NOBLE ONE BOTRYTIS SEMILLON 1993, DE BORTOLI WINES New South Wales	*Rich aromas of honeyed apricots carry over onto a luscious palate of baked citrus flavours.*	**£12.30**	Widely Available	(S)
MCGUIGAN BROTHERS PERSONAL RESERVE BOTRYTIS SEMILLON 1995 South Australia	*An attractive, honeyed citrus nose is followed by rich flavours on a well-balanced palate.*	**£12.50**	DBY IVY COK VNO GLY JAG	(B)

AUSTRALIA • SPARKLING

SEPPELT GREAT WESTERN BRUT ROSÉ NV, SEPPELT WINES South Australia	*A lovely fresh and delicate fizz from Australia. The palate is full of rich, red appley flavours.*	**£5.50**	Widely Available	(B)
DEAKIN ESTATE BRUT NV, WINGARA WINES Victoria	*A fresh, fruit driven nose, while the palate is soft with good yeast and fruit on the finish.*	**£6.40**	BI GGW CHF OD	(B)
SEAVIEW BRUT ROSÉ NV, SOUTHCORP WINES South Australia	*Light, delicate aromas abound on the nose backed up by gentle redcurrant fruit on the palate. Finishes well.*	**£6.50**	Widely Available	(B)
ANGAS BRUT NV, YALUMBA WINERY South Australia	*Yeasty, lemony, earthy and light tangerine biscuit aromas with a lengthy, mouth-cleansing, dry finish.*	**£6.60**	Widely Available	(B)

SEPPELT PINOT NOIR CHARDONNAY 1991, SEPPELT WINES South Australia	*Toasty, yeasty aromas with vanilla honey notes. Dry citrus flavours with some age giving refreshing finish.*	**£8.20**	Widely Available	B
YALUMBA CUVÉE TWO SPARKLING CABERNET NV, YALUMBA WINERY South Australia	*An unusual but delicious deep red sparkling wine with intense blackcurrant aromas and mature tannins on the finish.*	**£8.30**	TO JN OD	B
SEAVIEW PINOT NOIR CHARDONNAY 1994, SOUTHCORP WINES South Australia	*A dry, biscuity yeast influenced nose with crisp, citrus acidity on the lingering palate.*	**£8.40**	Widely Available	B
YALUMBA CUVÉE ONE PINOT NOIR CHARDONNAY NV, YALUMBA WINERY South Australia	*Malic, yeasty aromas predominate the nose with an elegant palate displaying a sophisticated biscuit finish.*	**£8.60**	Widely Available	B
HARDY'S SPARKLING PINOT NOIR CHARDONNAY NV, BRL HARDY South Australia	*Gentle, smoky aromas are backed up by clean, juicy fruit on the lightly toasted palate.*	**£8.70**	DBY WTS JMC	B
SEAVIEW EDWARDS & CHAFFEY PINOT NOIR CHARDONNAY 1993, SOUTHCORP WINES South Australia	*Creamy mousse, with yeasty, biscuity aromas and clean lemon and lime flavours on the long palate.*	**£8.80**	JS MTL HOU ABY SAF OD	B
SEPPELT SPARKLING SHIRAZ 1993, SEPPELT WINES South Australia	*Sweet, sparkling red wine with rich aromas of blackcurrant and yeasty spice repeated for a refreshing palate.*	**£9.50**	Widely Available	S
SEAVIEW EDWARDS & CHAFFEY PINOT NOIR CHARDONNAY 1992, SOUTHCORP WINES South Australia	*A yeasty nose with crisp, fruit characters and zesty, lemony acidity on the palate giving a clean finish.*	**£10.00**	POR HOU SAF	B

BERRY'S QUALITY AUSTRALIAN SPARKLING WINE NV, TALTARNI VINEYARDS Tasmania	*Delicate mousse with yeasty, creamy, fruity aromas. Autolytic, new oak notes add to refreshing lemon zest on the palate.*	£10.30	BBR	(S)
BROWN BROTHERS PINOT NOIR & CHARDONNAY NV, BROWN BROTHERS Victoria	*Attractive mousse, clean citrusy, fresh lemon nose with yeast characters. Zesty palate with vibrant fruit.*	£10.50	Widely Available	(S)
GREEN POINT BLANC DE BLANCS 1993, DOMAINE CHANDON Victoria	*Crisp, clean palate with malic apple notes; good length. Attractive mousse, with yeast oak characters and a creamy finish.*	£11.20	DIR VLW	(S)
GREEN POINT 1994, DOMAINE CHANDON Victoria	*Attractive mousse, autolytic characters to nose, tropical fruits, nutty pastry flavours on this well-made wine.*	£11.30	Widely Available	(S)
GREEN POINT ROSÉ 1993, DOMAINE CHANDON Victoria	*The winemaker, Dr Tony Jordan, has produced a lovely wine with a yeasty nose and vanilla overtones.*	£12.30	Widely Available	(B)
CROSER 1994, PETALUMA WINES South Australia	*A light, yeasty aroma with nuances of citrus and fresh bread. A rich, creamy palate.*	£12.30	TH NEI PHI EOO	(B)
CROSER 1993, PETALUMA WINES South Australia	*Sweet American cream soda aromas with a yeast infuenced oak and apple palate and a clean finish.*	£12.50	BEN	(B)
YALUMBA CUVÉE "D" 1994, YALUMBA WINERY South Australia	*Good yeasty, marmite aromas with delicate autolytic, tart apple flavours. Good length, balanced finish.*	£12.50	OD GRA FRT	(S)

WINE OF THE YEAR

E&E SPARKLING SHIRAZ NV, BRL HARDY South Australia	*A unique Australian style, this sparkling red wine is full of spice and tannins. Good with Kangaroo!?*	**£17.10**	VLW IVY VDV WRW	**B**

AUSTRALIA • FORTIFIED

MICK MORRIS RUTHERGLEN LIQUEUR MUSCAT, ORLANDO WYNDHAM GROUP Victoria	*Bags of rich orange and raisiny fruits combine with fair acidity to form this immense wine.*	**£5.60**	Widely Available	**S**
SEPPELTSFIELD SHOW PALOMINO DP117, SEPPELT WINES South Australia	*Attractive fresh nose. Well structured with zippy acidity. Light style with plenty of appeal.*	**£6.10**	Widely Available	**B**
YALUMBA MUSEUM SHOW RESERVE RUTHERGLEN MUSCAT, YALUMBA WINERY Victoria	*The palate is well structured with bitter chocolate and treacle fruit balanced by fine acidity.*	**£6.30**	VWC VLW JN GRA FRT	**S**
CARLYLE LIQUEUR MUSCAT, PFEIFFER WINES Victoria	*Christmas pudding in a glass: stacks of sultanas combining with rich, tangy orange fruit.*	**£6.50**	GNW WOI IRV	**S**
YALDARA RESERVE OLD TAWNY, YALDARA WINES South Australia	*This superb orange, gold tawny wine has a rich, juicy raisiny palate and beautiful length.*	**£6.90**	Widely Available	**S**
STANTON & KILLEEN RUTHERGLEN MUSCAT, STANTON & KILLEEN Victoria	*Luscious raisined fruits with coffee characteristics show on a rich, warm nose and round, mouth-filling palate.*	**£7.70**	Widely Available	**G**

SEPPELT RUTHERGLEN SHOW MUSCAT DP 63, SEPPELT WINES Victoria	*Bitter treacle leaps out of the glass and is nicely balanced by good acidity, with good length on the lingering palate.*	**£7.90**	Widely Available	**S**
CAMPBELLS RUTHERGLEN MUSCAT, CAMPBELLS Victoria	*Sweet stewed raisins and figs leap out of the glass in this intensely flavoured wine.*	**£8.30**	Widely Available	**S**
DE BORTOLI LIQUEUR MUSCAT, DE BORTOLI WINES New South Wales	*Attractive caramel toffee on the nose precedes a rich treacle finish with balanced acidity.*	**£9.00**	IVY	**B**
CHAMBERS RUTHERGLEN MUSCAT, CHAMBERS ROSEWOOD WINERY Victoria	*A mouthful of sweet toffee balances well with good acidity in this lovely clean wine.*	**£9.30**	Widely Available	**B**
OLD VINE MUSCADELLE, CHAMBERS ROSEWOOD WINERY Victoria	*Intense barley sugar fruit nose follows through to a warm, rich palate and citrus finish.*	**£11.40**	WSG VDV ODF OD	**S**
BROWN BROTHERS LIQUEUR MUSCAT, BROWN BROTHERS Victoria	*Incredible dark mahogany colour, with huge treacle and orange fruit aromas leading to a rich, demerera palate.*	**£12.30**	Widely Available	**G**
CAMPBELLS OLD RUTHERGLEN MUSCAT, CAMPBELLS Victoria	*Dense and raisiny with rich toffee fruit aromas coming through on the nose and palate.*	**£14.60**	WSG NI ODF OD NY	**S**
CHAMBERS OLD VINE SPECIAL MUSCAT, CHAMBERS ROSEWOOD WINERY Victoria	*Rich aromas of toffee apples and marmalade lead to a mouthfilling palate of raisined fruit.*	**£14.70**	WSG NY VDV	**G**

McWilliam's Liqueur Muscat, McWilliam's Wines New South Wales	*Lovely complex fruit with stacks of floral, orange and chocolate flavours, following through on the palate. An eternal finish.*	**£19.90**	DBY CDT	(G)

AUSTRIA

THE DESSERT WINES OF AUSTRIA are some of the best value in Europe. Having shaken off its unfavourable past image, this country now produces an impressive range of noble varietals, including Chardonnay, Pinot Noir and Cabernet Sauvignon. Small producers continue to experiment with a rich concoction of differing styles, culminating in great wines at competitive prices. Austria is definitely a country to watch for the future.

AUSTRIA • RED

BLAUFRANKISCH 1993, PAUL & MARIA BRAUNSTEIN Burgenland	*Pleasant, brambly fruit on the nose is followed by juicy, black cherry and clove flavours.*	£3.90	VIL	(B)

AUSTRIA • WHITE

PINOT BLANC 1995, ENGELBERT PRIELER Burgenland	*An austere, minerally style of wine with soft, peachy aromas and a smoky palate.*	£8.10	FW CES	(B)
WEINGUT SONNHOF JURTSCHITSCH GRÜNER VELTLINER LOISERBERG 1995 Nieder-Osterreich	*Biscuit and grapefruit characteristics come through on the nose of this attractive spicy wine.*	£9.00	CES	(B)
WEINGUT KOLLWENTZ-RÖMERHOF CHARDONNAY VON LEITHAGEBIRGE 1995 Burgenland	*Clean, fresh, slightly green fruits emerge to form a minerally, long-lasting finish.*	£10.00	GI	(B)

AUSTRIA • SWEET

Gewürztraminer TBA 1995, Helmut Lang Burgenland	*A lush, ripe wine. Parma violets and sweet floral flavours; oily and refined, yet delicate.*	£10.80	DIR FW	(B)
Sämling 88 BA 1994, Helmut Lang Burgenland	*Lusciously sweet, this wine has a nicely-balanced combination of rich fruit and acidity.*	£11.90	TAN FW CES	(B)
Sämling 88 BA 1991, Helmut Lang Burgenland	*Aromas of lychees and crushed peaches predominate, leading to an elegant palate with soft, balancing acidity.*	£13.30	FW	(S)
Welschriesling BA 1994, Helmut Lang Burgenland	*The intensity of fruit on the nose is reflected on the concentrated, luscious palate and finish.*	£15.00	FW	(S)
Grüner Veltliner BA 1991, Helmut Lang Burgenland	*Toasted oak character on the nose leads into a golden wine with honey and melon flavours.*	£15.50	FW	(B)
Sämling 88 TBA 1995, Weinbau Nekowitsch Burgenland	*Some lovely citrus fruit characteristics coming through on this nicely-structured, well-balanced wine. Excellent!*	£16.00	NY	(S)
Sämling 88 Ausbruch 1995, Helmut Lang Burgenland	*Richly sweet with a good dose of balancing acidity adding freshness to this attractive wine.*	£16.10	TAN FW	(B)

GEWÜRZTRAMINER BA 1994, HELMUT LANG Burgenland	*Rich, spicy fruit on the nose. In the mouth, a wine of richness and great elegance.*	£16.60	FW	(B)
WELSCHRIESLING TBA 1995, JOHAN MUNZENRIEDER Burgenland	*A sweet and refined wine offering honeyed fruit on a creamy palate. A reassuringly smooth finish.*	£17.00	RS	(B)
SÄMLING 88 AUSBRUCH 1993, HELMUT LANG Burgenland	*The luscious, rich palate has some wonderful lemon and honey flavours, balanced by fresh acidity.*	£17.10	FW	(S)
CHARDONNAY AUSBRUCH 1995, HELMUT LANG Burgenland	*Light and delicate, this wine has a subtlety of fruit with citrus characteristics shining through on the finish.*	£18.20	FW	(B)
PINOT GRIS AUSBRUCH 1992, HELMUT LANG Burgenland	*The honey and nut characteristics on the nose follow through to the well-balanced, concentrated palate.*	£18.70	FW	(B)
WELSCHRIESLING AUSBRUCH 1991, HELMUT LANG Burgenland	*Intense flavours of honey and grapefruit with a rich, lingering finish. A wine to savour.*	£20.90	FW	(B)
SÄMLING 88 AUSBRUCH 1991, HELMUT LANG Burgenland	*Stacks of honey fruit flavours stick to the well-rounded palate of this rich, sweet wine.*	£22.00	FW	(S)
WELSCHRIESLING No1 ZWISCHEN DEN SEEN TBA 1995, ALOIS KRACHER Burgenland	*Citrus fruit character on the nose; following through to the smooth, seemingly ever-lasting finish. Wonderful!*	£22.00	NY	(G)

SÄMLING 88 TBA 1994, HELMUT LANG Burgenland	*Some lovely, grapey fruit is balanced by some superb, woody characteristics on the nose.*	£23.00	FW	(B)
SCHEUREBE No.6 ZWISCHEN DEN SEEN TBA 1995, ALOIS KRACHER Burgenland	*Soft, ripe, candied fruits come through on the palate of this nice, gentle wine. A wonderfully tasty aperatif!*	£23.00	NY	(B)
WELSCHRIESLING AUSBRUCH 1989, HELMUT LANG Burgenland	*This deep orange wine has marmalade and apricot fruit combining on both the nose and palate.*	£23.00	FW	(S)
SÄMLING 88 TBA 1995, HELMUT LANG Burgenland	*A wonderful concentration of citrus fruit with some woody, buttery notes dominating the palate.*	£23.00	FW	(S)
MUSCAT No.5 ZWISCHEN DEN SEEN TBA 1995, ALOIS KRACHER Burgenland	*Good, soft fruit nose with lots of honey; this wine has an excellent, firm structure.*	£23.80	NY	(B)
WELSCHRIESLING No2 ZWISCHEN DEN SEEN TBA 1995, ALOIS KRACHER Burgenland	*A rich, toffeed nose is followed by a well-balanced palate with marmalade overtones.*	£23.80	NY	(S)
GRÜNER VELTLINER TBA 1995, HELMUT LANG Burgenland	*Marzipan on the nose is backed up by a luscious palate of almonds and orange marmalade.*	£24.70	FW	(S)
WELSCHRIESLING TBA 1994, HELMUT LANG Burgenland	*Honey and melon fruit flavours combine on the palate. Richly opulent in character. Delightful.*	£25.20	FW	(S)

SÄMLING 88 TBA 1991, HELMUT LANG Burgenland	*Richly sweet with some nice, fresh acidity balancing the fruit on this attractive wine.*	£26.00	FW	**B**
SCHILFWEIN TRADITION 1995, WEINBAU NEKOWITSCH Burgenland	*Lovely apricot and honey aromas leaping out of the glass. A battle of extremes results in an extraordinary wine!*	£26.00	NY	**S**
SCHILFWEIN TRADITION 1994, WEINBAU NEKOWITSCH Neusiedlersee	*A full, rich wine; raisiny sweet fruits with under-lying acidity and a long, elegant finish.*	£26.00	NY	**S**
WELSCHRIESLING TBA 1995, HELMUT LANG Burgenland	*Intense fruit characteris-tics come through on the nose and palate of this lusciously sweet wine.*	£26.30	FW	**B**
CHARDONNAY TBA 1995, HELMUT LANG Burgenland	*Rich, dried figs and cream comes across with a very good intensity of flavour.*	£26.30	FW	**S**
NO.11 MUSKAT TBA 1995, ALOIS KRACHER Burgenland	*Spicy, botrytis nose with honey notes; rich, round-ed glycerine palate with a sweet, unctuous finish*	£28.00	NY	**B**
NOUVELLE VAGUE CHARDONNAY WELSCH-RIESLING NO.7 TBA 1995, ALOIS KRACHER Burgenland	*A spicy, heady nose follows through to a sweetly honeyed palate balanced by tangy acidity.*	£28.00	NY	**B**
SCHEUREBE NO3 ZWISCHEN DEN SEEN TBA 1995, ALOIS KRACHER Burgenland	*Bags of honeyed fruit come through on this lovely sweetie. A well-made wine.*	£28.00	NY	**S**

PINOT NOIR TBA 1995, HELMUT LANG Burgenland	*Lightly aromatic rose petals are found on the nose of this attractive pink, sweet wine.*	**£28.40**	FW	(B)
SÄMLING 88 AUSBRUCH 1989, HELMUT LANG Burgenland	*Bags of potential can be seen in this rich, attractive wine; lovely, balanced acidity.*	**£28.40**	FW	(S)
OPITZ GOLDACKERL TBA 1995, WILLI OPITZ Burgenland	*Ripe peach and apricot fruit add to the excellent structure of this well-balanced wine.*	**£28.90**	T&W	(S)
ZWEIGELT ROSÉ NO.9 NOUVELLE VAGUE TBA 1995, ALOIS KRACHER Burgenland	*A good ripe, spiced fruit quality comes through on both the nose and palate. Lasts and lasts!*	**£29.00**	NY	(B)
ZWEIGELT ROSÉ NO.10 NOUVELLE VAGUE TBA 1995, ALOIS KRACHER Burgenland	*Attractively pink in colour, this intensely unctuous wine has stacks of rich, sticky fruit.*	**£29.00**	NY	(S)
NOUVELLE VAGUE TRAMINER NO.8 TBA 1995, ALOIS KRACHER Burgenland	*An intense flavour of caramelised fruits and marzipan combines with fresh, zesty acidity.*	**£29.00**	NY	(S)
SCHEUREBE NO.4 ZWISCHEN DEN SEEN TBA 1995, ALOIS KRACHER Burgenland	*Ripe, honeyed botrytis fruit shines through on the nose of this stunning, golden wine.*	**£29.00**	NY	(G)
PINOT BLANC TBA 1990, HELMUT LANG Burgenland	*Rich honey aromas are backed up by smooth caramel flavours on the lingering palate.*	**£30.60**	FW	(B)

PINOT BLANC TBA 1993, HELMUT LANG Burgenland	*Delicate acidity with hints of pink grapefruit and soft brown sugar. A wine with finesse.*	£30.60	FW	S
CHARDONNAY AUSBRUCH 1992, HELMUT LANG Burgenland	*Orangy citrus fruit aromas combine with warm honey notes on a lingering palate.*	£32.80	FW	B
NOUVELLE VAGUE CHARDONNAY No.13 TBA 1995, ALOIS KRACHER Burgenland	*Late harvest Chardonnay! Harmonious richness of fruit matched by restrained acidity. Paradise in a glass.*	£33.00	NY	B
PINOT GRIS TBA, WILLI OPITZ Burgenland	*Light, citrus fruit appears on the well-balanced, delicate palate which has immense length.*	£33.30	T&W	S
NOUVELLE VAGUE SCHEUREBE No.14 TBA 1995, ALOIS KRACHER Burgenland	*Big, rich, concentrated wine with a lovely marmalade character balanced by some great, fresh acidity.*	£34.00	NY	S
PINOT BLANC AUSBRUCH 1991, HELMUT LANG Burgenland	*A refreshing wine with ripe lemon and lime flavours on the soft nose and palate.*	£34.90	FW	B
SÄMLING 88 WELSCHRIESLING EISWEIN 1990, HELMUT LANG Burgenland	*Toffee-fruit aromas are backed up by powerful acidity on the smooth caramel palate.*	£34.90	FW	S
WELSCHRIESLING No.15 ZWISCHEN DEN SEEN TBA 1995 Burgenland	*On the palate, rich, syrupy toffee-fruit attacks the senses, giving an enormous mouthful.*	£35.00	NY	S

AUSTRIA • SWEET

GEWÜRZTRAMINER TBA 1995, WILLI OPITZ Burgenland	*The palate has rich 'turkish delight', balanced by fresh acidity and a wonderfully clean finish.*	**£39.50**	T&W	(S)
WELSCHRIESLING TBA 1994, WILLI OPITZ Burgenland	*The palate has a well-balanced, marmalade fruit character which floods the mouth.*	**£44.00**	T&W	(S)
OPITZ ONE TBA 1994, WILLI OPITZ Burgenland	*Figs and prunes come through on the nose of this well-balanced attractive wine. Luxurious!*	**£46.50**	RBS	(B)

EASTERN EUROPE

Traditional wine growing areas of Eastern Europe, such as Bulgaria, Romania and Hungary, are experimenting with both indigenous and classic grape varieties. Following the injection of capital investment and increased freedom within these countries we can expect even higher standards in future vintages. From rich Bulgarian Cabernet Sauvignon to fresh Hungarian Sauvignon Blanc, these wines continue to represent good value for money.

BULGARIA • RED

SAFEWAY YOUNG VATTED MERLOT 1996, VINPROM ROUSSE Rousse	*Juicy, fresh, soft, red fruit aromas with pleasant raspberries on the palate and drying tannins.*	£3.00	SAF	(B)
DOMAINE BOYAR LOVICO ROSSINA CABERNET MERLOT COUNTRY WINE NV, LOVICO ROSSINA Pavlikeni	*Light, cherry aromas on the nose and palate on this youthful wine with rich tannins.*	£3.00	BUD VW	(B)
DOMAINE BOYAR IAMBOL CABERNET SAUVIGNON 1996, VINIS IAMBOL Iambol	*Rich, plummy aromas on a deeply-coloured wine with concentrated, jammy flavours and a delightfully soft finish.*	£3.00	TH DBY	(B)
SAFEWAY YOUNG VATTED CABERNET SAUVIGNON 1996, VINI SLIVEN	*Generous, crunchy raspberry aromas lead onto lovely crisp, almost tart, red berry flavours and a balanced palate.*	£3.00	SAF	(S)
BVC YANTRA VALLEY CABERNET SAUVIGNON CONTROLIRAN 1992, VINPROM ROUSSE Rousse	*Mature blackcurrant fruit aromas with old wood, spice and tar nuances and sweet berry fruit on the palate.*	£3.70	JS	(B)

BVC SLIVEN CABERNET SAUVIGNON RESERVE 1991, VINI SLIVEN Sliven	*A sweet herbal, cherry jam nose leads to a palate of mature fruit with mint notes.*	£4.00	SAF	(B)
BVC GORCHIVKA CABERNET SAUVIGNON ESTATE SELECTION 1993, VINPROM SVISCHTOV Svischtov	*An intense bouquet of jammy, herbaceous aromas. A deep coloured wine with lingering blackcurrant flavours.*	£4.30	SAF	(S)
BVC TWIN PEAKS CABERNET SAUVIGNON 1991, VINPROM ROUSSE Rousse	*Sweet plum jam bouquet leads onto an intense palate of minty black-currants and soft tannins.*	£4.50	TH	(B)
DOMAINE BOYAR CZAR SIMEON CABERNET SAUVIGNON SPECIAL RESERVE 1990, LOVICO SUHINDOL Vinenka	*Sweet plummy nose and palate with hints of oak and a rounded, ripe, pleasing finish.*	£7.00	JS	(B)

HUNGARY • RED

DOMAINE TIFFAN'S VILLANYI CABERNET SAUVIGNON BARRIQUE 1995 Villany	*A ripe, bell-pepper, minty nose leads to a mouth-filling herbaceous, black cherry, fruit palate.*	£5.00	DBY	(B)

HUNGARY • WHITE

NAGYREDE WINERY PINOT GRIGIO 1996, NAGYREDE WINERY Mátraalja	*Ripe lime fruit on the nose with buttery, melon flavours on a long finish. A great example.*	£3.20	JS SAF	(B)

SPAR HUNGARIAN COUNTRY DANUBE WHITE NV, INTERCONSULT Dunaszentmikols	*A well-made wine, showing beautiful, fruity flavours and crisp acidity on the palate.*	£3.20	SPR	(B)
MATRA MOUNTAIN OAKED CHARDONNAY 1996, NAGYREDE WINERY	*Tropical fruit and vanilla flavours, enhanced by crisp acidity on a well-rounded palate.*	£3.50	SAF	(B)
PINOT GRIS OAKED RESERVE 1996, NAGYREDE WINERY Mátraalja	*Intense lime aromas on the nose, with a hint of earthiness and a well-structured palate.*	£3.50	WWI OD	(S)
LAKESIDE OAKED CHARDONNAY 1996, BALATONBOGLAR WINERY Balatonboglar	*Oaky aroma on the nose, backed by plenty of fruit and good integration of drying acidity.*	£3.60	W	(B)
THE GYÖNGYÖS ESTATE CHARDONNAY 1996, DANUBIANA BT BONYHAD Mátraalja	*Lemon drops and crisp acidity show on the palate with a good, long finish full of fruit.*	£3.80	TH FUL TO U CWS	(B)
THE GYÖNGYÖS ESTATE BARREL FERMENTED CHARDONNAY 1996, DANUBIANA BT BONYHAD Mátraalja	*Balanced acidity and restrained, ripe, citrus fruit with rich oak notes in this soft, yet full wine.*	£4.00	A	(B)

HUNGARY • SWEET

DISZNOKO TOKAJI ASZU 4 PUTTONYOS 1992, DOMAINE DISZNOKO Tokay	*Rich, intense and nutty, packed with tropical fruit, displaying concentrated flavours in the mouth.*	£10.80	DBY TRO	(B)

TOKAJI ASZU 5 PUTTONYOS 1992, DOMAINE DISZNOKO Tokay	*Unctious, honeyed nose which follows through onto the palate with lovely fresh, zesty fruit.*	£12.70	DBY MWW IVY SHJ WSO OD	**S**
TOKAJI ASZU 5 PUTTONYOS 1993, CHATEAU MEGYER Tokay	*Monumental, creamy fruit on the nose follows through to the very well-balanced palate.*	£13.00	MFS ENO	**G**
BLUE LABEL ASZU 5 PUTTONYOS 1993, ROYAL TOKAJI WINE COMPANY Tokay	*Floral fruit is balanced by some good acidity and honeyed marmalade. An attractive wine.*	£14.40	MWW SV BBR LEA EP	**G**
TOKAJI ASZU 6 PUTTONYOS 1992, DOMAINE DISZNOKO Tokay	*A wonderful waxy, lanolin quality adds to complex fruit characters in this sweetly-balanced wine of class.*	£15.40	DBY IVY	**S**
BLUE LABEL ASZU 5 PUTTONYOS 1991, ROYAL TOKAJI WINE COMPANY Tokay	*Intense rich, nutty characteristics show through on the nose and palate of this impressive wine. Mouth-coating!*	£16.90	RBS SV EP	**S**
TOKAJI 6 PUTTONYOS ASZU 1981, BODEGAS OREMUS Tokay	*This lovely, delicate wine has rich, interesting fruit which is balanced by some good acidity.*	£20.80	DIR	**S**
BETSEK TOKAJI ASZU 5 PUTTONYOS 1990, ROYAL TOKAJI WINE COMPANY Tokaji	*This richly-sweet wine has a good weight of well-balanced fruit on the palate. Great finish!*	£25.00	BBR	**B**
NYULASZO 6 PUTTONYOS 1ST GROWTH 1700 1993, ROYAL TOKAJI WINE COMPANY Tokay	*Clean, smoky, delicately-fragrant wine with lovely balanced acidity and a superb, lingering palate.*	£27.50	EP LEA	**B**

NYULASZO 5 PUTTONYOS 1ST GROWTH 1700, 1991 ROYAL TOKAJI WINE COMPANY Tokay	*The palate of rich caramel fruit is balanced by some very attractive, crisp acidity.*	**£39.40**	TAN	**G**

MONTENEGRO

MONTE CHEVAL VRANAC 1993, PLANTAZE Zeta White Paul Valley	*Ripe, citrus fruit aromas on a zingy lemon and lime palate balanced with floral notes.*	**£4.50**	MUK	**B**

ROMANIA • RED

MALT HOUSE VINTNERS TOHANI ROMANIAN MERLOT 1995, TOHANI Dealul Mare	*Leafy, vegetal and oak aromas with chocolate and cherries on the medium-bodied, balanced palate.*	**£3.20**	MHV	**B**
IDLEROCK PINOT NOIR RESERVE 1996, THE HANWOOD GROUP Dealul Mare	*Lovely summer fruit characters dominate the nose and are carried over onto a soft palate.*	**£3.80**	JS	**B**
IDLEROCK MERLOT RESERVE 1996, THE HANWOOD GROUP Dealul Mare	*Spicy, rhubarb jam aromas; these ripe characters carry over onto the soft, medium-bodied palate.*	**£3.80**	JS	**B**
SAHATENI VINEYARDS BARREL MATURED MERLOT SPECIAL RESERVE 1994, VINEXPORT Dealul Mare	*A deep, purple colour with sweet cherry aromas carrying over to a smooth palate with spicy notes.*	**£5.00**	HAE TRO CWS NRW LES	**B**

ROMANIA • WHITE

MURFATLAR CHARDONNAY 1996, VIE VIN MURFATLAR SA Dobrudjea	*A big, fat wine with lots of tropical fruit, lavish acidity and good length. A real mouthful!*	**£3.50**	HAE	(B)
RIVER ROUTE PINOT GRIGIO 1996, CARL REH Cernavoda	*An aromatic wine with a rich, earthy nose and a lemon and cooked apple palate. Fresh and zingy.*	**£3.50**	CRS	(S)

ENGLAND

ENGLISH WINES ARE STARTING TO COMPETE on individuality and quality and this has resulted in a collection of impressive medals. English producers have adapted their style of wine-making and introduced recently-developed grape varieties. The Germanic style has been left behind and the future for English vineyards lies in the continuing development of a classic, distinctive style.

ENGLAND • RED

CHAPEL DOWN WINES EPOCH RESERVE 1995, CHAPEL DOWN WINES Sussex	*Soft, berry fruits predominate the nose and palate of this impressive English red wine.*	£6.80	BNK W CDO CES GNW NRW	**B**

ENGLAND • WHITE

TENTERDEN ESTATE DRY NV, TENTERDEN VINEYARD Southern Counties	*A delightful pineapple nose with a hint of tropical fruit that is attractively well-balanced with a full finish.*	£5.00	BNK CDO TO CES	**S**
WYKEN SONATA 1994, WYKEN ESTATE VINEYARD Suffolk	*A rich and delicious wine offering a lemon palate with overtones of marzipan and asparagus.*	£5.50	WKV	**B**
NUTBOURNE VINEYARDS SCHONBURGER 1992, NUTBOURNE VINEYARDS Southern Counties	*Attractive, grapey nose with a good depth of fruit and plenty of body on the palate.*	£6.00	NBV	**B**

THORNTON HOLMES MERSEA 1995, THORNTON HOLMES Southern Counties	*Off-dry white wine. Gooseberries and a great tropical fruit aroma up to a lingering aftertaste.*	£7.40	L&W MSA W TH WR BU WBE	(B)
BREAKY BOTTOM SEYVAL BLANC OAKED FUME 1992, BREAKY BOTTOM VINEYARD East Sussex	*A good intensity of fresh, clean fruit on the palate. Subtle with elegance and gentle style.*	£7.50	BBV RBS BBU GDU HAR	(B)
BREAKY BOTTOM MULLER THURGAU 1992, BREAKY BOTTOM VINEYARD East Sussex	*Pale, yellow colour. Fairly smoky, ripe nose with uplifting acidity and well-rounded finish.*	£7.50	BBV BBU GDU HAR	(B)
BREAKY BOTTOM MÜLLER-THURGAU 1995, BREAKY BOTTOM VINEYARD East Sussex	*Aromatic honey, floral aroma. Intense on the palate with profound acidity and good length.*	£7.50	BBV BBU GDU	(B)
HIDDEN SPRING GOTHIC DRY TABLE WINE 1995, HIDDEN SPRING VINEYARD East Sussex	*A lively, clean wine with a limey bouquet and apple flavours on the crisp finish.*	£8.00	HSV HAC EWC	(B)
SHAWSGATE BACCHUS 1994, SHAWSGATE VINEYARD East Anglia	*The tasters noted a rush of nettle. They found the wine rounded and balanced up to the finish.*	£8.50	SHA	(B)
SHAWSGATE BACCHUS 1996, SHAWSGATE VINEYARD East Anglia	*Clean, crisp, well-made, medium-bodied wine, with intense fruitiness and good length.*	£8.80	SHA	(B)

Pinpoint who sells the wine you wish to buy by turning to the stockist codes. If you know the name of the wine you want to buy, use the alphabetical index. If the price is your motivation, refer to the invaluable price guide index; red and white wines under £5, sparkling wines under £10 and champagne under £15. Happy hunting!

ENGLAND • SWEET

DENBIES SPECIAL LATE HARVESTED 1995, DENBIES WINE ESTATE Surrey	*The rich, honeyed sweetness is balanced by excellent acidity and barley-sugar fruit flavour.*	**£6.20**	DBY VIL TO DBS OD	(S)

ENGLAND • SPARKLING

WOOLDINGS VINEYARD QUALITY SPARKLING 1994, WOOLDINGS VINEYARD Hampshire	*Lemony, yeasty aromas follow a good mousse and ripe, citrus fruits palate with a clean finish.*	**£12.50**	WOO	(B)
NYETIMBER PREMIER CUVÉE 1992, NYETIMBER VINEYARD Sussex	*Hints of honey on the nose; good mousse, aged flavours showing length and a dry, appley finish.*	**£15.00**	NYE	(B)

FRANCE

Facing increased competition from around the world, France has managed to hold its own in this year's Challenge. Winemakers have adapted their styles of wine to attract a new wave of consumers towards interesting grape varieties from lesser known regions. Grande Marque Champagnes continue to lead the field, with vintage wines predominating. Where Appellation Contrôlée laws are not enforced some award winning wines have emerged.

FRANCE • ALPINE

SAVAGNIN FRUITIÈRE VINICOLE D'ARBOIS 1990, FRUITIÈRE VINICOLE D'ARBOIS Arbois	*Stylish wine, that opens up fully onto a fruity palate with good length.*	£15.00	NIC	**B**

FRANCE • ALSACE • WHITE

PINOT BLANC 1996, CAVE INGERSHEIM, JEAN GEILER Alsace	*Deep aromas of grass and lemon zest lead to a spicy palate with herbaceous notes.*	£5.00	CRS	**B**
PINOT BLANC ROTENBERG 1995, BERNARD STAEHLE Alsace	*An intense spicy, peachy nose is followed by mouthfilling ripe lychee flavours on the palate.*	£5.00	PAV	**S**
GEWURZTRAMINER GRAND CRU BRAND 1994, CAVE VINICOLE DE TURKHEIM Alsace	*Stacks of ripe fruit and rich spice overflow on the nose of this heady wine.*	£8.00	DBY U BKW	**B**

MUSCAT D'ALSACE RESERVE PERSONELLE SIGELLE 1995, KUENTZ-BAS Alsace	*A delicate floral Muscat nose with spice notes on a dry palate with honeyed overtones.*	£10.00	PNA U JEM WIM	**B**
GEWURZTRAMINER WINZERHEIM 1995, DOMAINE ZIND-HUMBRECHT Alsace	*Ripe, aromatic nose with gentle spiciness. Lightly honeyed flavours with lingering floral notes on palate.*	£11.00	DBY ABY	**B**
GEWURZTRAMINER CUVÉE KARINE VEILLE VIGNES RES.1993, DOMAINE MITTNACHT-KLACK Alsace	*Powerful lychee and spice characters on the nose are mirrored on the rich, lasting palate.*	£11.00	WIN	**B**
TOKAY PINOT GRIS VIEILLES VIGNES 1995, DOMAINE SCHOFFIT Alsace	*Elegant soft spicy aromas moving on to a palate of smoky richness and a long, aromatic finish.*	£12.00	HBJ	**B**
RIESLING CLOS ST THEOBALD GRAND CRU 1995, DOMAINE SCHOFFIT Alsace	*Fresh petrol nose having floral notes with a crisp cirus finish to the balanced palate.*	£12.00	HBJ	**B**
RIESLING WINECK-SCHLOSSBERG GRAND CRU 1995, MEYER-FONNÉ Alsace	*Aromas of lighty spiced apples lead onto a concentrated floral palate with hints of petrol on the nose.*	£12.30	L&W	**B**
RIESLING CLOS HAUSEREN 1995, DOMAINE ZIND-HUMBRECHT Alsace	*Displays an incredible concentration of fruit which is perfectly in balance with the crisp acidity on the finish.*	£14.70	DBY ABY PHI	**G**
GEWURZTRAMINER CUVÉE ALEXANDRE 1994, DOMAINE SCHOFFIT Alsace	*Honey, spiced apples, freshly cut flowers and a stab of zesty acidity give this plenty of finesse.*	£15.00	HBJ	**S**

GEWURZTRAMINER 1994, DOMAINE SCHOFFIT Alsace	*Luscious, spicy peach and honeyed fruit. Great verve from citrus acidity and ripe, tropical fruits.*	**£15.00**	HBJ	(S)
PINOT GRIS VIEILLES VIGNES 1995, DOMAINE ZIND-HUMBRECHT Alsace	*A pungent nose precedes the palate with gooseberry undertones on a long, lingering finish.*	**£16.40**	ABY	(B)
PINOT GRIS HEIMBOURG 1994, DOMAINE ZIND-HUMBRECHT Alsace	*Intense herbaceous aromas with spicy, floral notes. A powerful palate dominated by ripe, citrus flavours.*	**£18.10**	DBY ABY	(G)
GEWURZTRAMINER HEIMBOURG 1995, DOMAINE ZIND-HUMBRECHT Alsace	*Smooth, creamy and rich. A ripe style full of tropical fruit. Will develop further.*	**£18.80**	JN ABY	(S)
PINOT GRIS CLOS WINSBUHL 1995, DOMAINE ZIND-HUMBRECHT Alsace	*Clean, crisp wine with green nettle and tangy gooseberry fruit clinging on the palate.*	**£19.80**	DBY ABY	(B)
GEWURZTRAMINER GRAND CRU EICHBERG 1994, KUENTZ-BAS Alsace	*Soft lychee and honey aromas flow onto a gentle spicy palate with a zesty finish.*	**£23.50**	PNA U JEM WIM PF BBR	(B)
GEWURZTRAMINER CLOS WINDSBUHL 1995, DOMAINE ZIND-HUMBRECHT Alsace	*Sweet peachy fruit aromas. Palate is drier with good zippy acidity. Full of character and class.*	**£26.50**	DBY MTB JN ABY	(B)
GEWÜRZTRAMINER HEIMBOURG 1994, DOMAINE ZIND-HUMBRECHT Alsace	*Intense, aromatic, floral nose. Elegant wine with a steely, mineral character and rich, oily, violet flavours on the finish.*	**£27.10**	DBY JN ABY	(B)

GEWURZTRAMINER HERRENWEG TURKHEIM 1995, DOMAINE ZIND-HUMBRECHT Alsace	*Full and rounded, this concentrated wine has plenty of ripe, tropical fruit. Warm, spicy finish.*	£35.90	JN ABY	(S)

FRANCE • ALSACE • SWEET

GEWURZTRAMINER 1994, CVPG PFAFFENHEIM Alsace	*This has an exotically ripe nose with hints of melons and grapefruit shining through.*	£6.40	SHJ	(S)
PINOT D'ALSACE 1995, DOMAINE ZIND-HUMBRECHT Alsace	*Strong flavours of rich stewed fruits with underlying subtle acidity culminate in a long, generous finish.*	£11.20	CEB RBS JN ABY	(G)
TOKAY PINOT GRIS SGN 1992, DOMAINE MITTNACHT-KLACK Alsace	*There is some wonderful complex apple fruit showing through on this excellent golden wine.*	£20.00	WIN	(B)
GEWURZTRAMINER GRAND CRU ALTENBERG VEND-AGE TARDIVE 1989, CHARLES KOEHLY ET FILS Alsace	*Wonderful late harvested wine full of ripe tropical fruits, creamy nuttiness and a dash of spice. Perfectly balanced.*	£20.00	HW SV	(S)
GEWURZTRAMINER SGN 1994, DOMAINE MITTNACHT-KLACK Alsace	*Rich spice infused with lychee aromas. Opulent fruit on the palate with a good, long, rich finish.*	£20.00	WIN	(S)
PINOT GRIS HEIMBOURG 1994, DOMAINE ZIND-HUMBRECHT Alsace	*Sweet grapefruit character on the palate with some lovely balancing acidity. Refreshing fruit.*	£27.90	ABY	(S)

TOKAY PINOT GRIS CLOS ST THEOBALD GRAND CRU SGN 1994, DOMAINE SCHOFFIT Alsace	*Caramel and crystallised fruits leap out of the glass in this rich, sweet wine.*	**£30.00**	HBJ	B
RIESLING CLOS ST THEOBALD GRAND CRU SGN 1994, DOMAINE SCHOFFIT Alsace	*Spicy aromas with floral undertones. This wine exudes flavours of ripe, caramalised, citrus fruits.*	**£30.00**	HBJ	S
PINOT GRIS CLOS JEBSAL 1994, DOMAINE ZIND-HUMBRECHT Alsace	*Intense, ripe, honeyed pears on the nose. Subtle fruit flavours on a developing palate.*	**£67.60**	ABY	G

FRANCE • ALSACE • SPARKLING

CRÉMANT D'ALSACE CUVÉE PRESTIGE NV, RENÉ MURE Alsace	*Rich, yeasty aromas with notes of exotic fruits carry over onto the well-balanced palate.*	**£9.10**	DIR LNR NIC NICOLAS	B

FRANCE • BEAUJOLAIS • RED

MALT HOUSE VINTNERS DOMAINE CHARPENAY BEAUJOLAIS VILLAGES 1996, CAVE DE BULLY Beaujolais	*Delightfully made wine with juicy fruit flavours, leading to clear cherry flavours on the finish.*	**£4.00**	MHV	B
MALT HOUSE VINTNERS BEAUJOLAIS VILLAGES 1995, HENRI LA FONTAINE Beaujolais	*Seductive, sweet strawberry fruit aromas on the nose, which follow through on a well-rounded palate.*	**£4.00**	MHV	B

BEAUJOLAIS VILLAGES 1996, BARTON & GUESTIER Beaujolais	*An attractive, jammy nose precedes a lively palate. Superbly-structured with good acidity and backing tannins.*	£4.00	SEA	(S)
ST MICHAEL BEAUJOLAIS 1996, PAUL SAPIN Beaujolais	*Light cherry colour in glass. With attractive raspberry fruit, uplifting acidity and excellent length, finishing well.*	£5.00	M&S	(B)
MORGON DOMAINE JAMBON 1996, MICHEL JAMBON Beaujolais	*Attractive cherries on the nose, leading to a well-structured fruity palate with good weight.*	£6.50	A	(B)
BROUILLY 1996, JEAN-PAUL SELLES Beaujolais	*Cherry red wine shows an attractive, peppery Gamay nose, with juicy fruit on a lively palate.*	£6.70	PLB SMF	(S)
MORGON 1996, CHÂTEAU DE PIZAY Beaujolais	*Freshly crushed berry nose and ripe summer fruit flavours on a medium length finish.*	£7.00	CNL	(B)
REGNIE 1995, GILLES DUCROUX Beaujolais	*A young wine with a fruity, slightly closed nose, that opens up nicely on the palate.*	£7.00	WSC	(B)
CHIROUBLES 1996, GEORGES DUBOEUF Beaujolais	*Good, juicy fruit aroma, followed by light zesty blackberry flavour and uplifting acidity.*	£7.00	DBY LNR PAG	(B)
MALT HOUSE VINTNERS FLEURIE 1996, HENRI LA FONTAINE Beaujolais	*Youthful, quite peppery nose, backed with beautiful rounded, jammy fruits on the palate. Well made wine.*	£7.30	MHV	(B)

Wine	Notes	Price	Stockist	
BROUILLY 1996, LOUIS TÊTE Beaujolais	*Light, fragrant nose with elegant grapey and jammy aromas, that are well-balanced to perfection.*	£7.60	ENO	B
CHÉNAS CHÂTEAU DU LORON 1996, JEAN LORON Beaujolais	*Gentle, delicate nose that is softly balanced in a good, attractive style of fruity wine.*	£7.80	DIR NIC	B
MORGON 1995, GEORGES DUBOEUF Beaujolais	*Stylishly-made wine, with a rounded cherry nose, precedes up-lifting fruity flavours on the palate.*	£7.80	Widely Available	B
MOULIN A VENT 1995, GEORGES DUBOEUF Beaujolais	*Creamy vanilla aromas on the nose, with medium fruit and a hot spicy oak finish.*	£8.80	DBY LNR GDS CST U JN WER	B
FLEURIE DOMAINE VERT-PRÉ 1996, PAUL BEAUDET Beaujolais	*Light violet aromas, with hints of ripe banana and juicy fruit on a delightfully round palate.*	£9.00	GI NAD	B
MOULIN-A-VENT 1995, DOMAINE JACKY JANODET Beaujolais	*Attractive, spicy nose with structured fruit and up-lifting tannins on a long, creamy finish.*	£9.00	DIR AMW	B
FLEURIE CHÂTEAU DU FLEURIE LORON 1996, LORON Beaujolais	*Jammy nose with ripe, clean, juicy fruit and light, subtle tannins on the palate.*	£9.00	DIR SHJ	B

Pinpoint who sells the wine you wish to buy by turning to the stockist codes. If you know the name of the wine you want to buy, use the alphabetical index. If the price is your motivation, refer to the invaluable price guide index; red and white wines under £5, sparkling wines under £10 and champagne under £15. Happy hunting!

FRANCE • BORDEAUX • RED

CLARET CALVET NV, BENOIT & VALERIE CALVET Bordeaux	*Rich, chocolate nose with a berried, plummy style on both nose and palate, and a light finish.*	£3.00	ALD	**B**
CLARET CALVET 1996, J CALVET Bordeaux	*Deep fruits of the forest aromas lead to a structured palate of red fruit flavours with a vanilla finish.*	£3.90	VWC FUL MAJ VW OD	**B**
CHATEAU CAVILLE 1995, ALAIN VAURIGAUD Bordeaux	*Mature, spicy cedarwood aromas with concentrated fruit on a lingering, well-balanced palate.*	£4.60	ABY	**B**
RIVERS MEET MERLOT CABERNET 1996, GINESTET Bordeaux	*Fresh plum and damson notes on the nose with good oak and fruit balance on the palate.*	£4.80	W CWS OD	**B**
CHÂTEAU SAINT GALIER ST EMILION GRAND CRU 1995, GINESTET Bordeaux	*A broad, plum jam nose leads onto a complex, medium-bodied, creamy, fruity, herbaceous palate.*	£5.00	MRN	**B**
YVECOURT PREMIUM 1995, YVON MAU Bordeaux	*Deep colour and cedary, blackcurrant aromas with meaty, savoury, fruit flavours on a lingering palate.*	£5.00	OD	**B**
BORDEAUX CAVE BEL AIR 1995, PETER A SICHEL Bordeaux	*Deep, cherry fruit aromas on the nose with chewy, jammy, fruit flavours. Rich and complex.*	£5.20	CNL BAB	**B**

Wine	Description	Price	Stockists	
BORDEAUX SUPERIEUR 1994, CHATEAU GAMAGE Bordeaux	*Light aromas of black fruits with a delicately flavoured palate, which has a cedary finish.*	£5.40	DIR WW SIJ POR AWS	**B**
CHATEAU DUCLA PERMANENCE 1995, YVON MAU Bordeaux	*Structured blackcurrant fruit flavours dominate the palate after a subtle nose.*	£6.00	OD	**B**
CHÂTEAU MANSENOBLE CABERNET SAUVIGNON 1995, JANSEGERS DE WIT. Coteaux De Miramont	*Aromas of crushed red fruits with soft tannins on a rich, fruit palate with balanced acidity.*	£6.30	CES H&D	**B**
ARTHUS CÔTES DE CASTILLON 1994, R DUBOIS Bordeaux	*A fruit and oak nose leads onto a light, blackcurrant palate with big tannins.*	£7.00	GRT BFW	**B**
CHÂTEAU LA MOULIERE FUTS DE CHÉNE 1995, BLANCHETON FRERES Cotes De Duras	*A simple nose of soft black fruits and oak followed by attractive flavours on the palate.*	£7.30	CES	**B**
ST EMILION 1994, BARON PHILIPPE DE ROTHSCHILD Bordeaux	*Brick red wine with soft fruit, herbaceous notes and light flavours of blackcurrant and cedar.*	£7.70	VIL CST IVY ROB EDC BAB JSS D	**B**
CHATEAU COMBES CANON BORDEAUX SUPERIEUR 1995, COMBES CANON Bordeaux	*An oak and fruit nose followed by a light, smoky, fruit palate that has elegance.*	£8.00	W	**B**
CÔTES DE CASTILLON 1993, CHATEAU DE BELCIER Bordeaux	*Concentrated nose of minty oak leads to an integrated palate of cedar and jammy fruits.*	£8.00	DBY BOO AMW NRW WER EP	**S**

BERRY'S ST JULIEN NV, CH. LAGRANGE Bordeaux	*Rich, black fruit aromas with herbaceous notes followed by a fruity palate with fine tannins.*	£8.50	BBR	(B)
CHÂTEAU MAGNOL CRU BOURGEOIS MÉDOC 1994, BARTON ET GUESTIER Bordeaux	*Nose of stewed fruits with herb notes leads to a structured palate of bitter cherry fruits.*	£8.80	CLA OD	(B)
CHÂTEAU BEAU-SITE CRU BOURGEOIS 1991, BORIE MANOUX Bordeaux	*A classic Médoc nose with cedary, cassis notes and pleasant juicy flavours on a soft, balanced palate.*	£8.80	CDT	(S)
CHÂTEAU HAUT BAGES MONPELOU CRU BOURGEOIS 1993, BORIE MANOUX Bordeaux	*Cedar and herb highlights on a red fruits nose with meaty, savoury flavours. A balanced palate .*	£9.00	FUL CDT	(B)
CHÂTEAU MAGNOL CRU BOURGEOIS MÉDOC 1993, BARTON ET GUESTIER Bordeaux	*Minty, black fruit and cedar bouquet and a deep palate of blackcurrant flavours with earthy tannins on the finnish.*	£9.00	OD	(B)
CHÂTEAU PALOUMEY HAUT MEDOC CRU BOURGEOIS 1994, MARTINE CAZENEUVE Bordeaux	*Attractive minty, cassis aromas Light, cherry flavours with oak notes on a well-knit palate.*	£9.00	M&V SOM RAV	(B)
'L' DE LA LOUVIÈRE 1994, CHÂTEAU LA LOUVIÈRE Bordeaux	*Rich, ripe, spicy fruit on the nose of this dark, concentrated wine with blackcurrant flavours.*	£10.00	JN W	(B)
GRAVES 1994, CHÂTEAU DU SEUIL Bordeaux	*Rich plum, fruit aromas with a hint of cedar followed by a soft balanced palate.*	£10.00	DIR	(B)

Château La Barde-les Tendoux Bergerac 1993, Socav Bordeaux	Deep purple, oak, mint and cedar aromas. On the palate flavours of blackcurrant, vanilla and sweet tannins.	£10.20	ABY	(S)
Château Ramage La Batisse Haut Medoc Cru Bourgeois 1993 Bordeaux	Elegant blackcurrant vanilla nose and a palate of minty berry fruit and soft lingering tannins.	£10.80	Widely Available	(S)
Château Côtes de Rol St Emilion Grand Cru 1995, Robert Giraud Bordeaux	Ripe summer fruit aromas appear on the soft, lengthy, palate of this balanced wine.	£12.00	AV	(B)
Sarget de Château Gruaud-Larose St Julien 1993, Domaines Cordier Bordeaux	Spicy, black cherry fruit on the nose and palate. Nuances of oak and tar with balanced acidity and tannins.	£13.90	U SHJ H&W FSW WFL HOL SEL	(S)
Château Batailley Pauillac 5ième Cru 1993, Borie Manoux Bordeaux	Smokey, ripe, cedar and blackcurrant nose moves to a ripe cassis and rich oak vanilla palate.	£15.00	DIR CDT	(B)
Château d'Armailhac Pauillac 5ième Cru 1992, Baron Philippe De Rothschild Bordeaux	The tasters found an attractive nose with integrated oak and a firm, yet rounded, palate.	£15.90	Widely Available	(S)
Château Clerc Milon Pauillac 5ième Cru 1992, Baron Philippe de Rothschild Bordeaux	The farmyardy, herby qualities on the nose were followed by black fruits and cedar flavours.	£17.70	Widely Available	(B)
Chateau Malescot-St-Exupéray Margaux 3ième Cru 1993, Bordeaux	This wine's herbaceous nose and rich velvety fruit on the palate demanded the panel's attention.	£18.00	DBY BNK CLA POR	(B)

CHÂTEAU HAUT MARBUZ-ET ST ESTÈPHE CRU BOURGEOIS EXCEP. 1994, HENRI DUBOSCQ ET FILS Bordeaux	*Minty, chocolate aromas, with oak hints persist on a sweet palate with ripe tannins and blackcurrant flavours.*	£18.30	DBY COK HVW MHW	**S**
CHÂTEAU POTENSAC MEDOC CRU BOURGEOIS 1990, Bordeaux	*Vivid colour, intense blackberry and cassis bouquet. Concentrated palate with ripe flavours and oak integration.*	£18.60	MTR DBY L&W COK EP	**G**
CHÂTEAU DE MEYNEY 1994 ST ESTÈPHE CRU BOURGEOIS 1994, DOMAINES CORDIER Bordeaux	*A restrained blackcurrant and liquorice nose with ripe cassis and damsons on the palate.*	£19.00	WWS FSW VIW UWM	**B**
CHÂTEAU LA LAGUNE HAUT MEDOC 3IÈME CRU 1993, Bordeaux	*A rich, berry fruit nose on this structured wine with light currant and oak flavours.*	£23.50	W	**B**
CHÂTEAU CORDEILLAN BAGES PAUILLAC 1988, JEAN MICHEL CAZES Bordeaux	*Rich cedar, cigar box aromas. Concentrated blackcurrant flavours with farmyard undertones. Classic Bordeaux palate.*	£24.00	ODF	**S**
CHÂTEAU TROTTEVIEILLE ST EMILION GRAND CRU CLASSÉ 1990, BORIE MANOUX Bordeaux	*Leathery, minty, jammy nose leads to long, structured palate of compote of oaked black fruits on the finish.*	£27.00	DIR CDT	**B**
VIEUX CHÂTEAU CERTAN POMEROL 1993, THIENPONT Bordeaux	*Ripe, minty, cabernet nose with a complex sweet liquorice and cherry palate with big tannins.*	£30.40	RAE DIR	**B**
CHÂTEAU BEAUSEJOUR DUFFAU-LAGARROSSE ST EMILION 1ER GRAND CRU CLASSÉ 1989 Bordeaux	*Elegant nose of black fruits and cigar box tobacco. Complex palate of mature fruits, mint and spice.*	£37.50	MTR J&B	**G**

FRANCE • BORDEAUX • RED – WHITE

CHÂTEAU L'EVANGILE POMEROL 1993 Bordeaux	*Packed with summer fruits and cedarwood aromas. Ripe plum and blackcurrant flavours on the palate.*	**£40.00**	J&B	**B**
CHÂTEAU PICHON LONGUEVILLE COMTESSE-DE-LALANDE PAUILLAC 2IÈME CRU 1990 Bordeaux	*A smoky, spicy, vegetal nose followed by ripe, sweet, berry fruit on a well-integrated, elegant palate. A classic!*	**£57.70**	MTR DBY J&B DIR L&W SEB	**G**
CHÂTEAU LATOUR PAUILLAC 1ÈR CRU 1991 Bordeaux	*Earthy, woody aromas. Intense fruit and an excellent structure are complimented by youthful tannins.*	**£63.50**	MTR J&B	**S**
CHÂTEAU LÉOVILLE-LASCASES ST JULIEN 2IÈME CRU 1989 Bordeaux	*Rich fruit and terroir on the nose; the palate reflects this with some brisk tannins.*	**£66.60**	MTR DBY J&B	**B**

FRANCE • BORDEAUX • WHITE

CASCADE BORDEAUX SAUVIGNON BLANC 1996, YVES PAGES Bordeaux	*Pleasant, ripe gooseberry aromas on the nose, with crisp, grassy undertones on the palate.*	**£3.00**	DBY MRN	**B**
WAITROSE BORDEAUX SAUVIGNON BLANC 1996, J CALVET Bordeaux	*A lemon, grassy nose, with hints of tropical fruit that follow though on a mouth-watering, fruity palate.*	**£3.50**	W	**B**
CHÂTEAU PIERROUSSELLE 1996, GINESTET Bordeaux	*Simple yet refreshing wine, with a soft, well-structured palate displaying lemony, gooseberry flavours.*	**£4.00**	CWS	**B**

SAUVIGNON BLANC 1996, J CALVET Bordeaux	*Classic steely aromas of under-ripe gooseberries lead to a dry palate, with a crisp mineral finish.*	**£4.00**	W MWW VW WCR FUL	**B**
GEMINI SAUVIGNON BLANC 1996, YVES PAGES Bordeaux	*Delightful aroma of gooseberry and grape-fruit on the nose leading to a lively, zesty palate.*	**£4.10**	Widely Available	**B**
TWO RIVERS SAUVIGNON SEMILLON 1996, J CALVET Bordeaux	*Elegantly-made wine that shows plenty of fine acidity and lovely, ripe citrus fruit.*	**£5.00**	CEL WCR BKW	**B**
LAMBERHURST MILLENNIUM SAUVIGNON BLANC 1996, YVON MAU Bordeaux	*Fine example of a Sauvignon, with a subdued nose and mouthwatering palate; filled with fruit.*	**£5.00**	TO	**B**
SAUVIGNON GRIS 1996, YVON MAU Bordeaux	*A superb wine, with a good concentration of fruit and profound acidity on the palate.*	**£5.00**	TO U OD	**S**
CHÂTEAU TIMBERLAY CUVÉE PRÉSTIGE 1996, ROBERT GIRAUD Bordeaux	*Herby, fruity bouquet, leading to a rich, spicy, palate of summer fruits with a long finish.*	**£7.00**	AV	**B**
CHÂTEAU CARSIN CUVÉE BLANC SEC 1995, Bordeaux	*Light, good structured wine with a smoky, toasty nose, and a lingering finish.*	**£7.50**	W	**B**

Pinpoint who sells the wine you wish to buy by turning to the stockist codes. If you know the name of the wine you want to buy, use the alphabetical index. If the price is your motivation, refer to the invaluable price guide index; red and white wines under £5, sparkling wines under £10 and champagne under £15. Happy hunting!

CHÂTEAU DU SEUIL GRAVES BLANC SEC 1995 Bordeaux	*A well-crafted, fresh and aromatic wine with beautiful lemon and lime overtones.*	**£7.70**	DIR	**(S)**
VIN SEC DU CHÂTEAU COUTET 1993 Bordeaux	*The tasters loved this scrumptious wine, due to its fruity nose and beautifully balanced palate. Very clean.*	**£7.90**	TH MWW MM WIN EP SEL BB SHJ	**(B)**

FRANCE • BORDEAUX • SWEET

CHÂTEAU DE LA CHARTREUSE SAUTERNES 1994, FACCHETTI RICARD Bordeaux	*Lovely, nutty fruit with sweet toffee undertones lingers on a well-structured palate showing good length.*	**£10.00**	W	**(B)**
SAUTERNES BARON PHILIPPE DE ROTHSCHILD 1991 Bordeaux	*A powerful marmalade fruit character enhanced by uplifting acidity on a powerful, well-rounded palate with good length.*	**£10.80**	Widely Available	**(S)**
SAUTERNES CUVÉE ARISTIDE 1989, MAISON MAU Bordeaux	*Lovely fresh, elegant botrytis nose precedes a long-lingering palate with honey undertones.*	**£14.00**	WSC	**(B)**
CHÂTEAU LOUBENS STE CROIX DU MONT GRAND CRU 1990 Bordeaux	*A very attractive wine with classic botrytis fruit character showing on the nose and palate.*	**£15.70**	L&W NIC	**(S)**
CHÂTEAU COUTET BARSAC 1ER CRU 1992 Bordeaux	*The burnt-toffee, fruit character is balanced by some good acidity on this attractive wine.*	**£28.80**	TH U GRO GAG HAC PHI EP	**(B)**

FRANCE • BURGUNDY • RED

HAUTES CÔTES DE NUITS PRESTIGE DU VAL DE VERGY 1995, YVES CHALEY Burgundy	*Aromas of vanilla, oak and jammy fruit dominate. A soft youthful strawberry palate follows.*	£6.00	LES	Ⓑ
HAUTES CÔTES DE NUITS LES MOUCHOTTES TÊTE DE CUVÉE 1995, DOM. DES MOUCHOTTES Burgundy	*Jammy fruit and racy acidity dominate the balanced, lengthy palate of this impressive wine.*	£7.00	BUG	Ⓑ
HAUTES CÔTES DE NUITS 1995, DENIS PHILIBERT Burgundy	*Huge aromas of ripe fruits are apparant with an attractive cherry finish. Very satisfying.*	£7.00	FUL	Ⓑ
SANTENAY 1995, ANTOINE DE PEYRACHE Burgundy	*Light cherry and floral aromas lead onto rich earthy flavours with a drying finish.*	£8.00	A	Ⓑ
BEAUNE 1995, COTTIN FRÈRES Burgundy	*Warm spicy nose on this young, well-structured wine. Nuances of cherry and violet flavours.*	£10.20	SMF	Ⓑ
NUITS-ST-GEORGES 1995, COTTIN FRÈRES Burgundy	*Aromas of soft, red fruits come to the fore of this youthful yet extremely approachable wine.*	£10.20	SMF	Ⓑ
BEAUNE CLOS DU ROI 1ÈR CRU CHÂTEAU PHILIPPE LE HARDI 1995 Burgundy	*An attractive, clean, raspberry and violet nose carries over to a big palate with firm tannins.*	£11.90	ABY	Ⓑ

ALOXE-CORTON 1994, CHÂTEAU PHILLIPE LE HARDI Burgundy	*A lovely, creamy nose with excellent cherry fruit which follows through to the soft palate.*	£11.90	ABY	(S)
ANDRÉ SIMON NUITS-ST-GEORGES 1994, ALBERT BICHOT Burgundy	*Delicate bouquet of soft red fruits leads to cherry and vegetal flavours on the palate.*	£12.00	WRT	(B)
MALT HOUSE VINTNERS NUITS-ST-GEORGES HENRI LA FONTAINE 1994, JEAN C BOISSET Burgundy	*Ripe strawberry and violet aromas are reflected on a chocolatey Pinot palate with light tannins.*	£12.00	MHV	(B)
CÔTE DE BEAUNE 1995, MAISON JOSEPH DROUHIN Burgundy	*Attractive cherry and strawberry fruit aromas are mirrored in the soft lengthy palate.*	£12.10	MM NEI OD EOO	(B)
ALOXE-CORTON 1995, CHÂTEAU PHILIPPE LE HARDI Burgundy	*Attractive vanilla and oak integrating with the classic Pinot fruit; summer fruits and floral notes dominate.*	£12.30	ABY	(B)
BEAUNE LES EPENOTTES 1ÈR CRU DOMAINE PARENT 1994 Burgundy	*Clean and fresh aromas with ripe, fruity, floral characters coming through on the palate.*	£13.00	SAF	(B)
BEAUNE 1ÈR CRU LES AVAUX 1995, JEAN-MICHEL JACOB Burgundy	*Supple tannins predominate the ripe, red-fruit and vegetal palate of this young wine.*	£14.00	3D	(B)
BEAUNE CENT VIGNES 1ÈR CRU 1995, DOMAINE RENÉ MONNIER Burgundy	*Rich aromas and flavours of ripe cherries combine with noticable tannins in this attractive wine. Smooth and clean.*	£15.00	ENO	(S)

Wine	Description	Price	Stockists	
NUITS-ST-GEORGES 1ÈR CRU 1993, DOMAINE DE L'ARLOT Burgundy	*Soft, summer fruit aromas develop on the nose and palate with nuances of old oak.*	£16.20	TH ABY	(S)
BEAUNE LES EPENOTTES 1ÈR CRU 1991, VALLET FRÈRES Burgundy	*Soft fruits with farmyard overtones dominate the nose. Ripe fruits and brisk tannins on the palate and finish.*	£17.30	DBY AMW TRO POR COK WCS	(S)
VOLNAY CLOS DE LA ROUGEOTTE 1ÈR CRU 1992, DOMAINE FRANCOIS BUFFET Burgundy	*Rich aromas of red fruits. Palate dominated by softening tannins showing on-going development.*	£18.00	ABB	(G)
NUITS-ST-GEORGES CLOS DE L'ARLOT 1994, DOMAINE DE L'ARLOT Burgundy	*Ripe, red cherry fruit floods the nose of this attractive wine with. A soft, balanced palate is then to follow.*	£21.00	TH ABY	(S)
GEVREY-CHAMBERTIN AUX COMBOTTES 1ÈR CRU 1995, DOMAINE AMIOT Burgundy	*Concentrated fruit flavours on the palate are balanced by big tannins and ripe acidity.*	£22.50	BD	(S)
DOMAINE DE LA POUSSE D'OR 1992, GERARD POTEL Burgundy	*Complex fruit and vegetable aromas precede a palate of lingering, mouthfilling flavours and softening tannins.*	£24.50	DIR T&W CNL GON HOL BLS	(B)
NUITS-ST-GEORGES FORETS ST GEORGES 1ÈR CRU, 1994, DOMAINE DE L'ARLOT Burgundy	*Sweet strawberry fruit on the palate is balanced by good acidity and ripe, grippy tannins.*	£25.60	TH ABY	(S)
DOMAINE DE LA POUSSE D'OR 1ÈR CRU 1993, GERARD POTEL Burgundy	*Raspberry fruit characters are balanced by big tannins and refreshing acidity on a long palate.*	£26.90	DIR T&W CNL GON HOL BLS	(B)

FRANCE • BURGUNDY • RED – WHITE

MOREY-ST-DENIS CLOS DES LAMBRAYS GRAND CRU 1989, F ET L SAIER Burgundy	*This has an excellent Pinot nose, filled with fat truffles and vegetal fruit flavours. Smooth and full.*	**£38.50**	NIC DBY	**B**
NUITS-ST-GEORGES AUX BOUDOTS 1ER CRU 1990, MEO-CAMUZET Burgundy	*A complex combination of vegetal characteristics and luscious sweet fruit on the nose and palate.*	**£49.00**	J&B	**S**
VOSNE-ROMANÉE AUX BRULEES 1ER CRU 1993, MEO-CAMUZET Burgundy	*Attractive wine with hints of violets on the nose; gamey characters on the softening palate.*	**£55.00**	J&B	**S**

FRANCE • BURGUNDY • WHITE

MÂCON SOLUTRÉ 1996, MAISON AUVIGNE Burgundy	*This wine shows real finesse; the fresh fruit on the nose carries through strongly to the palate.*	**£7.00**	W	**S**
CHABLIS CHÂTEAU DE MALIGNY 1995, JEAN DURUP Burgundy	*There is a good weight of citrus fruit giving a rich, ripe and well-structured wine. Subtle yet strong.*	**£8.20**	TH CST ABY	**S**
CHABLIS CUVÉE LA CHABLISIENNE 1995, LA CHABLISIENNE Burgundy	*Attractive sweet oak compliments the delicate soft peach-fruit character on this stunning wine.*	**£8.40**	GI GNW WIN NAD EOO	**G**
CHABLIS 1995, BERNARD LEGLAND Burgundy	*Toasty nose with good rich flavours, well-integrated oak and a long, clean, crisp finish.*	**£9.00**	VIL BI CHF GRT HAR	**B**

CHABLIS VIEILLES VIGNES LA CHABLISIENNE 1994, LA CHABLISIENNE Burgundy	*Nutty, complex aromas following through onto the palate with tight acidity and fine structure.*	£9.50	TH GI NAD	(B)
CHABLIS 1ÈR CRU VAU DE VEY CHÂTEAU DE MALIGNY 1995, JEAN DURUP Burgundy	*Sweet honey, marshmallow and floral aromas with a good, crisp flavour and reasonable length.*	£9.80	ABY	(B)
MALT HOUSE VINTNERS CHABLIS BEAUROY PREMIER CRU 1995, LES PRODUCTEURS DE CHABLIS Burgundy	*Some fresh, grassy fruit combines with a buttery mouth-feel on this promising wine.*	£10.20	MHV	(B)
CHÂTEAU DE CHAMIREY 1995, ANTONIN RODET Burgundy	*Elegant on both nose and palate; subtle integrated oak and rich opulent fruit predominate.*	£10.30	MWW SV PF EP	(B)
MALT HOUSE VINTNERS POUILLY FUISSÉ HENRI LA FONTAINE 1995, JEAN CLAUDE BOISSET Burgundy	*A clean, fresh, light-style of wine with hints of honey combining with citrus fruit.*	£10.30	MHV	(B)
POUILLY FUISSÉ VIEILLES VIGNES 1994 DOMAINE MANCIAT PONCET Burgundy	*Smoky and lemony on the palate. Rounded, soft, marzipan fruit; good, balanced fruit and acidity on the finish.*	£10.90	PAV J&B VIL ENO	(B)
CHABLIS 1ÈR CRU 1994, JEAN MARC BROCARD Burgundy	*Closed and tight on the nose, there is much more structure and complexity on the palate.*	£11.00	W HOU FTH	(S)
CHABLIS 1ÈR CRU MONT DE MILIEU 1993, LA CHABLISIENNE Burgundy	*Good creamy palate with zingy apple and pear fruit character and well-integrated oak.*	£11.50	GI NAD	(B)

CHABLIS FOURCHAUME 1ÈR CRU 1995, DOMAINE DES MALANDES Burgundy	*This well-made wine comes across as having a great concentration of fruit on the palate.*	**£11.60**	Widely Available	(S)
POUILLY FUISSÉ 1994, DOMAINE CORSIN Burgundy	*The palate shows very good extraction of fruit and is nicely balanced with good length.*	**£12.00**	GI NAD	(B)
CHABLIS 1ÈR CRU FOURCHAUME CHÂTEAU DE MALIGNY 1995, JEAN DURUP Burgundy	*Bags of citrus fruit with a rich, minerally edge and well-balanced crisp acidity. Made to make your mouth water!*	**£12.20**	TH CWI CST ABY	(B)
CHABLIS 1ÈR CRU MONT DE MILIEU 1992, LA CHABLISIENNE Burgundy	*This wine is subtle and has the potential to open into something absolutely wonderful. A great example of its type.*	**£12.20**	VWC GI NAD	(S)
CHABLIS VIEILLES VIGNES 1ÈR CRU DOMAINE BERNARD DEFAIX ET FILS 1994 Burgundy	*Soft, light green fruit with racy acidity and a fresh overall feel in the mouth. Subtle fruit.*	**£12.50**	L&W RBS HRV	(B)
CHABLIS LES VAILLONS 1ÈR CRU 1995, DOMAINE LONG DEPAQUIT Burgundy	*Some interesting tropical coconut fruit coming through on the palate of this pleasant wine.*	**£13.50**	DBY U ALL	(B)
CHABLIS CÔTE DE LECHET 1ÈR CRU 1992, DOMAINE DANIEL-ETIENNE DEFAIX Burgundy	*This is a ripe, elegant wine with nicely integrated oak, good acidity and clean fruit.*	**£17.00**	TH DBY CNL RBS SHJ	(S)
CHABLIS GRAND CRU VAUDÉSIR 1993, DOMAINE DE LA MALADIÈRE Burgundy	*Smooth balance of fruits and oak, with fairly intense acidity. Stimulates the palate.*	**£18.00**	DBY HBJ	(G)

MEURSAULT 'LES CHEVALIERES' 1995, DOMAINE RENÉ MONNIER Burgundy	*Toasted oak aromas lead on to a palate of creamy richness. This will age well but drinks well now.*	**£18.80**	BUT ENO	**B**
CHABLIS GRAND CRU VAUDÉSIR 1992, DOMAINE DES MALANDES Burgundy	*Creamy, honeyed tropical fruit comes through forming an broad, intense wine with good length.*	**£20.00**	MTR HAL T&W TBW	**B**
CHABLIS GRAND CRU LES CLOS 1995, J MOREAU ET FILS Burgundy	*There is some elegance shown on the nose; the palate has a mouthful of fruit and covers well.*	**£20.00**	MTL	**B**
MEURSAULT 1993, DOMAINE CHÂTEAU DE MEURSAULT Burgundy	*Matured, honeyed aromas; toasted oak with full, ripe, fruit flavours leave a slightly spicy aftertaste on the palate.*	**£20.70**	POR NRW	**S**
WAITROSE PULIGNY-MONTRACHET 1ER CRU 1994, GERARD CHAVY Burgundy	*A clean pear-drop nose, with strong oak under-tones leading to a lingering aftertaste.*	**£22.00**	W	**B**
NUITS ST GEORGES CLOS DE L'ARLOT 1ER CRU 1994, DOMAINE DE L'ARLOT Burgundy	*Intense nose of toasty creamy oak with subtle buttered undertones: with rich nutty flavours to follow.*	**£23.00**	TH ABY	**G**
PULIGNY-MONTRACHET SOUS LE PUITS 1ER CRU 1994, VERGET Burgundy	*The panel describe this well-made wine as complex and striking with beautiful uplifting oak.*	**£26.30**	DBY L&W SEB JN	**B**
BÂTARD MONTRACHET GRAND CRU 1994, JEAN NOEL GAGNARD Burgundy	*Melony, ripe fruit and citrus nose followed by a lemony palate with high-toned, fresh acidity on the finish.*	**£65.00**	J&B	**B**

FRANCE • BURGUNDY • SPARKLING

SOMERFIELD CRÉMANT DE BOURGOGNE 1991, CAVES DE BAILLY Burgundy	*Attractive yeasty aromas dominate the nose followed by a crisp, dry and refreshing palate.*	**£7.20**	SMF	**B**

FRANCE • CHAMPAGNE • WHITE

MALT HOUSE VINTNERS CHAMPAGNE PAUL LANGIER BRUT NV, F BONNET Champagne	*Tight bubbles on yeasty nose with complex biscuit, citrus flavours, leading to clean, lingering finish.*	**£11.00**	MHV	**B**
CHAMPAGNE PAUL HERARD DEMI-SEC NV, Champagne	*A very well put together wine, with a clean, light nose and very fine balancing acidity.*	**£11.40**	MRN	**B**
CHAMPAGNE DUVAL LEROY FLEUR DE CHAMPAGNE BRUT NV Champagne	*Rounded fruit aromas with autolytic led palate, attractive length and balanced, crisp acidity in the finish.*	**£12.60**	JS TP MRN	**B**
CHAMPAGNE DRAPPIER CUVÉE SPECIAL BRUT 1990 Champagne	*Persistant mousse with obvious yeast notes leads onto a rich apple flavour with a refreshing finish.*	**£13.00**	ABY	**B**
TESCO CHAMPAGNE BRUT NV, Champagne	*Crisp yeasty nose. Extra sweet honeyed flavours on the rounded palate, attractive finish.*	**£13.00**	TO	**B**

CHAMPAGNE JEAN MOUTARDIER CARTE D'OR BRUT NV Champagne	*Good mousse and sparkle. Autolysis aromas with tropical fruits on the delicate nose and palate.*	£13.70	GRT CFT	B
TESCO BLANCS DE BLANCS CHAMPAGNE NV, Champagne	*Nutty, appley, yeasty nose with fresh tart flavours on a balanced palate with a clean finish.*	£14.00	TO	B
CHAMPAGNE CHARTOGNE TAILLET BRUT NV Champagne	*Sound, yeast aroma and clean, biscuity, balanced palate followed by crisp underlying acidity.*	£14.90	DBY AMW EWD SOH PEA CEN	B
CHAMPAGNE ALBERT ETIENNE BRUT 1991, MARNE ET CHAMPAGNE Champagne	*Lingering mousse, sour, tart aromas with yeasty notes. Green apple flavours and a clean finish.*	£15.00	SHJ MCD	B
CHAMPAGNE BAUGET-JOUËTTE CARTE BLANCHE BRUT NV Champagne	*Lasting mousse, a full, yeasty nose with good, crisp, richly flavoured palate with refreshing acidity.*	£15.00	AMW JBV GRO	B
CHAMPAGNE H BLIN ET CIE BRUT TRADITION NV Champagne	*Rich nose, good autolytic characters, complex flavours of zesty fruit and toasty, yeast with a clean finish.*	£15.00	OD	B
CHAMPAGNE PATRICK ARNOLD BRUT RESERVE GRAND CRU NV Champagne	*Well-made, with good character. A mouthfilling wine with generous bead and a lively finish.*	£15.00	TO	B
CHAMPAGNE DRAPPIER CUVÉE SPECIAL BRUT NV Champagne	*Good mousse, baked bread aromas with balanced yeasty and marmite flavours, refreshing end to palate.*	£15.30	DBY COK ABY	B

CHAMPAGNE BONNET BLANC DE BLANCS BRUT NV Champagne	*An appealing nose with a yeasty touch and a clean palate of apple, lime and soft fruit.*	£15.40	MTR W P	(B)
CHAMPAGNE NICOLAS FEUILLATTE CUVÉE PALMES D'OR BRUT 1990 Champagne	*Light nose with yeast highlights, green apple flavours on the autolysis influenced palate, fresh, clean finish.*	£16.00	U HCK	(B)
CHAMPAGNE NICOLAS FEUILLATTE DEMI-SEC NV Champagne	*Rich toffee on the nose followed by ripe, vanilla oak balanced by clean, zippy acidity.*	£16.00	A	(B)
CHAMPAGNE NICOLAS FEUILLATTE BLANC DE BLANCS BRUT NV Champagne	*100% Chardonnay showing yeasty character on the nose and a rich doughy palate to follow.*	£16.00	A VW WCR	(B)
J M GREMILLET CHARDONNAY BRUT 1991, Champagne	*Yeasty, herbal nose with a full-flavoured palate of green grass. Refreshing, tart, acidity balances.*	£16.50	CPW MHW	(B)
CHAMPAGNE DRAPPIER BLANC DE BLANCS BRUT 1990 Champagne	*Good mousse, small bubbles, fresh, lemony, yeasty nose, complex ripe fruit, biscuity palate, great balance.*	£17.00	ABY	(S)
CHAMPAGNE PIPER HEIDSIECK CUVÉE BRUT NV Champagne	*Fresh on the nose with crisp acidity moving through to a fresh, clean, appley palate.*	£17.10	Widely Available	(B)
CHAMPAGNE DUVAL LEROY FLEUR DE CHAMPAGNE 1988 Champagne	*Aggressive mousse, with rich, tropical fruit aromas and flavours and yeast highlights. Clean, acid finish.*	£17.30	BD TAN TP	(B)

CHAMPAGNE LE BRUN DE NEUVILLE CUVÉE BRUT 1990 Champagne	*Lingering mousse in glass and mouth. Toasty yeast aromas with herbal notes and similar palate, balancing acidity.*	£17.30	WAW PV	(S)
CHAMPAGNE LANSON DEMI-SEC NV, MARNE ET CHAMPAGNE Champagne	*A beautifully integrated wine with crisp, fresh acidity, dry, peachy fruit and a soft, sweet finish.*	£17.30	CLA CST U MCD MRN	(S)
CHAMPAGNE HENRIOT BLANC DE BLANCS BRUT NV Champagne	*Clean, ripe aromas with autolytic notes and a complex palate of clean lemon and lime flavours.*	£17.40	NY ABY	(S)
CHAMPAGNE LE BRUN DE NEUVILLE CUVÉE ROI CLOVIS BRUT NV Champagne	*Light mousse, yeasty, green apple aromas and flavours with underlying depth, very long finish.*	£17.50	WAW PV	(B)
CHAMPAGNE BONNET BRUT 1989 Champagne	*Classic Chardonnay aromas, yeasty, biscuit notes on nose and palate, good concentrated fruit, elegant finish.*	£17.60	MTR	(B)
CHAMPAGNE MUMM CORDON ROUGE BRUT NV Champagne	*Good mousse, delicate nose, crisp flavours on the palate with a hint of dosage on the finish.*	£17.70	Widely Available	(B)
CHAMPAGNE HENRIOT BRUT SOUVERAIN NV Champagne	*Bready, creamy nose and soft mousse lead to an open, easy palate with a clean finish.*	£17.80	NIC ABY	(B)
CHAMPAGNE JACQUART BRUT 1990 Champagne	*Creamy pineapple, herbaceous and vanilla aromas mingle on the nose, followed by a soft, rounded, fruity palate.*	£18.00	POR	(B)

CHAMPAGNE JOSEPH PERRIER CUVÉE ROYALE BRUT 1989 Champagne	*Good mousse, concentrated yeasty, meaty aromas, clean zesty palate, complex notes of biscuit, apple and buttered fruit.*	**£18.20**	RBS CES GNW GRT TAN ES WON	(S)
CHAMPAGNE LANSON BLACK LABEL NV, MARNE ET CHAMPAGNE Champagne	*Lasting mousse, rich malic apple aromas with autolytic notes carry over to balanced palate.*	**£18.30**	Widely Available	(B)
CHAMPAGNE POMMERY BRUT ROYAL NV Champagne	*Strong autolytic character, creamy, lingering mousse, smooth flavours that last and last on a balanced palate.*	**£18.40**	Widely Available	(B)
CHAMPAGNE HENRIOT BRUT 1989 Champagne	*Clean, attractive nose with earthy, yeasty notes on a medium-length, refreshingly balanced palate.*	**£18.50**	ABY	(B)
CHAMPAGNE ALFRED GRATIEN BRUT NV Champagne	*Green apple aromas on a pleasant mousse, tart, appley flavours on palate with a clean finish.*	**£18.60**	JS WSO EOR OD ODF	(B)
CHAMPAGNE DUVAL LEROY BRUT 1990 Champagne	*Fine bubbles with elegant autolytic aromas, fresh, appealing palate with lively acidity giving a crisp finish.*	**£19.00**	L&W	(B)
CHAMPAGNE GERMAIN PRESIDENT SIGNATURE BRUT NV Champagne	*Ripe maturing fruit on a bready nose with autolysis notes; some rich acidity giving length.*	**£19.00**	BUD	(B)
CHAMPAGNE VILMART BRUT NV Champagne	*Clean yeasty aromas with a delicate mousse, leading to sweet fruit with good acid balance and length.*	**£20.00**	DIR NY BEN GON GRO SEL	(B)

CHAMPAGNE CHARLES HEIDSIECK BRUT RESERVE NV Champagne	*A rich, generous nose leads on to a palate of biscuit flavours and a ripe finish.*	£20.00	Widely Available	**B**
CHAMPAGNE MOËT & CHANDON BRUT IMPÉRIAL NV Champagne	*Lively, fruity wine with a fresh and yeasty, dry palate and a clean brisk finish. Very drinkable!*	£20.00	Widely Available	**S**
CHAMPAGNE BILLECART-SALMON BRUT RÉSERVE NV Champagne	*Small bubbles, minerally, yeasty, musky bouquet with fresh crisp, citrusy flavours leading to a soft apple finish.*	£20.20	J&B DBY V&C HW RBS JN BIL OD	**B**
CHAMPAGNE DRAPPIER BRUT 1989 Champagne	*Warm, smooth and well-structured champagne with yeast and biscuit highlights and a dry finish.*	£20.40	ABY	**B**
PHILIPPONNAT LE REFLET BRUT NV Champagne	*Pronounced bready, yeasty aromas with a palate full of zingy citrus fruit. Creamy finish.*	£20.50	CDT HAR SEL	**B**
CHAMPAGNE MUMM CORDON ROUGE BRUT 1989 Champagne	*Toasty, earthy aromas contribute towards a herbaceous nose. Rich apple flavours and a soft mousse and finish.*	£20.70	TH CLA OD AV	**B**
CHAMPAGNE R. RENAUDIN RÉSERVE SPECIAL CD 1985 Champagne	*Delicate fizz, autolysis notes on nose and tart apple flavoured palate, clean acid finish.*	£21.50	MTB	**B**
CHAMPAGNE PERRIER-JOUËT GRAND BRUT NV Champagne	*A light floral nose with a palate full of citrus fruit, yeast and a delicate finish.*	£21.90	Widely Available	**B**

CHAMPAGNE VEUVE CLICQUOT PONSARDIN WHITE LABEL DEMI-SEC NV Champagne	*The palate is beautifully balanced with some yeast influence, good acidity and a waxy feel.*	£21.90	Widely Available	(S)
CHAMPAGNE VEUVE CLICQUOT PONSARDIN YELLOW LABEL BRUT NV Champagne	*Complex, subtle yeast and biscuit aromas, attractive mousse, creamy lingering finish to balanced dry palate.*	£22.00	Widely Available	(B)
CHAMPAGNE DUVAL LEROY FLEUR DE CHAMPAGNE BLANC DE BLANCS BRUT 1990 Champagne	*This wine is rich on the nose with ripe flavours of toasty apples on a generous, creamy palate.*	£22.00	TP	(B)
CHAMPAGNE JACQUART CUVEE MOSAIQUE BLANC DE BLANCS 1990 Champagne	*Tight mousse, complex biscuity, citrusy notes on nose and palate, clean zesty finish with finesse.*	£22.00	EP PCC MWI PRS	(S)
CHAMPAGNE GOSSET BRUT EXCELLENCE NV Champagne	*Splendid mousse, restrained, austere yeasty nose, malic tart flavours with a dry, rich finish.*	£22.30	Widely Available	(B)
CHAMPAGNE POL ROGER WHITE FOIL BRUT NV Champagne	*Tight mousse, pleasant yesty, bready, vegemite characters, rounded mouthful of creamy, zesty fruit, intense finish.*	£22.30	Widely Available	(S)
CHAMPAGNE GAUTHIER 1988, MARNE ET CHAMPAGNE Champagne	*Persistant mousse; dry toasty, biscuity nose. Complex citrus fruit flavours and yeast notes balance on the palate.*	£23.00	NRW MCD	(S)
CHAMPAGNE POMMERY BRUT 1990 Champagne	*A mature, farmyardy nose with delicate mousse, citric fruity palate with soft acids. A yeasty finish.*	£24.10	CLA FUL RBS ALL EOO OD	(B)

CHAMPAGNE BOLLINGER SPECIAL CUVÉE NV Champagne	*Sweet, perfumed nose; clean, long palate with citrus bready flavours. A pleasant apple finish.*	£24.30	Widely Available	B
PHILIPPONNAT GRAND BLANC CHARDONNAY BRUT 1988 Champagne	*Aromas of fresh bread: in the mouth a palate of rich fruit and nuttiness abound.*	£24.50	CDT HAR SEL	B
CHAMPAGNE PERRIER-JOUËT 1990 Champagne	*Tight mousse, small bubbles; elegant autolytic nose with fresh appealing palate of citrus zest.*	£24.50	TH MWW CLA FUL RBS CPW ABY OD	B
CHAMPAGNE MOËT & CHANDON BRUT IMPÉRIAL 1992 Champagne	*Fresh and yeasty aromas are then followed by a delicate citrussy and lightly toasted palate.*	£24.80	Widely Available	S
CHAMPAGNE PIPER HEIDSIECK BRUT 1989 Champagne	*A sherbety nose with hints of mint. Delicate lime flavours fill the palate of this vintage champagne.*	£25.00	REM	B
CHAMPAGNE CHARLES HEIDSIECK BRUT 1990 Champagne	*Light, yeasty aromas precede a palate of creamy melon fruit with some underlying earthiness.*	£25.30	J&B CLA REM CPW WSC HAR FEN	S
CHAMPAGNE DEUTZ BLANC DE BLANCS BRUT 1989 Champagne	*Creamy, nougat, biscuity aromas; good fruit flavours and acid balance on finish.*	£26.00	FTH	B
CHAMPAGNE ALFRED GRATIEN BRUT 1988 Champagne	*Lasting mousse, fresh, lively biscuity nose; rich, sweet nougat and baked dough flavours. Tart acid in the finish.*	£26.00	WSO EOR	B

CHAMPAGNE CANARD-DUCHENE CHARLES VII NV Champagne	Yeasty, developing nose and palate with good weight of meaty fruit, aggressive, drying palate.	£26.90	VIL B&B JUS OD	(B)
CHAMPAGNE HENRIOT BRUT 1985 Champagne	Persistant mousse, strong bread aromas reflected on yeast dominated apple flavoured palate, refreshing tart finish.	£27.00	ABY	(S)
CHAMPAGNE VEUVE CLICQUOT PONSARDIN RÉSERVE 1989 Champagne	A gentle mousse with small slow rising bubbles. On the palate intense bready flavours and soft, mellow acidity.	£29.40	Widely Available	(G)
CHAMPAGNE NICOLAS FEUILLATTE CUVÉE SPECIALE BRUT 1989 Champagne	Complex Pinot aromas and flavours on a light grapey, autolysis influenced palate with a long, soft finish.	£30.00	V	(B)
CHAMPAGNE POL ROGER BRUT 1990 Champagne	An impressive vintage champagne, with a honeyed nose and balanced yeast fruit on a nutty, biscuity palate.	£30.10	Widely Available	(S)
CHAMPAGNE VEUVE CLICQUOT PONSARDIN RICH RESERVE 1989 Champagne	Rich honeyed nose, while on the palate there is well balanced yeasty fruit and acidity.	£30.50	Widely Available	(B)
CHAMPAGNE POMMERY CUVÉE LOUISE POMMERY BRUT 1988 Champagne	Lingering mousse, characteristic biscuity nose, ripe fruit flavours and autolytic influences, good acid balance rich finish	£30.80	CLA	(S)
CHAMPAGNE BOLLINGER GRANDE ANNÉE 1989 Champagne	Good mousse and acidity giving length to a developing palate with fresh tart acidity	£36.50	Widely Available	(B)

CHAMPAGNE LANSON NOBLE CUVÉE BRUT 1988, MARNE ET CHAMPAGNE Champagne	A rich and toasty champagne with yeasty flavours on the palate and a long finish.	£41.00	TH V&C MM U MCD	S
CHAMPAGNE CHARLES HEIDSIECK BLANC DES MILLENAIRES BRUT 1985 Champagne	Attractive mousse, leading to light, yeasty, appley aromas, reflected on creamy apple palate, lingering flavours..	£41.20	REM CPW WSC HAR FEN	G
PHILIPPONNAT CLOS DES GOISSES BRUT 1986 Champagne	Yeasty complexity to rich fruit palate and nose, lasting mousse and clean acidity, good length	£45.00	CDT HAR SEL	B
CHAMPAGNE PERRIER-JOUËT BELLE EPOQUE BRUT 1989 Champagne	Good fruit, aged character on the nose and palate, heavy yeast influence, good, crisp balancing acidity.	£45.30	Widely Available	B
CHAMPAGNE VEUVE CLICQOUT PONSARDIN LA GRANDE DAME BRUT 1989 Champagne	Clean, delicate scents of yeast and liquorice leads to rich, nutty, biscuity fruit, tart finish.	£57.50	Widely Available	B
CHAMPAGNE DOM PÉRIGNON PRESTIGE CUVÉE 1990, MOËT & CHANDON Champagne	Rich biscuity nose, sweet ripe apple and lemon flavours, palate has integrated acidity, sherbet and honey notes.	£60.10	Widely Available	S

CHAMPAGNE • ROSÉ

CHAMPAGNE F. BONNET BROSSAULT ROSÉ NV Champagne	Soft, summer berry fruit with balancing acidity and a rounded soft finish. Well made!	£12.00	FUL	B

MALT HOUSE VINTNERS CHAMPAGNE PAUL LANGIER BRUT ROSÉ NV, F. BONNET Champagne	*A compote of summer fruits soft on the nose with just enough balancing acidity on the palate.*	£13.00	MHV	(B)
SAFEWAY CHAMPAGNE ALBERT ETIENNE BRUT ROSÉ NV MARNE ET CHAMPAGNE Champagne	*Soft strawberry fruit and a persistent mousse combine with gentle acidity for an elegant wine.*	£14.00	SAF	(B)
CHAMPAGNE LE BRUN DE NEUVILLE BRUT ROSÉ NV Champagne	*This wonderful wine is elegant and delicate with a palate of strawberries, caramel and biscuit.*	£16.60	WAW TRO PV	(G)
CHAMPAGNE BESSERAT DE BELLEFON CUVÉE DES MOINES BRUT ROSÉ NV Champagne	*An elegant wine with soft fruits and gentle acidity moving on to a generous rounded finish.*	£18.00	MCD	(B)
CHAMPAGNE CHARTOGNE-TAILLET BRUT ROSÉ NV Champagne	*Generous on the nose, with slow rising mousse this wine has classy flavours of soft berry fruits.*	£18.50	DIO CDE WTR PEA CEN	(B)
CHAMPAGNE HENRIOT BRUT ROSÉ 1988 Champagne	*Bready strawberry aromas and a gentle mousse lead on to a wonderful elegant wine.*	£19.70	ABY CEL BKW WCE	(B)
CHAMPAGNE POMMERY BRUT ROSÉ NV Champagne	*A delicate pink with a strawberry bouquet. Peachy flavours follow on a long lasting palate.*	£19.90	CLA RBS ALL EOO	(B)
CHAMPAGNE LANSON BRUT ROSÉ NV, MARNE ET CHAMPAGNE Champagne	*Deep orange coral in colour with a rich, apricot palate. It will benefit from ageing.*	£21.90	U MCD MRN	(B)

CHAMPAGNE BILLECART-SALMON BRUT ROSÉ NV Champagne	*A pale pink fizz offering a red fruit nose followed by summer pudding fruit on the palate.*	£25.70	J&B DBY HW RBS JN BIL	(S)
CHAMPAGNE MOËT & CHANDON BRUT IMPÉRIAL ROSÉ 1990 Champagne	*Tawny pink, close to brick red. Redcurrants and strawberry fruit make up the complex palate.*	£27.10	DBY CLA VLW CST RBS U	(B)
VEUVE CLICQUOT PONSARDIN RESERVE BRUT ROSÉ 1989 Champagne	*Salmon pink in colour, this fizz offers a lovely red fruit nose and creamy finish.*	£30.40	Widely Available	(B)
CHAMPAGNE DOM PÉRIGNON ROSÉ PRESTIGE CUVÉE BRUT 1985, MOËT & CHANDON Champagne	*This wonderful wine from Moët offers a creamy palate with toffee and biscuit flavours.*	£169	M&C	(G)

FRANCE • LANGUEDOC • RED

SOMERFIELD MERLOT VDP NV, JEANJEAN Languedoc Roussillon	*A simple wine with instrinsic soft damson fruit and fresh lively tannins to finish.*	£3.40	SMF	(B)
CABERNET SAUVIGNON VDP 1996, VAL D'ORBIEU Languedoc Roussillon	*Ripe minty blackcurrants leading to a palate of warm berry fruit and restrained tannins.*	£3.40	SMF	(B)
MALT HOUSE VINTNERS CÔTES DU ROUSSILLON NV, Languedoc Roussillon	*An approachable soft wine, lifted by just a touch of volatile acidity on the nose.*	£3.60	MTL SMF	(B)

TESCO CABERNET SAUVIGNON RESERVE 1996, FREDERIC ROGER Languedoc Roussillon	*Green berry fruit minty overtones on the nose. A palate of blueberries and lively tannins.*	£3.70	TO	B
FORTANT DE FRANCE GRENACHE ROUGE VDP 1996, SKALLI Languedoc Roussillon	*Soft and fruity a sympathetically put together easy going, commercial style of wine.*	£3.70	BNK MWW HOU	B
BELLEFONTAINE MERLOT 1996, PAUL BOUTINOT Languedoc Roussillon	*Flavours of blackberries and jammy tannins on the nose backed by a palate of minty damson, berry fruits.*	£3.80	Widely Available	B
DOMAINE DE LA COMMANDÈRIE DE ST JEAN VDP 1996, CHATEAU DE GREZAN Côteaux de Laurens	*Blackberries and spice on the nose. A palate of peppery fruit and underlying tannins.*	£4.00	Widely Available	B
CHÂTEAU VILLESPASSANS 1995, LES GRANDS VINS DU SAINT CHINIAN Languedoc Roussillon	*Warm, black pepper aromas lead to a big spicy palate with a brisk tannin finish.*	£4.00	DLA	B
GEMINI MERLOT VDP 1996, YVES PAGES Languedoc Roussillon	*A nose of cooked fruits and racy tannins and a palate of pleasing balanced berry fruit.*	£4.10	Widely Available	B
LES ARBOUSIERS CABERNET SAUVIGNON 1995, LES ARBOUSIERS Languedoc Roussillon	*Gamey blackcurrants and leafy tannin aromas with a palate of ripening berry fruits to follow.*	£4.50	ENO	B
DOMAINE LE DEVOIS 1995, LES VIGNERONS DE ROUEIRE Languedoc Roussillon	*Soft and round with medium weight and length a slightly curious but appealing wine.*	£4.50	CES	B

DOMAINE DU RIVAGE MERLOT CUXAC VDP 1996, VAL D'ORBIEU Languedoc Roussillon	*Soft fruit and rounded warm tannins combine to produce a rich brambley wine of some class.*	£4.50	SPR	**B**
CHÂTEAU HELENE CUVEE PENELOPE 1993, MARIE-HELENE GAU Languedoc Roussillon	*With a warm peppery nose, a lightweight wine with quite aggressive tannins and reasonable peppered length.*	£4.80	WAW TP PV	**B**
GALET VINEYARDS SYRAH RESERVE VDP 1996, GABRIEL MEFFRE Languedoc Roussillon	*Gamey fruit and spice on the nose with a grippy palate with restrained power and tannin.*	£5.00	WCR CEL BKW	**B**
JAMES HERRICK CUVÉE SIMONE 1995, JAMES HERRICK Languedoc Roussillon	*Deep purple in colour a spicy fruity red wine with a good long finish.*	£5.00	VWC W FUL TO A U SMF	**B**
DR. ABBOTT'S SHIRAZ 1996, ST AURIOL. Languedoc Roussillon	*An intense round wine with a complex animal nose, fine tannins and a good finish.*	£5.00	MAJ VW	**S**
MINERVOIS DOMAINE DE BUADELLE 1996, Languedoc Roussillon	*A very good complex but approachable wine with depth concentration and a good finish.*	£5.50	BD	**S**
SELECTION SALVATERRE SYRAH 1995, CHATEAU D'OPOUL Languedoc Roussillon	*Medium weight with good fruit and tannins, a spicy wine on the nose and palate.*	£5.80	BD	**B**
CHÂTEAU ROQUEBRUN ST CHINIAN 1994, CAVE LES VINS DE ROQUEBRUN Languedoc Roussillon	*An aromatic possibly carbonic maceration nose is followed by blackcurrant fruit and big grippy tannins.*	£5.80	CRM NIC B&B	**B**

DOMAINE LA TOUR BOISEE CUVÉE MARIE CLAUDE 1994, JEAN-LOUIS POUDOU Languedoc Roussillon	*A highly extracted, big complex wine with savoury blackfruit palate and dusty tannins.*	£5.90	WAW PV	Ⓢ
CHÂTEAU DE CALCE 1993, CHÂTEAU DE CALCE Languedoc Roussillon	*This wine has a well developed smoky nose and a good balanced firm structure.*	£6.00	BD	Ⓑ
CHÂTEAU ROQUEBRUM PRESTIGE ST CHINIAN 1995, CAVES LES VINS DE ROQUEBRUN Languedoc Roussillon	*A peppery wine with confected spicy fruit aromas and a long soft finish.*	£6.00	CRM	Ⓑ
L' EXCELLENCE DE CHÂTEAU CAPENDU 1995, SA CAPENDU Languedoc Roussillon	*Deeply coloured, full of spicy fruit, a medium weight wine with big rich tannins.*	£6.00	VLW	Ⓑ
CHÂTEAU MINE L'ETANE 1995, Languedoc Roussillon	*Opulent and generous on the nose with a palate of balanced fruit and spicy tannins.*	£6.00	U BTH	Ⓑ
CHÂTEAU FLAUGERGUES 1995, HENRY DE COLBERT Languedoc Roussillon	*Deep purple in colour this wine has rich vibrant fruit, moderate oak and solid tannins.*	£6.50	MWW	Ⓑ
CHÂTEAU DE COMBEBELLE 1995, E.A.R.L. EMILY EDEN Languedoc Roussillon	*Warm aromas of smoke and spice lead to a gamey, peppery, full bodied palate.*	£6.50	VR	Ⓑ
CHÂTEAU DE LASTOURS CUVÉE FÛTS DE CHÊNE 1991, Languedoc Roussillon	*A warm savoury style of wine, quite chewy with nicely balanced spicy fruit and tannin.*	£6.80	Widely Available	Ⓑ

DOMAINE ST.JEAN DE VILLECROZE CABERNET SAUVIGNON 1992, Languedoc Roussillon	*A nose of rich fruit and oaky tannins in the mouth rounded and full.*	£7.00	POR MK TW CES	B
CHÂTEAU DE COMBEBELLE COMTE CATHARE 1994, E.A.R.L EMILY EDEN Languedoc Roussillon	*Cherry red with cherry fruit on the palate, a warm balanced wine with soft tannins.*	£7.80	VR	B
DOMAINE DE VILLEMAJOU 1994, GERARD BRETRAND Languedoc Roussillon	*A chewy wine with a rich spice nose and a good earthy palate.*	£8.50	NIC	B
DOMAINE SAINT ANTONIN FAUGERES 1995, DOMAINE SAINT ANTONIN Languedoc Roussillon	*A well-balanced wine exhibiting good complex plummy flavours and soft tannins.*	£9.00	M&V	B

FRANCE • LANGUEDOC • WHITE

SKYLARK HILL CHARDONNAY VDP 1996, VIENNET Languedoc Roussillon	*A lovely combination of crisp light peachy fruit, cloves, nutmeg and kernels balancing well together.*	£3.40	KWI	B
TERRET VDP 1996, J & F LURTON Languedoc Roussillon	*Bright and clear fresh acidity with a palate of crisp fruit and an off dry finish*	£3.60	JN HVW OD MRN	B
TERROIR CLUB CHARDONNAY VDP 1996 Languedoc Roussillon	*Quite an austere, yet elegant style of wine which is nicely balanced with good length.*	£4.00	PEC	B

TERROIR CLUB SAUVIGNON VDP 1996 Languedoc Roussillon	*Subtle start, that gradually changes into a soft style, with good upfront fruity flavours on the palate.*	£4.00	PEC	(S)
ST MONT D'ANDRE DAGUIN 1996, PRODUCTEURS DE PLAIMONT Languedoc Roussillon	*Pungent, soft fruit aromas followed by a weighty palate of rich pineapple and peach.*	£4.10	ABY	(B)
DOMAINE SALICES SAUVIGNON VDP 1996, J & F LURTON Languedoc Roussillon	*An intense gooseberry nose with, abundant character lead into a juicy palate with, zingy acidity.*	£4.40	JN OD	(S)
CHAIS CUXAC VAL D'ORBIEU 1996 Languedoc Roussillon	*Appealing fresh pear, smoky oak aromas. Concentration of fruits on a full palate.*	£4.70	COK MRN	(B)
LAPEROUSE VDP D'OC BLANC 1995, PENVAL Languedoc Roussillon	*A big, intense wine on the nose with hints of nuttiness, pears and soft fruit.*	£4.80	CWS TH OD EP SMF	(B)
DOMAINE DE FARELLES 1996, LES VIGNERONS DE CERESSOU Languedoc Roussillon	*Creamy butterscotch oak on the nose with tropical fruit, tinned peaches and toasty undertones lingering to smooth finish.*	£4.90	PLB BBR	(B)
TANNERS SAUVIGNON BLANC VDP 1995, J&F LURTON Languedoc Roussillon	*Clean, but intense varietal nose, with a dry grassy undertone on the palate. Crisp, green finish.*	£4.90	TAN	(B)

Pinpoint who sells the wine you wish to buy by turning to the stockist codes. If you know the name of the wine you want to buy, use the alphabetical index. If the price is your motivation, refer to the invaluable price guide index; red and white wines under £5, sparkling wines under £10 and champagne under £15. Happy hunting!

DOMAINE DE LA BAUME PHILIPPE DE BAUDIN SAUVIGNON BLANC 1996, BRL HARDY Languedoc Roussillon	*Describe by many tasters as a excelant stylish wine, with a sherberty nose, and a long, dry lingering aftertaste.*	**£5.00**	Widely Available	**B**
LA DOMEQUE TÊTE DE CUVÉE VIEILLES VIGNES 1996, FREDERIC ROGER Languedoc Roussillon	*A rich and creamy wine with a palate of ripe peach, apricot, mango and passion fruit.*	**£5.00**	A	**S**
MUSCAT SEC VAL D'ORBIEU VDP 1996, VAL D'ORBIEU Languedoc Roussillon	*Fresh grapey aromas are reflected on the dry palate of this approachable wine.*	**£5.00**	VDO	**B**
DLC CHARDONNAY TERRET, CHEVALIÈRE RÉSERVE VDP 1996, DOMAINE LA CHEVALIÈRE Languedoc Roussillon	*Deep yellow in colour with gentle tropical fruit on the palate and nutty, woody overtones.*	**£5.20**	DIR TRO TP POR	**B**
DLC SAUVIGNON, CHEVALIÈRE RÉSERVE VDP 1996, DOMAINE LA CHEVALIÈRE Languedoc Roussillon	*Clear, distinct asparagus flavour abounds on the nose, leading to good fruit that clings together.*	**£5.20**	DIR TRO POR EOO	**S**
VIOGNIER VDP D'OC 1996, MAUREL VEDEAU Languedoc Roussillon	*Attractive light, spicy nose, precedes a lively palate with apple and pear undertones.*	**£6.00**	SMF	**B**
CHATEAU DE LANCYRE "LA ROUVIÈRE" 1996 Languedoc Roussillon	*A crisp wine with grassy aromas and a palate full of fresh asparagus and gooseberry flavours.*	**£6.00**	VER	**G**
DOMAINE DE LA BAUME PHILIPPE DE BAUDIN CHARDONNAY VIOGNIER 1995, BRL HARDY Languedoc Roussillon	*A melon aroma on a well-rounded nose, leading to a vibrant finish.*	**£6.50**	W CHF L&W AWS A	**B**

DLC LA CHEVALIÈRE CUVÉE PREMIÈRE VDP 1995, DOMAINE LA CHEVALIÈRE Languedoc Roussillon	*A full, rich wine offering spicy aromas and a well rounded buttery palate.*	£7.00	DIR	**B**

FRANCE • LANGUEDOC • FORTIFIED

MUSCAT DE RIVESALTES CHAPOUTIER 1995, MARK CHAPOUTIER Languedoc Roussillon	*A beautifully integrated wine with a sweet, spicy nose which although delicate, shows great length of finish.*	£5.30	DIR W	**S**
NOILLY PRAT DRY Provence	*Distinct herb qualities abound in this fresh wine. Attractive grapiness balances the fruit and fresh alcohol.*	£6.40	Widely Available	**S**

FRANCE • LOIRE • RED

CAVE DU HAUT POITOU GAMAY 1996 Loire	*Attractive fresh strawberry and Gamay nose with young lively fruit and well-balanced tannin.*	£5.00	TBA	**B**
REUILLY ROUGE 1996, CLAUDE LAFOND Loire	*Minty leaf aromas on the nose. A palate of hebaceous tannins and a lean finish.*	£7.50	NIC	**B**
BOURGEUIL VIEILLES VIGNES 1993, PIERRE CASLOT Loire	*A light and simple Cabernet, pale red in colour with an earthy, oaky palate.*	£7.80	3D	**B**

BOURGUEIL VIEILLES VIGNES 1990, DOMAINE HUBERT Loire	*An earthy, spicy wine offering medium tannins and ripe red fruit on the lingering palate.*	£8.50	GI NAD	(B)
CHINON JEUNES VIGNES 1996, CHARLES JOYUET Loire	*Bright, youthful colour with a cooked raspberry nose and hints of violet on the palate.*	£8.80	DIR	(B)
SANCERRE ROUGE 1995, SERGE LALOUE Loire	*Elegant spicy nose with good gentle cherry fruit, this wine has an excellent structure.*	£8.90	ABY	(B)
SANCERRE ROUGE 1995, DOMAINE VACHERON Loire	*Raspberry fruit on the nose and flavours of loganberries in the mouth. Well made.*	£10.50	Widely Available	(B)
CHATEAU DE LA GRILLE 1993, LAURENT GOSSET Chinon	*Light and fresh with a toasted nose and ripe raspberry fruit on the generous palate.*	£11.60	PAV MK TW	(B)
CHINON VARENNES DU GRAND CLOS 1995, CHARLES JOYUET Loire	*A lovely rich nose is followed by a palate of raspberry fruit and gentle tannins.*	£12.00	DIR	(B)
SANCERRE ROUGE BELLES DAMES 1995, DOMAINE VACHERON Loire	*A light style of wine with delicate summer fruits and soft rose petal aromas on its juicy palate.*	£17.90	GI NAD	(B)

Pinpoint who sells the wine you wish to buy by turning to the stockist codes. If you know the name of the wine you want to buy, use the alphabetical index. If the price is your motivation, refer to the invaluable price guide index; red and white wines under £5, sparkling wines under £10 and champagne under £15. Happy hunting!

FRANCE • LOIRE • WHITE

ASDA MUSCADET 1996, BAUD Loire	*Dry aromas of fresh lemons lead to delicate palate full of fresh fruit with a yeasty prickle at the finish.*	**£3.00**	A	**B**
SAUVIGNON BLANC 1996, BRL HARDY Touraine	*Aussie knowledge on French terroir produces a fine, fruity, balanced wine with great length.*	**£3.90**	VWC DBY W CHF NEI WWI SAF VW	**B**
TESCO MUSCADET SUR LIE 1996, Loire	*Slightly fragrant, medium bodied wine with profound acidity and an attractive length.*	**£4.00**	TO	**B**
SAUMUR CHÂTEAU DE MONTGUERET 1996, LACHETEAU Loire	*Very young crisp wine. Rich in fruit that lingers through to the well-balanced finish.*	**£5.00**	WST OD	**B**
LE MONTAILLANT CHARDONNAY 1995, LES CAVES DES HAUTES DE SEYR Loire	*Fresh flinty nose following to a good palate of clean ripening fruit and nice acidity.*	**£5.30**	PMA	**B**
MUSCADET DE SÈVRE ET MAINE DOMAINE DE BASSE-VILLE SUR LIE 1996 Loire	*Clean and aromatic with a fresh, buttery nose and crisp apple flavours on the palate.*	**£5.50**	GI NAD	**B**
MUSCADET DE SÈVRE ET MAINE DOMAINE DE L'ECU SUR LIE 1996, GUY BOSSARD Loire	*A dry nose with yeasty autolytic notes from lees contact giving complexity to the citrus palate.*	**£5.70**	VER VR SAF	**B**

REUILLY BLANC 1996, HENRI BEURDIN & FILS Loire	*A lively nose precedes the palate which is filled with ripe gooseberry fruit and soft herbs.*	£5.90	GI MWW NAD EBA GC	(B)
REUILLY 1996, CLAUDE LAFOND Loire	*A fine, subtle wine. Brackish on the nose with a delightfully light finish of cut grass.*	£7.00	CES NIC	(S)
VOUVRAY SEC 1995, DIDIER CHAMPALOU Loire	*Honeyed, ripe and clean; with a concentration of good, balanced flavours; this is definitely medal-winning stuff.*	£7.30	ENO	(S)
LA GRAVELIÉRE 1995, JOSEPH MELLOT Loire	*Ripe gooseberry and grassy aromas dominate the nose, definate 'terroir' influence on the palate.*	£7.50	GRA	(B)
SANCERRE DOMAINE DU CARROU 1996, DOMINIQUE ROGER Loire	*A medium-weight wine, showing good Sancerre fruit, in an attractive style with a crisp finish.*	£8.00	ENO	(B)
WAITROSE POUILLY FUMÉ 1996, DOMAINE MASSON-BLONDELET Loire	*Aromas of asparagus and nettles on the nose with a good concentration of fruit on the palate.*	£8.00	W	(S)
POUILLY FUMÉ LES GRIOTTINES 1996, MICHEL BAILLY Loire	*A refined wine. Pale to the eye, it freshens the palate with subtle, well-balanced fruit.*	£8.50	U	(B)
SANCERRE CHÂTEAU FAVRAY 1996, QUENTIN DAVID Loire	*Clear, gooseberry style with a ripe, fruity background and succulent acidity on the finish.*	£9.00	ENO	(B)

FRANCE • LOIRE • WHITE

SANCERRE LES BARONNES BONNES BOUCHES 1996, HENRI BOURGEOIS Loire	*A strong asparagus aroma lingers on the nose, while the palate shows persistence and profound acidity.*	£9.00	SAF	(B)
DOMAINE DU CARROIR 1996, PIERRE RIFFAULT Loire	*A balanced wine showing dry acidity and gooseberry fruit on the palate. A thoroughly becoming wine.*	£9.00	3D	(B)
DOMAINE DE CHATENOY 1996, PIERRE CLEMENT Menetou Salon	*Fragrant gooseberry fruit on the nose; well-structured palate showing good weight and depth.*	£9.20	DIR NIC ENO	(B)
SANCERRE LA CLEMENCE DOMAINE PINARD 1996, VINCENT PINARD Loire	*A palate that is full of fresh, gooseberry characteristics and zingy, mouthwatering acidity on the finish.*	£9.20	J&B FUL grt ABY	(G)
SANCERRE BLANC LES ROCHES 1996, DOMAINE VACHERON Loire	*The panel found this wine to be full-bodied, with a concentrated flavours of gooseberry with gunflint notes.*	£9.70	GI GNW U BEN NAD BBR F&M	(S)
SANCERRE 1996, HENRI BOURGEOIS Loire	*Bright, lightly coloured appearance, with a beautiful herbaceous nose, finishing with a palate of cut grass and gooseberry.*	£9.70	CNL	(S)
POUILLY FUMÉ 1996, HENRI BOURGEOIS Loire	*A delicate wine with an elegant herbaceous fruit aroma on the nose which carries over onto the citrus palate.*	£9.70	CNL	(S)
POUILLY FUMÉ DOMAINE DAGUENEAU 1996, SERGE DAGUENEAU Loire	*Youthful wine, showing well-structured fruit on the palate, with pear drops on the aftertaste.*	£10.10	J&B PO WIN ABY	(B)

POUILLY FUMÉ CHÂTEAU DE TRACY 1995, CHÂTEAU DE TRACY Loire	*Rich fruity gooseberry aromas on a vibrant nose, leading to a young attractive palate.*	£10.80	MTL DBY L&W MM CES POR HOU WSO	(B)
SANCERRE LES CAILLOTTES 1995, PASCAL JOLIVET Loire	*The tasters thought this wine offered a harmonious ensemble of elegant, exotic fruit on the palate.*	£13.50	BDT UNC	(S)
SANCERRE GRAND CUVÉE COMTE LAFOND 1993, DE LADOUCETTE Loire	*This Sancerre opens up nicely on the nose, with unpretentious gooseberry and grassy aromas.*	£18.00	MWW NEI NIC PAL EDC EP	(G)

FRANCE • LOIRE • SWEET

LES DEUX ANÉES 1995, DE FESLES BERNARD GERMAIN Bonnezeaux	*Attractive botrytis fruit character shines through on this rich, subtle, well-balanced wine, with good length.*	£13.50	PO	(B)

FRANCE • LOIRE • SPARKLING

GRATIEN & MEYER CUVÉE FLAMME NV, GRATIEN & MEYER Saumur	*Straw yellow in colour with a strawberry, appley nose and rich, firm, fairly heavy palate.*	£9.20	CNL CAR OD	(B)

Pinpoint who sells the wine you wish to buy by turning to the stockist codes. If you know the name of the wine you want to buy, use the alphabetical index. If the price is your motivation, refer to the invaluable price guide index; red and white wines under £5, sparkling wines under £10 and champagne under £15. Happy hunting!

FRANCE • PROVENCE

DOMAINE TERRES BLANCHES CUVÉE AURELIA 1990, NOEL MICHELIN Provence	*This wine of outstanding quality has a cigar box nose and herbal, fleshy fruit palate.*	£9.00	VR	(G)
CLOS D'IERE CUVÉE I 1992, DOMAINE RABIEGA Provence	*Spicy aromas lead to a warm palate of smoked game and pepper with ripe tannins.*	£13.00	NY	(B)
CHÂTEAU DE PIBARNON BANDOL 1993, COMTE DE ST VICTOR Provence	*A superbly made wonderfully deep and complex wine with rich liquorice and tar aromas.*	£13.70	WIN ABY	(G)
CLOS D'IERE CUVÉE I 1993, DOMAINE RABIEGA Provence	*Dark plum in colour with warm, leathery, spicy fruit aromas. Will improve further still.*	£18.60	ENO	(S)
LANGUE GARDE ROUGE 1993, DOMAINES OTT Provence	*Dark and brooding, opening to an enticing, warm palate of tarry spice and plum fruit.*	£25.00	DAV	(B)

FRANCE • RHÔNE • RED

SAFEWAY COTES DE LUBERON ROUGE 1995, CELLIER DE MARRENON Rhône	*Light purple with good berry fruit aromas, a mid-weight wine with a gentle tannic finish.*	£3.30	SAF	(B)

CROZES HERMITAGE 1995, JEAN-PAUL SELLES Rhône	*A strawberry nose leads onto a lively fruit palate, a long finish with soft, juicy tannins.*	**£5.10**	PLB SMF SMF	**B**
VACQUEYRAS, CUVÉE DU MARQUIS DE FONSEGUILLE 1995, CAVE DE VACQUEYRAS Rhône	*A nicely balanced clean fresh wine with pepper on the nose and a lengthy finish.*	**£5.50**	CWS	**B**
CÔTES DU RHÔNE 1995, DOMAINE BRUSSET Rhône	*A vibrant, structured, intensely fruity wine with good length and pleasant blackberry nose.*	**£5.50**	ENO	**S**
CÔTES DU RHÔNE VILLAGES DOMAINE DE LA GRANDE BELLANE VALREAS 1996, EARL GAIA Rhône	*Very fresh and peppery, a wine with clean black-currant fruit and attractive, firm acidity.*	**£5.80**	JS VER CWS T BRP VW	**S** WINE OF THE YEAR
ST JOSEPH 1994, JEAN-PAUL SELLES Rhône	*A lovely well-balanced wine with soft spicy pep-pery plum fruit on the structured palate.*	**£6.20**	PLB SMF	**B**
CÔTES DU RHÔNE VILLAGES DOMAINE DE LA BERTHETE 1995, PASCAL MAILLET Rhône	*A well made wine with rich spicy fruit, a ripe strawberry nose and a clean finish.*	**£6.90**	NIC	**B**
GIGONDAS DOMAINE STE LUCIE 1995, CAVE VIGNERONS GIGONDAS Rhône	*A firm wine with a powerful fruity nose and a rich, spicy, plum and redcurrant palate.*	**£7.00**	W IVY	**B**
CÔTES DU RHÔNE VILLAGES BEAURENARD RASTEAU 1995, PAUL COULON & FILS Rhône	*Jammy aromas of cooked fruit lead to a spicy palate with raisined fruit flavours.*	**£7.00**	LNR PAG	**B**

SAINT JOSEPH 1990, GEORGES DUBOEUF Rhône	*A wine with an attractive fruit tannin balance, smoked bacon nose and a lingering, balanced palate.*	£7.00	LNR PAG	(B)
CÔTES DU RHÔNE VILLAGES CAIRANNE 1996, DOMAINE RICHAUD Rhône	*A well-structured, purple wine with a rich, peppery nose and intense blackberry fruit flavours.*	£7.00	HOU LIB	(S)
CÔTES DU RHÔNE VILLAGES CAIRANNE 1995, DOMAINE BRUSSET Rhône	*Complex and well-balanced with a meaty nose, dried fruit flavours come to the fore.*	£7.10	NY CHF ENO	(B)
ROUX LAITHWAITE S5 VDP NV, CAVES DE CHUSCLAN Rhône	*A nicely balanced, cherry red wine with a spicy, meaty nose, firm structure and good length.*	£7.40	BD	(G)
CHÂTEAU VAL JOANIS LES GRIOTTES 1993, CHRISTIAN DUPORT Rhône	*This wine has a herby spice nose, nicely balanced palate, attractive fruit and good grip.*	£7.60	ABY	(B)
CÔTES DU RHÔNE CUVÉE PRESTIGE VIELLES VIGNES 1995, DOMAINE ROGER PERRIN Rhône	*A vibrant and lively wine with peppery, fruity aromas and ripe fruit cake flavoured palate.*	£7.60	HRV	(S)
CÔTES DU RHÔNE VILLAGES CAIRANNE CUVÉE PRESTIGE 1995, DOMAINE DE L'ORATOIRE Rhône	*Smoky, slightly rustic on the nose. A soft, ripe and juicy palate makes this an approachable wine.*	£7.70	COK SWS L&W	(S)
LIRAC DOMAINE DE LA MORDORÉE 1996, DELORME Rhône	*Rich spicy aromas lead to concentrated flavours of baked fruit and a lingering brisk finish.*	£7.80	NIC BEN	(G)

ANDRÉ SIMON CHÂTEAUNEUF-DU-PAPE 1994, JEAN-PAUL SELLES Rhône	*A spicy plum and raspberry nose leads to a chewy wine with good pepper and fruit.*	£8.50	MTL WRT	**B**
ST. JOSEPH 1995, CAVE DE TAIN Rhône	*Rich smoky aromas lead to intense black pepper and game flavours on a mouthfilling palate.*	£8.70	DBY NIC COK WCS NRW SWS MRN	**B**
GIGONDAS DOMAINE DES ESPIERS 1995, PHILIPPE CARTOUX Rhône	*Spicy leathery aromas lead to well combined fruit flavours, tannins and acids on the palate.*	£9.00	CRM B&B BEL	**B**
CÔTES DU RHÔNE VILLAGES 1991, J. VIDAL-FLEURY Cotes De Rhône	*Excellent gritty fruit bouquet is followed by rich raisined fruit flavors on the dry palate.*	£9.00	WIN MK TW HCK	**B**
GIGONDAS LE GRAND MONTIRAIL 1995, DOMAINE BRUSSET Rhône	*Full and rich, this wine has a spicy peppery nose and well-integrated ripe lingering tannins.*	£9.80	CHF SWS ENO	**B**
GIGONDAS 1995, DOMAINE DE FONT-SANE Rhône	*A wine with smoky spicy aromas displaying good fruit on the palate and a long finish.*	£10.00	BI	**B**
GIGONDAS 1994, ETIENNE GUIGAL Rhône	*A dark wine with a bubblegum style, fruit nose and a simple palate with firm tannins.*	£10.00	DBY MWW SHG GGW OD IRV	**B**
CHÂTEAUNEUF-DU-PAPE CLOS SAINT MICHEL 1995, GUY MOUSSET Rhône	*A rich wine with warm aromas of stewed plums and spice on a light palate with a soft finish.*	£10.00	W	**B**

FRANCE • RHÔNE • RED

GIGONDAS DOMAINE RASPAIL-AY 1994, DOMINIQUE AY Rhône	*Rich spicy aromas lead to a fruit dominated palate with good depth and a soft finish.*	£10.50	GGW HVW	(B)
GIGONDAS DOMAINE RASPAIL-AY 1993, DOMINIQUE AY Gigondas	*Jammy fruit aromas on a rich spicy palate with overtones of baked fruit and grippy tannins.*	£10.60	L&W GGW	(B)
CHÂTEAUNEUF-DU-PAPE LAURUS 1995, GABRIEL MEFFRE Rhône	*This Southern Rhône wine exhibits extremely ripe, peppery fruit cake characteristics with well integrated oak.*	£11.00	GA	(S)
ST JOSEPH BERNARD GRIPA 1995, BERNARD GRIPA Rhône	*Needing some age an intense wine with good ripe fruit, firm tannins and good length.*	£11.30	MTR MWW	(B)
CÔTES DU RHÔNE VILLAGES CAIRANNE 1996, DOMAINE RICHAUD EBRESCADE Rhône	*A young complex ,spicy, peppery wine with medium tannins and lengthy fruit flavours on the dryish palate.*	£11.50	LIB	(B)
HERMITAGE LES BESSARDS 1994, DELAS FRÈRES Rhône	*Showing signs of maturity with a lovely animal pepper nose and an impressive medium weight palate.*	£11.80	FTH	(S)
CHÂTEAUNEUF-DU-PAPE DOMAINE LA ROQUETTE 1993, BRUNIER FILS Rhône	*Complex aromas and flavours of rich fruit cake and spice dominate this Southern Rhône wine.*	£12.50	DIR L&W SHJ	(B)
CHÂTEAUNEUF-DU-PAPE DOMAINE FONT DE MICHELLE 1995, JEAN ET MICHEL GONNET Rhône	*A juicy ripe palate with firm chewy tannins and a spicy nose characterise this wine.*	£13.20	DBY J&B HVW WR BU BLS	(G)

FRANCE • RHÔNE • RED

CORNAS 1994, MARK CHAPOUTER Rhône	*Medium dark, a gutsy wine with an earthy nose, meaty palate and Christmas pudding fruit.*	**£13.30**	DIR W MM	(B)
CHÂTEAUNEUF-DU-PAPE 1994, CHÂTEAU LA NERTHE Rhône	*Big spicy, fruitcake aromas are repeated on the concentrated palate with a brisk tannin finish.*	**£14.00**	JN OD	(B)
CHÂTEAUNEUF-DU-PAPE DOMAINE DU PEGAU 1994, DOMAINE DU PEGAU Rhône	*Rich, complex aromas of Christmas cake are followed by a soft palate of spicy fruit.*	**£14.70**	NY AMW HVW	(B)
CHÂTEAUNEUF-DU-PAPE CHAUPIN 1995, DOMAINE DE LA JANASSE Rhône	*A delicate nose leads to a full palate of rich spicy fruit, attractive easy drinking wine.*	**£15.00**	ENO	(B)
CHÂTEAUNEUF-DU-PAPE 1995, DOMAINE DU VIEUX TELEGRAPHE Rhône	*Concentrated spicy Dundee cake aromas, intense juicy flavours on the lingering palate with brisk tannins.*	**£16.10**	DBY J&B DIR L&W CWI MM RBS CPW	(S)
HERMITAGE 1995, DOMAINE FAYOLLE Rhône	*Peppery on the nose, a rich concentrated fruity wine with powerful tannins and acid.*	**£20.50**	BD	(S)
CÔTE ROTIE 1993, ETIENNE GUIGAL Rhône	*Good structure and weight, a delicate wine with cool climate characteristics and a subtle smoky, spicy nose.*	**£21.00**	Widely Available	(B)
CÔTE ROTIE CÔTEAUX DES BASSENON 1994, DOMAINE CUILLERON Rhône	*A concentrated savoury nose with rich smoky flavours finishes with an attractive fresh acidity.*	**£23.50**	BUT ENO	(B)

FRANCE • RHÔNE • RED

VIOGNIER 1996, GEORGES DUBOEUF Rhône	*Peaches and cream aromas. Ripe fruit gives it a smooth texture. Attractive soft, underlying acidity.*	£6.90	BNK LNR NY RBS JN PAG JS	(B)
CONDRIEU 1995, ETIENNE GUIGAL Rhône	*This wine shows style, with crisp clear grape and lychees aromas that linger on the finish.*	£20.20	GGW CEB U HVW V IRV J&B	(B)
CONDRIEU LYS DE VOLAN 1995, ALAIN PARET & GÉRARD DEPARDIEU Rhône	*Lightly oaky, floral nose, leading to a well-made wine with good weight, and a rich texture.*	£23.00	WSG RD	(B)
CONDRIEU LA COTE 1996, DOMAINE CUILLÈRON Rhône	*Excellent nose of apricot and peach. Succulent on the palate - a wonderful change from the norm.*	£25.00	BUT WIN ENO OD	(B)
CONDRIEU LES CHAILLETS VIEILLES VIGNES 1996, DOMAINE CUILLÈRON Rhône	*Typical peachy character. Hints of oak too. Ripe and rounded with a soft, creamy finish.*	£25.50	NY ENO OD	(B)

FRANCE • SOUTH WEST • RED

FOLONVIE CABERNET MERLOT 1996, YVON MAU Côtes de Gascogne	*Négociant-bottled; both on the nose and palate this shows blackcurrant damson fruit with pleasant drying tannins.*	£3.40	WWI	(B)

FRANCE • SOUTH WEST • WHITE

GAILLAC BLANC 1996, BRL HARDY WINE COMPANY Gaillac	*This pale yellow wine offers an earthy nose with rich tropical fruit and buttery flavours.*	**£3.90**	DBY CHF NEI PTR JHL	(S)
VIN DE PAYS BLANC 1996, JACQUES VERITIER Côtes du Tarn	*Citrussy on the nose with hints of eucalyptus. The palate offers soft appley flavours and a crisp finish.*	**£4.00**	ENO	(B)
DOMAINE DU GRAND MAYNE 1996, ANDREW GORDON Côtes de Duras	*Pale and crystal clear, this is fresh with good fruit and a pleasant, steely finish.*	**£4.00**	WSA	(B)
MALT HOUSE VINTNERS BERGERAC DRY 1996, LES CAVES ST GERMAIN Bergerac	*Fresh dry yet slightly aromatic on the nose this wine shows good soft citrus fruit.*	**£4.00**	MHV	(B)
DOMAINE DE MAUBET 1996, DOMAINE DE MAUBET Côtes de Gascogne	*It has delightful green, grassy aromas on the nose, following through to a well-rounded palate.*	**£4.30**	Widely Available	(B)
CHÂTEAU GRINOU GRANDE RÉSERVE 1996, CATHERINE & GUY COISSET Bergerac	*A light, leafy gooseberry nose leading to a structured palate showing uplifting fruit and acidity.*	**£5.80**	ALZ	(B)
DOMAINE DE TARIQUET CUVÉE BOIS 1994, DOMAINES GRASSA Côtes de Gascogne	*Clean, juicy nose, leading to a lively palate, with creamy oak and melon aromas.*	**£6.00**	U	(B)

CHÂTEAU DE MINUTY DOMAINE FARNET 1996, J.E. MATTON Provence	*Rich lanolin flavours on the palate are toned down by the influence of the Clairette grape.*	£7.00	ABY	(S)
JURANÇON SEC CHANT DES VIGNES 1996, DOMAINE CAUHAPÉ South West	*Powerful floral nose, with a smoky, melony aroma leading to a crisp, grapefruity finish.*	£8.00	GI NAD TAN	(B)

FRANCE • SOUTH WEST • SWEET

MONBAZILLAC DOMAINE DU HAUT RAULY 1994, PIERRE ALARD South West	*Intense honey and caramel fruit flavours showing on this elegant, well-balanced, old fashioned wine.*	£8.00	CWS	(B)
SAUSSIGNAC CHÂTEAU GRINOU 1995, CATHERINE & GUY COISSET South West	*Herbal lemon character on the nose with a powerful weight of fruit and rich complexity.*	£9.50	ALZ	(B)
SAUSSIGNAC CUVÉE MARIE JEANNE 1994, CHÂTEAU LE PAYRAL South West	*A delicious wine with stacks of complex fruit characteristics coming through on the nose and palate.*	£10.00	ENO	(G)

FRANCE • SOUTH WEST • SPARKLING

SOMERFIELD CHARDONNAY BRUT NV, CAVES DE LANDIRAS South West	*A light, zesty nose produces a refreshing wine with gooseberry fruit and a biscuity palate.*	£5.00	SMF	(B)

SOREVI SPARKLING CHARDONNAY NV, SOREVI Côtes de Gascogne	*Good mousse, creamy, yeasty, lemony aromas, attractive, apple flavours, fresh bread notes and a delicate finish.*	**£5.80**	GI NAD	**S**
DOMAINE COLLIN BLANQUETTE DE LIMOUX NV, PHILIPPE COLLIN Languedoc Roussillon	*Delicate biscuit and autolysis notes with zesty fruit on a well-balanced, lingering palate.*	**£8.00**	CRM B&B W&V	**B**
CUVÉE DU PRESIDENT 1991, CAVE DU SIEUR D'ARQUES Languedoc Roussillon	*Ripe, fruity nose with citrus tones and good yeast characters, reflected on a clean refreshing palate.*	**£9.80**	BD	**B**

GERMANY

THE UK IS DRINKING INCREASING AMOUNTS of German wine from crisp, dry whites to rich dessert wines. Incredible determination is required to produce these wines from steep slopes in regions where obtaining full ripeness of the grape is not always guaranteed. Despite the apparently overwhelming labels, these wines are well worth seeking out and are becoming readily accessible in the British market.

GERMANY • WHITE

MALT HOUSE VINTNERS MAINZER DONNHERR SPÄTLESE 1995, OBERMEISTER Rhienhessen	*Soft, appealing apricot fruit on the nose leading to appealing acidity on a well-structured palate.*	£4.00	MHV	B
WAITROSE MÖNCHHOF ZELTINGER HIMMELREICH QBA 1988, ROBERT EYMAEL Mosel-Saar-Ruwer	*Very attractive floral notes showing on the nose, with soft, grapey fruit on the palate.*	£5.00	W	B
TESCO SCHLOSS-BÖCKEL-HEIM KUPFERGRUBE RIESLING, STAATELICHE, NIEDERHAUSEN Nahe	*Light apricot and flowery fruit aromas on the nose, leading to a crisp, clean finish.*	£5.90	TO	B
PIESPORTER GOLDTROPFCHEN RIESLING 1992, GRANS FASSIAN Mosel-Saar-Ruwer	*Spicy, floral fruit, beautifully balanced with fresh, uplifting acidity with crisp lime finish.*	£6.00	SPR	G
RIESLING TROCKEN 1995, GRANS FASSIAN Mosel-Saar-Ruwer	*Mouth-watering juicy acids combine with elegant fruity flavours on the palate to produce a zesty apple finish.*	£6.40	TO WMK	S

GERMANY • WHITE

Wine	Tasting Note	Price	Codes	
BERNKASTELER BADSTUBE RIESLING KABINETT 1994, VON KESSELSTATT Mosel-Saar-Ruwer	*Pale, young slightly vegetal nose with soft fruit flavours coming through on the palate.*	£8.20	GI CWS	**B**
RÜDESHEIMER MAGDALENENKREUZ RIESLING KABINETT 1996, JOSEF LEITZ Rheingau	*This wine shows some clean, fresh and grapey fruit with lovely balanced light acidity.*	£8.30	WSG CPW SWS ADN	**B**
FREINSHEIMER RIESLING HALBTROCKEN SPÄTLESE 1994, RAINER LINGENFELDER Pfalz	*Slightly closed nose, that opens up beautifully on the palate, showing good length and finish.*	£8.30	JN	**S**
GRAACHER DOMPROBST RIESLING SPÄTLESE 1994, MAX FERDINAND RICHTER Mosel-Saar-Ruwer	*Fresh green apples show on both the nose and the palate along with racy lime acidity.*	£9.10	DBY	**B**
SCHLOSS JOHANNISBERGER KABINETT 1995, WEINGUTER Rheingau	*This wine shows a beautiful perfumed nose and ripe honey flavours on the palate.*	£10.40	DBY GNW WIN LLV	**B**
J.L WOLF WACHENHEIMER GERUMPEL RIESLING SPÄLESE 1996, LOOSEN Pfalz	*Pleasantly balanced fruity aromas that follow through on a lively palate with uplifting lemon acidity.*	£10.80	WSG ADN	**B**
MAXIMIN GRÜNHAUS RIESLING KABINETT 1995, CARL VON SCHUBERT Mosel-Saar-Ruwer	*A graceful wine with a good concentration of fruit character which balances well with fresh, zippy acidity.*	£12.70	MAY J&B L&W	**G**
SCHLOSS JOHANNISBERGER SPÄTLESE 1995, WEINGUTER Rheingau	*Attractive fruity flavours on the nose, with honey, apricots and buttery undernotes on the finish.*	£13.60	DBY GI	**B**

SCHLOSS JOHANNISBERGER SPÄTLESE 1993, WEINGUTER Rheingau	*Aged, aromatic, diesel characteristics on the nose, while the palate shows complex flowery citrus fruit.*	**£14.20**	DBY GI WIN BEN LLV	(S)
ERDENER PRÄLAT RIESLING AUSLESE 1996, DR LOOSEN Mosel-Saar-Ruwer	*Very attractive flavours showing on the nose and palate, well-balanced wine with uplifting acidity.*	**£18.70**	WSG NY DBY BBR TAN	(B)

GERMANY • SWEET

ST URSULA RIESLING AUSLESE 1993, ST URSULA WEINKELLERI Pfalz	*Pale straw yellow in colour with crisp green apple flavours creating a light, pleasant wine.*	**£3.90**	KWI	(B)
KIRCHHEIMER SCHWARZERDE BA 1994, ZIMMERMANN GRAEFF Phalz	*A very attractive perfumed nose with lovely balanced citrussy fruit, showing on the palate.*	**£4.90**	MWW W FUL CWS MRN	(B)
KOBERNER WEISENBERG RIESLING BA 1995, FREIHERR VON SCHLEINITZ Mosel-Saar-Ruwer	*Some lovely fresh citrus aromas precedes the crisp palate, of this attractive, clean wine.*	**£17.00**	WSC	(B)
SCHLOSS JOHANNISBERGER AUSLESE 1995, WEINGUTER Rheingau	*Lovely peach and grapefruit character on the nose precedes a lively, well-integrated palate, with good length.*	**£19.10**	DBY GI	(B)

Pinpoint who sells the wine you wish to buy by turning to the stockist codes. If you know the name of the wine you want to buy, use the alphabetical index. If the price is your motivation, refer to the invaluable price guide index; red and white wines under £5, sparkling wines under £10 and champagne under £15. Happy hunting!

ITALY

The world's largest producer of wine, Italy is currently experimenting with new styles of Vini da Tavola. The influx of flying winemakers combined with inspired local knowledge is resulting in rich Super Tuscans and fresh styles from the south. The top estates in Brunello, Chianti and Barolo continue to perform well and offer excellent value for money.

ITALY • PIEDMONT

BARBERA D'ASTI ALASIA 1994, ARALDICA VINI PIEMONTESI Piedmont	*This is a complex, interesting wine with a typical nose, rich fruit and firm tannins.*	£6.30	V&C CWI GGW BEN LIB	**B**
BARBERA D'ALBA 1995, PRUNOTTO Piedmont	*A powerful wine with pleasant bitter cherry characters on the nose with chocolate on the palate.*	£7.40	V&C RBS SHJ SV W	**B**
BAROLO 1993, TERRE DEL BAROLO Piedmont	*A rich meaty, powerful wine with a herbal nose and long finish.*	£8.50	BNK CWS SMF	**B**
DOLCETTO D'ALBA "PRIAVINO" 1995, ROBERTO VOERZIO Piedmont	*A wonderfully balanced wine with an intensely flowery, truffley nose and clean, ripe fruit.*	£10.50	V&C ENO	**S**
BARBERA D'ALBA VIGNOTA 1995, CONTERNO FANTINO Piedmont	*With an intense smoked raspberry nose, this wine is exceptionally well-made and balanced. Lovely soft fruit!*	£11.00	V&C ENO	**S**

BARBARESCO 1994, MARINA MACARINO Piedmont	*This is a rich wine with a bitter cherry nose, soft fruit and firm tannins.*	**£11.80**	WAW PV DIR	(B)
BAROLO 1993, FONTANAFREDDA Piedmont	*This is rich and dry with a wonderful balance of savoury fruit and firm, grippy tannins.*	**£11.80**	TH V&C VIL MM CLA COK WWI ENO	(B)
BARBERA D'ASTI SUPERIORE 1994, BAVA Piedmont	*An older style of wine with a slightly floral nose and good weight of fruit.*	**£12.00**	VIN	(B)
BAROLO RISERVA 1990, VILLA LANATA Piedmont	*This is a wine with well-developed colour, an earthy nose, good fruit and firm tannins.*	**£13.00**	WMK GRA	(B)
BARBERA PASSUM 1991, CASCINA CASTLE'T Piedmont	*Classy wine with bitter cherry liquorice aromas and onto a long, drying finish.*	**£13.20**	V&C NY LU SAW	(G)
BAROLO VIGNETI ROCCHE 1993, AURELIO SETTIMO Piedmont	*A tarry, figgy wine with some straw aromas and a powerful, yet balanced, tannic structure.*	**£15.70**	WAW PV DIR	(B)
BAROLO 1993, AURELIO SETTIMO Piedmont	*A dry wine with prune and tobacco overtones and a firm, bold tannic finish.*	**£15.90**	DIR WAW PV	(B)
BARBERA D'ALBA "VIGNASSE DEL POZZO" 1994, ROBERTO VOERZIO Piedmont	*This wine with its berry fruit and classy oak nose has a tight fruity palate.*	**£17.00**	V&C ENO	(S)

BAROLO CONTEISA CEREQUIO 1989, ANGELO GAJA Piedmont	*A savoury, chewy wine packed with ripe fruit. The finish is long, and truly Italian - a favorite.*	£33.60	DBY L&W HVW	G

ITALY • TUSCANY

MALT HOUSE VINTNERS CHIANTI 1996, PICCINI Tuscany	*A dry, medium bodied wine with peppery, nettley tones, pronounced tannins and a medium finish.*	£3.90	MHV	B
SAFEWAY CHIANTI 1995, ROCCA DELLE MACIE Tuscany	*A richly coloured wine with a ripe, plummy nose, soft palate and a dry finish.*	£4.00	SAF	B
SAFEWAY CHIANTI CLASSICO 1995, ROCCA DELLE MACIE Tuscany	*This wine has an almondy, animal nose, a pleasant soft fruit palate and good length.*	£5.30	SAF	B
CHIANTI CLASSICO VILLA CAFAGGIO 1995, CASA GIRELLI SPA Tuscany	*A deeply coloured wine with morello cherries on the nose, fruity palate and zingy finish.*	£6.80	VEX WCS M&S BAB VD CHF RTW WRW	B
CHIANTI CLASSSICO CASTELLO DI NIPOZZANO RISERVA 1994, FONTANAFREDDA Tuscany	*Aromas of ripe morello cherries with liquorice, tarry notes are followed by a velvety palate.*	£7.70	V&C MWW MM OD	B
CHIANTI CLASSICO RISERVA 1993, GESTIONI PICCINI Moreto	*A classy, sophisticated wine with subtle aromas, good balance of flavours and long finish.*	£7.70	CST A SAF UWM WRT MAK SMF	G

CHIANTI CLASSICO RISERVA ROCCA DI CASTAGNOLI 1991, WALTER FILIPUTI Tuscany	*Quite a mature wine with earthy character, some ripe fruit and overtones of tar, wood and dark chocolate.*	**£8.00**	W	(B)
CHIANTI CLASSICO 1994, CASTELLO DI FONTERUTOLI Tuscany	*A wine with a slightly bitter fruit nose, sweet cherry palate and light, easy tannins.*	**£8.20**	VWC CWI VW RD BBR	(S)
LE VOLTE 1995, TENUTA DELL'ORNELLAIA Tuscany	*A well-balanced wine with a clean cherry and raspberry nose, full and recognisable tannins on a rich palate.*	**£8.70**	Widely Available	(B)
CHIANTI RUFINA 1994, FATTORIA SELVAPIANA Tuscany	*A creamy, oaky nose leads to a palate full of ripe fruit with a clean, supple finish.*	**£8.90**	DBY V&C DIR GGW VLW RBS BEN LIB	(B)
BARCO REALE 1996, TENUTA DI CAPELLANA Tuscany	*An earthy, bitter cherry nose precedes a ripe fruit palate with a drying long finish.*	**£8.90**	DBY LIB	(B)
CHIANTI CLASSICO 1994, CASA EMMA Tuscany	*A light wine with cherry and raspberry aromas before a medium palate of floral, fruity flavours.*	**£8.90**	FLW	(B)
CHIANTI CLASSICO 1994, FATTORIA ISOLE E OLENA Tuscany	*Vegetal aromas, excellent morello cherry and blackcurrant flavours with firm tannins on a lengthy palate .*	**£9.80**	Widely Available	(S)
CHIANTI CLASSICO RISERVA 1993, CASTELLO DI BROLIO Tuscany	*Stylish nose with rich fruit and liquorice notes this wine has a complex fruit palate.*	**£10.30**	V&C VIL NY ENO	(S)

CHIANTI CLASSICO 1994, FATTORIA FELSINA BERARDENGA Tuscany	*This wine has a smoky tobacco nose and soft ripe berry and bitter cherry flavours.*	£10.70	V&C DIR NY RBS CPW BEN LIB	(S)
CHIANTI CLASSICO BARRIQUE 1994, TENUTA SAN VITO, FIOR DI SELVA Tuscany	*A rich, soft full wine with a lovely violet nose and complex, earthy, chocolatey fruit.*	£11.00	VER	(S)
CHIANTI CLASSICO RISERVA DUCALE 'ORO' 1990, TENIMENTI RUFFINO Tuscany	*A well balanced, attractive wine with a powerful gamey nose and deep rich flavours.*	£14.00	V&C LU LLY WIM ALI	(S)
BRUNELLO DI MONTALCINO CASTELGIOCONDO 1992, M. DE' FRESCOBALDI Tuscany	*Definite signs of age; aromas of dried figs with leathery, spicy notes and a velvety palate.*	£14.60	MM OD	(B)
CHIANTI CLASSICO SER LAPO RISERVA 1994, CASTELLO DI FONTERUTOLI Tuscany	*Seductive vanillin oak and flowery nose leads to a full, balanced palate of ripe, juicy fruit.*	£15.50	V&C	(G)
ANAGALIS 1994, TENUTA DI LILLIANO Tuscany	*Aromas of black fruits with cedar, oak, almond are repeated on the dry bitter finishing palate.*	£16.00	HBJ	(S)
CHIANTI CLASSICO RISERVA 1993, BADIA A COLTIBUONO Tuscany	*A full, rich wine, with earthy, herbal aromas, pleasant cherry fruit and light crisp tannins.*	£16.50	AV	(B)
BRUNELLO DI MONTALCINO 1992, CASTELLO BANFI Toscana	*Mature prune nose soft cedar oak rich and soft in the mouth with a drying finish.*	£16.60	DBY MWW GNW	(B)

POLIZIANO ELEGIA 1994, AZIENDA AGRICOLA POLIZIANO Tuscany	*Creamy plum aromas dominate a well structured wine with light cherry and liquorice flavoured palate .*	£17.10	V&C BOO COK WIN	(S)
CHIANTI CLASSICO MONTESODI 1993, MARCHESI DE' FRESCOBALDI Tuscany	*Elegant summer fruit pudding aromas lead to a rich palate with complex notes of tarry spice.*	£17.70	V&C GRA OD	(S)
BRUNELLO DI MONTALCINO RISERVA 1991, COL D'ORCIA Tuscany	*An approachable wine with spicy notes on a cherry nose, harmonious, well - balanced fruit palate.*	£18.00	CRM V&C RBS	(B)
CHIANTI CLASSICO RISERVA 1982, BADIA A COLTIBUONO Tuscany	*A tarry, earthy aged wine with good fruit flavours and quite high tannins. Ready to drink.*	£19.00	AV	(B)
BRUNELLO DI MONTALCINO 1992, AZIENDA AGRICOLA CAPRILLI Tuscany	*An aged wine with good oak characters, pleasant cherry fruit and lots of supple tannin.*	£19.00	ENO	(B)
CABREO RISERVA 1994, TENIMENTI RUFFINO Tuscany	*Aromas of dried cherries and tarry liquorice dominate the nose and palate of this powerful wine.*	£19.00	LU ALI LLY WIM	(S)
CEPPARELLO 1994, FATTORIA ISOLE & OLENA Tuscany	*A dry wine with herbaceous nose, spicy, tarry flavours and recognisable tannin finish.*	£19.10	V&C NY CWI GGW VLW BEN LIB	(B)
CHIANTI CLASSICO MORMORETO 1994, MARCHESI DE' FRESCOBALDI Tuscany	*Plummy, spiced black fruits nose reflected in elegant flavours that fill a lingering, palate.*	£20.00	V&C GRA	(S)

BRUNELLO DI MONTALCINO RISERVA 1990, COL D'ORCIA Tuscany	*Attractive wine with rich morello cherry aromas leading to a soft palate with a bitter finish.*	**£22.00**	DBY V&C NY RBS LU	(B)
ORNELLAIA 1993, TENUTA DELL'ORNELLAIA Tuscany	*With its highly herbaceous nose and soft berry flavours, this is a rich and tannic wine.*	**£28.50**	NY CWI VLW RBS CPW BUT ENO	(B)

ITALY • OTHER RED

COPERTINO 1992, F COLUCCI Puglia	*An uncomplicated wine with a cherry stone nose and raspberry fruit. Slightly rustic.*	**£3.60**	TO	(B)
NERO D'AVOLA ZAGARA DI SICILIA 1996, KYM MILNE Sicily	*A very attractive, youthful wine with a red fruit nose and soft fruit palate.*	**£4.00**	SAF OD	(B)
PRIMITIVO DEL SALENTO CANTELE LE TRULLE 1996, KYM MILNE Puglia	*Aromas of soft, bittersweet, red, dusty berry flavours and good balance. Very drinkable!*	**£4.50**	VWC TH TO CWS VW OD SMF	(B)
SOLTERO ROSSO VINO DA TAVOLA 1993, SETTESOLI Sicily	*A soft, fruity table wine with ripe cherry and vanilla flavours, slightly woody with some acidity.*	**£4.50**	SMF	(B)
MONTEPULCIANO D' ABRUZZO 1995, UMANI RONCHI Abruzzo	*Attractive wine with new oak nose, fresh juicy blackcurrant fruit, light tannin and good length.*	**£4.60**	Widely Available	(B)

BARDOLINO CHIARETTO CLASSICO LA SORTE 1996, NEGRAR Veneto	*Attractive pink/ purple colour, strawberry/ hay aromas with fruitgum flavours on a light, delicate palate*	**£5.00**	GRA	**B**
ROZZANO 1995, VILLA PIGNA Marches	*A rich well balanced, dense wine with a dark red colour and a flowery nose.*	**£5.00**	A UWM	**S**
SALICE SALENTINO 1994, AGRICOLE VALLONE Puglia	*This is a well-balanced wine with subtle mulberry flavours and good mouth feel. Quite classy.*	**£5.10**	Widely Available	**B**
TORRE DEL FALCO MURGIA ROSSO 1995, TORREVENTO Apulia	*Very pleasant, light straightforward young wine with a stalky nose and rich juicy fruit.*	**£5.50**	OD	**B**
SALICE SALENTINO RISERVA 1993, FRANCESCO CANDIDO Puglia	*A youthful, rustic wine with a spicy, peppery palate, quite high tannins and good length.*	**£6.00**	Widely Available	**B**
COPERTINO RISERVA 1994, CANTINA SOCIALE COPERTINO Puglia	*This is a mature red wine with meaty, chewy flavours, ripe tannins and lots of rich flavours.*	**£6.30**	DBY V&C VIL HVW ENO	**B**
VALPOLICELLA CLASSICO 1996, ALLEGRINI Veneto	*A youthful, magenta coloured wine with carbonic maceration type nose and lots of plummy fruit.*	**£6.40**	V&C VIL CWI NY PHI ENO	**B**
MONTEPULCIANO D'ABRUZZO BARRIQUE CHIERO DI LUNA 1995, MADONNA DEI MIRACOLI Marches	*Ripe, plummy cherry fruits and vanilla; a little toasty oak and good balance right to the finish.*	**£6.50**	A BC SAF SSM	**B**

ITALY • RED • OTHER

TEROLDEGO ROTALIANO 1995, ROBERTO ZENI Trentino	*A lean, sinewy wine with a good balance of fruit and oak and a medium finish.*	£7.50	CTL MWW	**B**
PELAVET 1995, TERRE DI GINESTRA Sicily	*With its warm fruit and soft tannins, this is an elegant wine with a good finish.*	£7.50	MWW	**B**
VIGNA PEDALE CASTEL DEL MONTE 1994, TORREVENTO Apulia	*A light, well-balanced wine with bright garnet colour, creamy nose, juicy palate and flinty tannins.*	£7.50	AV	**S**
CAPITEL SAN ROCCO ROSSO VDT VERONESE 1991, AGRICOLA F.LLI TEDESCHI Verona	*A slightly volatile rich savoury wine with a black cherry nose and a long finish.*	£8.00	SAF EP	**S**
NEXUS 1994, SAN SIMONE Fruili	*Aromas of dried cedar berry fruit. Burnt morello cherries with rich yet unobtrusive oak tannins.*	£8.00	BUD WIM	**S**
VALPOLICELLA CLASSICO SUPERIORE CORTEFORTE 1993, CARLO-MARIA CERRUTI Verona	*A dark, chewy, rustic wine with sweet, plummy fruit on the palate and some spice.*	£8.30	GGW LIB	**B**
CIRO CLASSICO RISERVA DUCA SAN FELICE 1991, LIBRANDI Calabria	*A mature, rich meaty wine, a bit smoky with surprisingly broad fruit characters and long warm finish.*	£8.90	V&C VIL L&W CWI HVW ENO	**B**
AGONTANO 1994, GAROFOLI Marches	*This wine has an attractive colour, loads of fruit, firm tannins and aromas of aniseed on the nose.*	£9.00	OD	**B**

CARIGNANO DEL SULCIS RISERVA ROCCA RUBIA 1993, CANTINA SOCIALE SANTADI Sardinia	*With its bright colour, aromatic bouquet, rich palate and high tannins this wine has plenty of bite.*	£9.30	Widely Available	(B)
REGIANO NV, PERLAGE Veneto	*Delicate cherry, raspberry aromas lead onto a medium bodied palate with a characteristic bitter finish.*	£9.90	VER	(B)
VALPOLICELLA CLASSICO PALAZZO DELLA TORRE 1993, ALLEGRINI Veneto	*A pleasing, well-balanced wine with an earthy spicy nose, ripe fruit and good finish.*	£10.10	V&C VIL CWI NY PHI ENO ODF	(S)
VALPOLICELLA CLASSICO LA GROLA 1993, ALLEGRINI Veneto	*This muscular wine has an almond and chocolate fudge nose and a savoury fruit palate.*	£10.60	V&C VIL CWI RBS CPW ABY PHI ENO	(S)
VALTELLINA SUPERIORE RISERVA GRUMELLO 1989, CASA VINICOLA NERA Lombardy	*A wine with an intense nut kernel and violet nose, good fruit flavours and soft tannins.*	£11.00	ALI	(B)
VALTELLINA SUPERIORE RISERVA INFERNO 1989, CASA VINICOLA NERA Lombardy	*A classy wine with subtle floral nose, intense mouth filling flavours, good weight and great length.*	£11.00	V&C ALI	(G)
AMARONE CLASSICO A SORTE 1993, NEGRAR Veneto	*A dry, mid-ruby colour wine with slightly green cherry fruit and pronounced tannins.*	£11.30	P TP GRA	(B)
ROSSO DEL SALENTO DUCA DI ARAGONA 1991, FRANCESCO CANDIDO Puglia	*A full-bodied wine with a complex fruit nose, clean ripe palate and a solid, dry finish.*	£11.50	DBY V&C VIL CWI CPW ENO	(S)

ITALY • RED • OTHER

CABERNET SAUVIGNON 1995, PLANETA Sicily	*A elegant wine with a vibrant colour, complex spicy nose, warm fruit and good length.*	£12.20	V&C VIL NY VLW ENO	(S)
RECIOTO CLASSICO DOMINI VENETI 1995, NEGRAR Veneto	*Sweet, rich aromas of ripe morello cherries leading to a luscious palate of complex fruits.*	£12.50	GRA	(B)
AMARONE BRIGALDA CLASSICO 1991, STEFANO CESAR Veneto	*A lean peppery wine with a tobacco, cherry nose and sweet dried fruit flavours.*	£13.00	VIN	(S)
AMARONE CLASSICO 1990, ZENATO Veneto	*An excellent wine with deep colour, great complexity and long finish.*	£13.30	V&C HW WIM	(G)
AMARONE CLASSICO 1993, F.LLI TEDESCHI Veneto	*A compact wine with cherry and leather on the nose, ripe fruit flavours and good length.*	£13.80	DBY MWW WIN SEL EP SAF AV	(B)
MERLOT 1995, PLANETA Sicily	*A delicious balanced wine with creamy aromas, a rich, warm palate and excellent finish.*	£14.20	V&C VIL NY VLW HVW ENO	(G)
VALTELLINA SFURZAT 1991, CASA VINICOLA NERA Lombardy	*Sweet, dried cherry aromas with liquorice hints, concentrated palate of morello cherries, bitter almond finish.*	£14.70	V&C ALV	(G)
RUBESCO ROSSO DI TORGIANO RISERVA 1987, LUNGAROTTI Umbria	*A rustic wine with a lifted toasted oak nose, moderately fruity palate and tannic finish.*	£15.00	V&C HN SEL	(S)

ITALY • RED • OTHER

AMARONE DELLA VALPOLICELLA 1993, BOSCAINI Veneto	*A rich, full, beefy wine with an earthy nose, dried fruit flavours and amazing length.*	**£16.00**	DIR A	(S)
RECIOTO CLASSICO DELLA VALPOLICELLA 1993, GIOVANNI ALLEGRINI Veneto	*A fruity wine with sweet, dried fruit flavours, a lifted nose and a bitter-sweet finish.*	**£16.10**	V&C VIL CWI NY DBY ENO ODF	(B)
TERRE BRUNE 1993, CANTINA SOCIALE SANTADI Sardinia	*Excellent aromas of ripe fruity oak. The palate of raisins, liquorice and fair tannin levels give a long finish.*	**£16.40**	Widely Available	(G)
MONTEPULCIANO D'ABRUZZO "PELAGO" 1994, UMANI RONCHI Marches	*A well-balanced, solid wine with spicy aromas, rich flavours and good tannin levels.*	**£16.70**	V&C VIL NY VLW NEI COK ENO	(G)
AMARONE CLASSICO DELLA VALPOLICELLA 1993 AMANDORLATO CORTEFORTE Verona	*A prickly Amarone with a fruity nose, concentrated flavours and a very good finish.*	**£16.70**	GGW LIB	(G)
AMARONE CLASSICO DELLA VALPOLICELLA 1991, ALLEGRINI Veneto	*A deep purple wine with lovely morello cherry, loganberry fruit and good length.*	**£17.10**	Widely Available	(B)
SFURSAT 5 STELLE 1995, NINO NEGRI Lombardy	*With a herbal nose and big fruit this wine has clean acidity and a good, rich finish.*	**£17.30**	VIL NY CWI ENO	(B)
TURRIGA 1992, VITIVINCOLA AGIOLAS Sardinia	*An uncomplicated wine with a good colour, firm tannins and chocolatey, strawberry fruit tones.*	**£17.50**	GI S & G C & B L & W RD RBS	(S)

RECIOTO CLASSICO MONTE FONTANA DOC 1993, F.LLI TEDESCHI Veneto	*This wine displays a warm herbal nose, sweet ripe dried fruit and good length.*	£18.00	DIR AV	(S)
AMARONE CLASSICO CAPITEL MONTE OLMI 1993, F.LLI TEDESCHI Veneto	*The intense colour, earthy truffly nose and richness of fruit make this an impressive wine.*	£18.70	DBY DIR AV	(S)
BRANCAIA 1994, CASTELLO DI FONTERUTOLI Tuscany	*A very full, rich, well-structured wine with intense aromas, ripe fruit and great length.*	£19.20	V&C BUT	(G)
CONCERTO DI FONTERUTOLI 1994, CASTELLO DI FONTERUTOLI Tuscany	*A restrained and elegant wine with very tight compact fruit and rounded tannins.*	£20.00	BUT	(B)

ITALY • WHITE

SAFEWAY SOAVE 1996, FABIANO Veneto	*A wine with good balance offering rich, concentrated apple fruit and a clean spritzy finish.*	£3.50	SAF	(B)
SOAVE CLASSICO LA SORTE 1996, NEGRAR Veneto	*Fresh lime on the nose leads into a citrusy palate with a green apple finish.*	£3.70	TP GRA	(B)
SOAVE CLASSICO COLOMBARA 1996, SERGIO ZENATO Veneto	*Light citrus notes on the smoky nose and palate create a fresh, spicy wine.*	£5.00	W	(B)

Wine	Description	Price	Stockist	
SALICE SALENTINO CANTELE LE TRULLE 1996, KYM MILNE Puglia	*Pleasant aromatic nose and quite complex fruit character coming through with good balancing acidity.*	£5.00	TO W	(B)
VERDICCHIO CLASSICO VILLA BIANCHI 1996, UMANI RONCHI Marches	*Waxy peardrops and green apple aromas lead into a palate of honeysuckle, melon and peaches.*	£5.30	Widely Available	(B)
MALVASIA DEL LAZIO TERRE DEI GRIFI 1996, FONTANA CANDIDA Lazio	*A floral nose is followed by a palate packed with fresh melon and spice.*	£5.60	VIL ENO	(B)
GRECHETTO DELL'UMBRIA 1996, LUIGI BIGI Umbria	*Grapefruit hints on a ripe, appealing nose with minerally and metallic flavours to follow.*	£5.90	VIL ENO	(B)
CATARRATTO ZAGARA BARRIQUE 1996, KYM MILNE & FIRRIATO Sicily	*Elegant wine, with good weight on the palate, leading to a long finish.*	£6.00	OD	(B)
VIGNETI DI CARAMIA CHARDONNAY CANTELE LE TRULLE 1996, KYM MILNE Puglia	*Exciting vanilla and lemon aromas make up the nose, with plenty of clean, fresh fruit on the well-balanced palate.*	£6.00	TH MWW FUL JS OD SAF	(S) WINE OF THE YEAR
VERDICCHIO DEI CASTELLI DI JESI CLASSICO SAN SISTO 1993, FAZI BATTAGLIA Marches	*Elegant use of oak, with some nice clean fruit beneath, leading to a good lemony finish.*	£6.20	FAB	(B)
FRASCATI SUPERIORE VIGNETO SANTA TERESA 1996, FONTANA CANDIDA Lazio	*Grapefruit and creamy vanilla aromas lead into a palate full of peach and pear flavours.*	£6.30	Widely Available	(S)

ORVIETO CLASSICO SALVIANO 1996, FATTORIA DI SALVIANO Umbria	*Honey and peach aromas with slightly nutty hints on the palate and a lemon finish.*	£6.70	GGW BEN LIB	**B**
SOAVE CLASSICO PRA 1996, AZIENDA AGRICOLA PRA Veneto	*A minerally nose is backed up by ripe peach and apricot flavours on the palate.*	£6.90	BOO GRT POR COK SWS COC	**S**
ARNEIS ROERO 1995, ARALDICA Piedmont	*A bright lemon yellow wine offering ripe pineapple fruit on the long lasting palate.*	£7.00	V&C ENO	**B**
MOSCATO D'ASTI CRU CARDINALE LANATA 1996, VILLA LANATA Piedmont	*A light sweet grapey nose with rich Muscat flavours and body on a clean palate.*	£7.50	GRA	**B**
SOAVE CLASSICO SUPERIORE 1995, NINO PIEROPAN Veneto	*Spicy and lime aromas open up a delicately floral wine with a dry, clean finish.*	£7.70	TH V&C CWI VLW SV ENO	**B**
ALASTRO PLANETA 1995, PLANETA Sicily	*Lemon yellow in colour creating a full style of wine with toasty and smoky flavours.*	£8.70	V&C VIL VLW HVW ENO	**B**
FONTESTELLA 1995, CASTELLO DI FONTERUTOLI Tuscany	*Integrated soft oak, aniseed and lanolin aromas, a palate of delicate fruit, light acid and a gentle finish.*	£8.80	ENO	**B**
CHARDONNAY 1995, PLANETA Sicily	*The tasters found this wine to be pleasantly-oaked and well-rounded.*	£12.20	TH V&C VIL VLW ENO	**B**

VINNAE JERMANN 1996, **VINNAIOLI JERMANN** Fruili	*A fresh, zippy and appley wine with peachy overtones and a lean, honeyed finish.*	£12.80	VIL MM VLW WCS ENO	(B)
PINOT BIANCO 1996, **VINNAIOLI JERMANN** Fruili	*Fresh, crisp appley fruit on the nose with a touch of nutty creaminess underneath.*	£13.30	V&C VIL VLW RBS JN ENO	(B)
SELLA DEL BOSCONE **CHARDONNAY 1994,** **BADIA A COLTIBUONO** Tuscany	*Lightly structured wine with excellent fruit and medium length.*	£13.50	AV	(B)
TERRE DI TUFI 1996, **TERUZZI E PUTHOD** Tuscany	*A spicy, toasty nose precedes a palate of light apple fruit and a delicate finish.*	£13.60	V&C NY CWI VLW BEN ENO	(B)
CHARDONNAY 1996, **VINNAIOLI JERMANN** Fruili	*Lemony floral, slightly honeyed nose. On the palate the wine is clean, young and lively.*	£13.60	V&C VIL VLW ENO	(B)
ALTESERRE 1995, **BAVA** Piedmont	*Fresh pineapples and lemons on the nose precede a round, peachy cream palate.*	£14.00	VIN	(B)
SAUVIGNON BIANCO **ISONZO 'VIERIS' 1995,** **VIE DI ROMANS** Fruili	*Creamy, vanilla aromas, with a slight oakiness on the nose. A skilfully made wine, with good character.*	£15.50	ENO	(B)
FLORS DI UIS 1995, **VIE DI ROMANS** Fruili	*Orange peel and cream aromas with a concentrated palate of butterscotch and peaches.*	£16.50	V&C ENO	(S)

PINOT GRIGIO ISONZO 'DESSIMIS' 1995, VIE DI ROMANS Fruili	*A relatively smoky and oaky wine with an oily, biscuity, creamy palate.*	£17.00	V&C ENO	**B**

ITALY • SPARKLING

PROSECCO SPUMANTE 1996, LA MARCA Veneto	*Soft and fruity this is a lovely light easy wine to drink and enjoy.*	£5.50	VWC TO	**B**
SOMINI VENETI RECIOTO SPUMANTE 1995, NEGRAR Veneto	*Vibrant ,rich ruby colour with yeasty strawberry, raspberry aromas, on a sweet sugar and spice palate.*	£13.00	GRA	**B**

ITALY • FORTIFIED

VINI SANTO 1990, CA'VIT Trentino Alto Adige	*A wonderfully grapey wine with stacks of intense syrupy sweetness balanced by some attractive acidity.*	£19.10	MFS BOO	**S**

Pinpoint who sells the wine you wish to buy by turning to the stockist codes. If you know the name of the wine you want to buy, use the alphabetical index. If the price is your motivation, refer to the invaluable price guide index; red and white wines under £5, sparkling wines under £10 and champagne under £15. Happy hunting!

NEW ZEALAND

NEW ZEALAND IS PRODUCING increasingly diverse styles of wine. The eleven Gold medal winners in this year's Challenge included a Riesling, a Gewürtztraminer and, reassuringly, a Cabernet Merlot blend. Sauvignon Blanc continued to perform well, confirming that this grape variety matched with the cool New Zealand climate creates wonderful, fresh, gooseberry wines.

NEW ZEALAND • CABERNET SAUVIGNON

DELEGAT'S PROPRIETORS RESERVE CABERNET MERLOT 1995, DELEGAT'S WINES Hawkes Bay	*A rich fruit nose with vegetal, oak overtones. Complex, minty fruit flavours with grippy, dense tannins.*	**£7.70**	DBY	**(B)**
MONTANA CHURCH ROAD CABERNET MERLOT 1994, MONTANA WINES Auckland	*Earthy notes to this rich cassis nose. Soft fruit and vanilla flavours on the long, warm palate.*	**£8.00**	Widely Available	**(B)**
CORBAN'S PRIVATE BIN CABERNET MERLOT 1995, CORBAN'S WINES Hawkes Bay	*A well-made wine with cigar box aromas. Sweet soft fruit flavours and good length.*	**£8.70**	DBY JCK WTR CEN MHW CDE	**(B)**
VIDAL ESTATES CABERNET MERLOT 1995, VIDAL ESTATES Hawkes Bay	*A cedary blackcurrant nose with ripe fruit and tannin on a soft palate. Good length.*	**£8.90**	FNZ NZD	**(B)**
MONTANA CHURCH ROAD RESERVE CABERNET MERLOT 1994, MONTANA WINES Auckland	*A deep colour, with an intense blackcurrant, mint nose. A palate offering spicy notes.*	**£9.00**	DBY W VLW	**(S)**

TE MATA ESTATE CABERNET MERLOT 1995, TE MATA ESTATE Hawkes Bay	*Intense cedar and blackcurrant aromas. A palate of good length, body and brisk tannins.*	**£9.20**	Widely Available	(S)
MORTON ESTATE BLACK LABEL CABERNET MERLOT RESERVE 1995, MORTON ESTATE Hawkes Bay	*Minty liquorice nose with plenty of new oak and jam, showing ripe blackcurrant fruit on the lingering palate.*	**£9.30**	DBY LNR PAG HAR OD	(B)
MATUA VALLEY DARTMOOR SMITH CABERNET SAUVIGNON 1995, MATUA VALLEY WINES Hawkes Bay	*Leafy and leather notes on the nose give way to figgy fruit and a fresh, minty palate.*	**£10.80**	VIL TP GRT WCS	(B)
MONTANA CHURCH ROAD RESERVE MERLOT 1994, MONTANA WINES Auckland	*Elements of fig and cedar aromas on the nose, reappearing on a palate offering firm, brisk tannins.*	**£12.00**	WR BU	(B)
C.J. PASK CABERNET SAUVIGNON RESERVE 1995, C.J. PASK WINERY Hawkes Bay	*Deep brick red, with spicy raisins, tar and cedar aromas. The palate offers concentrated red berry fruit.*	**£13.10**	CEB POR	(G)
ELSPETH CABERNET MERLOT 1995, MILLS REEF WINERY Hawkes Bay	*Attractive tobacco, leather and bitter chocolate aromas. Palate of herbal fruit with excellent length.*	**£14.00**	COK	(G)
ARARIMU CABERNET SAUVIGNON 1994, MATUA VALLEY WINES Auckland	*Minty, blackcurrant oak aromas. A balanced palate full of black fruits and vanilla flavours.*	**£17.10**	VIL TP	(S)
DUNLEAVY TE MOTU 1994, WAIHEKE VINEYARDS South Island	*Superb, deep cherry red with complex liquorice, black fruit aromas. Ripe fruit and cream flavours.*	**£22.40**	GI FNZ GNW VDV MWW PIM OD	(G)

NEW ZEALAND • PINOT NOIR

TE KAIRANGA PINOT NOIR 1995, TE KAIRANGA WINES Martinborough	*Ripe cherry fruit, strawberries and oak combine well to give a long-lasting aftertaste.*	£10.00	TH BI	Ⓑ
PALLISER ESTATE MARTINBOROUGH PINOT NOIR PINOT NOIR 1995, PALLISER ESTATE Martinborough	*There is some lovely cherry and raspberry fruit showing through on the palate.*	£10.50	DBY ABY TH UR BU	Ⓢ
BAZZARD ESTATE RESERVE PINOT NOIR 1996, CHARLES & KAY BAZZARD Kumeu	*A very classy wine with great fruit character and fresh red fruit on a lingering palate.*	£11.30	GGW	Ⓑ
TE KAIRANGA RESERVE PINOT NOIR RESERVE 1996, TE KAIRANGA WINES Martinborough	*Shows lovely soft, cherry fruit characters, and delicate oak qualities combining well on the long-lasting finish.*	£11.50	BI	Ⓑ
MARTINBOROUGH VINEYARDS PINOT NOIR 1995, MARTINBOROUGH VINEYARDS Martinborough	*This well-structured wine shows creamy, soft fruit characters on the palate. Fairly soft, yet has a smooth, prolonged finish.*	£12.20	Widely Available	Ⓑ
ATA RANGI PINOT NOIR 1995, ATA RANGI WINES Martinborough	*Attractive strawberry fruit is detected on the nose and complements the soft flavours of this sumptuous wine.*	£17.80	Widely Available	Ⓑ
MARTINBOROUGH VINEYARDS RESERVE PINOT NOIR 1995, MARTINBOROUGH VNYDS. Martinborough	*This wine has impressive ripe strawberry fruit on a weighty palate.*	£17.80	Widely Available	Ⓢ

NEW ZEALAND • OTHER RED

MATUA VALLEY DARTMOOR SMITH MERLOT 1995, MATUA VALLEY WINES Hawkes Bay	*A blackcurrant nose with oak overtones. Ripe fruits on the palate and balancing tannins.*	**£10.90**	VIL CLA TP TMW BEN EOO	**B**

NEW ZEALAND • CHARDONNAY

TESCO NEW ZEALAND CHARDONNAY	*Youthful, with light oak aromas and a rich concentration of fruit on the palate.*	**£5.00**	TO	**B**
KAITUNA HILLS CHARDONNAY 1996, AVERILL ESTATE Gisborne	*Soft yet full buttery fruit with stacks of lemony citrus characteristics on a rich palate.*	**£5.50**	M&S	**B**
DELEGAT'S HAWKES BAY CHARDONNAY 1996, DELEGAT'S WINES Hawkes Bay	*Buttercup gold in colour, this wine shows soft but tight fruit and young fresh elegance.*	**£5.90**	DBY MWW	**S**
VILLA MARIA PRIVATE BIN LIGHTLY OAKED CHARDONNAY 1996, VILLA MARIA ESTATE Marlborough	*Youthful wine showing fresh, zesty lemon and apple flavours with uplifting fruit and crisp acidity.*	**£6.50**	TH WR BU	**B**
STONELEIGH MARLBOROUGH CHARDONNAY 1995, CORBAN'S WINES Marlborough	*A well-balanced wine with passion fruit characters. Impressive body and a medium to long finish.*	**£7.00**	Widely Available	**B**

NEW ZEALAND • WHITE • CHARDONNAY

KIM CRAWFORD MARLBOROUGH CHARDONNAY 1996, KIM CRAWFORD Marlborough	*Stacks of sweet tropical fruit on the nose with a lovely buttery feel to the soft palate.*	**£7.00**	WCR	(B)
KIM CRAWFORD MARLBOROUGH UNOAKED CHARDONNAY 1996, KIM CRAWFORD Marlborough	*Buttery icing sugar nose leads into restrained peachy fruit flavours. Balanced by lovely full-structured acidity.*	**£7.00**	LIB WCR	(S)
TWIN ISLANDS UNWOODED CHARDONNAY 1996, NEGOCIANTS NEW ZEALAND Marlborough	*Honeyed, almost vibrant full palate with citrus acidity and good structure and length.*	**£7.30**	VDV MWW GRA FRT	(B)
HIGHFIELD ESTATE CHARDONNAY 1995, HIGHFIELD ESTATE South Island	*This medium-dry white is pale yellow in colour, with a busy lemony nose and fresh acidity.*	**£7.50**	U ES CTH	(B)
DELEGAT'S PROPRIETORS RESERVE CHARDONNAY 1995, DELEGAT'S WINE Hawkes Bay	*Pineapple and guava aromas, lead to a well-balanced palate offering integrated oak and uplifting acidity.*	**£7.70**	DBY	(S)
OYSTER BAY MARLBOROUGH CHARDONNAY 1996, OYSTER BAY VINEYARDS Marlborough	*Well-integrated creamy oak on the nose backed by a rich, buttery, citrus fruit finish.*	**£7.80**	Widely Available	(B)
MATUA VALLEY UNOAKED CHARDONNAY 1996, MATUA VALLEY WINES Hawkes Bay	*Ripe, honeyed nose, with rich pineapple fruit. Balanced by minerally acidity on the palate. A well-integrated wine.*	**£8.00**	JN	(B)
VIDAL HAWKES BAY CHARDONNAY 1996, ELSIE MONTGOMERY Hawkes Bay	*Good textured wine, with succulent fruit and firm acidity culminating into a warm finish.*	**£8.00**	FNZ NZD	(B)

NEW ZEALAND • WHITE • CHARDONNAY

MONTANA CHURCH ROAD CHARDONNAY 1995, MONTANA WINES Auckland	*Buttermilk and zesty citrus aromas leading to undertones of pineapple and grapefruit on the tropical fruit palate.*	**£8.00**	Widely Available	(S)
MONTANA RESERVE CHARDONNAY 1996, MONTANA WINES South Island	*Toasty oak and melon fruit on the nose, with creamy butterscotch flavours. Classic Gold medal wine.*	**£8.00**	Widely Available	(G) **WINE OF THE YEAR**
SELAK'S FOUNDER'S RESERVE CHARDONNAY, MATADOR ESTATE 1994, SELAK WINES Marlborough	*The palate offers well-rounded, juicy ripe fruit and fine toasted oak. A delightful melon nose.*	**£8.20**	GI WSC NAD	(S)
GIESEN ESTATE CHARDONNAY 1996, GIESEN WINES Canterbury	*The palate boasts bags of young lively citrus fruit backed up by a soft, long lasting finish.*	**£8.20**	MOR BOO JN EP	(S)
SOLJANS CHARDONNAY 1996, TONY SOWAN Auckland	*Distinctive vanilla Chardonnay nose, with a floral undertone, that lingers on the palate.*	**£8.30**	FRI	(B)
MORTON ESTATE MARLBOROUGH WHITE LABEL CHARDONNAY 1996, MORTON ESTATE Marlborough	*Excellent delicate appley fruit and oak, well-balanced, following through with impressive length in the mouth.*	**£8.40**	LNR PAG Har	(B)
THE MILLTON VINEYARD BARREL FERMENTED CHARDONNAY 1996, JAMES MILLTON Gisborne	*Rich oaky aromas followed by light fruit which develops well on the palate.*	**£8.50**	VER SAF	(B)
ESK VALLEY HAWKES BAY CHARDONNAY 1996, ESK VALLEY ESTATE Hawkes Bay	*Lengthy wine with pineapple fruit and soft oaky aromas that open up on the palate.*	**£8.50**	TP CEB WSC WCR EBA	(B)

NEW ZEALAND • WHITE • CHARDONNAY

WAIRAU RIVER CHARDONNAY 1994, WAIRAU RIVER WINES Marlborough	*Rich buttery nose, with toasted oak. Ripe tropical fruit on an attractively rounded palate.*	£9.00	SOM HLM BEN R	**B**
MORTON ESTATE HAWKES BAY WHITE LABEL CHARDONNAY 1996, MORTON ESTATE Hawkes Bay	*Critrus aromas on the nose backed by good acidity and limey undertones on the lingering palate.*	£9.00	DBY LNR RBS CPW PAG	**B**
CORBAN'S PRIVATE BIN GISBORNE CHARDONNAY 1995, CORBAN'S WINES Gisborne	*Elegant fruity flavours on the palate with well-integrated oak, showing good structure and body.*	£9.30	Widely Available	**S**
JACKSON ESTATE CHARDONNAY 1996, JACKSON ESTATE Marlborough	*Delicate lemony aromas abound on the nose, with creamy oaky flavours to follow.*	£9.40	Widely Available	**B**
C.J. PASK CHARDONNAY 1996, C.J. PASK WINERY Hawkes Bay	*Very lemony and fresh medium bodied wine. A lightly nutty finish with good length.*	£9.40	TAN POR SHJ	**B**
GOLDWATER CHARDONNAY 1993, GOLDWATER ESTATE Waiheke Island	*Overwhelming, generous wine. Wood tends to dominate, but is backed by plenty of fruit.*	£9.60	MWW IVY WCS CER AV	**B**
WAIPARA WEST CHARDONNAY 1995, TUTTON SIENKO HILL Waipara	*Delicate gooseberry and lime fruit come through in this fresh, clean and lively wine.*	£9.60	DIR WAW TRO GNW PV HOL	**B**
ALLAN SCOTT CHARDONNAY 1995, ALLAN SCOTT WINERY Marlborough	*Sweet honey finish on the nose. Soft oak and good acidity gives this wine an interesting character.*	£9.80	L&W	**B**

ORMOND ESTATE CHARDONNAY 1994, MONTANA WINES Gisborne	*An attractively, complete wine with superbly structured, fruit, acidity and oak on the palate.*	£9.80	Widely Available	**G**
PALLISER MARTINBOROUGH CHARDONNAY 1995, PALLISER ESTATE Martinborough	*Rich varietal nose, with intense fruit on the palate. Subtle oak on a well-balanced palate.*	£10.00	TH DBY ABY HVW BU WR	**B**
BABICH GISBORNE UNWOODED CHARDONNAY 1996, BABICH Hawkes Bay	*Clean, ripe apple fruit. Fresh, crisp flavours and nicely balanced acidity. A well-structured wine.*	£10.00	PF	**B**
MONTANA CHURCH ROAD RESERVE CHARDONNAY 1995, MONTANA WINES Auckland	*Oaky aromas, followed by good fruit on the palate, gives this wine a well-rounded touch.*	£10.00	DBY OD EP	**B**
HUNTAWAY CHARDONNAY 1995, CORBAN'S WINES Gisborne	*Pleasantly presented Chardonnay with a rich, oaky nose and a long lingering finish.*	£10.00	EWD SOH PEA	**S**
RENWICK ESTATE CHARDONNAY 1994, MONTANA WINES South Island	*A ripe, lime, fruity nose leading into a complex, full rich fruit salad and peachy palate.*	£10.00	DBY CLA VLW TMW OD EP WCR EP	**S**
WAIPARA SPRINGS CHARDONNAY 1995, MARK & MICHELLE RATTRAY Waipara	*A pleasant wine with attractive passion fruit flavours. Uplifting acidity on a well-rounded, lively palate.*	£10.10	DIR WAW PV	**B**
JUDD ESTATE CHARDONNAY 1996, MATUA VALLEY WINES Gisborne	*Elegant, well-rounded wine with a tropical fruit nose and subtle vanilla oak undertones.*	£10.60	VIL CLA GRT	**B**

Wine	Description	Price	Availability	
HUNTER'S CHARDONNAY 1996, HUNTER'S WINES Marlborough	*Nicely balanced fruit, with uplifting acidity on the palate, ending on a citrus note.*	£11.00	DBY NY JN FUL BBR	(S)
MARTINBOROUGH VINEYARD CHARDONNAY 1995, MARTINBOROUGH VINEYARD Martinborough	*Intense pineapple aromas on the nose, with warm ripe fruit. Balanced acidity follows on the palate.*	£11.20	Widely Available	(S)
MORTON ESTATE BLACK LABEL CHARDONNAY RESERVE 1995, MORTON ESTATE Hawkes Bay	*Smoky aromas on the nose. Enhanced by light, citrusy fruit and crisp, zingy acidity.*	£11.70	LNR BOO PAG HAR	(G)
TE KAIRANGA RESERVE CHARDONNAY 1996, TE KAIRANGA WINES Martinborough	*Well-rounded wine with an aromatic blend of tropical fruit and nicely balanced oak.*	£11.80	BI WOI	(B)
VIDAL HAWKES BAY RESERVE CHARDONNAY 1995, ELSIE MONTGOMERY Hawkes Bay	*Pale lemon in colour with a ripe fruity aroma and a creamy citrus fruit palate.*	£12.00	FNZ NZD	(B)
COLLARDS ROTHESAY CHARDONNAY 1995, LIONEL COLLARD Marlborough	*Attractive limey nose, which leads to a palate full of intense, ripe and fruity flavours.*	£12.00	LAW	(B)
HUNTER'S CHARDONNAY 1994, HUNTER'S WINES Marlborough	*Lively melon fruit aromas follow through onto a well-rounded palate. Integrated oak and firm acidity.*	£12.00	Widely Available	(S)
VIDAL HAWKES BAY RESERVE CHARDONNAY 1996, ELSIE MONTGOMERY Hawkes Bay	*The palate consists of well-blended flavours with a nice integration of acidity and good fruit.*	£12.00	FNZ NZD	(S)

ELSTON HAWKES BAY CHARDONNAY 1996, TE MATA ESTATE Hawkes Bay	*Intense nose of ripe pineapple and oak, leading to a full-bodied palate, with a rich, intense finish.*	£12.80	Widely Available	G
LINDEN ESTATE HAWKES BAY CHARDONNAY RESERVE 1995, LINDEN ESTATE Hawkes Bay	*This wine is distinguished by its crisp, youthful fruit and well-balanced oak.*	£13.00	MWW	B
GIESEN ESTATE CHARDONNAY RESERVE 1995, GIESEN WINES Canterbury	*This almost botrytis nose follows through to a very rich, sweet palate, with high acidity.*	£14.00	MOR BOO EP	B
VAVASOUR SINGLE VINEYARD CHARDONNAY 1996, VAVASOUR WINE LTD Marlborough	*Tropical pear drop nose with spicy, well-rounded fruit leads to a voluptuous finish.*	£14.20	FUL JN	B
COTTAGE BLOCK CHARDONNAY 1995, CORBAN'S WINES Gisborne	*Beautiful buttery, creamy nose, enhanced by a fine balance of tropical fruit and oak.*	£15.00	EWD PEA CEN MHW CDE	S
KIM CRAWFORD TIETJEN GISBORNE CHARDONNAY 1996, KIM CRAWFORD Gisborne	*Crisp acidity and rich fruitiness tingles on the palate, culminating into a satisfying finish.*	£15.00	LIB	S
ARARIMU CHARDONNAY 1994, MATUA VALLEY WINES Auckland	*Rich varietal nose, lightly oaked with elegant creamy fruit. An up-front, balanced wine.*	£19.00	MZ	B
ARARIMU CHARDONNAY 1993, MATUA VALLEY WINES Auckland	*A lighter style of Chardonnay, with uplifting oak and well-balanced fruit on a fresh finish.*	£21.20	VIL MZ	B

NEW ZEALAND • SAUVIGNON BLANC

COOKS SAUVIGNON BLANC 1996, CORBAN'S WINES Gisborne	*A wine that opens up nicely on the nose, with apple and pear aromas.*	**£5.10**	Widely Available	(B)
MONTANA MARLBOROUGH SAUVIGNON BLANC 1996, MONTANA WINES South Island	*Grassy on the palate with asparagus overtones. This wine shows a refreshing, zesty finish.*	**£5.60**	Widely Available	(B)
LONGRIDGE HAWKES BAY SAUVIGNON BLANC 1995, CORBAN'S WINES Hawkes Bay	*A ripe tropical fruit nose, with lingering gooseberry undertones on a well-integrated palate.*	**£6.00**	BNK CEN NRW DIO PES CDE EWD	(B)
STONELEIGH MARLBOROUGH SAUVIGNON BLANC 1996, CORBAN'S WINES Marlborough	*Pure in colour, with a fresh nose and a zippy, grassy palate. A wonderful Sauvignon Blanc.*	**£6.10**	Widely Available	(S)
TWIN ISLANDS SAUVIGNON BLANC 1996, NEGOCIANTS NEW ZEALAND Hawkes Bay	*Beautiful upfront, spicy aroma on the nose. Packed with crisp, tangy gooseberry fruit flavours.*	**£6.50**	JN VDV MWW GRA FRT	(S)
VIDAL HAWKES BAY SAUVIGNON BLANC 1996, ELSIE MONTGOMERY Hawkes Bay	*Rich coloured wine, in a mature style. Ripe and full in the mouth with good acidity.*	**£7.00**	FNZ VW	(B)
OMAKA SPRINGS ESTATE SAUVIGNON BLANC 1996, OMAKA SPRINGS ESTATE Marlborough	*A wine with bite. Rich grassy, gooseberry aromas on a rich, attractive nose.*	**£7.00**	WSC HLV HOT	(S)

MORTON ESTATE HAWKES BAY WHITE LABEL SAUVIGNON BLANC 1996, MORTON ESTATE Hawkes Bay	*A delicate tinned pea and asparagus nose, with well-rounded acidity and good fruit concentration.*	£7.00	LNR BOO CPW D PAG	(S)
NOBILO MARLBOROUGH SAUVIGNON BLANC 1996, NOBILO WINES Marlborough	*Intense flavours on the nose, leading to a clean, crisp palate, with a medium-long finish.*	£7.10	DBY GDS CEB HOU AV	(B)
MATUA VALLEY HAWKES BAY SAUVIGNON BLANC 1996, MATUA VALLEY WINES Hawkes Bay	*This wine shows sweet marshmallow, and pear drop aromas. Clean, crisp and well-balanced.*	£7.20	Widely Available	(S)
COOPERS CREEK SAUVIGNON BLANC 1996, COOPERS CREEK Marlborough	*This wine shows good concentration of gooseberry fruit on a full, rounded palate.*	£7.40	Widely Available	(B)
MONTANA RESERVE SAUVIGNON BLANC 1996, MONTANA WINES South Island	*Beautifully rounded nose, with rich pineapple aromas. Harmonious and balanced herbaceous palate.*	£7.50	TH BNK COK OD WR BU EP EP	(B)
OYSTER BAY MARLBOROUGH SAUVIGNON BLANC 1996, OYSTER BAY VINEYARDS Marlborough	*This wine offers a big, fat, fruity nose, bursting with gooseberry and honey tones.*	£7.50	MWW VLW FUL WIN EP	(G)
SHINGLE PEAK SAUVIGNON BLANC 1996, MATUA VALLEY WINES Marlborough	*Slightly tropical fruit aroma, leading to some richness and weight on the beautiful, fresh aspargus finish.*	£7.60	VWC GRT	(B)
GROVE MILL SAUVIGNON BLANC 1996, GROVE MILL South Island	*Crisp acidity, and a superbly structured palate, shows the quality of this structured wine.*	£7.60	JS DBY CNL OD	(S)

NEW ZEALAND • WHITE • SAUVIGNON BLANC

FORREST ESTATE SAUVIGNON BLANC 1996, FORREST ESTATE Marlborough	*An excellent example of a Marlborough wine, crisp and zingy, yet with lots of juicy fruit and balanced length.*	**£8.00**	DBY NY P CHF PHI BEN ADN OD	(B)
LAWSON'S DRY HILLS SAUVIGNON BLANC 1996, LAWSON'S DRY HILLS Marlborough	*Crisp youthful wine, with ripe banana aromas. Made in a soft pleasant, easy drinking style.*	**£8.30**	W SHG GGW CHF WIN VDV	(B)
GIESEN WINE ESTATE SAUVIGNON BLANC 1996, GIESEN WINES Canterbury	*Pale green in colour, with a crisp, clear nose that is loaded with ripe gooseberry flavours.*	**£8.40**	MFS MOR BOO POR JN EP	(S)
WAIRAU RIVER SAUVIGNON BLANC 1996, PHILIP ROSE South Island	*Soft on the nose, with a palate that shows plenty of herbaceous and mown grass characters.*	**£8.60**	TH NY BOO CFT WR LEA RAM R	(B)
NAUTILUS ESTATE SAUVIGNON BLANC 1996, NEGOCIANTS NEW ZEALAND Marlborough	*Full bodied wine with intense, ripe fruit aromas on the nose, and passion fruit characters.*	**£8.70**	Widely Available	(B)
JACKSON ESTATE SAUVIGNON BLANC 1996, JACKSON ESTATE Marlborough	*Nettley nose, with a hint of pickle. Good fruit concentration that lingers on the aftertaste.*	**£8.70**	Widely Available	(S)
TE KAIRANGA SAUVIGNON BLANC 1996, TE KAIRANGA Martinborough	*Pale lemon colour, with a youthful gooseberry, asparagus nose. Balanced acidity and great length.*	**£8.80**	TH BI WOI	(B)
WAIPARA WEST SAUVIGNON BLANC 1996, TUTTON SIENKO HILL Waipara	*Intense herbaceous nose that leads to an attractive palate with good length and depth.*	**£8.80**	DIR WAW TRO GNW PV HOL FNZ	(B)

NEW ZEALAND • WHITE • SAUVIGNON BLANC

GROVE MILL SAUVIGNON BLANC RESERVE 1996, GROVE MILL South Island	*This wine offers zesty varietal character, good forward fruit and a smoky flavour on the attractive citrus finish.*	£9.00	OD	(S)
COLLARDS MARLBOROUGH SAUVIGNON BLANC 1996, LIONEL COLLARD Marlborough	*This wine has a pleasant, fresh, grapefruity nose followed by plenty of zingy flavour.*	£9.00	NRW	(S)
VILLA MARIA WAIRAU VALLEY SAUVIGNON BLANC RESERVE 1996, VILLA MARIA ESTATE Marlborough	*Tangy green apple and gooseberry nose leading to a warm, ripe fruit palate with a cleansing finish.*	£9.10	TH PO MM CEB U POR WR BU	(G)
ALLAN SCOTT WINERY SAUVIGNON BLANC 1996, ALAN SCOTT Marlborough	*Characterful nose, with beautiful gooseberry and herbaceous flavours on a mouthwatering palate.*	£9.20	L&W NY	(R)
HIGHFIELD ESTATE SAUVIGNON BLANC 1996, HIGHFIELD ESTATE South Island	*Well-balanced mixed fruit on the nose, carries through onto a superbly structured palate.*	£9.20	RBS CPW ES WRI FLM	(B)
GOLDWATER DOG POINT SAUVIGNON BLANC 1996, GOLDWATER ESTATE Waiheke Island	*A nice upfront nose, with nettle and gooseberries. Well-balanced on a refreshing palate.*	£9.30	NY MWW CER AV	(B)
PALLISER ESTATE MARTINBOROUGH SAUVIGNON BLANC 1996, PALLISER ESTATE Martinborough	*Ripe and developed, with good gooseberry fruit. This Sauvignon Blanc is fresh and herbaceous.*	£9.60	TH DBY NY ABY PHI WSO BU UR	(S)
VAVASOUR AWATERE SAUVIGNON BLANC 1996, VAVASOUR WINE Awatere	*Bright, pale colour, with a fresh, lively nettle aroma. Dry acidity leading to a rounded finish.*	£10.30	Widely Available	(B)

NEW ZEALAND • WHITE • SAUVIGNON BLANC – OTHER

MONTANA BRANCOTT ESTATE SAUVIGNON BLANC 1996, MONTANA WINES South Island	*Showing strong asparagus tones on the nose, with underlying hints of freshly mown grass.*	**£10.30**	Widely Available	(B)
HUNTER'S SAUVIGNON BLANC 1996, HUNTER'S WINES South Island	*Medium intensity of fruit on the palate, enhanced by crisp acidity and beautiful gooseberry undertones on the finish.*	**£10.50**	Widely Available	(B)

NEW ZEALAND • OTHER WHITE

AZURE BAY SAUVIGNON BLANC SEMILLON 1996, MONTANA WINES South Island	*Slightly rich dessert, gooseberry nose. Good concentrated fruit, on the palate with appealing weight and length.*	**£5.00**	TH WR BU	(B)
MONTANA MARLBOROUGH RIESLING 1996, MONTANA WINES South Island	*Delicate floral characteristics show through on the nose, the palate has good weight and balance.*	**£5.30**	COK TO EP	(B)
VILLA MARIA PRIVATE BIN RIESLING 1996, VILLA MARIA ESTATE Marlborough	*A well-made wine with green tart aromas leading to petrol and floral flavours on a lingering palate.*	**£5.80**	TH MM WMK HOU VDV WR BU	(B)
WAIPARA SPRINGS RIESLING 1996, WAIPARA SPRINGS WINES Waipara	*Beautifully fragrant, slightly honeyed nose. Plenty of fruit on the palate balanced by crisp acidity.*	**£7.00**	WAW PV	(B)
MILLS REEF RESERVE RIESLING 1995, MILLS REEF WINERY Hawkes Bay	*Intense lime character with a decent zip of acidity and a good persistent finish.*	**£7.50**	FTH	(B)

THE MILLTON VINEYARD RIESLING OPOU 1996, JAMES MILLTON Gisborne	*A well-balanced wine showing ripe melons and some tropical fruit alongside crisp acidity.*	£8.00	VER	**B**
OMAKA SPRINGS ESTATE RIESLING 1996, OMAKA SPRINGS ESTATE Marlborough	*A delicate nose showing floral aromas. Which leads to a palate with good fruit concentration.*	£8.50	A&N SEL	**S**
MONTANA PATUTAHI ESTATE GEWURZTRAMINER 1995, MONTANA WINES Gisborne	*Fresh apricots, lychees and pink grapefruit. Clean spiciness. Slightly marmalady. Refreshing lemon zest finish.*	£10.30	Widely Available	**S**
HUNTER'S RIESLING 1996, HUNTER'S WINES South Island	*Delicate tropical fruit aromas abound on the nose, following through on a well-rounded floral palate.*	£10.40	DIR VDV NY	**B**
GLAZEBROOK NOBLE HARVEST RIESLING 1996, NGATARAWA WINES Hawkes Bay	*A lovely dried apricot and citrusy nose is followed by a delicate, flavoured palate.*	£15.00	WSG	**S**

NEW ZEALAND • SPARKLING

LINDAUER SPECIAL RESERVE NV, MONTANA WINES South Island	*Pink tinges, soft bramble fruits with yeast overtones. Clean finish to a rich fruity palate.*	£9.20	Widely Available	**B**
DANIEL LE BRUN BRUT NV, CELLIER LE BRUN Marlborough	*Good mousse, rich creamy aromas of yeasty bread and a lingering citrus palate.*	£15.40	Widely Available	**B**

NEW ZEALAND • WHITE • SPARKLING

JACKSON BRUT 1993, JACKSON ESTATE Marlborough	*Attractive green apple aromas. Showing age with a toasty palate with a dry fruit finish.*	**£17.70**	HW AMW POR SV	**B**
DANIEL LE BRUN BRUT 1991, CELLIER LE BRUN Marlborough	*Deep bready, yeasty nose with mellow smooth fruit and ripe flavours giving a soft finish.*	**£24.50**	HW	**B**

Washington and Oregon are following California's lead and the North American wine trade is enjoying a much lauded revival, moving towards more subtle and interesting styles of wine. Experimentation is taking place using more global grape varieties, including Mourvedre, Malvasia and Viognier. Canada is following suit and producing light, fruity reds, delicate whites and luscious dessert wines.

CALIFORNIA • CABERNET SAUVIGNON

SUTTER HOME CABERNET SAUVIGNON 1994, SUTTER HOME WINES California	*Concentrated, ripe plummy fruit aromas with herby notes lead to sweet berry flavours.*	£4.70	Widely Available	(B)
L A CETTO CABERNET SAUVIGNON 1994, LUIS CETTO Baja California	*A light, sweet cherry and chocolate nose with soft blackcurrant and creamy oak flavours.*	£4.90	Widely Available	(B)
REDWOOD TRAIL CABERNET SAUVIGNON 1994, STERLING VINEYARDS California	*Classy nose of ripe fruit, vanilla, oak and rich black fruits on a sweet oak flavoured palate.*	£5.70	CRM CPW COK OD	(S)
TRIERE CABERNET SAUVIGNON 1994, KAUTZ IRONSTONE VINEYARDS California	*Herbaceous aromas with meaty notes lead to a pleasant, jammy fruit palate with round, full, lingering tannins.*	£6.00	CLR HOT	(B)
LAUREL GLEN REDS 1994, LAUREL GLEN WINES California	*The rich nose of dried fruit leads to smooth ripe red fruits with a soft vanilla finish.*	£6.00	JN	(B)

Wine	Notes	Price	Availability	
GALLO TURNING LEAF CABERNET SAUVIGNON 1994, ERNEST & JULIO GALLO California	*A powerful blackcurrant nose combines with fresh, juicy currant flavours on a rounded, smooth palate.*	£6.00	Widely Available	(S)
FETZER EAGLE PEAK MERLOT 1995, FETZER VINEYARDS California	*The light cherry aromas follow through onto the palate which is youthful and light.*	£6.50	Widely Available	(B)
DUNNEWOOD BARREL SELECT CABERNET SAUVIGNON 1994, DUNNEWOOD VINEYARDS California	*Intense colour, peppery, vegetal aromas followed by good dry spicy fruit on the balanced palate.*	£6.50	CAN	(B)
MONTEVIÑA CABERNET SAUVIGNON 1993, MONTEVIÑA WINES California	*Ripe blackcurrant and green pepper on the nose, with oak influences on the spicy palate.*	£6.60	VIL TP DBY COE HOF C&H PG	(B)
FETZER VALLEY OAKS CABERNET SAUVIGNON 1994, FETZER VINEYARDS California	*Vibrant ruby, complex black cherry and new oak aromas. Long spicy fruit and vanilla flavours. Balanced acidity.*	£6.70	MWW W CWS HVW OD SMF	(S)
PEDRONCELLI CABERNET SAUVIGNON 1994, PEDRONCELLI VINEYARDS California	*Smoky ripe fruit aromas with cedar notes lead onto a simple creamy fruit palate.*	£7.00	DIR	(B)
PEDRONCELLI CABERNET SAUVIGNON 1993, PEDRONCELLI VINEYARDS California	*Spicy herbal notes on the nose with ripe jammy fruit flavours on the rich, mellow palate.*	£8.00	DIR RBS L&W	(B)
TERRA ROSA 1995, LAUREL GLEN WINES California	*Rich, ripe fruit with integrated oak on both the nose and palate of this attractive wine.*	£8.00	JN	(B)

DUNNEWOOD DRY SILK CABERNET SAUVIGNON 1993, DUNNEWOOD VINEYARDS California	*Ripe, jammy aromas with sweet oak lead to a palate with vanilla and black fruits flavours.*	£8.00	CAN	(B)
GALLO SONOMA COUNTY CABERNET SAUVIGNON 1992, ERNEST & JULIO GALLO California	*Generous tarry, resinous nose. Lots of ripe black fruits and vanilla on a palate with great length.*	£8.00	Widely Available	(S)
FETZER BONTERRA ORGANIC CABERNET SAUVIGNON 1994, FETZER VINEYARDS California	*Deep spicy, brambley aromas with intense flavours of ripe black fruits and sweet oak.*	£8.40	DBY VER FUL VR OD JS SAF GRA	(S)
BEAUCANON CABERNET SAUVIGNON 1988, BEAUCANON ESTATE WINES California	*Deep colour showing signs of age. Intense plum and tobacco aromas are reflected on a concentrated palate.*	£9.50	ALL	(G)
SONOMA CASK MERLOT 1994, AUGUST SEBASTIANI WINES California	*Blackcurrant leaves and spice aromas. Full ripe fruits and vegetal notes on a structured palate.*	£10.00	FBG EOR	(B)
FETZER RESERVE CABERNET SAUVIGNON 1994, FETZER VINEYARDS California	*Good ripe fruit and mint aromas. A palate with oak balance and green, spicy notes.*	£10.00	OD GRA SMF	(S)
KENWOOD YULUPA CABERNET SAUVIGNON 1992, KENWOOD VINEYARDS California	*Elegant aromas of currants, oak and mint lead to a chewy palate with black fruits and savoury tannins.*	£10.00	COK VNO GLY P&R WRK	(S)
NAPA VALLEY CABERNET SAUVIGNON 1992, WILLIAM HILL VINEYARDS California	*Rich damson, herbaceous aromas with a jammy, concentrated fruit palate and coffee, toasty oak, eucalyptus notes.*	£10.30	YWL	(S)

VILLA MOUNT EDEN CABERNET SAUVIGNON 1994, VILLA MOUNT EDEN WINES California	*Rich blackcurrant aromas with creamy black fruits on the palate. Drying finish with supple tannins.*	**£10.50**	LIB	(S)
BERINGER CABERNET SAUVIGNON 1994, BERINGER VINEYARDS California	*A soft rich peppery nose. Sumptuous palate with ripe black fruits, nuances of chocolate and vanilla.*	**£10.60**	DBY MWW LNR CPW VW SEL SMF EOO	(S)
KENDALL-JACKSON VINTNER'S RESERVE CABERNET SAUVIGNON 1994, KENDALL-JACKSON California	*Punchy, soft, creamy ripe fruits on the nose and palate, a well-made impressive wine.*	**£11.00**	DIR	(B)
RENAISSANCE CABERNET SAUVIGNON RESERVE 1993, RENAISSANCE VINEYARDS California	*Minty chocolate elements on a rich blackcurrant nose. Good body and ripe black fruits on the palate.*	**£11.90**	DBY CHF BUT	(S)
FREEMARK ABBEY CABERNET SAUVIGNON 1993, FREEMARK ABBEY CELLERS California	*An attractive musky, cedary nose leads onto full ripe berry flavours on the long palate.*	**£12.00**	PAT	(B)
GEYSER PEAK SONOMA CABERNET SAUVIGNON 1994, GEYSER PEAK WINES California	*Herbaceous aromas. A palate full of supple ripe tannins and deep blackcurrant flavours. A soft, lengthy finish.*	**£12.00**	HBJ	(S)
RENAISSANCE CABERNET SAUVIGNON 1994, RENAISSANCE VINEYARDS California	*Deep garnet in colour with cedar boxes on the nose and a lingering palate of mature Cabernet flavours.*	**£12.10**	P BUT	(B)
GALLO SONOMA THREE VINEYARD MERLOT 1993, ERNEST & JULIO GALLO California	*Full ripe fruits on the nose with a dry, slightly closed palate that will develop in time.*	**£12.60**	CST WMK ABY	(B)

Wine	Tasting Notes	Price	Codes	
CLOS DU BOIS SONOMA COUNTY MERLOT 1994, CLOS DU BOIS VINEYARD California	*Sweet, elegant fruit and flower aromas lead into lusciously smooth, hawthorn oak flavours on a developed palate.*	£13.00	YWL	(S)
GALLO SONOMA FREI RANCH CABERNET SAUVIGNON 1993, ERNEST & JULIO GALLO California	*Cherry purple, warm spicy fruit, oak notes on nose. Jammy, herbaceous flavours with mint and vanilla interlaced.*	£14.00	CST WMK EP	(S)
CLOS DU BOIS MARLSTONE 1993, CLOS DU BOIS VINEYARD California	*Soft, sweet, jammy nose with structure and length leading to a sweet berry and liquorice palate.*	£16.00	YWL	(B)
NAPA VALLEY CABERNET SAUVIGNON RESERVE 1993, WILLIAM HILL WINERY California	*Upfront fruit aromas with leafy notes and a fruit dominated palate which has brisk tannins.*	£16.00	YWL	(B)
KAUTZ IRONSTONE LIBRARY COLLECTION MERITAGE 1992, KAUTZ IRONSTONE VINEYARDS California	*Youthful colour develops black fruit and liquorice aromas. Intense fruit flavours dominate finish. Well structured.*	£16.00	CLR	(S)
DURNEY VINEYARDS CABERNET SAUVIGNON 1992, DURNEY VINEYARDS California	*Sweet vanilla aromas with deep, dark fleshy currants. Intense creamy, dark berry flavours on the palate.*	£16.10	MAY LEA SOB PAR LV	(S)
CLOS DU VAL CABERNET SAUVIGNON STAGS LEAP DISTRICT 1992, CLOS DU VAL VINEYARD California	*Herbaceous, vegetal edge to jammy aromas with dense, chocolate and plum flavours that linger on the palate.*	£16.50	CWI AV	(S)
STONESTREET CABERNET SAUVIGNON 1994, STONESTREET VINEYARD California	*An attractive warm cedary fruit nose with ripe black fruits and balance on the palate.*	£18.00	DIR RBS	(S)

Wine	Tasting Notes	Price	Codes	Award
Wente Murrieta's Well Vendimia 1992, Wente Vineyards California	Cigar box, herbaceous and ripe fruit aromas lead to a sweet, elegant fruit palate displaying lots of promise.	£19.00	EWD WFL AR VHW	B
Oakville District Cabernet Sauvignon 1993, Robert Mondavi Winery California	A stylish and complex wine, powerful summer fruits and oak aromas. Concentrated flavours with excellent length.	£19.50	DBY MWW MM CRM JN COK M EOO	G
Beringer Howell Mountain Merlot 1993, Beringer Vineyards California	Deep plummy fragrant oak aromas with a fat, sweet fruit palate and a young, developing, tannic finish.	£19.60	MWW LNR CPW SEL PAG	B
Kendall-Jackson Grande Reserve Cabernet Sauvignon 1994, Kendall-Jackson California	Some ageing in appearance with deep black fruits, pencil shavings and mature cigar box aromas.	£19.80	DIR	B
Freemark Abbey Cabernet Merlot Bosche 1991, Freemark Abbey Cellers California	The panel noted that delicate oak aromas were followed by intense berry fruit flavours on the palate.	£20.00	PAT	B
Cecchetti Sebastiani Cabernet Sauvignon 1993, Cecchetti Sebastiani Wines California	Ripe fruit, oak, mint and spice nuances on the nose with intense ripened black fruit and chocolate on the palate.	£20.00	TWB CAN	S
Freemark Abbey Cabernet Sauvignon Sycamore 1991, Freemark Abbey Cellers California	With firm cedar and liquorice bouquet, this wine displayed intense fruit flavours and excellent structure.	£20.00	PAT	G
Gallo Northern Sonoma Estate Cabernet Sauvignon 1992, Ernest & Julio Gallo California	Ripe jammy fruits, green pepper and cedar characters. Rich cassis and butter flavours on the palate.	£25.00	CST U WMK	S

ROBERT MONDAVI CABERNET SAUVIGNON RESERVE 1994, ROBERT MONDAVI WINERY California	*A blackcurrant nose leads to a lingering ripe fruit palate offering good balance and firm, lengthy tannins.*	£29.70	DBY MWW MM CLA JN M	(S)
CLOS DU VAL RESERVE CABERNET SAUVIGNON 1992, CLOS DU VAL VINEYARD California	*Rich minty, cassis aromas, nuances of toasted oak and tobacco. Sweet, chocolate, vanilla and cassis flavours.*	£30.00	AV	(S)
RIDGE MONTE BELLO 1993, RIDGE VINEYARDS California	*A deep colour, minty, baked fruit nose and intense palate containing ripe tannins, cassis and chocolate.*	£50.00	MFS M&V CNL TAN RBS JN BEN	(S)
OPUS ONE 1993, BARON PHILIPPE DE ROTHSCHILD AND ROBERT MONDAVI California	*An intensely rich blackcurrant and vanilla nose followed by a concentrated fruit and sandalwood palate.*	£59.10	Widely Available	(G)

CALIFORNIA • PINOT NOIR

REDWOOD TRAIL PINOT NOIR 1995, STERLING VINEYARDS California	*Attractive black cherry aromas are followed by concentrated fruit flavours on the egalitarian palate.*	£5.70	TRO CRM CRS CWS CPW COK OD	(B)
FETZER SANTA BARABRA PINOT NOIR 1994, FETZER VINEYARDS California	*A complex combination of aromas including fresh strawberries, violets and spice come across on the palate.*	£8.00	WCR MWW SAF GRA OD	(S)
FETZER BARREL SELECT PINOT NOIR 1994, FETZER VINEYARDS California	*A big youthfully vibrant wine with very good warm spice showing on the balanced palate.*	£9.50	DBY MWW GRA HAR SEL OD	(G)

KENDALL JACKSON VINTNER'S RESERVE PINOT NOIR 1995, KENDALL-JACKSON California	*Light violet fruit aromas lead to a soft raspberry palate with a hint of prickly nettles.*	**£11.00**	DIR	(B)
SANFORD PINOT NOIR 1995, SANFORD ESTATES California	*Hugely attractive bramble fruit aromas are mirrored on a soft, silky palate that offers underlying vanilla notes.*	**£15.00**	DBY COK	(S)
MARIMAR TORRES PINOT NOIR 1994, MARIMAR TORRES VINEYARDS California	*Lovely strawberry and raspberry fruit with some vegetal character is balanced by fresh acidity and tannins.*	**£16.90**	Widely Available	(S)
ROBERT MONDAVI CARNEROS PINOT NOIR 1994, ROBERT MONDAVI WINERY California	*An attractive vegetal nose with smooth herbaceous hints and intense flavours on a silky palate.*	**£17.20**	DBY MWW W MM TP JN BEN WM	(B)
ROBERT MONDAVI PINOT NOIR 1994, ROBERT MONDAVI WINERY California	*Rich raspberry and violet aromas are followed by an intense palate of soft red fruits and well-balanced tannins.*	**£19.10**	DBY MWW MM TAN CLA JN BEN MAJ	(B)

CALIFORNIA • ZINFANDEL

DUNNEWOOD ZINFANDEL 1994, DUNNEWOOD VINEYARDS California	*Ripe strawberries and pepper combine on the nose of this well-made, attractive wine.*	**£6.50**	CAN	(S)
SEGHESIO ZINFANDEL 1994, SEGHESIO VINEYARDS California	*Rich red strawberry fruit is balanced by firm tannins and fresh acidity giving a warm finish.*	**£7.00**	MWW NY	(B)

Wine	Tasting Notes	Price	Stockist	
PEDRONCELLI ZINFANDEL 1994, PEDRONCELLI VINEYARDS California	*Soft spicy fruit flavours come through in this simple, yet truly enjoyable wine.*	**£7.40**	L&W DIR	(B)
BERINGER ZINFANDEL 1994, BERINGER VINEYARDS California	*Chocolate and bramble jelly shows through with great intensity on both the nose and palate.*	**£7.40**	DBY MWW LNR CWS CPW SEL PAG	(S)
SUTTER HOME RESERVE ZINFANDEL 1991, SUTTER HOME WINES California	*Spiced oaky fruit. This rich wine shows excellent overall integration. Put it in your glass!*	**£7.70**	Widely Available	(B)
MOUNT EDEN ZINFANDEL 1995, VILLA MOUNT EDEN VINEYARDS California	*The soft spicy fruit on the nose shows through with good intensity on the palate.*	**£8.00**	U OD	(B)
KENWOOD ZINFANDEL 1994, KENWOOD VINEYARDS California	*The soft oak integrates well with light flowery berry fruit, showing appealing complexity.*	**£9.60**	Widely Available	(B)
GALLO SONOMA FREI RANCH ZINFANDEL 1994, ERNEST & JULIO GALLO California	*Smoky nose with plenty of fruit. Some concentration which leads to a rich, warm finish.*	**£13.00**	WMK EP	(B)
TOPOLOS PINER HEIGHTS ZINFANDEL 1995, TOPOLOS VINEYARDS California	*Cream and cherry fruit is balanced by soft tannins, recognisable acidity and good length.*	**£13.00**	DIR	(B)

Pinpoint who sells the wine you wish to buy by turning to the stockist codes. If you know the name of the wine you want to buy, use the alphabetical index. If the price is your motivation, refer to the invaluable price guide index; red and white wines under £5, sparkling wines under £10 and champagne under £15. Happy hunting!

CALIFORNIA • OTHER RED

PEPPERWOOD GROVE CABERNET FRANC 1995, PEPPERWOOD GROVE WINERY California	*Herbal, grassy aromas lead onto a light raspberry flavoured palate with firm tannins and length.*	£4.50	FUL A BUD	B
MONTEVIÑA BARBERA 1994, MONTEVIÑA WINES California	*Jammy fruit aromas are followed by an oak dominated palate with tarry fruit flavours.*	£6.90	VIL TP EP HAC JUS	B
SEGHESIO VITIGNO TOSCANO SANGIOVESE 1995, SEGHESIO VINEYARDS California	*A moderately light, ready to drink, fruity but also tannic wine with a ripe, long finish.*	£10.00	MWW	B
GEYSER PEAK MARIETTA CELLARS SHIRAZ 1994, GEYSER PEAK WINES California	*A complex, tough wine with a long finish comprising animalistic and ripe fruit flavours.*	£10.00	MWW	S
VOSS VINEYARDS MERLOT 1993, NEGOCIANTS USA California	*Crimson purple in colour with blackberry and apple aromas. Creamy oak and juicy redcurrant flavours.*	£10.70	HVW BU GRA FRT	B
QUPÉ BIEN NACIDO SYRAH RESERVE 1994, QUPÉ VINEYARDS California	*A dark, soft and balanced wine with a good fruit nose and long lasting complex palate.*	£14.10	M&V GRT HN NY	S
JADE MOUNTAIN LA PROVINCALE RESERVE 1995, JADE MOUNTAIN VINEYARDS California	*Deep ruby in colour. A slightly young wine, rich and complex with good structure and length.*	£15.00	Widely Available	S

RIDGE GEYSERVILLE 1995, RIDGE VINEYARDS California	*The concentration of fruit apparant on the palate is backed up by firm tannins and crisp, clean acidity.*	£15.50	Widely Available	G
RIDGE LYTTON SPRINGS 1994, RIDGE VINEYARDS California	*Intense spicy fruit nose with some oak. The palate offers similar fruit characters and big, hefty tannins.*	£15.60	Widely Available	B
JADE MOUNTAIN MOURVÈDRE RESERVE 1995, JADE MOUNTAIN VINEYARDS California	*A cleanly balanced wine with sweet berry fruit and good firm length on the finish.*	£17.30	M&V NY BEN SAN RD	B

CALIFORNIA • CHARDONNAY

SEBASTIANI CHARDONNAY 1995, AUGUST SEBASTIANI WINES California	*The palate is rich and vibrant, making a good classy wine with finesse.*	£5.30	MTL A	B
M. G. VALLEJO CHARDONNAY 1994, M.G VALLOJS WINES California	*Perfumy, slightly oaky nose. A superbly balanced wine with strong oak undertones on the palate.*	£5.30	CDT	B
CANYON ROAD CHARDONNAY 1996, CANYON ROAD VINEYARDS California	*The rich creamy characteristics which are found on the nose, follow through to the fruit dominated palate.*	£6.00	M&S	B
MONTEVIÑA CHARDONNAY 1994, MONTEVIÑA WINES California	*Hot vanilla and fig aromas complement each other on the nose of this complex wine.*	£7.00	VIL TP U NEI NIC	S

GALLO SONOMA COUNTY CHARDONNAY 1993, ERNEST & JULIO GALLO California	*Very smoky, oaked nose. Soft, quite rich fruit leading to a dry, but lingering finish.*	**£7.40**	Widely Available	**B**
MOUNT EDEN CHARDONNAY 1995, VILLA MOUNT EDEN California	*A rich nutty, oak aroma, followed by full-flavoured buttery melon nuances on the well-integrated palate.*	**£8.00**	NY U OD	**B**
J.LOHR CYPRESS CHARDONNAY 1994, J. LOHR WINES California	*Ripe buttery nose with intense tropical fruit flavours leaves a lingering aftertaste to be savoured.*	**£8.00**	NY VLW WIN ENO	**S**
FIRESTONE CHARDONNAY 1995, FIRESTONE VINEYARDS California	*Wonderful rich, inviting nose, full on the palate with round and soft buttery oaked fruit.*	**£8.00**	JS TDS MWW	**S**
FETZER BONTERRA ORGANIC CHARDONNAY 1995, FETZER VINEYARDS California	*Good fleshy full fruit with a tangy edge, clean fresh acidity, and a long, generous finish.*	**£8.20**	Widely Available	**B**
GALLO SONOMA LAGUNA RANCH CHARDONNAY 1995, ERNEST & JULIO GALLO California	*A good, earthy nose with, gentle, floral fruit and abundant oak on a lingering palate.*	**£8.40**	CST WMK	**S**
WENTE ESTATE GROWN CHARDONNAY 1995, WENTE VINEYARDS California	*Bags of flavours come through on the nose and palate, including creamy flowery fruit and toasty oak.*	**£8.80**	PO BAB WFL AR EWD HOU	**S**
JEKEL GRAVELSTONE CHARDONNAY 1995, JEKEL VINEYARDS California	*Vibrant tropical fruit balancing with lively acidity gives a surprising depth, weight and huge structure to this wine.*	**£9.00**	MWW GRA	**B**

Wine	Description	Price	Stockists	Rating
BEAUCANON CHARDONNAY 1995, BEAUCANON ESTATES California	*Displays a powerfully structured palate, with oak and lemon undertones after a rich tropical nose.*	£9.50	ALL	**B**
GALLO SONOMA STEFANI RANCH CHARDONNAY 1994, ERNEST & JULIO GALLO California	*A firm, nutty nose is followed by what the tasters described as 'an evocative mouthful'.*	£9.50	CST WMK ABY	**S**
SEBASTIANI SONOMA CASK CHARDONNAY 1994, AUGUST SEBASTIANI WINES California	*Pale wine, that is slightly oaked with pleasant fruit and buttery flavours on a lingering toasty palate.*	£10.00	FBG EOR	**B**
WENTE RIVA RANCH CHARDONNAY 1995, WENTE VINEYARDS California	*Ripe fruit aromas introduce this wine, with a lovely balance between oak and fruit on its rich palate.*	£10.00	END BAB HAM VHW	**S**
KENWOOD YULUPA CHARDONNAY 1995, KENWOOD VINEYARDS California	*This wine displays well-integated oak and an elegantly balanced palate with a lingering butterscotch aftertaste.*	£10.50	VNO GLY P&R WRK	**B**
BERINGER CHARDONNAY 1995, BERINGER VINEYARDS California	*A spicy, slightly oaked aroma, with smooth and subtle pineapple fruit on the palate.*	£10.50	Widely Available	**B**
J. LOHR RIVERSTONE CHARDONNAY 1995, J. LOHR WINES California	*Toasted oak and sweet toffee nose. A well-made wine, with heavy fruit flavours and balanced soft acidity.*	£10.80	NY VLW BUT ENO	**G**
CLOS DU BOIS SONOMA COUNTY CHARDONNAY 1995, CLOS DU BOIS VINEYARD California	*Well-rounded soft, creamy vanilla oak extracts on the palate, backed by a tropical fruit nose.*	£11.00	YWL	**B**

KENDALL-JACKSON VINTNER'S RESERVE CHARDONNAY 1995, KENDALL-JACKSON California	*A luscious, rounded cocktail of oak influenced lemon and lime is complemented by uplifting acidity.*	£11.00	DIR	(G)
RENAISSANCE CHARDONNAY RESERVE 1994, RENAISSANCE VINEYARDS California	*Classy flavoursome oak influenced nose follows through to a melony vanilla taste on the lengthy palate.*	£11.30	DBY P	(B)
CURTIS CHARDONNAY 1995, CURTIS WINERY California	*Light apples and zesty lemons combine with good acidity in this well balanced attractive wine.*	£12.00	GRA	(B)
GALLO SONOMA STEFANI RANCH CHARDONNAY 1995, ERNEST & JULIO GALLO California	*Fresh, lightly toasty nose with persistent soft vanilla oak on a dry fruity flavoured palate.*	£12.00	CST WMK	(G)
CRICHTON HALL CHARDONNAY 1994, CRICHTON HALL VINEYARDS California	*Bright golden colour, with very traditional butterscotchy flavours, elegant fruits and well-balanced acidity.*	£13.70	DIR GRT EP	(S)
AU BON CLIMAT CHARDONNAY 1995, AU BON CLIMAT California	*A medium-bodied Chardonnay that is slightly nutty on the nose, with ripe fruit flavours on the palate.*	£13.90	Widely Available	(B)
WILLIAM HILL CHARDONNAY RESERVE 1995, WILLIAM HILL WINERY California	*Well integrated aromas on the nose such as passionfruit, lemon and pear with a zingy finish.*	£14.00	YWL	(B)
SANFORD CHARDONNAY 1995, SANFORD ESTATES California	*Rich tropical fruit flavours abound on the palate. Good acidity follows building up to a memorable aftertaste.*	£14.30	DBY JN COK	(G)

MARIMAR TORRES CHARDONNAY 1994, MARIMAR TORRES WINES California	*Attractive varietal nose with well integrated oak and melon. Profound acidity on the palate*	£14.40	Widely Available	(S)
BERINGER PRIVATE RESERVE CHARDONNAY 1995, BERINGER VINEYARDS California	*Full bodied with a beautiful concentration of fruit on the palate and rich creamy aromas.*	£15.00	MWW LNR SEL PAG OD	(S)
ROBERT MONDAVI CARNEROS CHARDONNAY 1994, ROBERT MONDAVI WINERY California	*Full rounded palate which harmoniously integrates pineapple and apricot flavours with smoky oak.*	£15.60	DBY MM TAN CRM JN OD	(S)
KENDALL-JACKSON GRANDE RESERVE CHARDONNAY 1995, KENDALL-JACKSON California	*Well balanced melon and coffee aromas on the nose with a lingering sweet oak finish.*	£17.00	DIR	(B)
STONESTREET CHARDONNAY1995, STONESTREET VINEYARDS California	*Well structured body, with superb balance of fruit and distinctive vanilla undertones on the palate.*	£18.00	DIR RBS	(S)
CORLEY SELECT RESERVE CHARDONNAY 1994, MONTICELLO VINEYARDS California	*Powerful vanilla oak on the nose, with pleasant buttery tropical fruits on a lingering aftertaste.*	£18.50	L&W	(B)
GALLO NORTHERN SONOMA ESTATE CHARDONNAY 1994, ERNEST & JULIO GALLO California	*Toasty, buttery oak with lively zest and full tropical fruit flavours. Nicely balanced acidity*	£25.00	CST U	(G)

Pinpoint who sells the wine you wish to buy by turning to the stockist codes. If you know the name of the wine you want to buy, use the alphabetical index. If the price is your motivation, refer to the invaluable price guide index; red and white wines under £5, sparkling wines under £10 and champagne under £15. Happy hunting!

CALIFORNIA • OTHER WHITE

DRY CREEK CHENIN BLANC 1996, DRY CREEK VINEYARDS California	*Grassy, smooth balanced wine, with well-rounded lemon tea and peach aromas. A crisp finish.*	£7.10	DBY GNW	(B)
VOSS VINEYARDS SAUVIGNON BLANC 1996, NEGOCIANTS USA California	*Herbaceous but quite creamy on the nose, the palate is dry and full with crisp underlying acidity.*	£8.00	BU GRA FRT	(B)
DRY CREEK FUMÉ BLANC 1996, DRY CREEK VINEYARDS California	*Delightful gooseberry and varietal flavours on the nose, that follow through on to a slightly lemony finish.*	£9.00	GNW	(B)
ROCHIOLI SAUVIGNON BLANC 1996, ROCHIOLI WINERY California	*Slightly closed nose, that opens up on a well-rounded palate, with a good fruit structure and uplifting acidity.*	£9.10	RAE NY JN	(B)
IL PORDERE DELL 'OLIVOS' TOCAI FRIULANO 1995, AU BON CLIMAT California	*Warm aromas on the nose, fresh grapey fruit with added weight on the palate: excellent!*	£10.00	M&V HN	(B)
KENWOOD SAUVIGNON BLANC 1995, KENWOOD VINEYARDS California	*Nicely rounded palate, which at first is slightly sweet, enhanced by an excellent fresh acidity.*	£10.00	COK VNO GLY P&R WRK	(S)

Pinpoint who sells the wine you wish to buy by turning to the stockist codes. If you know the name of the wine you want to buy, use the alphabetical index. If the price is your motivation, refer to the invaluable price guide index; red and white wines under £5, sparkling wines under £10 and champagne under £15. Happy hunting!

CALIFORNIA • SWEET

RENAISSANCE SELECT LATE HARVEST SAUVIGNON BLANC 1994, RENAISSANCE VINEYARDS California	*A lovely wine offering refreshing zingy acidity and sweet marmalade flavours on its rich palate.*	**£9.60**	DBY BEN	**S**

CALIFORNIA • SPARKLING

CODORNIU NAPA BRUT NV, CODORNIU NAPA WINERY California	*A persistent mousse and tiny bubbles show in this gentle, well balanced yeasty fizz.*	**£8.10**	A PLB HVW	**R**
MUMM CUVÉE NAPA BRUT NV, MUMM NAPA VALLEY WINERY California	*Green, grassy aromas with a tight mousse. Tart flavours with sweet, creamy oak balance and a clean finish.*	**£9.20**	Widely Available	**B**
SCHARFFENBERGER BRUT NV, SCHARFFENBERGER CELLARS California	*Persistant mousse with autolytic notes to the citrus nose, repeated on the balanced palate.*	**£9.50**	A	**B**
MUMM CUVÉE NAPA BLANC DE BLANCS BRUT NV, MUMM NAPA VALLEY WINERY California	*Good mousse, lactic, yeasty aromas, mouthfilling fruit with autolytic highlights, a rounded, weighty palate.*	**£11.80**	VLW CRM ABY OD	**S**
DOMAINE CARNEROS BRUT NV, DOMAINE CARNEROS WINERY California	*Good mousse, ripe aromas of yeasty lemon lead to a creamy, zesty palate with long, citric acid finish.*	**£12.30**	TP SEL	**B**

SCHRAMSBERG BLANC DE NOIRS BRUT 1988, SCHRAMSBERG VINEYARDS California	*Pinkish tinges to good mousse, with green, tart fruit on the nose and palate, toasty finish.*	£13.00	L&W	B
SCHRAMSBERG BLANC DE BLANCS BRUT 1991, SCHRAMSBERG VINEYARDS California	*Vegetal style of wine. Yeasty, almond notes on the nose and palate, with a green tart finish.*	£13.70	L&W RBS	B
ROEDERER ESTATE QUARTET BRUT NV, ROEDERER ESTATES California	*Rich yeasty aromas lead to a creamy biscuit and citrus palate that lasts and lasts.*	£14.30	Widely Available	B
SCHRAMSBERG "J. SCHRAM" BRUT 1989, SCHRAMSBERG VINEYARDS California	*Persistent mousse, intense, toasty mature nose with big yeasty concentration. Bready palate with dosage finish.*	£20.00	L&W	B

CALIFORNIA • FORTIFIED

QUADY STARBOARD VINTAGE 1989, ANDREW QUADY California	*Full and fruity with a spicy nose and smooth ripe blackcurrants on the palate.*	£9.60	RBS JN COK	G

OREGON • SPARKLING

ARGYLE BRUT 1993, ARGYLE WINES Oregon	*Aromatic nose with bready, toasty fruit characters on the nose and palate. A clean acidic finish*	£12.40	TP NEI TMW SWS EOO	B

WASHINGTON • RED

COLUMBIA CREST CABERNET SAUVIGNON 1994, COLUMBIA CREST VINEYARDS Washington State	*Concentrated cherry fruit bouquet with a spice and oak depth to the weighty palate.*	**£7.00**	GGW IVY LIB	**B**
HEDGES CABERNET MERLOT 1994, TOM HEDGES Columbia Valley	*Minty, eucalyptus notes on an intense black fruits nose. Rich forest fruits flavours dominate the palate.*	**£7.70**	CWS	**B**
CHATEAU STE MICHELLE CABERNET SAUVIGNON 1994, CHATEAU STE MICHELLE Washington State	*Complex style, intense black fruits and cedar aromas. A palate of peppery blackcurrants with a creamy finish*	**£9.70**	GGW	**S**
CABERNET SAUVIGNON ESTATE SERIES 1993, COLUMBIA CREST VINEYARDS Washington State	*An attractive sweet blackcurrant nose leads to soft fruit and toasty oak flavours. Well-balanced palate.*	**£11.90**	GGW LIB	**B**
CHATEAU STE MICHELLE MERLOT 1994, CHATEAU STE MICHELLE Washington State	*Plum jam and new oak aromas followed by concentrated fruit and tannins. A wine to keep.*	**£12.90**	GGW IVY	**B**
CHATEAU STE MICHELLE COLD CREEK VINEYARD MERLOT 1994, CHATEAU STE MICHELLE Washington State	*The ripe fruit and oak elements on the nose are mirrored in the weighty palate.*	**£15.00**	LIB	**B**
INDIAN WELLS VINEYARDS MERLOT 1994, CHATEAU STE MICHELLE Washington State	*Attractive aromas of oak and black fruits. A simple jammy fruit palate with a pleasant soft finish.*	**£15.00**	LIB	**B**

WASHINGTON • WHITE

CHATEAU STE MICHELLE CHARDONNAY 1995, CHATEAU STE MICHELLE Washington State	*The golden ripe honeyed, creamy aromas provide a characterful wine with an enticing richness.*	£9.30	GGW	(B)
COLUMBIA CREST CHARDONNAY ESTATE SERIES 1995, COLUMBIA CREST Washington State	*This delicious wine is well balanced with toasty oak on the nose. Quite complex with medium length.*	£11.90	GGW LIB	(S)
CANOE RIDGE VINEYARD CHARDONNAY 1995, CHATEAU STE MICHELLE Washington State	*Deliciously complex palate full of good fruity flavours, well integrated with smoky oak and lemon zest tones.*	£17.10	DBY GGW	(S)
CHATEAU STE MICHELLE COLD CREEK VINEYARD CHARDONNAY 1995, CHATEAU STE MICHELLE Washington State	*Well integrated fruit flavours on the palate, lead to a soft, rounded finish, with peach undertones.*	£18.10	GGW	(S)

CANADA • RED

SOUTHBROOK CABERNET FRANC 1995, SOUTHBROOK FARMS Ontario	*Blackcurrant aromas lead into an oaky wine with cedar and vanilla hints on the palate.*	£7.00	AR	(B)
SOUTHBROOK LAILEY CABERNET SAUVIGNON 1995, SOUTHBROOK FARMS Ontario	*Aromas reminiscent of underripe blackcurrants, but the palate is ripe black fruit with oak notes.*	£8.50	AR	(B)

CANADA • WHITE

MISSION HILL PINOT BLANC RESERVE 1994, MISSION HILL VINEYARDS Okanagan Valley	*Lychees and peach aromas abound on the nose, with crisp acidity and a perfumy finish.*	**£7.50**	EOR	**B**
PILLITTERI CHARDONNAY BARREL AGED 1995, PILLITTERI ESTATES WINERY Ontario	*Stacks of oak, limes and coconut coming through on the nose of this powerful wine.*	**£9.60**	PMA	**S**
MISSION HILL CHARDONNAY 1995, MISSION HILL VINEYARDS Okanagan Valley	*Seductive vanilla nose, with light toasty oak on the palate, backed by integrated fruit and acidity.*	**£9.70**	DBY TP EOR EP	**B**

CANADA • SWEET

CHÂTEAU DES CHARMES LATE HARVEST RIESLING 1995, CHÂTEAU DES CHARMES Ontario	*Honeyed aromas are followed by melon fruit and sherbety flavours on a well balanced palate*	**£9.00**	GNW GI NAD	**S**
INNISKILLIN ICEWINE 1995, INNISKILLIN WINES Ontario	*Floral and elderflower aromas lead into a palate full of honeyed fruit and firm acidity.*	**£30.00**	DIR	**G**

Pinpoint who sells the wine you wish to buy by turning to the stockist codes. If you know the name of the wine you want to buy, use the alphabetical index. If the price is your motivation, refer to the invaluable price guide index; red and white wines under £5, sparkling wines under £10 and champagne under £15. Happy hunting!

CANADA • FORTIFIED

SOUTHBROOK CANADIAN FRAMBOISE NV, SOUTHBROOK FARMS Ontario	*Intense rich sweet raspberry jam fruit leaps out of the glass and lingers in the mouth.*	**£8.20**	Widely Available	(G)
SOUTHBROOK CANADIAN CASSIS NV, SOUTHBROOK FARMS Ontario	*Stacks of freshly picked blackcurrants combine with mint to give a glass of amazing power.*	**£8.30**	MWW DIR NY A CRS ASDA	(G)

PORTUGAL

REGIONAL AND VARIETAL IDENTITY IS now becoming a priority for the winemaker and Portugal is currently producing formidable wines. As evidence, one has to look no further than the Quinta do Crasto Douro Red - one of the International WINE Challenge Red Wines of the Year. The standard of Port entries was high with a number of top awards going to these famous wines. Several Madeira medals were also awarded.

PORTUGAL • RED

DONA ELENA NV, BENFICA Ribatejo	*Attractive oak and red berry aromas. Ripe and rounded with good fruit extract. Well-made.*	**£3.00**	SPR	(B)
RAMADA 1995, ADEGA CO-OP TORRES VEDRAS Estremadura	*Jammy sweet fruit with red cherries on a palate full of real character and style.*	**£3.20**	TH D&F VIL W U CWS WR	(B)
ESTEMADURA RED 1994, ADEGA COOPERATIVA DE SAO MAMEDE DA VENTO. Mamede	*Peppery fruit with leathery aspects. Sweet oak and good acidity produce a well-structured wine.*	**£3.40**	D&F VIL	(B)
J.P. RED VINHO DE MESA NV, J.P. VINHOS Terras Do Sado	*An easy drinking wine full of jammy sweet fruit and low tannins with a rounded full finish.*	**£3.50**	VWC TH FUL CST	(B)
J.P. BARREL SELECTION VINHO REGIONAL 1991, J.P. VINHOS Terras Do Sado	*Smoky and gamey aromas precede a big rich palate of plummy fruit, tobacco and leather.*	**£3.60**	TO	(S)

SOMERFIELD DOURO RED 1994, REAL COMPANHIA VINICOLA Douro	*A wonderfully harmonious wine, packed full of supple black fruits. Great balance and length.*	£3.70	SMF	**B**
JOSE NEIVA 1995, ADELA CO-OP DE SAO MAMEDE DA VENTOSA Estremadura	*Soft supple summer fruit character. Hints of marmite. Lovely creamy vanilla from well-handled oak.*	£4.00	D&F VIL P RBS BTH KWI	**B**
DOURO TINTO SOCIEDADE DOS VINHOS 1995, BORGES Douro	*A warm, rich and spicy wine offering jammy fruit and liquorice flavours on the palate.*	£4.00	D&D	**B**
LELLO RESERVA SOCIEDADE DOS VINHOS 1995, BORGES Douro	*A sweet blackcurrant and damson fruit nose precedes a fleshy palate of berry flavours.*	£4.00	D&D	**B**
VILA REGIA SOGRAPE 1995, SOGRAPE Douro	*Soft cherry fruit showing some signs of development. Well-structured with a lovely long finish.*	£4.20	GI BOO OD	**B**
ESPIGA 1996, QUINTA DA BOAVISTA Estremadura	*Vanilla and light oak on the nose with sweet berry fruit and strawberry flavours.*	£4.20	TH D&F WR BTH BU	**S**
FORAL DOURO RESERVA 1995, CAVES ALIANCA Douro	*Damson and blackberry fruit with hints of vanilla oak on the soft, fruity palate.*	£4.30	DIR COC AMW GNW WCS NRW	**B**
FORAL DOURO RESERVA 1996, CAVES ALIANCA Douro	*Youthful vibrant summer berry fruits. Quite sweet, yet well-balanced with a firm tannic backbone.*	£4.40	DIR WCS SAF COC GNW	**B**

ADEGA CO-OP COMENDA SANTIAGO REGIONAL 1995, ADEGA CO-OP DE ARRUDA DOS VINHOS Arruda dos Vinhos	*Gorgeous appealing nose showing some development. Fruit still held back by firm tannins.*	£4.80	BD	(B)
QUINTA DO RIBEIRINHO 1995, LUIS PATO Bairrada	*Delightful sweet ripe blackberry fruit with warming spiciness. Firm, mouthfilling palate, it has great potential.*	£5.10	WF U	(B)
BRIGHT BROTHERS DOURO 1996, BRIGHT BROTHERS Douro	*Wonderful chunky ripe blackberry, plum fruit with a sprinkling of black pepper. Rich and powerful.*	£5.10	Widely Available	(S)
MONTE DE TERRUGE ALENTEJO 1995, CAVES ALIANCA Alentejo	*Supple fragrant hedgerow fruit. Gentle tannins, with a ripe, fresh and clean dry finish.*	£5.30	DIR	(B)
PALHA CANAS 1996, QUINTA DA BOAVISTA Estremadura	*Generous sweet vanilla and spiced plum nose. Firm youthful berry fruit with a savoury dimension.*	£5.50	D&F P U BEL RBS	(S)
QUINTA DE LAGOALVA 1994, QUINTA DE LAGOALVA DE CIMA Ribatejo	*Rich plummy fruit with cinnamon and vanilla flavours. Still young with firm tannins.*	£5.60	D&F P RBS WCR BKW	(B)
LUIS PATO TINTO 1995, LUIS PATO Bairrada	*Sweet redcurrant fruit with hints of roses. Still youthful, it has a firm palate.*	£5.80	WF	(B)
LAGOALVA DE CIMA 1992, QUINTA DE LAGOALVA DE CIMA Ribatejo	*Rich concoction of plums and sweet toffee. Good stab of acidity to balance.*	£6.00	D&F P WCS B&B	(B)

DUQUE DE VISEU 1992, SOGRAPE Dao	*Concentrated spices on a complex nose. A good balance of juicy fruit and tannins.*	£6.20	GI BOO CWS WSO SEL	**B**
DOURO RED 1995, QUINTA DO CRASTO Douro	*Soft abundant juicy fruit, with a hint of spice. Well-balanced and very approachable.*	£6.40	FUL TMW PHI ENO OD	**S**
GALERIA CABERNET SAUVGNON 1995, CAVES ALIANCA Dao	*Deep black, purple colour. A perfumed wine with blackcurrant, cedar, and restrained oak flavours.*	£6.50	DIR	**B**
DOURO RED 1996, QUINTA DO CRASTO Douro	*This excellent wine is spicy and plummy and packed with concentrated deep black fruit.*	£5.90	PHI ENO	**S** WINE OF THE YEAR
DOURO RESERVA 1994, QUINTA DO CRASTO Douro	*Pleasant ripe berry fruit. Soft warm oak with a hint of smokiness. Good modern style.*	£7.50	ENO OD	**B**
DOURO RESERVA 1995, QUINTA DO CRASTO Douro	*Powerful chunky berry fruit with a lovely fragrance. Sweet new oak. Good length, with drying tannins.*	£7.50	ENO	**S**
SOGRAPE RESERVA DOURO 1992, SOGRAPE Douro	*Tobacco and plum aromas precede a fresh palate of red fruit and damson flavours.*	£7.90	GI BOO	**S**
LUIS PATO RESERVA 1995, LUIS PATO Bairrada	*Rich blackberry, redcurrant fruit. Quite soft and sweet, it has a firm tannic backbone.*	£8.50	WF U	**B**

QUINTA DOS BONS ARES 1994, ADRIANO RAMOS-PINTO Douro	*Sweet cherry aromas. Soft oak complements the rich crushed berry fruit. Attractive now, will develop.*	£9.00	J&B	(B)
TOURIGA NACIONAL DOURO RED 1995, QUINTA DO CRASTO Douro	*A mouthful of juicy summer fruit with liquorice and vanilla overtones. Good depth and complexity.*	£10.00	PHI ENO ODF	(S)
DUAS QUINTAS RESERVA 1994, ADRIANO RAMOS-PINTO Douro	*Rich and powerfully built with its melange of dark berry and cherry fruits. Spicy backbone.*	£11.50	SHG VLW J&B EP HWL PAR PTR	(S)

PORTUGAL • WHITE

ALVARINHO 1996, ADEGA COOPERATINA DE MONCAO	*Soft fruity aromas on the nose, backed by uplifting acidity and grassiness on the finish.*	£3.20	RBA	(B)
FIUZA CHARDONNAY VINHO REGIONAL 1996, FIUZA BRIGHT BROTHERS Ribatejo	*Creamy, buttery nose with some ripeness, followed by a fruity palate with crisp acidity.*	£4.30	FUL CWS CRS A	(B)
QUINTA DE AZEVEDO 1996, SOGRAPE Vinho Verde	*Grapey and aromatic. This is a crisp, zesty wine with pleasant spicy, apple flavours.*	£5.00	GI WSO SEL	(B)
COVA DA URSA CHARDONNAY VINHO REGIONAL 1995, J.P VINHOS Terras Do Sado	*A pronounced oaky nose, following through on a toasty vanilla palate with medium length.*	£7.20	TH DIR NY	(B)

PORTUGAL • MADEIRA

LEACOCKS FINE RICH MADEIRA NV Madeira	*A balanced wine with rich, nutty, intense, complex flavours and crisp, sherbet like acidity.*	**£9.00**	DIR WMK SOB C&B	(S)
HENRIQUES & HENRIQUES NV, Madeira	*A nicely balanced, nutty, toffee coloured wine with crisp acidity and great length.*	**£10.00**	HW	(B)
BLANDY'S 5 YEAR OLD BUAL Madeira	*A tawny slightly sweet nutty, figgy wine with orange, lemon and caramel nuances on the palate.*	**£10.90**	Widely Available	(S)
BLANDY'S 5 YEAR OLD SERCIAL Madeira	*An orange gold, off-dry wine, well balanced with a complex salty and nutty influenced palate.*	**£11.60**	Widely Available	(B)
BLANDY'S 5 YEAR OLD VERDELHO Madeira	*This is an off-dry, tawny, aromatic wine with soft tannins and a light caramel flavour.*	**£11.90**	DBY VIL BOO MM BEN SWS OD	(S)
COSSART & GORDON 5 YEAR OLD SERCIAL, Madeira	*Dry, well-structured wine with rich toffee apple flavours on a soft and moderately long finish.*	**£13.20**	Widely Available	(B)

Pinpoint who sells the wine you wish to buy by turning to the stockist codes. If you know the name of the wine you want to buy, use the alphabetical index. If the price is your motivation, refer to the invaluable price guide index; red and white wines under £5, sparkling wines under £10 and champagne under £15. Happy hunting!

Wine	Description	Price	Stockist	
COSSART & GORDON 5 YEAR OLD MALMSEY Madeira	*This well-integrated malmsey shows interesting complexity with apricot, toffee flavours and clean acidity.*	£13.50	Widely Available	S
HENRIQUES & HENRIQUES 10 YEAR OLD MALMSEY, Madeira	*Deep caramel colour, warm and complex fruit and toffee nose, balanced acidity on a rich palate.*	£15.80	Widely Available	S
BLANDY'S 10 YEAR OLD MALMSEY Madeira	*A mid-tawny colour, rich aroma, weight, fruit, oak flavours, clean acidity and excellent finish.*	£16.20	Widely Available	G
COSSART & GORDON 10 YEAR OLD VERDELHO Madeira	*Fresh and young with apricot fruit. A sweet well-balanced wine.*	£17.80	TH DIR GGW GNW BEN MIL ICL	B
HENRIQUES & HENRIQUES 15 YEAR OLD MALMSEY, Madeira	*Complex aromas of toffee, bramley apples and fig are followed by rich flavours of baked fruit.*	£18.40	DBY HW CPW SV IRW TAN	S
HENRIQUES & HENRIQUES 15 YEAR OLD VERDELHO, Madeira	*Rich caramel aromas with nuances of prunes and figs. A concentrated palate of raisined fruit follows.*	£18.50	HW SV IRW TAN	B
COSSART & GORDON 15 YEAR OLD MALMSEY Madeira	*This is a rich sweet wine with soft tannins, good acidity, high complexity, and long finish.*	£22.70	Widely Available	G

Pinpoint who sells the wine you wish to buy by turning to the stockist codes. If you know the name of the wine you want to buy, use the alphabetical index. If the price is your motivation, refer to the invaluable price guide index; red and white wines under £5, sparkling wines under £10 and champagne under £15. Happy hunting!

PORTUGAL • PORT

SANDEMAN VINTAGE 1994 SANDEMAN SANDERMAN & CO. Douro	*A soft, juicy port offering light fruit aromas and slightly grassy characters on the palate.*	£25.00	SEA WAV WTL	**B**
QUINTA DO SAGRADO RUBY PORT, A.A. CALEM Oporto	*A spicy nose is followed by plum and ripe black cherry fruit on a flavoursome palate.*	£4.50	LAU	**S**
QUINTA DO SAGRADO VINTAGE CHARACTER, A.A. CALEM Oporto	*Brick red with a traditional, rustic nose. Deep plummy flavours are backed up by strong tannins.*	£6.00	LAU	**B**
ROZES LBV 1992 ROZES & CO. Douro	*A wonderful soft, round wine offering fig and prune fruit on a peppery palate.*	£7.00	MRN	**S**
SOMERFIELD NAVIGATOR VINTAGE CHARACTER, REAL COMPANHIA VELA Oporto	*Concentrated fruit aromas with a Christmas cake palate offering rich black cherry and plum flavours.*	£7.20	SMF	**S**
QUINTA DO NOVAL COLHEITA 1984, QUINTA DO NOVAL Douro	*A wine showing promise for the future. Round in the mouth offering ripe jammy fruit.*	£7.50	VLW EP ETV PAL V&C	**B**
DOW'S FINE RUBY, SILVA & COSENS Douro	*The nose and palate are packed with jammy black cherry fruit and creamy vanilla oak.*	£7.50	Widely Available	**G**

CO-OP VINTAGE CHARACTER PORT, SMITH WOODHOUSE & CO Douro	*Plum and cherry flavours form the core of a well-rounded palate packed with fruit.*	£7.70	CWS NI	**G**
SAFEWAY SMITH WOODHOUSE LBV 1991, SMITH WOODHOUSE & CO. Douro	*Very deep red colour offering dried fruit on the nose. Velvety soft palate with black cherries.*	£7.90	SAF	**B**
MALT HOUSE VINTNERS REGIMENTAL LBV 1990, SILVA & COSENS Douro	*Forward fruit on the nose with concentrated sticky flavours and long length in the mouth.*	£7.90	MHV	**B**
TAYLOR'S FIRST ESTATE RESERVE, TAYLOR FLADGATE & YEATMAN Douro	*The palate offers rich plum, pepper and spicy flavours backed up by long firm tannins.*	£8.00	Widely Available	**S**
WARRE'S WARRIOR FINEST RESERVE, WARRE & CO Douro	*Smooth redcurrant and cinnamon spice flavours produce a delicious wine; perfect for drinking in two years.*	£8.30	Widely Available	**S**
COCKBURN'S SPECIAL RESERVE, COCKBURN SMITHES & CO. Douro	*Pale orange in colour and backed up by rich red fruit flavours on a soft palate.*	£8.40	Widely Available	**B**
QUINTA DO NOVAL COLHEITA 1981, QUITA DO NOVAL Douro	*Deep orange in colour with a prune and raisin nose and cinnamon flavours on the palate.*	£8.50	CER EP ETV EP	**B**
QUINTA DO NOVAL LBV 1990, QUINTA DO NOVAL Douro	*Nutty aromas are followed by massive ripe cherry and chocolate flavours on a well-balanced palate.*	£8.60	JS MTL VIL MM HOU HVW EOO EP	**S**

FONSECA BIN 27, TAYLOR FLADGATE & YEATMAN Douro	*A young wine with a purple rim, sweet floral aromas and a plum fruit palate.*	**£8.90**	Widely Available	(B)
QUINTA DO NOVAL COLHEITA 1982, QUINTA DO NOVAL Douro	*Marzipan aromas are followed by a palate of boiled sweets leading into a long, intense finish.*	**£9.00**	JS F&M SEL CMI	(S)
CALEM LATE BOTTLED VINTAGE 1992, A.A. CALEM Douro	*Some nice complexity showing on the nose with attractive spicy notes combining with rich plummy fruit.*	**£9.00**	BNK PNA U P&R WIM RAC WE	(S)
DOW'S TRADEMARK RESERVE NV, SILVA & COSENS Douro	*Extremely soft on the nose with spicy aromas. The jammy palate leads into a long, rich finish.*	**£9.10**	VIL RBS COK NEW LINE	(B)
RAMOS-PINTO QUINTA DA URTIGA, ADRIANO RAMOS-PINTO Douro	*The palate is full of plum and melted chocolate flavours which fill the mouth.*	**£9.10**	Widely Available	(G)
QUINTA DO LA ROSA FINEST RESERVE Douro	*Pepper and spice aromas lead into a weighty palate of herbal and chocolate flavours.*	**£9.50**	M&V NY VLW TRO TP CHF F&M HN	(S)
COCKBURN'S ANNO LBV 1992, COCKBURN SMITHES & CIA LTDA Douro	*A slightly stalky nose but showing perfect balance of ripe fruit, firm acidity and tannin.*	**£10.00**	CWS SB A MRS SAF W	(B)
RAMOS-PINTO LBV 1992, ADRIANO RAMOS-PINTO Douro	*Dark ruby in colour, impressive spicy nose. A thick, velvety palate, intense black cherry fruit and long lasting tannins.*	**£10.00**	VLW HHC PAG	(G)

QUINTA DO NOVAL COLHEITA 1976, QUINTA DO NOVAL Douro	*Very spirity nose but well-balanced and backed up by sweet toffee and caramel flavours.*	**£10.20**	VWC BEN F&M EP HN JS EP	**B**
SANDEMAN LBV 1991 SANDEMAN & CO. Douro	*A sweet and peppery wine offering violet tannins that round off the palate beautifully.*	**£10.30**	MTL OD	**S**
BERRY'S LBV 1990, CHURCHILL GRAHAM Douro	*Christmas spices on the nose backed up by juicy ripe berry fruit on a nutty palate.*	**£10.30**	BNK GDS WSC BBR	**S**
ADRIANO RAMOS-PINTO LBV 1989, ARIANO RAMOS-PINTO Douro	*Spicy aromas lead into a mature palate of ripe fruit with underlying hints of cherry fruit.*	**£10.50**	VLW FUL EP PAG BOO HHC EP	**B**
GRAHAM'S LBV 1991, W & J GRAHAM & CO Douro	*Nice depth of black red colour, showing warm youthful fruit. Well-balanced with ripe plum flavours.*	**£10.50**	Widely Available	**B**
FONSECA LBV 1991, TAYLOR FLADGATE & YEATMAN Douro	*Deep red in colour this port offers rich stewed berry fruits on the nose and palate.*	**£10.50**	DBY VIL DIR VLW RBS DAV	**B**
QUINTA DO LA ROSA LBV 1992 ROZES & CO. Douro	*Sweet and succulent in the rounded mouth with hints of coffee and melted chocolate.*	**£10.50**	M&V NY VLW TP	**S**
TAYLOR'S LBV 1991, TAYLOR FLADGATE & YEATMAN Douro	*A lovely nose packed with juicy red fruit preceding black cherries on the palate.*	**£10.60**	Widely Available	**S**

FONSECA LBV 1992, TAYLOR FLADGATE & YEATMAN Douro	*Christmas cake dried fruit on a rich nose with hints of spice and pepper on the finish.*	**£10.70**	DBY DIR VLW CST RBS NEI NIC RES	(G)
PORTO FEIST LBV 1990, H & CJ FEIST Oporto	*Caramel and spicy hints on the nose are followed by a palate of rich baked fruit.*	**£11.20**	D&F P	(B)
GRAHAM'S SIX GRAPES VINTAGE CHARACTER, W & J GRAHAM & CO. Douro	*Spicy fruit on the nose backed up by cherry fruit and medium tannins on the palate.*	**£11.40**	Widely Available	(S)
DELAFORCE HIS EMINENCE'S CHOICE TAWNY, DELAFORCE & CO. Douro	*This is a clean tawny with ripe fruit on the nose and sweet toffee flavours on the finish.*	**£12.40**	VIL	(B)
DOW'S 10 YR OLD TAWNY, SILVA & COSENS Douro	*A rich fruity wine with firm acidity backing a palate of spicy plums and black cherries.*	**£12.60**	Widely Available	(B)
NOVAL 10 YR OLD TAWNY, QUINTA DO NOVAL Douro	*An unusual pinky colour with a big rich nose. Splendid length on a palate of figs.*	**£12.70**	Widely Available	(B)
QUINTA DO PORTO 10 YR OLD TAWNY, A.A.FERREIRA Douro	*Light but concentrated this port boasts warm hazelnut and plummy flavours on a lingering balanced palate.*	**£12.90**	DBY BNK NY BOO WCS BPP P&R	(B)
WARRE'S SIR WILLIAM 10 YR OLD TAWNY, WARRE & CO. Douro	*Bright orange in colour this wine is rich and full flavoured with soft mellow red fruit characteristics.*	**£14.10**	Widely Available	(B)

TAYLOR'S 10 YR OLD TAWNY, TAYLOR FLADGATE & YEATMAN Douro	*An attractive wine showing potential with black cherry and plum flavours opening up on the palate.*	£14.10	Widely Available	(S)
SMITH WOODHOUSE TRADITIONAL LBV 1984, SMITH WOODHOUSE & CO. Douro	*Delicate floral aromas are backed up by a huge palate of ripe blackcurrants, plums and spices.*	£14.90	Widely Available	(G)
QUINTA DA ERVAMOIRA VINTAGE PORT 1994, ADRIANO RAMOS-PINTO Douro	*Glorious red fruit on the nose is followed by a long lasting round and soft palate.*	£15.30	Widely Available	(B)
QUINTA DO INFANTADO ORGANIC VINTAGE CHARACTER, JOAO ROSEIRA Douro	*Rich cassis aromas are followed by full and spicy fruit flavours and a chewy finish.*	£15.90	FRI	(S)
BERRY'S WILLIAM PICKERING, QUINTA DO NOVAL Douro	*A rich and soft wine with a palate showing good acidity balanced by jammy fruit.*	£16.00	BBR	(S)
FONSECA GUIMARENS 1986, TAYLOR FLADGATE & YEATMAN Douro	*Slight metallic and spirity nose leading into a long lasting palate of sweet summer fruits.*	£17.50	VIL DIR RES	(B)
FONSECA GUIMARENS 1984, TAYLOR FLADGATE & YEATMAN Douro	*Cassis and Christmas cake aromas followed by sweet, ripe succulent fruit on a minty palate.*	£18.50	Widely Available	(S)
BERRY'S VINTAGE 1980, WARRE & CO. Douro	*Dark coffee and spicy aromas are backed up by ripe redcurrants and long lingering juicy finish.*	£18.50	BBR	(G)

TAYLOR'S QUINTA DO VARGELLAS VINTAGE 1986, TAYLOR FLADGATE & YEATMAN Douro	*Spicy fruit and chocolate on the nose leads into a weighty palate of sweet rich caramel.*	£19.00	Widely Available	(B)
QUINTA DO VARGELLAS VINTAGE 1984, TAYLOR FLADGATE & YEATMAN Douro	*Rich warm nose backed up by a palet of rich raisin fruit and a rounded finish.*	£19.00	Widely Available	(G)
QUINTA DO CRASTO VINTAGE 1994, QUINTA DO CRASTO Douro	*A traditional port, deep ruby in colour with Christmas cake flavours dominating the palate.*	£19.50	FUL ENO ODF	(S)
GRAHAM'S 20 YR OLD TAWNY, W & J GRAHAM & CO. Douro	*Herbal and grassy aromas are backed up by smooth, hot redcurrant fruit on a rich palate.*	£20.00	DBY VIL CST JN HAR	(S)
ROZES VINTAGE 1994, ROZES & CO. Douro	*Rich, sweet flavours on a jammy fruit palate with positive tannins providing a firm backbone.*	£20.00	ROZ	(S)
DOW'S QUINTA DO BOMFIM VINTAGE 1984, SILVA & COSENS Douro	*A well balanced wine with a slightly floral nose and light summer fruits on the palate.*	£20.20	TH DBY VIL RBS JS HAR RVA OD	(B)
GRAHAM'S MALVEDOS VINTAGE 1984, W & J GRAHAM & CO. Douro	*A wonderful complex wine offering powerful concentration of mint aromas and spicy fruit flavours.*	£20.20	Widely Available	(G)
WARRE'S QUINTA DA CAVADINHA VINTAGE 1986, WARRE & CO. Douro	*A wine for the future with juicy redcurrants balanced out by medium tannins on the palate.*	£20.80	Widely Available	(S)

Dow's 20 Yr Old Tawny, Silva & Cosens Douro	*Young bramble fruit on a soft, ripe nose is followed by a sweet caramel palate.*	£21.50	CWS WMK W CRS BBR	(B)
Sandeman 20 Yr Old Tawny, Sandeman & Co. Dourol	*Orange in appearance this port posses a palate of vanilla oak and light redcurrant fruit.*	£21.70	MTL V&C LEA OD	(B)
Ramos-Pinto Vintage 1994, Adriano Ramos-Pinto Douro	*Deep, dark fruit on a rich nose with concentrated jammy flavours on the palate.*	£22.00	VLW EP CLA L&W LLT N&P EP	(S)
Churchill's Vintage 1991, Churchill Graham Douro	*Deep red in colour, this port has a jammy palate with underlying hints of banana fruits.*	£24.00	Widely Available	(S)
Duque de Braganca 20 Yr Old Tawny, A.a.Ferreira Douro	*Soft caramel flavours melt on a berry fruit palate ending with an excellent nutty finish.*	£24.40	DBY BOO NI COK NRW SCA	(S)
Quinta do Noval 20 Yr Old, Quinta Do Noval Douro	*Light in colour with a complex nose of caramelised orange peel and sweet fruit flavours.*	£25.90	VIL JCB JAK BUY P&R HAC	(B)
Ramos-Pinto Vintage 1983, Adriano Ramos-Pinto Douro	*Intense peppery cinnamon aromas. The palate offers dense black cherry fruit, damson and plum flavours.*	£26.20	SHG CLA VLW POR COK WFL	(G)
Ramos-Pinto Vintage 1982, Adriano Ramos-Pinto Douro	*A dense ruby wine: offering dark, black fruit on the palate but an easy finish.*	£27.40	CLA VLW	(B)

QUINTA DO BOM-RETIRO 20 YR OLD TAWNY, ADRIANO RAMOS-PINTO Douro	*A rich boneyed nose precedes nutty flavours and light raspberry fruit on the palate.*	**£28.00**	VLW RBS TMW BEN BEL SEL HAR FSW	Ⓢ
PORTO FEIST COLHEITA 1987, H & CJ FEIST Douro	*Orangey brown in colour offering damson aromas. The palate is rich and smooth with good body and length.*	**£29.00**	D&F	Ⓑ
'CHURCHILL'S VINTAGE 1985, CHURCHILL GRAHAM Douro	*Dark in colour. Aromas of spice, tar and sweet fruit. A palate of bitter sweet chocolate and fruit cake.*	**£29.60**	Widely Available	Ⓖ
TAYLOR'S 20 YR OLD TAWNY, TAYLOR FLADGATE & YEATMAN Douro	*A nose of caramel, toffee and coffee precedes a strawberry fruit and nutty palate.*	**£31.10**	Widely Available	Ⓢ
CALEM VINTAGE 1970, A.A. CALEM Douro	*Pepper and spice on the nose are backed up by ripe cherry flavours on the palate.*	**£35.00**	PNA U P&R WIM RAC WE	Ⓖ
RAMOS-PINTO 30 YR OLD TAWNY, ADRIANO RAMOS-PINTO Douro	*A mature nose is backed up by excellent concentration of plummy fruit on a forward palate.*	**£36.50**	VLW CES EP KM SEL CVR EP	Ⓑ
CALEM COLHEITA 1960, A.A. CALEM Douro	*Rich buttery aromas are followed by caramel and ripe cherry fruit flavours on the palate.*	**£56.00**	MM U P&R WIM RAC WE	Ⓢ
QUINTA DO NOVAL OVER 40 YR OLD TAWNY, QUINTA DO NOVAL Douro	*A port which is orangey in colour and has a rich, alcoholic nose and palate.*	**£58.00**	VIL BBR F&M HAM P&R	Ⓢ

PORTUGAL • PORT				
QUINTA DO NOVAL VINTAGE 1966, QUINTA DO NOVAL Douro	*Aromas of old oak are followed by vanilla and sweet red fruit flavours on the palate.*	**£62.00**	VIL SHJ CCC D UNC	**S**
QUINTA DO NOVAL COLHEITA 1937, QUINTA DO NOVAL Douro	*Yellow, amber in colour with a creamy, caramel palate blessed with smooth toffee flavours that last and last!*	**£170**	F&M	**G**

SOUTH AFRICA

ONE OF THE MOST BEAUTIFUL VITICULTURAL regions in the world, producing exciting and diverse styles of wine. Increased foreign investment has encouraged the expansion of a successful existing industry. The Pinotage grape is a particular asset to this rising nation. The large number of entries and medals awarded this year re-affirms South Africa's popularity in the UK market.

SOUTH AFRICA • RED

SIMONSVLEI SHIRAZ RESERVE 1996, SIMONSVLEI Paarl	*A very spicy, peppery wine with a good farmyardy palate. Will develop with time.*	£4.30	W SAF	(B)
TESCO PAARL CABERNET SAUVIGNON, PAUL & HUGO DE VILLIERS Paarl	*Blackcurrant, cedarwood nose. Crisp mint and oak nuances lead to a structured palate of ripe blackcurrant fruit.*	£4.30	RSS	(S)
ROOIBERG PINOTAGE 1994, ROOIBERG CO-OP CELLARS Robertson	*This full bodied wine has bags of rich spices and over ripe strawberries on the nose.*	£.4.95	MK	(B)
NEIL JOUBERT CABERNET SAUVIGNON 1996, NEIL JOUBERT Paarl	*A soft and jammy wine which develops into a complex palate of liquorice and blackcurrants.*	£5.00	CAP SOA MRN	(B)
KYM MILNE ROSENVIEW CABERNET SAUVIGNON 1996, KYM MILNE Stellenbosch	*Predominate tar and ceder aromas leading to rich black brambles and damson flavours on the dense palate.*	£5.00	SAF	(B)

SOUTH AFRICA • RED

VINFRUCO OAK VILLAGE PINOTAGE MERLOT 1996, VINFRUCO Coastal Region	*Wonderfully fruit driven on the nose with a lovely balanced palate and good length.*	**£5.00**	TO	(B)
TESCO BEYERS TRUTER PINOTAGE NV, BEYERS TRUTER Stellenbosch	*Fresh spicy, slightly green fruit is balanced well by light oak. This shows on the good length.*	**£5.20**	VLW TO RSS	(B)
KWV MERLOT 1993, KWV Western Cape	*Soft plums and smoky oak are followed by fresh, elegant fruit with a slightly tart finish.*	**£5.70**	FUL GDS CST WMK SEL BCL CAP	(B)
RAILROAD RED 1996, GRAHAM BECK MADEBA Robertson	*A mild red. Soft berry fruit on the nose followed by a strawberry and raspberry palate.*	**£5.70**	EP	(S)
BACKSBERG PINOTAGE 1995, BACKSBERG ESTATE Paarl	*Stacks of rich blackberry fruit on the nose follows through to the palate showing excellent length.*	**£5.90**	DBY TP ADN JEH L&W IRV BBU	(B)
BACKSBERG MERLOT 1995, BACKSBERG ESTATE Paarl	*Aromas of ripe red berry fruit with oak highlights and a rich vanilla flavoured, soft palate.*	**£5.90**	DBY TP EP IRV CHH BBU	(S)
SAXENBURG CABERNET MERLOT 1996, SAXENBURG Stellenbosch	*Attractive ripe fruit aromas give complexity to a wine offering sweet fruit and spice flavours.*	**£6.00**	BBR IRV EP	(B)
DIEMERSDAL MERLOT 1996, SONOP WINE FARM Coastal Region	*Ripe blackcurrant fruit aromas lead onto a sweet, appealing and generous palate with light tannins.*	**£6.00**	TO SSM WSO	(B)

SOUTH AFRICA • RED

HUGH RYMAN JACANA PINOTAGE 1995, HUGH RYMAN Stellenbosch	*A wonderfully complex wine with stacks of black fruit, pepper, smoke and tar showing through.*	**£6.00**	OD	(S)
BAY VIEW CABERNET SAUVIGNON PINOTAGE 1995, LONGRIDGE Stellenbosch	*Hints of spice on the nose. Nicely balanced fruit, with softening tannins and medium length palate.*	**£6.20**	VIL HW BCW TPA H&W	(B)
FAIRVIEW CABERNET SAUVIGNON 1995, CHARLES BACK Paarl	*Tarry, concentrated raspberry fruit aromas with a luscious sweet berry flavour and a good tannin finish.*	**£6.30**	JS VWC A GRT VW	(B)
FAIRVIEW SHIRAZ 1995, CHARLES BACK Paarl	*A herbal wine with super, soft fleshy fruit and a slightly medicinal finish to a rich, spicy palate.*	**£6.50**	J&B FUL TO A GNW	(B)
CLOS MALVERNE PINOTAGE 1996, CLOS MALVERNE Stellenbosch	*A good nose showing brambles and white pepper, following through to a spicy palate.*	**£6.50**	W BOO FUL GNW POR COK	(B)
VERGELEGEN CABERNET SAUVIGNON 1995, VERGELEGEN Stellenbosch	*Mature blackcurrant aromas with oaky herbaceous elements, and a complex palate of vanilla berry fruit.*	**£6.50**	JS OD	(G)
RUST EN VREDE MERLOT 1996, RUST EN VREDE ESTATE Stellenbosch	*Ripe black fruits on the nose with soft aromatic characters on a well structured palate.*	**£7.00**	L&W	(B)
STELLENZICHT CABERNET SAUVIGNON 1994, STELLENZICHT WINES Stellenbosch	*Aroma of underripe red-currants followed by an intensely flavoured palate of tart summer and bramble fruits.*	**£7.00**	IRV CAP SOA	(B)

SOUTH AFRICA • RED

TESCO PREMIUM SHIRAZ 1995, JOHN WORONTSCHAK MADEBA FARMS Western Cape	*Aromas of spice and mint. On the palate flavours of smoked bacon and peppered dry tannins.*	£7.00	TO	(S)
BLAAUWKLIPPEN SHIRAZ 1995, BLAAUWKLIPPEN Stellenbosch	*A purple, gamey wine with plenty of up-front fruit and a toasted oak nose.*	£7.00	OD	(S)
KLAWERVLEI ESTATE PINOTAGE 1995, KLAWERVLEI ESTATE Stellenbosch	*Stacks of warm spicy fruit is balanced on the palate by firm tannins and crisp acidity.*	£7.00	AMW ISW GRO NY	(S)
KWV CATHEDRAL CELLAR CABERNET SAUVIGNON 1994, KWV Coastal Region	*The nose reminds one of soft leather chairs followed by spicy weighty fruit on the palate.*	£7.20	DBY MRN	(B)
BACKSBERG CABERNET SAUVIGNON 1994, BACKSBERG ESTATE Paarl	*A blackcurrant and minty nose leads into a big expansive wine with ripe tannins.*	£7.30	TP WMK IRV BBU EP VAU WTL EP	(B)
LA MOTTE SHIRAZ 1994, LA MOTTE ESTATE Franschhoek	*A simple, friendly, fruity wine with soft tannins and a good palate of spicy fruit.*	£7.40	DBY MFS QR CAP SOA LAY	(B)
NEETHLINGSHOF SHIRAZ 1993, NEETHLINGSHOF ESTATE Stellenbosch	*Good colour and green pepper aromas lead to a smoky, spicy palate with a dry finish.*	£7.40	TP IRV CAP SOA	(B)
KWV CATHEDRAL CELLAR TRIPTYCH 1993, KWV Coastal Region	*A nutty oak, cigar box aroma leads to leathery, dried out soft fruit flavours.*	£7.40	DBY	(B)

SIMONSIG SHIRAZ 1994, SIMONSIG ESTATE Stellenbosch	*A spicy lean wine with firm tannins and lively peppery flavours on the palate.*	£7.40	Widely Available	(B)
VILLIERA CRU MONRO 1995, VILLIERA ESTATE Paarl	*A gorgeous nose of vanilla and cigar boxes. The fruit flavours are rich and creamy.*	£7.40	VWC TH OD	(S)
STELLENZICHT SHIRAZ 1994, STELLENZICHT WINES Stellenbosch	*Green, leafy herbaceous notes on the spicy nose with rich gamey, pepper flavours and smoky notes.*	£7.50	TP IRV CAP SOA FVM EP	(B)
BACKSBERG KLEIN BABYLONSTOREN 1994, BACKSBERG ESTATE Paarl	*Simple fresh fruits on the nose and palate. Balanced with a soft lingering finish.*	£7.70	TP CPW EDR CHH ABY IRV	(B)
VILLIERA MERLOT 1996, VILLIERA ESTATE Paarl	*Deep ruby wine with youthful raspberry aromas and creamy plum fruits. A soft velvety finish.*	£7.80	TH	(B)
ZANDVLIET SHIRAZ 1990, ZANDVLIET ESTATE Robertson	*Rich and mellow. A very attractive wine offering complex peppery and ripe fruit characters.*	£9.00	HBJ	(B)
SIMONSIG CABERNET SAUVIGNON 1993, SIMONSIG ESTATE Stellenbosch	*Aromas of chocolate and underripe fruit leading to full-bodied blackcurrant flavours with fine tannins.*	£9.00	COE ALE PS	(B)
HUGH RYMAN JACANA PINOTAGE RESERVE 1995, HUGH RYMAN Stellenbosch	*A melting pot of flavours with mint, leather, liquorice, spice and ripe strawberries all combining on the palate.*	£9.00	CWS SAF	(G)

ROGER JORGENSEN RED WELLINGTON 1994, ROGER JORGENSEN Wellington	*Sweet nose of black cherry and apple fruits is reflected on the palate of this wine.*	£9.50	GNW L&W	B
UITERWYK PINOTAGE 1994, UITERWYK Stellenbosch	*Tar, fig and rich smoky aromas precede a lengthy, well-balanced, spicy palate.*	£9.90	DBY L&W NY RBS	B
SAXENBURG MERLOT PRIVATE COLLECTION 1994, SAXENBURG ESTATE Stellenbosch	*Deep aromas of underripe plums and tobacco, with sweet oak, intense plum and cream flavours.*	£10.00	EP IRV EP	B
PLAISIR DE MERLE CABERNET SAUVIGNON 1995, STELLENBOSCH FARMERS' WINERY Paarl	*Deep colour. Rich aromas of summer fruits and new oak preceding a mouthful of blackcurrant.*	£10.00	BNK CAP FUL PEA	S
PLAISIR DE MERLE MERLOT 1995, STELLENBOSCH FARMERS' WINERY Paarl	*Rich vanilla, mint and fruit aromas lead to integrated ripe berry fruit on the palate.*	£10.00	CAP SOA MHW PEA EWD	S
RUST EN VREDE SHIRAZ 1994, RUST EN VREDE ESTATE Stellenbosch	*A medium purple wine with complex, smoky fruit characters on a ripe, juicy palate.*	£10.30	L&W NY NI	B
GROOT CONSTANTIA GOUVERNEURS RESERVE 1994, GROOT CONSTANTIA Constantia	*Sweet, jammy nose with pepper notes. A rich, medium bodied palate dominated by soft black fruits.*	£10.30	TP G&M CAP SOA EP	B
VEENWOUDEN CLASSIC 1994, VEENWOUDEN Paarl	*Ripe fruits and violets on the nose with a concentrated palate of soft black fruits.*	£13.00	OD	B

VEENWOUDEN MERLOT 1994, VEENWOUDEN Paarl	*A powerful oak nose is followed by a structured palate of rich fruit and tannins.*	**£13.00**	OD	**B**
STELLENZICHT SYRAH 1994, STELLENZICHT WINES Stellenbosch	*An opaque, ripe, juicy wine offering concentrated red fruit flavours and medium tannins.*	**£13.70**	TP BBR CAP SOA EP	**B**
SAXENBERG CABERNET SAUVIGNON PRIVATE COLLECTION 1992, SAXENBERG ESTATE Stellenbosch	*An interesting cassis and oak nose with powerful, juicy fruit on the balanced palate.*	**£20.00**	BBR	**S**

SOUTH AFRICA • WHITE

TABLE BAY EARLY RELEASE CHENIN BLANC 1997, KYM MILNE AT WELMOED CO-OP Stellenbosch	*A very young wine that is slightly aromatic. Fresh and clean on a delicate fruit palate.*	**£3.70**	VWC SAF	**B**
BOTTELARY CO-OP EARLY RELEASE CHENIN BLANC 1997, KYM MILNE AT BOTTELARY CO-OP Stellenbosch	*An off-dry white. Gooseberry and tropical fruit aromas lead onto a lingering aftertaste.*	**£4.40**	TH FUL OD	**B**
WATERSIDE WHITE 1996, GRAHAM BECK MADEBA Robertson	*Fresh, lemon aromas with underlying hints of almond, followed by a creamy, buttery palate.*	**£4.90**	EP SAF EP	**S**
BELLINGHAM SAUVIGNON BLANC 1996, DOUGLAS GREEN BELLINGHAM Paarl	*Strong Sauvignon aromas leap out at you from the glass. Good depth on the gooseberry dominated palate.*	**£5.10**	Widely Available	**B**

WELMOED CHARDONNAY 1996, WELMOED COOP CELLARS Stellenbosch	*Melons and honey shine through attractively on the nose of this fresh yet weighty wine.*	£5.30	MFS GNW HOU WWI	(B)
SAXENBURG SAUVIGNON BLANC 1996, SAXENBURG ESTATE Stellenbosch	*A skilfully - made wine that shows crisp fruit. A beautiful gooseberry aroma and pleasant uplifting acidity.*	£5.40	DBY CPW CHH D FUL BBR ABY	(B)
VERGELEGEN SAUVIGNON BLANC 1995, VERGELEGEN Stellenbosch	*A delightful nose with young gooseberry fruit on the palate. Excellent structure and skilfully made.*	£6.00	JS TO OD	(B)
MÔRESON UNWOODED CHARDONNAY 1995, MÔRESON FARM Franschhoek	*Citrus lemon nose leading into bags of huge apple custard fruit on the palate.*	£6.60	TP CAP NG SEL SOA	(B)
STELLENZICHT CHARDONNAY 1996, STELLENZICHT WINES Stellenbosch	*Oaky vanilla flavours on the nose, leading to a mouthwatering blend of tropical fruit.*	£6.90	TP IRV CAP SOA OD	(B)
SPECIAL CUVÉE SAUVIGNON BLANC 1996, SPRINGFIELD ESTATE Robertson	*Lengthy nettle nose, on a soft and full palate. Good fruity structure and long finish.*	£7.00	VWC W BI GGW WIN VW	(B)
NEIL ELLIS SAUVIGNON BLANC 1996, NEIL ELLIS WINES Stellenbosch	*Pale green in colour, with underlining herbaceous aromas on a full bodied, ripe palate,*	£7.10	MTL DBY BOO FUL RBS COK FTH	(B)
SAXENBURG CHARDONNAY 1996, SAXENBURG ESTATE Stellenbosch	*There is a hint of oiliness showing alongside the fruit in this well-integrated wine.*	£7.20	U BBR IRV EP	(B)

SOUTH AFRICA • WHITE

CATHEDRAL CELLARS CHARDONNAY 1996, KWV Coastal Region	*This stylish Chardonnay, displays a beautiful aroma of smoky, ripe, toasted oak and seductive fruit.*	**£7.20**	DBY ABY CAP SOA MRN	(S)
BACKSBERG CHARDONNAY 1995, BACKSBERG ESTATE Paarl	*This off-dry white has rich tropical fruit aromas and a lingering palate of melon flavours.*	**£7.30**	TP EP CHH IRV BBR BBU EP	(B)
KLEIN CONSTANTIA ESTATE CHARDONNAY 1995, KLEIN CONSTANTIA ESTATE Constantia	*Toasty oaked fruit flavours are superbly integrated with good acidity on an appealing palate.*	**£7.50**	DBY DIR MM U SHJ EOO	(S)
VERGELEGEN CHARDONNAY RESERVE 1995, VERGELEGEN Stellenbosch	*Delicate toasty oaked nose, superbly balanced with a good integration of oak and acidity.*	**£8.70**	JS OD	(B)
BOSCHENDAL CHARDONNAY RESERVE 1995, BOSCHENDAL Franschhoek	*A light, smoky, fruity nose precedes a lively complex palate of grapefruit characters.*	**£8.90**	GI VIL PO U HOU ROD EDC	(B)
PLAISIR DE MERLE CHARDONNAY 1996, STELLENBOSCH FARMERS' WINERY Paarl	*Pleasant peach and lemon aromas abound on the nose, leading to a well-rounded palate.*	**£9.20**	DBY EP BNK TO MHW MWW SEL SOA	(B)
HAMILTON RUSSELL CHARDONNAY 1996, HAMILTON RUSSELL Walker Bay	*Stylish wine, with a harmonious mixture of fruit and subtle oak on a well-integrated palate.*	**£10.90**	Widely Available	(B)

Pinpoint who sells the wine you wish to buy by turning to the stockist codes. If you know the name of the wine you want to buy, use the alphabetical index. If the price is your motivation, refer to the invaluable price guide index; red and white wines under £5, sparkling wines under £10 and champagne under £15. Happy hunting!

SOUTH AFRICA • SPARKLING

LA COTTE SPARKLING DEMI SEC 1996, FRANSCHHOEK COOP CELLARS Franschhoek	*A lovely flowery bouquet, following through to aromatic fruit on the palate balanced with good acidity.*	£5.80	ABB AP G&G	**B**
LA COTTE SPARKLING SAUVIGNON BLANC BRUT 1996, FRANSCHHOEK COOP CELLARS Franschhoek	*Slightly lighter style, that shows good fruity flavours on a clear and refreshing palate.*	£6.00	BUT ABB G&G SMF	**B**
TESCO ROBERTSON SPARKLING, JOHN WORONTCHAK Robertson	*Starting with a burst of yeasty fruit on the nose, and following through to the palate.*	£7.00	TO	**S**
GRAHAM BECK BRUT BLANC DE BLANC 1991, GRAHAM BECK MADEBA Robertson	*Foaming mousse, delicate and clean aromas and flavours of citrus and apples with autolytic notes.*	£9.00	OD	**B**
LONGRIDGE BRUT 1993, LONGRIDGE WINES Stellenbosch	*Tight mousse, rich toasty yeast, with complex citrus flavours, on a long, balanced palate.*	£9.90	VIL HW RBS BCW TPA H&W	**S**

SOUTH AMERICA

Prudence and alacrity in the vineyards of South America is resulting in the production of drier, more traditional-style, New World wines. Bordelais blends and fresh Sauvignon Blancs predominate along with cooler climate Chardonnays. Chile and Argentina have gained from an influx of European winemakers prepared to share their knowledge in this emerging market. New wine styles continue to excite the British consumer.

SOUTH AMERICA • ARGENTINA • RED

GRAFFIGNA SHIRAZ CABERNET 1995, BODEGAS SANTIAGO DE GRAFFIGNA Mendoza	*Lovely sweet, berry fruit coming through with an attractive intensity and weight on the palate.*	**£3.50**	VWC CWS VW	**B**
BALBI VINEYARD SYRAH MALBEC 1996, ALLIED DOMECQ Mendoza	*Spicy aromas combine with the silky soft tannins of malbec, to give a earthy mouthfilling wine.*	**£3.70**	MOR KWI MRN	**B**
BRIGHT BROTHERS CABERNET MALBEC 1996, PEÑAFLOR Mendoza	*A well-structured Cabernet, Malbec blend with mouthwatering blackcurrant fruit and spicy aroma on the nose.*	**£3.70**	A CWS CRS	**S**
VICUÑA PEAK MALBEC TEMPRANILLO 1996, BODEGAS SANTA ANA Mendoza	*Dense wine with lots of gripping tannins balanced by rich fruit characters on a lingering vanilla palate.*	**£4.00**	CRS CDT	**B**
TOSO SYRAH 1995, PASCUAL TOSO Mendoza	*A restrained wine of medium weight offeringa palate of mature oak and baked fruit characteristics .*	**£4.50**	PLB TO	**B**

ETCHART CABERNET SAUVIGNON 1995, ARNALDO ETCHART Mendoza	*Intense aromas of cassis, eucalypt and pencil shavings are reflected in a well-concentrated , soft drying palate.*	£4.80	Widely Available	G
SANTA JULIA ALAMOS RIDGE MALBEC 1994, BODEGAS ESMERALDA Mendoza	*A minty blackcurrant nose, with pleasant uplifting fruit and a deep ruby red colour.*	£5.00	GGW BI FUL WSO SAF	B
MALBEC OAK RESERVE 1994, LA AGRICOLA 1994, Mendoza	*The classic grape variety of Cahors has produced a richly flavoured wine with soft tannins.*	£5.00	TO	B
SANTA JULIA CABERNET SAUVIGNON OAK RESERVE 1994, LA AGRICOLA Mendoza	*Minty rich fruit aromas lead to rounded mulberry flavours with marzipan notes and ripe, juicy tannins.*	£5.00	T&T	B
CORREAS CABERNET SAUVIGNON 1996, BODEGA CORREAS Mendoza	*A glossy, ripe blackcurrant aroma with an appetising palate of ripe fruits and firm tannins.*	£5.00	MOR	B
NORTON BARBERA 1995, BODEGA NORTON Mendoza	*This is a warm, robust, tannic wine with excellent texture and a bitter sweet finish.*	£5.10	LNR BOO FUL OD PAG	B
NORTON CABERNET SAUVIGNON 1996, BODEGA NORTON Mendoza	*Light ripe berry nose leading to rich loganberry flavours dominated by sweet oak on the palate.*	£5.80	LNR BOO CPW PAG OD	B
GRAN LURTON CABERNET RESERVE 1995, J & F LURTON Mendoza	*Compote of fruit and coffee aromas lead to dry raspberry flavours with hints of spice.*	£6.00	FUL	B

NORTON MALBEC 1994, BODEGA NORTON Mendoza	*Beautifully rounded flavours of berries and sweet oak that sticks to the palate on the finish.*	**£6.10**	LNR NY BOO NI CPW JN PAG EP	**B**
TRAPICHE OAK CASK CABERNET SAUVIGNON 1993, BODEGAS TRAPICHE Mendoza	*Fragrant, herbaceous nose with young and elegant ripe fruit flavours on a lingering, palate.*	**£6.20**	DBY GI TP CRM WIN NAD JS	**B**
VALENTIN BIANCHI MALBEC RESERVE 1991, VALENTIN BIANCHI Mendoza	*Good warm alcohol; a very deeply coloured chewy wine with a powerful, long finish.*	**£8.00**	OD	**B**
CATEÑA MALBEC 1995, BODEGAS ESMERALDA Mendoza	*An attractively coloured wine, warm, rich and ripe with an excellent nose and finish.*	**£8.50**	DBY GGW BI FUL WSO	**S**
WEINERT MALBEC 1991, BODEGA Y CAVAS DE WEINERT Mendoza	*A sophisticated nose that lingers through on a lively palate with an underlying touch of spice.*	**£8.90**	Widely Available	**S**

SOUTH AMERICA • ARGENTINA • WHITE

VINAL CAYEN CHARDONNAY 1995, BODEGAS CHANDON Mendoza	*Vanilla and butter aromas lead to an attractively rounded citrus finish, with complexity and depth.*	**£7.00**	CWS	**S**
CATEÑA CHARDONNAY 1995, BODEGAS ESMERALDA Mendoza	*Honey and sherbety nose with medium acidity and good concentrated fruit on the palate.*	**£8.60**	BI GGW FUL CHF WSO SAF	**B**

CATEÑA ALTA CHARDONNAY 1995, BODEGAS ESMERALDA Mendoza	*Delightful lemon and toasted oak on the nose, followed by well-rounded fruit and crisp acidity.*	£19.80	BI GGW (S)

SOUTH AMERICA • CHILE • RED

SANTA CAROLINA TIERRA DEL REY 1996, SANTA CAROLINA Maipo	*A young ruby.coloured red, with medium intensity and a slightly tannic, dry finish.*	£3.00	CWS BKI (B)
LA PALMA CABERNET SAUVIGNON 1996, VIÑA LA ROLA Rapel	*Rich jammy, herbal aromas on a deeply flavoured fresh blackcurrant palate with balanced ripe tannins.*	£4.00	FUL CWS SMF (B)
MALT HOUSE VINTNERS CARTA VIEJA CHILEAN MERLOT 1996, VIÑA CARTA VIEJA Maule	*Plum jam and cedar aromas lead to a balanced palate of soft black fruits ending with vanilla notes.*	£4.00	MWW PIM OD (B)
LA PALMA MERLOT 1996, VIÑA LA ROSA Rapel	*Plum jam nose developing to a soft palate with sweet fruit, cedarwood, mint and dry tannins.*	£4.00	W FUL OD (S)
LA PALMA MERLOT 1996, VIÑA LA ROSA Cachapoal	*Purple and ruby, fresh ripe fruit on the nose and palate with spice and tannin.*	£4.10	W HW FUL SV OD (S)
SPAR CHILEAN MERLOT 1996, CANEPA Maipo	*Vibrant purple colour with red fruit aromas and a rich plum flavour on the palate.*	£4.20	SPR SMF (B)

VALDIVIESO CABERNET SAUVIGNON 1996, VALDIVIESO Lontue	*Plummy and vanilla nose with bints of raisins, sweet dark fruit and oak undertones.*	**£4.40**	JS VWC BI GGW SB VW	**B**
ANDES PEAKS MERLOT 1996, VIÑA SANTA EMILIANA Rapel	*A minty berbaceous nose with blackcurrant and oak flavours to the fore of the palate.*	**£4.40**	Widely Available	**B**
FOUR RIVERS CABERNET SAUVIGNON 1995, VIÑA GRACIA Maipo	*A sweet and berbaceous nose is followed by ripe black fruits and mint on the palate.*	**£4.50**	CWS EP	**S**
GATO NEGRO 1995, VIÑA SAN PEDRO Lontue	*Smoky blackcurrant aromas and a rounded, soft, creamy plum flavoured palate.*	**£4.60**	MTL RBS NIC MRS WST MRN	**B**
VALDIVIESO MERLOT 1996, VALDIVIESO Lontue Valley	*Strong, aromatic berries and cedar, creamy plum fruit flavours on a youthful wine with strong tannins.*	**£4.70**	JS TH DBY BI GGW FUL SB	**B**
CALITERRA CABERNET SAUVIGNON 1995, CALITERRA Maipo	*Mint and oak scented aromas with a soft blackcurrant palate and light structure. Simple balanced finish.*	**£4.70**	Widely Available	**B**
DOMAINE ORIENTAL CABERNET SAUVIGNON 1996, AGRICOLA SALVE Maule Valley	*Sweet blackcurrant aromas with light oak notes on an impressive palate of chewy black fruits and vanilla.*	**£4.90**	PNA U ALL JEM WIM EP	**B**
LA PALMA CABERNET MERLOT RESERVE 1996, VINA LA ROSA Rapel	*Impressive purple colour with a leafy, cedar nose and youthful plummy fruit and smooth finish.*	**£5.00**	FUL CWS JS OD	**B**

VIU MANENT CABERNET SAUVIGNON RESERVE 1993, VIU MANENT Colchagua	*Ripe blackberry and spicy tobacco aromas, creamy oak and black fruit flavours on long, balanced palate.*	£5.00	HW	B
ROWAN BROOK CABERNET MERLOT 1995, VINICOLA LAS TAQUAS Central Valley	*A subdued blackcurrant nose leading to a New World herbaceous and blackcurrant palate with 'grippy' tannins.*	£5.00	A	B
VINA BISQUERTT VINEYARDS MERLOT 1995, BISQUERTT VINEYARDS Colchagua	*An intense nose of black cherry and tarry spice with rich flavours and good balance.*	£5.00	SHG BOO CRS	B
VIÑA GRACIA CABERNET PREMIUM 1994, VIÑA GRACIA Maipo	*Pronounced berry fruit nose with cedar and tobacco notes, ripe berry fruit and spice on a warm palate.*	£5.00	CWS	B
VIÑA CARTA ANTIGUAS SELECTION CABERNET SAUVIGNON 1995, VIÑA CARTA VIEJA Maule	*Ripe plum and spice aromas with minty leather notes on a rich spicy palate with a buttery finish.*	£5.00	MWW PIM OD	B
CASA LEONA CABERNET SAUVIGNON RESERVE 1995, VIÑA PEUMO Rapel	*Intense plum colour, spicy, tobacco and oak nose, concentrated palate of ripe black fruits, soft tannins.*	£5.00	M&S	S
CASA LEONA MERLOT RESERVE 1996, VIÑA PEUMO Rapel	*Deep plum colour, intense cherry and spice aromas, powerful flavours of red berries and vanilla balance tannins.*	£5.00	M&S	S
VIU MANENT CABERNET SAUVIGNON RESERVE 1994, VIU MANENT Colchagua	*Deep purple with mint and blackcurrant aromas, mouthful of sweet creamy oak and ripe plummy fruit flavours.*	£5.00	HW	S

ROWAN BROOK CABERNET SAUVIGNON 1994, VINICOLA LAS TAQUAS Central Valley	*Deep plum wine, intense blackcurrant, eucalyptus aromas, rich soft black fruit flavours, lingering balanced palate.*	£5.00	A	(S)
VILLA MONTES MALBEC 1996, DISCOVER WINES Colchagua	*A warm, ripe fruity nose with attractive secondary flavours on the palate. Well-balanced by light, structured tannins.*	£5.20	Widely Available	(B)
ERRAZURIZ ESTATES CABERNET SAUVIGNON 1996, ERRAZURIZ ESTATES Aconcagua	*A mulberry, plummy nose introduces this wine of some complexity and good fruits on the palate.*	£5.20	Widely Available	(B)
SANTA DIGNA CABERNET SAUVIGNON 1995, MIGUEL TORRES Curico	*A pleasant plummy bouquet precedes a palate of ripe, juicy blackcurrant fruit with peppery overtones.*	£5.40	Widely Available	(B)
MERLOT GRAN TARAPACA RESERVE 1995, VIÑA TARAPACA Maipo	*Warm spicy style wine with elements of oak and black fruits on the nose and palate.*	£5.40	CDT	(B)
SANTA CAROLINA CABERNET SAUVIGNON RESERVA 1994, SANTA CAROLINA Maipo	*Some signs of age with rich, herbaceous, jammy plum notes on the nose and a sweet palate.*	£5.50	TH DBY YWL WMK OD	(B)
MONTES OAK AGED CABERNET SAUVIGNON 1994, DISCOVER WINES Curico	*Leafy blackcurrant and vanilla aromas. Well-balanced, lingering ripe fruit flavours with a raspberry finish.*	£5.60	Widely Available	(B)
PRIMA DE MARTINO CABERNET SAUVIGNON RESERVE 1995, DE MARTINO Maipo	*Rich aromas of blackcurrant jammy lead onto a berby, black fruit palate with a sweet finish.*	£5.60	LNR BOO PAG	(B)

VIÑA GRACIA CABERNET SAUVIGNON 1996, VIÑA GRACIA Maipo Valley	*A jammy, summer fruits bouquet carries onto a deeply flavoured fruit-gum palate with a sweet finish.*	£5.60	TP COK EP	Ⓑ
DOMAINE ORIENTAL MERLOT CLOS CENTENAINE 1996, AGRICOLA SALVE Maule Valley	*Herbaceous plummy notes on the nose and a deep plum jam flavour mark this wine.*	£5.60	PNA U ALL JEM WIM EP	Ⓑ
SANTA CAROLINA MERLOT RESERVA 1996, SANTA CAROLINA San Fernando	*Purple with leafy, spicy aromas, big blackberry fruit and oak flavours on a medium palate.*	£5.60	YWL WMK	Ⓑ
TORREON DE PAREDES CABERNET SAUVIGNON RESERVE 1989, TORREON DE PAREDES Rengo	*Herbaceous notes interlink with fruit aromas. Blackcurrant and mint flavours soften and develop in the mouth.*	£5.70	DBY FTH	Ⓑ
CARMENERE RESERVE LEGADO DE ARMIDA 1996, SANTA INES Maipo	*Minty red berries, liquorice aromas and flavours with dominant oak. Good fruit finish.*	£6.00	TH TO IWS	Ⓑ
SANTA INES LEGADO DE ARMIDA MERLOT RESERVE 1996, SANTA INES Maipo	*A herbaceous nose with good colour, flavours of dried fruit and spice predominate the palate.*	£6.00	FUL IWS	Ⓑ
HACIENDA SAN CARLOS CABERNET SAUVIGNON 1996, VIU MANENT Colchagua	*Intense crunchy red fruit aromas lead to a palate with eucalyptus, ripe fruits and tannins.*	£6.00	BD	Ⓑ

Pinpoint who sells the wine you wish to buy by turning to the stockist codes. If you know the name of the wine you want to buy, use the alphabetical index. If the price is your motivation, refer to the invaluable price guide index; red and white wines under £5, sparkling wines under £10 and champagne under £15. Happy hunting!

PROSPERITY MERLOT NV, FIRESTONE VINEYARDS Colchagua	*Fresh crushed berry fruit aromas, enhanced on the palate with hints of oak and spice.*	**£6.00**	GRA	(B)
CASTILLO DE MOLINA CABERNET SAUVIGNON RESERVA 1995, VIÑA SAN PEDRO Lontue	*Ripe sweet fruit on a nose with terroir influences, rich fruit on palate, brisk tannins.*	**£6.00**	RBS	(B)
CASTILLO DE MOLINA CABERNET SAUVIGNON RESERVA 1994, VIÑA SAN PEDRO Lontue	*A nose full of ripe cherries followed by sweet black fruits on a creamy vanilla finish.*	**£6.00**	RBS WRS WRT	(S)
UNDURRAGA CABERNET SAUVIGNON RESERVA 1995, VIÑA UNDURRAGA	*Herbaceous black fruit nose leads to an intensely fruity soft palate with sweet oak, chocolate nuances.*	**£6.40**	DBY WES GRA MWW AV	(S)
VIÑA PORTA CABERNET SAUVIGNON 1996, VIÑA PORTA Cachapoal	*A spicy, jammy nose leads to delicate dark fruit flavours on the long balanced palate.*	**£6.50**	A CRM TMW OD CRS	(B)
VIÑA PORTA CABERNET SAUVIGNON RESERVA 1995, VIÑA PORTA Rapel	*Dense, black ruby colour with a restrained, cedary nose and soft blackcurrant flavours. Long finish.*	**£6.50**	DBY OD	(B)
CARMEN MERLOT RESERVE 1995, CARMEN VINEYARDS Rapel	*Aromas of plum and cedar on the nose with soft plummy fruit on a gentle palate.*	**£6.60**	Widely Available	(B)

Pinpoint who sells the wine you wish to buy by turning to the stockist codes. If you know the name of the wine you want to buy, use the alphabetical index. If the price is your motivation, refer to the invaluable price guide index; red and white wines under £5, sparkling wines under £10 and champagne under £15. Happy hunting!

CARMEN RESERVE CABERNET SAUVIGNON 1995, CARMEN VINEYARDS Maipo	*Perfumed nose of plum, raspberry, characteristics of terroir cedar. Soft fruit flavours, green pepper highlights.*	£6.60	Widely Available	(S)
ECHEVERRIA MERLOT RESERVA 1995, VIÑA ECHEVERRIA Molina	*Deep nose with rhône style spice aromas, sweet ripe fruit flavours on the medium palate.*	£6.70	AV	(B)
CALITERRA RESERVADO CABERNET SAUVIGNON 1995, CALITERRA Maipo	*Garnet appearance with a warm appealing fruit nose leading to a jammy soft fruit palate.*	£6.70	TH VWC PTR OD	(B)
VALDIVIESO CABERNET SAUVIGNON RESERVA 1995, VALDIVIESO Lontue	*Intense plum colour. Complex aromas of black-currants, cedar and chocolate, powerfully reflected on a long palate.*	£6.70	JS DBY BI GGW FUL SB	(S)
CARMEN GRANDE VIDURE CABERNET SAUVIGNON 1995, CARMEN VINEYARDS Maipo	*Deep bramble, redcurrant nose followed by lingering mellow flavours of creamy black fruits, chocolate and mint.*	£6.70	Widely Available	(S)
MONT GRAS RESERVA CABERNET SAUVIGNON 1996, MONT GRAS VINEYARDS Rapel	*A vegetal nose leads onto a palate of rich red fruits slightly masked by medium tannins.*	£6.80	VIL NY JN BUT HVW	(B)
MONT GRAS RESERVA CABERNET MERLOT 1996, MONT GRAS VINEYARDS Rapel	*Rich berry fruit on nose. A wonderful balance between fruit, acidity and oak on palate.*	£6.80	NY JN HVW	(S)
ERRAZURIZ CABERNET SAUVIGNON RESERVE 1995, ERRAZURIZ ESTATES Aconcagua	*A jammy blackcurrant nose is followed by compote of fruit flavours on the soft palate.*	£6.90	VWC TH DBY TO U OD WR BU	(B)

MONT GRAS RESERVA MERLOT 1996, MONTGRAS Rapel	*Intense brick red, powerful pepper and spice aromas, commanding spicy black fruit palate, well-balanced and long lasting.*	**£6.90**	VIL NY FUL CHF JN BUT HVW	(S)
VALDIVIESO MERLOT RESERVA 1995, VALDIVIESO Lontue	*Tobacco notes on a fruity, blackcurrant nose with ripe tannins on the lengthy, damson palate.*	**£7.00**	BI GGW	(B)
LA PALMA RESERVA MERLOT 1996, VIÑA LA ROSA Rapel	*Deep colour with a jammy, chocolate nose and a fruity palate with vanilla, chocolate notes.*	**£7.00**	FUL OD	(B)
LA PALMA RESERVA CABERNET SAUVIGNON 1996, VINA LA ROSA Rapel	*A rounded bramble jam nose with fruity fresh currant flavours and soft tannins and acidity.*	**£7.00**	HW	(B)
ERRAZURIZ ESTATES CABERNET SAUVIGNON RESERVA 1994, ERRAZURIZ ESTATES Aconcagua	*Rich minty eucalypt notes on the nose match pleasant, structured cassis and bramble, mint flavours.*	**£7.50**	VWC TO WCR	(B)
SANTA CAROLINA MERLOT GRAN RESERVA 1995, SANTA CAROLINA San Fernando	*Pungent berry fruits, with a good tannin, structure and acidity, on a sweet oaky finish.*	**£7.50**	DBY YWL WMK	(B)
CASABLANCA SANTA ISABEL CABERNET 1996, VIÑA CASABLANCA Casablanca	*Deep ruby wine. Youthful plummy aromas leading to soft fruit flavours on a balanced, sweet palate.*	**£8.00**	DBY MOR BOO HVW OD EP	(B)
CASABLANCA SANTA ISABEL MERLOT 1996, VIÑA CASABLANCA Casablanca	*Ripe jammy aromas with mint and cedar notes lead onto a deep plum jam flavoured palate*	**£8.40**	NY MOR HVW OD	(B)

DON MAXIMIANO CABERNET SAUVIGNON RESERVA 1993, ERRAZURIZ ESTATES Aconcagua	*Fresh minty blackcurrant aromas dominate soft sweet flavours of blackcurrant jam with oak and tobacco nuances.*	£8.40	VWC DBY FUL TO WMK	(S)
MONTES ALPHA MERLOT 1995, DISCOVER WINES Curico	*Blackcurrant and mint aromas on the nose and a delicately fruit flavoured palate mark this wine.*	£8.70	Widely Available	(B)
MONTES ALPHA CABERNET SAUVIGNON 1994, DISCOVER WINES Curico	*Light, mulberry, oak and cassis aromas are reflected on the elegantly balanced, lingering palate.*	£8.70	Widely Available	(B)
VIÑA PORTA CASA PORTA CABERNET SAUVIGNON 1996, VIÑA PORTA Cachapoal	*Dark cherry fruit leading to a soft rich palate with fine tannins and an elegant finish.*	£9.00	DBY CRS OD	(B)
SANTA CAROLINA CABERNET SAUVIGNON RESERVA DE FAMILIA 1993, SANTA CAROLINA Maipo	*A Chilean cabernet offering cedar and herbaceous notes followed by attractive blackcurrant and eucalypt characters.*	£9.00	THW	(B)
VALDIVIESO CABERNET FRANC RESERVA 1995, VALDIVIESO Lontue	*Deep tarry nose with blackcurrant aromas leading to a big palate. Sweet juicy fruit and fine tannins.*	£9.00	TH BI GGW FUL SAF	(S)
CASA LAPOSTOLLE MERLOT CUVEE ALEXANDRE 1996, CASA LAPOSTOLLE Rapel	*Deep purple colour. Passion fruit and oak aromas with powerful cedary, blackcurrant flavours on a lingering palate.*	£9.20	DBY VLW FUL HVW OD	(S)
VALDIVIESO CABALLO LOCO NUMERO UNO NV, VALDIVIESO Lontue	*Blackcurrants on the nose and palate. A nicely balanced wine, approachable; with oomph.*	£9.80	W GGW BI FUL SAF TH	(B)

ECHEVERRIA FAMILY RESERVA CABERNET SAUVIGNON 1994, VIÑA ECHEVERRIA Molina	*Rich, fruity, cedarwood and jam aromas with firm structured cassis and integrated oak flavours.*	£9.80	VIL MFS NY IVY HVW E&B AV	(S)
VALDIVIESO CABALLO LOCO NV, VALDEVIESO Lontue	*Rich plum nose with herbaceous notes, ripe plum flavours on a full palate with gripping tannin finish.*	£9.90	TH W BI GGW FUL	(S)
ERRAZURIZ ESTATES SYRAH RESERVA 1996, ERRAZURIZ ESTATES Aconcagua	*Black and rich; a soft fruity wine with ripe tannins, an easily appreciated Chilean wine.*	£10.00	FUL VWC OD	(B)
DON MAXIMIANO CABERNET SAUVIGNON RESERVA 1994, ERRAZURIZ ESTATES Aconcagua	*Leafy, jammy style aromas with masses of black fruits and mint on the palate.*	£10.00	VWC FUL	(B)
ERRAZURIZ ESTATES MERLOT RESERVA 1996, ERRAZURIZ ESTATES Aconcagua	*Soft, spicy nose with herbaceous notes. Prolonged, peppery, black-berry flavoured palate with chocolate characters.*	£10.00	WMK OD	(S)
MANSO DE VELASCO 1995, MIGUEL TORRES Curico	*Herby, peppery aromas: black liquorice notes followed by deep, long flavours of ripe fruit and oak.*	£11.30	Widely Available	(S)
CANEPA MAGNIFICUM CABERNET SAUVIGNON 1993, VINICOLA LAS TAGUAS Central Valley	*Loganberry and pepper nose with herbaceous and juicy fruit flavours: in the mouth mint and blackberries.*	£13.00	T&T	(B)
DON MAXIMIANO CABERNET SAUVIGNON RESERVA 1995, ERRAZURIZ ESTATES Aconcagua	*Intense perfume of herbaceous, plums and eucalyptus. Complex palate of mulberry with oak and cinnamon characters.*	£15.00	VWC OD	(G)

SOUTH AMERICA • CHILE • WHITE

SOMERFIELD CHILEAN CHARDONNAY 1996, VIÑA LA ROSA Rapel	*Fresh, clean nose with full buttery flavours coming through and showing some elegance.*	**£4.00**	SMF	(B)
CASA LEONA CHARDONNAY 1996, VIÑA PEUMO Rapel	*There is stacks of citrus fruit coming through on both the nose and the palate.*	**£4.00**	M&S	(S)
LA PALMA CHARDONNAY 1996, VIÑA LA ROSA Rapel	*Rich toasty oak and fruit aromas follow through with a good concentration in the mouth.*	**£4.30**	FUL SV OD	(B)
ANDES PEAKS SAUVIGNON BLANC 1996, VIÑA SANTA EMILIANA Mulchen	*Fresh, lively, grassy aromas backed up by ripe gooseberry fruit and rich honey flavours.*	**£4.40**	Widely Available	(B)
TORREON DE PAREDES SAUVIGNON BLANC 1996, TORREON DE PAREDES Rengo	*Delicate fruity nose gives way to a palate of uplifting acidity and rounded gooseberry fruit flavours.*	**£4.40**	DBY GNW FTH	(B)
UNDURRAGA GEWÜRZTRAMINER 1996, VIÑA UNDURRAGA Maipo Valley	*Lively citrus fruit. Grapefruit and limes balanced by a swirl of honey. Intense and ripe texture.*	**£4.50**	TO	(B)
SAUVIGNON BLANC DE MARTINO 1997, SANTA INES Maipo	*Mid gold colour. Gooseberry and peach fruit aromas followed by concentrated fruit on the palate.*	**£4.80**	LNR PAG	(B)

CASA LAPOSTOLLE SAUVIGNON BLANC 1996, CASA LAPOSTOLLE Rapel	*A great New World example, filled with gooseberries, elderflowers and fresh, zingy limes flavours.*	**£4.90**	DBY VLW HVW OD	(B)
VIU MANENT CHARDONNAY 1996, VIU MANENT Colchagua	*There is some reasonable citrus character coming through on this attractive full, yet soft wine.*	**£5.00**	HW	(B)
CARTA VIEJA ANTIGUAS SELECTION CHARDONNAY 1996, VIÑA CARTA VIEJA Maule Valley	*Gooseberry and green fruit aromas. Skilfully made wine with a well-held finish.*	**£5.00**	MWW PIM OD	(B)
CANEPA CHARDONNAY 1997, VINOCOLA LAS TAGUAS Central Valley	*Creamy, fat fruit, balances well with crisp acidity to give a big, weighty wine.*	**£5.20**	SPR SWS BES TO	(S)
TRIO CHARDONNAY 1996, VIÑA CONCHA Y TORO Aconcagua	*Brilliant greeny gold in colour with stacks of round, spicy floral fruit and crisp acidity.*	**£5.50**	TH TDS WR BU	(S) WINE OF THE YEAR
CASABLANCA WHITE LABEL SAUVIGNON BLANC 1996, VIÑA CASABLANCA Lontue	*Clear, soft wine with a well-developed fruity aroma. Showing intense fruit on a ripe palate.*	**£5.60**	Widely Available	(B)
CASABLANCA WHITE LABEL CHARDONNAY 1996, VIÑA CASABLANCA Casablanca	*A mixture of lemons and apples with some tropical fruit aromas leads to a well-rounded wine.*	**£5.70**	Widely Available	(S)
SANTA CAROLINA CHARDONNAY RESERVA 1996, SANTA CAROLINA Maipo	*Lychee and fruit aromas combine well to produce a soft palate with integrated oak.*	**£5.90**	YWL WMK OD	(B)

ECHEVERRIA CHARDONNAY RESERVA 1996, VIÑA ECHEVERRIA Molina	*Delicate fruit and sherbet nose. Very dry, but shows good fruit and length on the finish.*	£6.00	Widely Available	B
VIÑA TARAPACA CHARDONNAY 1996, VIÑA TARAPACA Maipo	*Crisp gooseberry fruit is balanced by fair acidity giving the wine a ripe intensity on the palate.*	£6.00	SHG BD	B
UNDURRAGA CHARDONNAY RESERVA 1996, VIÑA UNDURRAGA Maipo	*Rich, intense aromas of citrus and wood, enhanced by a well-integrated palate.*	£6.60	DBY MWW IVY U WES AV	B
VALDIVIESO CHARDONNAY 1996, VALDIVIESO Lontue	*Youthful smoky, earthy aroma with dry, but nicely balanced, soft easy fruit on the palate.*	£6.90	DBY BI GGW FUL W	S
VILLARD RESERVE CHARDONNAY 1996, THIERRY VILLARD Casablanca	*Sweet toasted oak and honey nose. Firmly rounded fruit on the palate with good concentration and length.*	£7.00	DBY IVY GNW NEI POR NRW HVW OD	B
LA PALMA CHARDONNAY RESERVE 1996, VIÑA LA ROSA Rapel	*Lime and ripe fruit on a very upfront nose. Lightly oaked characters dominate a weighty yet subtle palate.*	£7.00	FUL HW	S
ERRAZURIZ ESTATES RESERVE CHARDONNAY 1996, ERRAZURIZ ESTATES Casablanca	*Ripe, fragrant fruit lingering on an oaky, concentrated palate. A long lasting, rich finish.*	£7.20	DBY TO CEB WMK HOU FUL WCR OD	B
CASABLANCA SANTA ISABEL CHARDONNAY 1996, VIÑA CASABLANCA Casablanca	*Lemon vanilla and grapefruit aromas on the nose. Peach and cream flavours on the palate.*	£7.20	NY MOR BOO HOU HVW OD	G

SANTA CAROLINA CHARDONNAY GRAN RESERVA 1996, SANTA CAROLINA Maipo	*Fresh, zesty fruit flavours, strongly integrated with toasted oak. Medium intensity on the long palate.*	**£7.50**	TH CST YWL WMK OD	(G)
CASABLANCA SANTA ISABEL SAUVIGNON BLANC 1996, VIÑA CASABLANCA Casablanca	*Deep yellow colour, with open grassy aromas and green fruits on the nose. Ripe forward palate and a creamy finish.*	**£7.70**	DBY MOR BOO WSO HVW OD	(B)
PEDRO GRAND CHARDONNAY 1996, DISCOVER WINES Colchagua	*Yeast characters with hints of floral fruit. Good acidity shows on this reasonably long wine.*	**£8.00**	BD	(B)
CASA LAPOSTOLLE CHARDONNAY CUVÉE ALEXANDRA 1996, CASA LAPOSTOLLE Rapel	*Rich golden colour. Ripe fruit and honey on the nose followed by well-rounded oak flavours.*	**£8.40**	DBY VLW FUL OD EP	(B)
MONTES ALPHA CHARDONNAY RESERVE 1995, DISCOVER WINES Curico	*Well integrated fruit and oak; rich, toasty and ripe. Great structure with well-balanced acidity.*	**£8.60**	Widely Available	(S)
CASABLANCA CHARDONNAY BARREL FERMENTED 1996, VIÑA CASABLANCA Casablanca	*Clean, new oak aroma on nose softens with butterscotch flavours on the creamy palate.*	**£8.70**	NY MOR HVW OD	(B)
CASABLANCA CHARDONNAY BARREL FERMENTED 1995, VIÑA CASABLANCA Casablanca	*Lemon and grapefruit aromas followed by ripe peaches and cream on the palate.*	**£8.80**	JS MOR BOO HVW EP	(B)
ERRAZURIZ ESTATES 'WILD FERMENT' CHARDONNAY 1996, ERRAZURIZ ESTATES Casablanca	*The palate shows good clean earthy fruit. A stylish soft mouthful, enhanced by balanced oak and acidity.*	**£9.00**	OD	(S)

SANTA CAROLINA CHARDONNAY RESERVA DE FAMILIA 1996, SANTA CAROLINA Maipo	*A delicate floral, blossomy nose followed by mouthwatering ripe, juicy fruit and subtle toasty oak palate.*	£9.40	YWL WMK OD	**B**

SOUTH AMERICA • CHILE • ROSÉ

SANTA DIGNA CABERNET SAUVIGNON ROSÉ 1996, MIGUEL TORRES Curico	*Rosé pink colour, fresh gooseberry, green pepper aromas carry over onto a grassy, spicy palate*	£5.00	Widely Available	**B**

SPAIN

Renowned for its traditional, oaky reds from Rioja, Spain is now producing delicious alternatives from Navarra, Somontano and Valdepeñas. Deeply-entrenched conservative attitudes to wine making are giving way to fresh, original ideas. Consequently winemakers are understanding the importance of individuality and flavour in their modern day style of winemaking.

SPAIN • RED

VILLARTA TEMPRANILLO VIÑO DE LA TIERRA 1996, JOHN WORONTSCHAK VILLARTA Manchuela	*Young and fruity this wine offers lively flavours of morello cherry, marzipan and vanilla.*	£3.30	VWC SMF	(B)
SAINSBURY'S LA MANCHA TEMPRANILLO 1996, VINICOLA DE CASTILLA La Mancha	*An easy drinking red with cherry fruit on the nose and a rich earthy palate.*	£3.50	JS	(B)
PERGOLA 1996, JOHN WORONTSCHAK VILLARTA Manchuela	*This wine offers lovely juicy fruit with a spicy palate of black cherries and vanilla oak.*	£3.50	SMF	(B)
PALACIO DE LEON 1994, BODEGAS VINOS DE LEON Leon	*Bright cherry and plum coloured followed by strawberry and black fruit on the round palate.*	£4.00	TH WCR	(B)
HERMANOS LURTON TEMPRANILLO CRIANZA VINO DE MESA 1994, J & F LURTON Castilla Y Leon	*Gamey, soft and rich. A concentrated wine with plummy fruit and new oak influence.*	£4.30	TH	(B)

AGAPITO JUMILLA RESERVA 1993, AGAPITO RICO Jumilla	*Sweet, ripe tobacco fruit on the nose with chocolate and toffee flavours. An intense finish!*	£4.50	JS	(B)
EL MESON NV, BODEGAS EL MESON Rioja	*Deep purple in colour with an appealing mature nose. Showing ripe strawberry fruit.*	£4.50	A	(B)
MARQUÉS DE GRIÑON DURIUS COLLECION PERSONAL VIÑO DE MESA 1994, BOD. BERBERANA Ribera Del Duero	*A rich, slightly spicy nose is followed by a palate of chocolate, ripe fruits and coconut.*	£4.50	NY FUL SMF	(B)
VISCONDE DE AYALA RIOJA RESERVA 1990, BODEGAS RIOJA SANTIAGO Rioja	*An oaky, leathery and traditional nose is followed by ripe cherry fruit on the palate.*	£5.00	HAE	(B)
AGRAMONT TEMPRANILLO 1995, BODEGAS PRINCIPE DE VIANA Navarra	*Well-balanced with great depth of red fruit on the palate and a spicy well rounded finish.*	£5.00	VWC TH BNK VLW L&S VN JOV OD	(B)
SANTARA CABERNET MERLOT 1995, CONCAVINS & HUGH RYMAN Conca De Barbera	*Raspberry aromas with hints of cedar and pine lead to light apple and blackcurrant flavours, tightly structured.*	£5.10	JS VLW FUL CWS	(B)
TORRES SANGRE DE TORO 1995, MIGUEL TORRES Penedes	*Light fruit on the nose is followed by a palate of spicy and cherry flavours.*	£5.40	Widely Available	(B)
TORRE DEMONTALBO 1996, BODEGAS AMEZOLA DE LA MORA Rioja	*A youthful wine, filled with blackberries and jammy aromas, all wrapped up in balanced, soft tannins.*	£5.50	TH WR BU	(B)

MARQUÉS DE GRIÑON RIOJA 1995 BODEGAS BERBERANA Rioja	*Vanilla oak on the nose is followed by well-balanced raspberry fruit and spicy flavours.*	£5.50	Widely Available	(B)
CASTILLO LABASTIDA OAK-AGED 1996, UNION COSECHEROS LABASTIDA Rioja	*Young, bright blackcurrant colours with rich plum, mulberry and new oak flavours on the palate.*	£5.60	BD	(B)
CAMPILLO CRIANZA 1993, BODEGAS CAMPILLO Rioja	*A pronounced smoky and toffee nose precedes a spicy, jammy palate with light tannins.*	£5.80	VWC DBY A PLB VW	(B)
EL PORTICO RIOJA 1994, BODEGAS PALACIO Rioja	*A light fruit nose with lovely oak and rich redcurrant flavours on the palate.*	£6.00	HVW OD	(B)
MARQUÉS DE CACERES RESERVA 1992, MARQUÉS DE CACERES Rioja	*Peppery fruit emerges from a simple start. This jammy wine keeps on improving in the mouth.*	£6.20	Widely Available	(B)
LAS TORRES MERLOT 1996, MIGUEL TORRES Penedes	*Sophisticated creamy, cherry nose, with young fruit on palate and a good tannic structure.*	£6.20	DIR GGW SWS ES ICL	(S)
RAIMAT MERLOT 1991, RAIMAT Costers del Ségre	*Age on rim, with deep plum aromas. Oak cedar notes, intense black fruit on a chewwy palate.*	£6.20	TH DBY PLB HVW TO	(S)
CAMPO VIEJO RESERVA 1992, BODEGAS Y BEBIDAS Rioja	*Opulent, full bodied and spicy this wine has pruney and ripe berry fruit flavours.*	£6.20	TH CLA CST POR A&A NRW SWS	(S)

GUELBENZU CRIANZA 1994, BODEGAS GUELBENZU Navarra	*Ruby colour wine offering a soft, well-rounded oaky palate of ripe brambley fruit.*	**£6.30**	Widely Available	**B**
GRAN SANGRE DE TORO RESERVA 1993, MIGUEL TORRES Penedes	*Berried aromas and jammy fruit join together with soft, smooth tannins to provide a lasting finish.*	**£6.40**	Widely Available	**B**
CONDE DE VALDEMAR CRIANZA 1994, MARTINEZ BUJANDA Rioja	*A big spicy and smoky wine with real generosity of creamy ripe red fruit.*	**£6.40**	Widely Available	**B**
COSME PALACIO Y HERMANOS TINTO 1995, BODEGAS PALACIO Rioja	*A pronounced jammy nose with concentrated ripe raspberry and cherry fruit on the palate.*	**£5.90**	W NIC OD	**S** WINE OF THE YEAR
CHATELDON RESERVE 'JUAN TETAS' 1993, BODEGAS PINORD Penedes	*Wine has brown rim indicating age. Nose; traditional cabernet cedar aromas with a stylish palate.*	**£6.50**	WCS	**G**
NAVAJAS RESERVA 1990, MANUEL MORENS Rioja	*Ruby in colour followed by mulberry, strawberry and old oak on a long, ripe palate.*	**£6.60**	MOR BOO HVW MRN	**B**
PALACIO DE LA VEGA MERLOT CRIANZA 1994, PALACIO DE LA VEGA Navarra	*New American oak dominates this wine with sweet ripe cherry fruit on the palate.*	**£6.70**	Widely Available	**B**
AÑARES RESERVA 1990, BODEGAS OLARRA Rioja	*Soft and creamy with exotic fruit aromas. Sweet vanilla oak flavours with underlying hints of leather.*	**£6.70**	VIL C&D	**B**

SPAIN • RED

ENATE CRIANZA 1994, VIÑEDOS Y CRIANZAS DEL ALTO ARAGÓN Somontano	*A stewed fruit nose is followed by a soft black cherry palate with hints of vanilla.*	£6.70	Widely Available	(S)
ESTOLA GRAN RESERVA 1985, BODEGAS AYUSO. La Mancha	*Deep ruby with hints of coconut nut and warm liquorice flavours on the finish.*	£6.80	PLB TBC	(B)
EVENTUM 1992, BODEGAS MAGAÑA Navarra	*Deep colour, stewed plum aromas with a cedary edge. Firm tannins with ripe fruit give good length.*	£7.10	BD C&D BBR	(S)
NAVAJAS RESERVA 1990, BODEGAS NAVAJAS Rioja	*Brick red orange with chocolate and strawberry flavours, gentle tannins and a vanilla finish.*	£7.50	MOR NY HVW MRN	(B)
COTO DE IMAZ GRAN RESERVA 1987, BODEGAS EL COTO DE IMAZ Rioja	*A slightly savoury nose is followed by herbal and strawberry flavours on the palate.*	£7.90	CKB GGW WCS EOO	(B)
HERENCIA LASANTA CRIANZA 1994, BODEGAS HERENCIA LASANTA Rioja	*Plummy and juicy this slightly oaky wine offers spice, cinnamon and ripe fruit flavours.*	£8.00	MOR	(B)
SANTARA CARBONELL CABERNET SAUVIGNON 1995, CONCAVINS & HUGH RYMAN Conca De Barbera	*A concentrated, tarry, cedary nose with intense dark forest fruit flavours and a spicy finish.*	£8.00	RYM	(B)
MARQUÉS DE RISCAL RESERVA 1993, MARQUÉS DE RISCAL Rioja	*Following a light nose the palate is full of soft oak and ripe black cherry fruit.*	£8.20	Widely Available	(B)

SOLAGUÉN RESERVA 1989, UNION DE COSECHEROS LABASTIDA Rioja	*Deep garnet in colour with mint aromas leading into a berried palate of sweet fruit.*	£8.70	BD	(S)
CAMPILLO RESERVA 1990, BODEGAS CAMPILLO Rioja	*This wine has jammy aromas with rich damson and spicy oak flavours to follow.*	£8.80	DBY PLB TBC	(B)
SENORIO DE NAVA RESERVA 1990, BODEGAS SENORIO DE NAVA Ribera del Duero	*Sweet, berry fruit aromas are balanced with fine tannins on a uplifting palate, showing good length.*	£9.00	FUL PEC	(B)
MARQUÉS DE GRIÑON RIOJA RESERVA 1990, BODEGAS BERBERANA Rioja	*A smoky nose is followed by a palate of blackberry fruit and relatively high tannins.*	£9.20	LNR NY FUL TH	(B)
MARQUÉS DE GRINON SYRAH VIÑO DE MESA 1995, BODEGAS BERBERANA Toledo	*A very fruity, well-balanced wine showing good length, weight, concentration and use of oak.*	£9.30	TH FUL A&A TO MWW W	(S)
MARQUÉS DE MURRIETA TINTO RESERVA 1992, DOMINIOS DE CREIXELL Rioja	*A rich damson fruit bouquet offers sweet berry fruit on the soft, creamy palate.*	£9.40	Widely Available	(B)
CHIVITE COLECCION 125 GRAN RESERVA 1990, BODEGAS JULIAN CHIVITE Navarra	*A mellow and mature wine with soft berry fruit on a well-balanced palate through to the finish.*	£9.40	XXBJC DBY DIR COK OD	(B)
BODEGAS BERBERANA GRAN RESERVA 1987, BODEGAS BERBERANA Rioja	*This is a stylish wine with an excellant balance of fruit and oak. Ready now.*	£9.60	DBY W MWW LNR WMK ALL A&A	(B)

Wine	Description	Price	Stockists	
CAMPO VIEJO GRAN RESERVA 1982, BODEGAS Y BEBIDAS Rioja	*Rich, ripe wine with a fresh fruit character exhibiting strawberry, minty and old oak flavours on the finish.*	£9.60	IVY HOU WCS	Ⓑ
PAGO DE CARRAOVEJAS 1995, PAGO DE CARRAOVEJAS Ribera Del Duero	*A delicious wine which is rich, soft and plummy with spicy red fruits on the palate.*	£9.90	VWC TH NY MOR POR EP	Ⓑ
BARON DE CHIREL RESERVA 1991, MARQUÉS DE RISCAL Rioja	*Soft vanilla oak on the nose precedes creamy redcurrant and stra berry fruit in the mouth.*	£10.00	MFS	Ⓑ
MILENIO RESERVA 1992, FAMILIA MARTINEZ BUJANDA Rioja	*Toffee aromas lead into a long lasting palate of cedar and plummy flavours on the finish .*	£10.00	BD	Ⓢ
VIÑA ARANA RESERVA 1989, LA RIOJA ALTA Rioja	*Glowing garnet in colour this wine has a rich gamey and ripe fruit palate.*	£10.60	Widely Available	Ⓢ
GUELBENZU EVO CRIANZA 1993, BODEGAS GUELBENZU Navarra	*Clean, lightly vegetal nose with a lofted palate of herbaceous, eucalyptus fruit. Dry tannic finish*	£10.70	DBY MWW MOR BOO HVW EP	Ⓑ
FAUSTINO I GRAN RESERVA 1988, FAUSTINO Rioja	*Mulberry ripe fruit with soft tannins make this wine long lasting and rich.*	£10.70	Widely Available	Ⓑ
CONDE DE VALDEMAR GRAN RESERVA 1990, MARTINEZ BUJANDA Rioja	*Medium brick red colour with liquorice aromas and long lasting spicy fruit flavours.*	£10.90	TH PAV DBY VEX JN WSC HVW	Ⓑ

MARQUÉS DE GRIÑON CABERNET SAUVIGNON VIÑO DE MESA 1995, BODEGAS BERBERANA Toledo	*Ripe berry fruit aromas with complex, sweet fruit and vanilla flavours on a lengthy palate.*	£10.90	TH FUL RBS A&A MWW W	(B)
CAMPILLO GRAN RESERVA 1988, BODEGAS CAMPILLO Rioja	*An intense liquorice nose is followed by a palate of mature red fruit and old oak.*	£11.00	DBY W PLB TO	(B)
VIÑA ARDANZA RESERVA 1989, LA RIOJA ALTA Rioja	*Glowing garnet in colour, this Spanish red wine offers concentrated cherry fruit on the palate.*	£11.10	Widely Available	(B)
VALDUERO RESERVA 1991, BODEGAS VALDUERO Ribera Del Duero	*A soft style of wine offering juicy, upfront red fruit and soft, long tannins on the finnish.*	£11.10	VLW L&S WOI BEN BEL GLY	(B)
MAURO 1994, BODEGAS MAURO Tubela De Duero	*A lovely soft spicy style of wine with juicy blackcurrant fruit on a long palate.*	£11.10	CES JN	(B)
JEAN LEON CABERNET SAUVIGNON RESERVA 1990, JEAN LEON Castilla Y Leon	*Deep mulberry colour with excellent blackcurrant nose and rich black berry palate with lovely length.*	£12.10	DBY DIR GGW HOL MRF PTR	(B)
MARTINEZ BUJANDA GARNACHA RESERVA 1990, MARTINEZ BUJANDA Rioja	*A jammy, garnet wine offering intense blackcurrant and vanilla flavours on a spicy palate.*	£12.10	TH VEX TP JN HVW	(B)
PESQUERA RESERVA 1993, ALESANDRO FERNANDEZ Ribera Del Duero	*The fresh perfumed fruit and relatively high tannins balance out perfectly in this juicy wine.*	£12.30	DIR JN WIN	(B)

MARTINEZ BUJANDA CABERNET SAUVIGNON GRAN RESERVA 1990, MARTINEZ BUJANDA Rioja	*Spicy and leathery aromas lead into a dark cherry, rich and well-balanced palate.*	£12.70	TH VEX WSC	**B**
ALDEANUEVA AZABACHE RIOJA CRIANZA 1994, ALDEANUEVA Rioja	*A full and fruity wine offering cherry characters on the palate and a warm finish.*	£13.00	MFS	**B**
LAGUNILLA GRAN RESERVA 1987, BODEGAS LAGUNILLA Rioja	*A chocolate and redcurrant nose with orange spice and dense plummy flavours on the palate at the finish.*	£15.00	J&B CDT BUD	**S**
RIOJA GRAN RESERVA 904 1987, LA RIOJA ALTA Rioja	*Sweet oaky aromas lead into juicy plum and black cherry flavours on the palate.*	£18.00	Widely Available	**B**
TORRES MAS LA PLANA 1994, MIGUEL TORRES Penedes	*Deep purple, blackcurrant and mint aromas. Full flavoured palate of fruit cake, with softening tannins.*	£18.20	Widely Available	**S**
TORRES MAS LA PLANA 1990, MIGUEL TORRES Penedes	*Light, oak and vegetal nose leads to a jammy fruit palate with good acidity and balancing tannins.*	£19.40	VIL DIR MM GGW SEL L&S	**B**
CLOS DE L'OBAC TINTO DE GUARDA 1994, COSTERS DEL SIURANA Cataluña	*A juicy, sweet nose leads into a palate of light black cherry and old oak.*	£26.80	DBY VLW L&S NI J&B GNW WIM	**B**

Pinpoint who sells the wine you wish to buy by turning to the stockist codes. If you know the name of the wine you want to buy, use the alphabetical index. If the price is your motivation, refer to the invaluable price guide index; red and white wines under £5, sparkling wines under £10 and champagne under £15. Happy hunting!

SPAIN • WHITE

GANDIA CASTILLO DE LIRIA MOSCATEL NV, GANDIA Valencia	*Pale golden appearance, clean, honeyed, grapey aromas with a sweet, lingering palate and good acidity*	£3.50	VWC KWI PLB CRS CWS COK BRP VW	**B**
RUEDA WHITE 1996, BODEGAS C D N Rueda	*Ripe gooseberry aromas carry over onto a youthful fruit dominated, lengthy palate with citrus notes.*	£3.50	KWI	**B**
REMONTE CHARDONNAY 1996, COOPERATIVA VINICOLA MURCHANTINA Navarra	*Youthful wine, with a stalky nose, precedes good oak and butter flavours on the palate.*	£5.00	VER	**B**
VIÑA CALERA SAUVIGNON BLANC 1996, MARQUÉS DE RISCAL Rueda	*Classic Sauvignon Blanc with a crisp, gooseberry nose and palate followed by a fresh finish.*	£5.00	TH BU WR	**B**
MARQUÉS DE RISCAL RUEDA 1996, MARQUÉS DE RISCAL Rueda	*Pale and clean this wine offers perfumed aromas and lemon freshness with a long finish.*	£5.50	MWW TP U HOU A&A SV A+A	**B**
ALBACORO VERDEJO CHARDONNAY 1996, MARQUÉS DE LA RISCAL Rueda	*A zesty, up front nose, leading to a well-structured palate, with a good fruit concentration.*	£5.50	CWS	**B**
VEGA SINDOA BARREL-FERMENTED CHARDONNAY 1996, BODEGAS NEKEAS Navarra	*This lightly oaked Chardonnay with a clean, fruity taste is highly recommended.*	£6.00	OD	**B**

MARQUÉS DE RISCAL SAUVIGNON 1996, MARQUÉS DE RISCAL Rueda	*An elegant Spanish wine with perfumed, slightly talc like aromas and a light, clean finish.*	£5.70	SV	**B**
TORRES GRAN VIÑA SOL 1996, MIGUEL TORRES Penedes	*Apple and pear abounds on the nose, with uplifting acidity and well-rounded, soft fruit.*	£6.00	Widely Available	**S**
VIÑO DEL VERO CHARDONNAY 1995, VIÑAS DEL VERO Somantano	*Aromas of butter and rich toasty oak balance well with good acidity and fleshy floral fruit on a forward palate.*	£6.10	VWC DBY TP GRT GNW CRS EOO OD	**B**
RAIMAT CHARDONNAY 1996, RAIMAT Costers del Segre	*Well put-together with firm, fresh fruit and crisp acidity; a good all-round wine.*	£6.20	MTL DBY A U	**S**
MARQUÉS DE ALELLA CHARDONNAY 1994, MARQUÉS DE ALELLA Alella	*Strong lemony sensation on the nose, with uplifting acidity and reasonable fruit.*	£6.70	DIR MOR	**B**
SANZ RUEDA SUPERIOR 1996, VIÑOS SANZ Rueda	*A clean and minerally nose produces a well-balanced wine with soft ripe fruit overtones.*	£7.00	TBC	**B**
ALBARIÑO CONDES DE ALBAREI "CLASSICO" JOVEN 1996, BODEGAS SALNESUR Galicia	*An appley nose leads into a crisp and mouth-watering wine, with a spicy finish on the zippy palate.*	£7.00	TH VEX CHF	**B**

Pinpoint who sells the wine you wish to buy by turning to the stockist codes. If you know the name of the wine you want to buy, use the alphabetical index. If the price is your motivation, refer to the invaluable price guide index; red and white wines under £5, sparkling wines under £10 and champagne under £15. Happy hunting!

LA VAL ALBARIÑO 1995, VIÑA LUDY Rias Baixas	*Lime in colour with light pear aromas and green fruit on the well-balanced palate.*	**£7.00**	CKB GGW CES	**B**
MIGUEL TORRES WALTRAUD 1996, MIGUEL TORRES Penedes	*Clean pale lemon nose. Honey and orange flavours on the palate combine with racy acidity on the finish.*	**£7.60**	DIR JEF	**B**
LAGAR DE CERVERA ALBARIÑO 1996, LAGAR DE FORNELOS Rias Baixas	*Herby aromas on a delicate nose are followed by an intense flavour of lemon on the palate*	**£7.70**	VWC VLW L&S RBS GNW VW J&B SEL	**B**
ALBARIÑO CONDES DE ALBAREI "CARBALLO GALEGO" 1995, BODEGAS SALNESUR Galicia	*Honey aromas with buttery ripe fruit and hints of cinnamon on the broad palate.*	**£7.80**	VEX	**G**
MARQUÉS DE ALELLA CHARDONNAY 1995, MARQUÉS DE ALELLA Alella	*Ripe melon and tropical fruit bouquet on a rich creamy, well-balanced palate.*	**£8.30**	DIR MOR EP	**B**
VIONTA ALBARIÑO RESERVA 1995, VILANOVA DE ARONSA Rias Baixas	*A silky nose with some grassiness precedes a creamy butterscotch palate with good weight.*	**£9.00**	Widely Available	**B**
ENATE BARREL-FERMENTED CHARDONNAY 1995, VINEDOS Y CRIANZAS DEL ALTO ARAGÓN Somontano	*This Chardonnay shows delicate pear and grape-fruit flavours, with good length and a clean finish.*	**£9.70**	DBY DIR HOU L&W	**B**
ALBARIÑO PAZO DE BARRANTES 1995, DOMINIOS DE CREIXELL Galicia	*A long juicy wine with ripe apple and honey flavours on a well-rounded palate.*	**£10.20**	MFS HOL PTR WFL EP BOO	**S**

BELONDRADE YENSE LURTON 1994, BRIGITTE LURTON Rueda	*Soft textured wine, that is well-balanced, smooth and packed with ripe, tropical flavours.*	**£10.50**	RAE W	(B)
TORRES MILMANDA 1995, MIGUEL TORRES Penedes	*Elegant tropical flavours, with subtle oak on the palate leading to a creamy finish.*	**£15.60**	Widely Available	(B)

SPARKLING

SAFEWAY CAVA BRUT NV, FREIXENET Penedes	*This shows an attractive lemony nose with hints of spice on a fresh zingy palate.*	**£5.30**	SAF	(S)
MALT HOUSE VINTNERS GRAN TROYA CAVA BRUT NV, San Sadurni	*Warm aromas of ripe fruit lead to a dry yeasty palate with a refresing citrus finish.*	**£5.50**	BNK	(B)
BONOVAL CAVA GRAN RESERVA BRUT 1991, BODEGAS INVIOSA Exremaura	*Ripe toasty flavours combine well with orange peel fruit in this well-made wine.*	**£6.00**	ADN	(B)
L'HEREU CAVA BRUT NV, JOSÉ MARIA RAVENTOS I BLANC Penedes	*Yeasty aromas lead to a ripe and rounded style of sparkling wine which lasts well in the mouth.*	**£6.70**	WAW PV	(B)
MARRUGAT CAVA GRAN RESERVA BRUT NV, BODEGAS PINORD Penedes	*Fresh and light with citrus characteristics coming through on the lemony, limey palate.*	**£6.90**	WCS	(B)

HEREDAD CAVA BRUT RESERVA NV SEGURA VIUDAS Penedes	*Clean, fresh fruit. Yeasty aromas with intense warm climate fruit on a pleasantly acidic, rich palate.*	**£11.50**	DIR HOF	**S**

WINE OF THE YEAR

FORTIFIED

MALT HOUSE VINTNERS GRAN CAPATAZ EQUILAZ AMONTILLADO, Jerez	*Appealing amontillado with rich hazelnuts, raisins and caramel. Soft and smooth with good underlying acidity.*	**£3.00**	MHV	**B**
TESCO SUPERIOR OLOROSO SECO, SANCHEZ ROMATE Jerez	*Ripe raisiny aromas. Smooth caramel and soft brown sugar flavours mixed with a rich nutty character.*	**£3.40**	TO	**B**
TESCO SUPERIOR MANZANILLA, SANCHEZ ROMATE Jerez	*Rich and zesty with an attractive salty tanginess. Very refreshing. Fine length on the finish.*	**£3.40**	TO	**S**
SOMERFIELD FINE OLD AMONTILLADO SHERRY, EMILIO LUSTAU Jerez	*Excellent aged style combining rich nuttiness and creamy vanilla with hints of honey and toffee.*	**£3.70**	SMF	**S**
CO-OP FINO SHERRY, LUIS CABALLERO Jerez	*Lovely nose of yeasty overtones which carries through to combine with wildly crisp acidity.*	**£4.00**	CWS	**B**
SOMERFIELD AMONTILLADO SHERRY, ESPINOSA DE LOS MONTEROS Jerez	*Stylish amontillado with dried fruits, roasted nuts and smooth caramel. Lovely creamy finish.*	**£4.40**	SMF	**S**

CABRERA AMONTILLADO, D G GORDON Jerez	*Rich concentration of dried fruit and smooth caramel. Complex, with great balance and richness.*	£4.40	WRT	(S)
TESCO SUPERIOR PALO CORTADO, SANCHEZ ROMATE Jerez	*Rare style with roasted nutty character balanced by rich creamy caramel. Lovely dried fruit finish.*	£4.50	TO	(B)
SAFEWAY FINO, GARCIA DE LEANIZ Jerez	*Fresh lively nose. Tangy salty fino character. Clean fresh slightly nutty fruit. Finely balanced.*	£4.70	SAF	(B)
SAFEWAY AMONTILLADO, GARCIA DE LEANIZ Jerez	*Creamy nutty nose with hints of dried apricots. Rewarding smooth caramel texture with plenty of appeal.*	£4.70	SAF	(B)
DOM RAMOS MANZANILLA, WISDOM & WARTER LTD. Jerez	*Fresh, tangy citrus fruit nose. Typical saltiness with a hint of nuts.*	£4.70	U	(B)
TESCO FINEST AMONTILLADO, SANCHEZ ROMATE Jerez	*Intense amontillado style. Quite fat and creamy with good walnut character and a sprinkling of brown sugar.*	£5.00	TO	(B)
TRES CANDIDAS PEDRO XIMÉNEZ, BODEGAS J FERRIS Jerez	*Intensely sweet packed palate full of soft toffee and treacle. Hints of dark chocolate and ground coffee.*	£5.20	STB	(B)
DOUBLE CENTURY OLOROSO SHERRY, PEDRO DOMECQ Jerez	*Packed full of rich nutty fruit balanced by good acidity. Good complexity, very well balanced.*	£5.20	TH PLB TO SMF VW SMF	(S)

LA CONCHA, GONZÁLEZ BYASS Jerez	*Smooth caramel poured over chopped nuts and sultanas. Rich and refined with good acidity to give balance.*	£5.50	Widely Available	(S)
PANDO FINO SHERRY, WILLIAMS & HUMBERT Jerez	*Fresh zippy fino style showing lovely clean tangy fruit. Very refreshing and uplifting.*	£5.90	W NY MM CST CES WWI CFT	(B)
MANZANILLA LA GOYA, DELGADO ZULETA Jerez	*Fresh, clean tangy nose. Typical salty palate with refreshing zesty character. Good length of flavour.*	£6.00	C&D CRM	(B)
TANNERS MARISCAL MANZANILLA, VINICOLA HIDALGO Jerez	*Typical manzanilla nose of salty sea air and bitter almonds. Fresh clean tangy style. Attractive clean finish.*	£6.20	TAN	(B)
HARVEYS BRISTOL CREAM, JOHN HARVEY Jerez	*Sweet orange peel aromas. Rich nuttiness and sweet raisins with a swirl of smooth caramel.*	£6.50	Widely Available	(B)
BARBADILLO SOLEAR MANZANILLA PASADA, ANTONIO BARBADILLO Jerez	*Stylish manzanilla with its characteristic tangy saltiness. Concentrated minerally palate length to the finish.*	£6.70	Widely Available	(B)
ALFONSO, GONZÁLEZ BYASS Jerez	*Intense, luscious ripe palate full of rich flavours; dark muscovado sugar, sultanas and figs. Classy and complex.*	£7.10	DBY MM VLW CST OD ODF	(G)
TIO PEPE GONZÁLEZ BYASS Jerez	*Clean salty nose. Fresh tangy style exhibiting good fino character. Very attractive floral and citrus fruit.*	£7.50	Widely Available	(B)

LUSTAU PUERTO FINO SOLERA RESERVA, EMILIO LUSTAU Jerez	*Clean tangy fresh nose. Light and refreshing on the palate with a soft finish. Appealing tangy character.*	**£8.20**	Widely Available	(B)
DOS CORTADOS SHERRY PALO CORTADO, WILLIAMS & HUMBERT Jerez	*Complex hedonistic mix of sweetmeats, crushed nuts, caramel and cream. Full of verve.*	**£8.40**	Widely Available	(G)
LUSTAU EAST INDIA SOLERA, EMILIO LUSTAU Jerez	*Dark and luscious, with raisins and demerara sugar giving fantastic length - goes on and on!*	**£9.50**	Widely Available	(B)
PEDRO XIMÉNEZ, CREAM OF CREAMS, MANUEL DE ARGUESO Jerez	*Sweet, enticing aromas lead to a wonderfully raisiny, creamy palate with hints of toasted hazlenuts.*	**£10.10**	Widely Available	(S)
MATUSALEM, GONZÁLEZ BYASS Jerez	*Fabulously rich with delightful dried fig, nuts and raisin flavours. Wonderful zesty acidity to balance.*	**£17.30**	Widely Available	(G)
APOSTOLES, GONZÁLEZ BYASS Jerez	*Intense raisiny fruit, rich nuttiness and soft caramel combine to make a rich and sensational wine.*	**£19.20**	Widely Available	(S)
NÖE, GONZÁLEZ BYASS Jerez	*Muscovado sugar, figs, raisins and a dash of smooth caramel combine to make a stunningly sexy sherry.*	**£20.60**	MM VLW OD ODF	(S)
SANDEMAN ROYAL CORREGIDOR RARE RICH OLOROSO, THE HOUSE OF SANDEMAN Jerez	*Lots of complexity with mouthfilling rich nutty and raisin flavours and hints of dark chocolate and coffee.*	**£43.00**	RBS	(G)

OTHER COUNTRIES

WIDENING THE CHOICE FOR THE CONSUMER, wines from Greece to Morocco have impressed this years tasters enhancing the history and diversity of Mediterranean Coastal regions as quality wine producing areas. Wine makers strive to maintain intrinsic local and national characteristics in a continuous pursuit of excellence; long may this continue allowing the consumer an even broader choice of wines!

CYPRUS

COMMANDARIA ST. JOHN, KEO WINERY Commandaria	*Delicate, nutty aromas with intense treacle and toffee fruit coming through on the palate.*	**£21.00**	DBY NEI SHJ CFT MCK	**B**

GREECE

MAVRODAPHNE OF PATRAS, KOURTAKIS Patras	*A complex nose with sweet raisin and damson fruit following through to the palate.*	**£3.90**	JS W KWI CST CRS MRN	**B**
PORFYROS 1996, BROTHERS SPIROPOULOS Peloponnese	*Velvety smooth, spicy nose and ripe tannins, leading to medium-long, warming finish.*	**£7.10**	GWC VR	**B**
MEGAS OENOS WHITE 1996, GEORGE SKOURAS Peloponnese	*A rich honeyed and floral nose with peachy overtones and good acidity on the finish.*	**£7.50**	GWC	**B**

RAPSANI TSANTALIS 1993, TSANTALIS Rapsani	*Rich, full-bodied red. Recognise by smoky bacon crisp on the nose leading to plenty of fruit on the aftertaste.*	£7.80	CRM	**B**
AMETHYSTOS RED 1995, DOMAINE CONSTANTIN LAZARIDI Drama	*Fresh berry fruits on the nose with hints of chocolate, rich round black fruit flavours.*	£8.00	GWC	**B**
HATZIMICHALIS CABERNET SAUVIGNON 1995, DOMAINE HATZIMICHALIS Opuntia Locris	*Deep colour, some age, earthy aromas, concentrated creamy forest fruits flavours, lengthy, balanced palate.*	£8.00	GWC	**S**
CHATEAU JULIA CHARDONNAY 1996, DOMAINE CONSTANTIN LAZARIDI Drama	*Peachy aromas develop into a well-rounded, full-bodied wine, with good maturation potential.*	£8.50	GWC	**B**
AMETHYSTOS FUMÉ 1996, DOMAINE CONSTANTIN LAZARIDI Drama	*Slightly closed nose gives way to a sensation of fruit and oak on a lively, well-balanced palate.*	£8.50	GWC	**S**
AMETHYTOS ROSÉ 1996, DOMAINE CONSTANTIN LAZARIDI Drama	*Great complexity of yeasty character, combining with outstanding fruit and flavour giving a weighty wine.*	£9.00	GWC	**B**
MAVRODAPHNE PATRAIKI RESERVE 1993, PATRAIKI CO-OPERATIVE Peloponnese	*Soft strong well-integrated fruit with complex tar notes and a good long finish.*	£9.90	GWC	**B**
HATZIMICHALIS KAPNIAS 1994, DOMAINE HATZIMICHALIS Opuntia Locris	*Ripe blackcurrant bouquet with oak highlights leads to deep fruity palate with a vanilla ending.*	£14.00	GWC	**B**

| **HATZIMICHALIS MERLOT 1995, DOMAINE HATZIMICHALIS** Atalanti Valley | *Deep herbaceous, plummy aromas are mirrored on the intense, fruity, palate of this softening wine.* | £15.50 | GWC | **B** |

ISRAEL

| **GOLAN CHARDONNAY 1994, GOLAN HEIGHTS WINERY** Galilee | *Huge aromas of flower blossom, honey, melons and pears on the nose which continue onto the rich palate.* | £5.99 | M&S | **S** |

MALTA

| **ANCHOR BAY ROSÉ NV, EMMANUEL DELICATA** | *Salmon pink colour, strawberry aromas with fresh, grapy flavours and refreshing acidity on the soft palate.* | £4.00 | CRS | **B** |

MEXICO

| **L A CETTO NEBBIOLO 1993, LOUIS CETTO** | *Rich aromas of cherries and tar carry over to a creamy, lingering palate.* | £7.90 | DBY DIR P TAN GNW VDV WOI | **B** |

Pinpoint who sells the wine you wish to buy by turning to the stockist codes. If you know the name of the wine you want to buy, use the alphabetical index. If the price is your motivation, refer to the invaluable price guide index; red and white wines under £5, sparkling wines under £10 and champagne under £15. Happy hunting!

MONTENEGRO

Monte Cheval Vranac 1993, Plantaze Zeta White Paul Valley	*Ripe citrus fruit aromas on a zingy lemon, lime palate balanced with floral notes.*	**£4.50**	MUK	**B**

MOROCCO

Domaine Cigogne 1996, Sincomar Parlier et Fermaud Berkane	*The palate shows smoky, blackberry fruit and firm, full oak with massive concentration.*	**£3.00**	VW	**S**

REDS • £5 AND UNDER

Claret Calvet NV, *Benoit & Valerie Calvet*	£ 3.00	B
Domaine Boyar Cabernet Sauvignon 1996, *Vinis Iambol*	£ 3.00	B
Domaine Boyar Cabernet Merlot Country Wine NV *Lovico*	£ 3.00	B
Dona Elena NV, *Benfica*	£ 3.00	B
Safeway Young Vatted Merlot 1996, *Vinprom Russe*	£ 3.00	B
Santa CarolinaTierra del Rey 1996, *Santa Carolina*	£ 3.00	B
Domaine Cigogne 1996, *Sincomar Parlier et Fermaud*	£ 3.00	S
Safeway Young Vatted Cabernet Sauvignon 1996, *Vini sliven*	£ 3.00	S
Malt House Vintners Romanian Merlot 1995, *Tohani*	£ 3.20	B
Ramada 1995, *Adega Co-op Torres Vedras*	£ 3.20	B
Safeway Cotes de Lubéron 1995, *Cellier de Marrenon*	£ 3.30	B
Tempranillo Vino de la Tierra 1996, *John Worontschak Villarta*	£ 3.30	B
Cabernet Sauvignon VDP 1996, *Val d'Orbieu*	£ 3.40	B
Folonvie Cabernet Merlot 1996, *Yvon Mau*	£ 3.40	B
Somerfield Merlot VDP NV, *Jeanjean*	£ 3.40	B
Estemadura Red 1994, *Adega Co-op de Sao Mamede da Ventosa*	£ 3.40	B
Dos Santos Vino de la Tierra 1996, *John Worontschak Villarta*	£ 3.50	B
Shiraz Cabernet 1995, *Bordegas Santiago De Graffigna*	£ 3.50	B
J.P. Red Vinho de Mesa NV, *J.P. Vinhos*	£ 3.50	B
Sainsbury's La Mancha Tempranillo 1996, *Vinicola de Castilla*	£ 3.50	B
Copertino 1992, *F Colucci*	£ 3.60	B
Malt House Vintners Côtes du Roussillon NV,	£ 3.60	B
J.P. Barrel Selection Vinho Regional 1991, *J.P. Vinhos*	£ 3.60	S
Balbi Vineyard Syrah Malbec 1996, *Allied Domecq*	£ 3.70	B
BVC Yantra Valley Cabernet Sauvignon Controliran 1992, *Vinprom Rousse*	£ 3.70	B
Fortant de France Grenache Rouge VDP 1996, *Skalli*	£ 3.70	B
Somerfield Douro Red 1994, *Real Companhia Vinicola*	£ 3.70	B
Tesco Cabernet Sauvignon Reserve 1996, *Frederic Roger*	£ 3.70	B
Bright Brothers Cabernet Malbec 1996, *Peñaflor*	£ 3.70	S
Bellefontaine Merlot 1996, *Paul Boutinot*	£ 3.80	B
Idlerock Merlot Reserve 1996, *The Hanwood Group*	£ 3.80	B
Idlerock Pinot Noir Reserve 1996, *The Hanwood Group*	£ 3.80	B
Claret J Calvet 1996, *J Calvet*	£ 3.90	B
Malt House Vintners Chianti 1996, *Piccini*	£ 3.90	B

Mavrodaphne Of Patras Nv, *Kourtakis*	£ 3.90	B
Braunstein Blaufrankisch 1993, *Paul & Maria Braunstein*	£ 3.90	B
BVC Cabernet Sauvignon Reserve 1991, *Vini sliven*	£ 4.00	B
Château Villespassans 1995, *Les Grands Vins du Saint Chinian*	£ 4.00	B
Domaine de la Commanderie de St Jean VDP 1996, *Château de Grezan*	£ 4.00	B
Douro Tinto 1995, *Sociedade dos Vinhos Borges*	£ 4.00	B
Malt House Vintners Beaujolais Villages 1995, *Henri La Fontaine*	£ 4.00	B
Jose Neiva 1995, *Adela Co-op De Sao Mamede Da Ventosa*	£ 4.00	B
Kanarie Creek Cabernet Shiraz NV, *Angoves Pty. Ltd.*	£ 4.00	B
Kingston Print Shiraz Mataro 1996, *Kingston Estate*	£ 4.00	B
La Palma Cabernet Sauvignon 1996, *Vina la Rola*	£ 4.00	B
Lello Reserva Sociedade dos Vinhos Borges 1995, *Sociedade dos Vinhos Borges*	£ 4.00	B
Malt House Vintners Chilean Merlot 1996, *Vina Carta Vieja*	£ 4.00	B
Nero d'avola Zagara Di Sicilia 1996, *Kym Milne*	£ 4.00	B
Palacio de Leon 1994, *Bodegas Vinos de Leon*	£ 4.00	B
Safeway Chianti 1995, *Rocca Delle Macie*	£ 4.00	B
Vicuna Peak Malbec Tempranilla 1996, *Bodegas Santa Ana*	£ 4.00	B
Beaujolais Villages 1996, *Barton & Guestier*	£ 4.00	S
La Palma Merlot 1996, *Vina la Rosa*	£ 4.00	S
Nanya Estate Malbec Ruby Cabernet 1996, *Angove's Pty. Ltd.*	£ 4.00	S
Gemini Merlot VDP 1996, *Yves Pages*	£ 4.10	B
La Palma Merlot 1996, *Vina la Rosa*	£ 4.10	S
Spar Chilean Merlot 1996, *Canepa*	£ 4.20	B
Vila Regia 1995, *Sogrape*	£ 4.20	B
Espiga 1996, *Quinta da Boavista*	£ 4.20	S
Foral Douro Reserva 1995, *Caves Alianca*	£ 4.30	B
Hermanos Lurton Tempranillo Crianza 1994, *J & F Lurton*	£ 4.30	B
Simonsvlei Shiraz Reserve 1996, *Simonsvlei*	£ 4.30	B
Tesco Australian Shiraz Cabernet	£ 4.30	B
BVC Gorchivka Cabernet Sauvignon Estate Selection 1993, *Vinprom Svischtov*	£ 4.30	S
Tesco Paarl Cabernet Sauvignon, *Paul & Hugo de Villiers*	£ 4.30	S
Andes Peaks Merlot 1996, *Vina Santa Emiliana*	£ 4.40	B
Foral Douro Reserva 1996, *Caves Alianca*	£ 4.40	B
Valdivieso Cabernet Sauvignon 1996, *Valdivieso*	£ 4.40	B
Jumilla Reserva 1993, *Agapito Rico*	£ 4.50	B
BVC Twin Peaks Cabernet Sauvignon 1991, *Vinprom Rousse*	£ 4.50	B
Co-op Australian Cabernet Sauvignon 1995, *Angoves Pty. Ltd.*	£ 4.50	B
Domaine du Rivage Merlot Cuxac VDP 1996, *Val D'Orbieu*	£ 4.50	B
Domaine de Devois 1995, *Les Vignerons de Roueire*	£ 4.50	B
El Meson Cvc NV, *Bodegas El Meson*	£ 4.50	B
Les Arbousiers Cabernet Sauvignon 1995, *Les Arbousiers*	£ 4.50	B

Marques de Grinon Durius Collecion		
Personal Vino de Mesa 1994, *Bodegas Berberana*	£ 4.50	B
Monte Cheval Vranac 1993, *Plantaze*	£ 4.50	B
Pepperwood Grove Cabernet Franc 1995, *Pepperwood Grove*	£ 4.50	B
Primitivo del Salento Cantele Le Trulle 1996, *Kym Milne*	£ 4.50	B
Soltero Rosso Vino da Tavola 1993, *Settesoli*	£ 4.50	B
Syrah 1995, *Pascual Toso S.a.*	£ 4.50	B
Four Rivers Cabernet Sauvignon 1995, *Vina Gracia*	£ 4.50	S
Château Caville 1995, *Alain Vaurigaud*	£ 4.60	B
Gato Negro 1995, *Vina San Pedro*	£ 4.60	B
Montepulciano d'Abruzzo 1995, *Umani Ronchi*	£ 4.60	B
Caliterra Cabernet Sauvignon 1995, *Caliterra*	£ 4.70	B
Sutter Home Cabernet Sauvignon 1994, *Sutter Home*	£ 4.70	B
Valdivieso Merlot 1996, *Valdivieso*	£ 4.70	B
Adega Co-op Comenda Santiago Regional 1995, *Adega Co-op De Arruda dos Vinhos*	£ 4.80	B
Chateau Helene Cuvee Penelope 1993, *Marie-Helene Gau*	£ 4.80	B
Kingston Estate Jarrah Ridge Shiraz Mataro 1995, *Kingston Estate*	£ 4.80	B
Rivers Meet Merlot Cabernet 1996, *Ginestet*	£ 4.80	B
Etchart Cabernet Sauvignon 1995, *Arnaldo Etchart*	£ 4.80	G
Domaine Oriental Cabernet Sauvignon 1996, *Agricola Salve*	£ 4.90	B
L A Cetto Cabernet Sauvignon 1994, *Luis Cetto*	£ 4.90	B
Sahateni Vineyards Barrel Matured Merlot Special Reserve 1994, *Vinexport Sahateni*	£ 4.90	B
Bardolino Chiaretto Classico La Sorte 1996, *Negrar*	£ 5.00	B
Agramont Tempranillo 1995, *Bodegas Principe de Viana*	£ 5.00	B
Visconde de Ayala Rioja Reserva 1990, *Bodegas Rioja Santiago*	£ 5.00	B
Gamay 1996, *Cave du Haut Poitou*	£ 5.00	B
Château Saint Galier St Emilion Grand Cru 1995, *Ginestet*	£ 5.00	B
Correas Cabernet Sauvignon 1996, *Viños Correas*	£ 5.00	B
Villanyi Cabernet Sauvignon Barrique 1995, *Domaine Tiffan's*	£ 5.00	B
Galet Vineyards Syrah Reserve VDP 1996, *Gabriel Meffre*	£ 5.00	B
James Herrick Cuvee Simone 1995, *James Herrick*	£ 5.00	B
Kym Milne Rosenview Cabernet Sauvignon 1996, *Kym Milne*	£ 5.00	B
La Palma Cabernet Merlot Reserve 1996, *Vina la Rosa*	£ 5.00	B
Malbec Oak Reserve 1994, *La Agricole*	£ 5.00	B
Neil Joubert Cabernet Sauvignon 1996, *Neil Joubert*	£ 5.00	B
Rowan Brook Cabernet Merlot 1995, *Vinicola las Taquas*	£ 5.00	B
Santa Julia Alamos Ridge Malbec 1994, *Bodegas Esmeralda*	£ 5.00	B
Santa Julia Cabernet Sauvignon Oak Reserve 1994, *La Agricola*	£ 5.00	B
St Micheal Beaujolais 1996, *Paul Sapin*	£ 5.00	B
Vina Bisquertt Vineyards Merlot 1995, *Bisquertt Vineyards*	£ 5.00	B

Viña Carta Antiguas Selection Cabernet Sauvignon 1995, *Viña Carta Vieja*	£ 5.00	B
Viña Gracia Cabernet Premium 1994, *Vina Gracia*	£ 5.00	B
Vinfruco Oak Village Pinotage Merlot 1996, *Vinfruco*	£ 5.00	B
Viu Manent Cabernet Sauvignon Reserve 1993, *Viu Manent*	£ 5.00	B
Yvecourt Premium 1995, *Yvon Mau*	£ 5.00	B
Casa Leona Cabernet Sauvignon Reserve 1995, *Vina Peumo*	£ 5.00	S
Casa Leona Merlot Reserve 1996, *Vina Peumo*	£ 5.00	S
Dr. Abbott's Shiraz 1996, *St Auriol.*	£ 5.00	S
Rowan Brook Cabernet Sauvignon 1994, *Vinicola las Taquas*	£ 5.00	S
Rozzano 1995, *Villa Pigna*	£ 5.00	S
Stockmans Bridge Cabernet Shiraz 1995, *Southcorp Wines*	£ 5.00	S
Viu Manent Cabernet Sauvignon Reserve 1994, *Viu Manent*	£ 5.00	S

WHITES • £5 AND UNDER

Asda Muscadet 1996, *Baud*	£ 3.00	B
Cascade Bordeaux Sauvignon 1996, *Yves Pages*	£ 3.00	B
Alvarinho 1996, *Adega Cooperatina De Moncao*	£ 3.20	B
Pinot Grigio 1996, *Nagyrede Winery*	£ 3.20	B
Spar Hungarian Country Danube White NV, *Interconsult*	£ 3.20	B
Skylark Hill Chardonnay VDP 1996, *Viennet*	£ 3.40	B
Gandia Castillo de Liria Moscatel NV, *Gandia S.a.*	£ 3.50	B
Matra Mountain Oaked Chardonnay 1996, *Nagyrede*	£ 3.50	B
Murfatlar Chardonnay 1996, *Vie Vin Murfatlar SA*	£ 3.50	B
Rueda White 1996, *Bodegas Bodegas C D N*	£ 3.50	B
Safeway Soave 1996, *Fabiano*	£ 3.50	B
Waitrose Bordeaux Sauvignon Blanc 1996, *J Calvet*	£ 3.50	B
Pinot Gris Oaked Reserve 1996, *Nagyrede Winery*	£ 3.50	S
River Route Pinot Grigio 1996, *Carl Reb*	£ 3.50	S
Lakeside Oaked Chardonnay 1996, *Balatonboglar Winery*	£ 3.60	B
Terret J & F Lurton VDP 1996, *J & F Lurton*	£ 3.60	B
Malt House Vintners Scenic Ridge Australian White NV, *Redello Wines*	£ 3.70	B
Soave Classico La Sorte 1996, *Negrar*	£ 3.70	B
Table Bay Early Release Chenin Blanc 1997, *Kym Milne At Welmoed Co-op*	£ 3.70	B
The Gyöngyös Estate Chardonnay 1996, *Danubiana Bt*	£ 3.70	B
Jarrah Ridge Dry White 1996, *Kingston Estate*	£ 3.90	B
Sauvignon Blanc BRL Hardy Wine Company 1996, *BRL Hardy Wine Company*	£ 3.90	B
St Ursula Riesling Auslese 1993, *St Ursula Weinkekker G M B H*	£ 3.90	B
Gaillac Blanc 1996, *BRL Hardy Wine Company*	£ 3.90	S
Château Pierrousselle 1996, *Ginestet*	£ 4.00	B
Domaine du Grand Mayne 1996, *Andrew Gordon*	£ 4.00	B
Fontanario de Pegoes White Vqprd 1996, *Santo Isidro De Pegoes*	£ 4.00	B
Mainzer Donnherr Spätlese 1995, *Obermeister*	£ 4.00	B
Malt House Vintners Bergerac Dry 1996, *Les Caves St Germain*	£ 4.00	B
Sauvignon Blanc 1996, *J Calvet*	£ 4.00	B
Somerfield Chilean Chardonnay 1996, *Vina La Rosa*	£ 4.00	B
Terroir Club Chardonnay VDP 1996, *Terroir Club*	£ 4.00	B
Tesco Muscadet Sur Lie 1996,	£ 4.00	B

The Gyöngyös Estate Barrel Fermented Chardonnay 1996, *Danubiana Bt Bonyhad*	£ 4.00	B
Vin de Pays Blanc 1996, *Jacques Veritier*	£ 4.00	B
Casa Leona Chardonnay 1996, *Vina Peumo*	£ 4.00	S
Terroir Club Sauvignon VDP 1996, *Terroir Club*	£ 4.00	S
Gemini Sauvignon Blanc 1996, *Yves Pages et Associes*	£ 4.10	B
St Mont d'Andre Daguin 1996, *Producteurs de Plaimont*	£ 4.10	B
Domaine de Maubet 1996, *Domaine de Maubet*	£ 4.30	B
Fiuza Chardonnay Vinho Regional 1996, *Fiuza Bright*	£ 4.30	B
La Palma Chardonnay 1996, *Vina La Rosa*	£ 4.30	B
Viognier des Caves St Pierre VDP 1996, *Caves Saint Pierre*	£ 4.30	B
Andes Peaks Sauvignon Blanc 1996, *Vina Santa Emiliana*	£ 4.40	B
Early Release Chenin Blanc 1997, *Kym Milne At Bottelary Co-op*	£ 4.40	B
Torreon de Paredes Sauvignon Blanc 1996, *Torreon de Paredes*	£ 4.40	B
Domaine Salices Sauvignon VDP 1996, *J & F Lurton*	£ 4.40	S
Undurraga Gewurztraminer 1996, *Vina Undurraga*	£ 4.50	B
Chais Cuxac Val d'Orbieu 1996, *Val d'Orbieu*	£ 4.70	B
Jacob's Creek Semillon Chardonnay 1996, *Orlando Wyndham Group*	£ 4.70	B
Cawarra Unoaked Chardonnay 1996, *Lindemans*	£ 4.70	B
Laperouse Vin de Pays d'Oc Blanc 1995, *Penval*	£ 4.80	B
Sacred Hill Semillon Chardonnay 1996, *De Bortoli Wines*	£ 4.80	B
Sauvignon Blanc de Martino 1997, *Santa Ines*	£ 4.80	B
Casa Lapostolle Sauvignon Blanc 1996, *Casa Lapostolle Sa*	£ 4.90	B
Domaine de Farelles 1996, *Les Vignerons De Ceressou*	£ 4.90	B
Kirchheimer Schwarzerde BA 1994, *Zimmermann Graeff*	£ 4.90	B
Tanners Sauvignon Blanc 1995 *J & F Lurton*	£ 4.90	B
Waterside White 1996, *Graham Beck Madeba*	£ 4.90	S
Azure Bay Sauvignon Blanc Semillon 1996, *Montana Wines Ltd.*	£ 5.00	B
Carta Vieja Antiguas Selection Chardonnay 1996, *Vina Carta Vieja*	£ 5.00	B
Pinot Blanc 1996, *Cave Ingersheim, Jean Geiler*	£ 5.00	B
Cuckoo Hill Viognier 1996, *Nick Butler*	£ 5.00	B
Domaine de la Baume Philippe de Baudin Sauvignon Blanc 1996, *BRL Hardy Wine Company*	£ 5.00	B
Lamberhurst Millennium Sauvignon 1996, *Yvon Mau*	£ 5.00	B
Pioneers Raisined Muscat Bin 168 1996, *Miranda Wines*	£ 5.00	B
Quinta de Azevedo 1996, *Sogrape Sa*	£ 5.00	B
Remonte Chardonnay 1996, *Cooperativa Vinicola Murchantina*	£ 5.00	B

Salice Salentino 1996, *Cantele Le Trulle & Kym Milne*	£ 5.00	B
Saumur Château de Montgueret 1996, *Lacheteau*	£ 5.00	B
Soave Classico Colombara 1996, *Sergio Zenato*	£ 5.00	B
Tesco New Zealand Chardonnay,	£ 5.00	B
Two Rivers Sauvignon Semillon J Calvet 1996, *J Calvet*	£ 5.00	B
Vina Calera Sauvignon Blanc 1996, *Marques De La Riscal*	£ 5.00	B
Viu Manent Chardonnay 1996, *Viu Manent*	£ 5.00	B
Waitrose Mönchhof QBA 1988, *Robert Eymael*	£ 5.00	B
Pinot Blanc Rotenberg 1995, *Bernard Staeble*	£ 5.00	S
La Domeque Tête de Cuvée Vieilles Vignes 1996, *Frederic Roger Sdva*	£ 5.00	S
Tenterden Estate Dry NV, *Tenterden Vineyard*	£ 5.00	S
Yvon Mau Sauvignon Gris 1996, *Yvon Mau*	£ 5.00	S

SPARKLING • £10 AND UNDER

Somerfield Chardonnay Brut NV, *Caves de Landiras*	£ 5.00	B
Safeway Cava Brut NV, *Freixenet*	£ 5.30	S
Malt House Vintners Gran Troya Cava NV, *St Sadurni*	£ 5.50	B
Prosecco Spumante La Marca 1996, *La Marca*	£ 5.50	B
Seppelt Great Western Brut Rosé NV, *Seppelt*	£ 5.60	B
Franschhoek Vineyards Coop La Cotte Sparkling Demi Sec 1996, *Franschhoek Vineyards Coop*	£ 5.80	B
Sorevi Sparkling Chardonnay NV, *Sorevi*	£ 5.80	S
Bonoval Brut Gran Reserva 1991, *Bodegas Inviosa*	£ 6.00	B
La Cotte Sparkling Sauvignon Blanc Brut 1996, *Franschhoek Vineyards Coop*	£ 6.00	B
Deakin Estate Brut NV, *Wingara Wine*	£ 6.40	B
Seaview Brut Rosé NV, *Southcorp Wines*	£ 6.50	B
Angas Brut NV, *Yalumba Winery*	£ 6.60	B
Raventos I Blanc L'hereu NV, *Jose Maria Raventos I Blanc*	£ 6.70	B
Marrugat Gran Brut Reserve NV, *Juan Tetas Bodegas Pinord*	£ 6.90	B
Tesco Robertson Sparkling , *John Worontchak*	£ 7.00	S
Somerfield Cremant de Bourgogne 1991, *Caves de Bailly*	£ 7.20	B
Domaine Collin Blanquette de Limoux NV, *Philippe Collin*	£ 8.00	B
Codorniu Napa Brut NV, *Codorniu Napa*	£ 8.10	B
Seppelt Pinot Noir Chardonnay 1991, *Seppelt*	£ 8.20	B
Seaview Pinot Noir Chardonnay 1994, *Southcorp Wines*	£ 8.40	B
Hardy's Sparkling Pinot Noir Chardonnay NV, *BRL Hardy Wine Company*	£ 8.70	B
Yalumba Cuvée One Pinot Noir Chardonnay NV, *Yalumba*	£ 8.70	B
Yalumba Cuvée Two Sparkling Cabernet NV, *Yalumba*	£ 8.70	B
Seaview Edwards & Chaffey Pinot Noir Chardonnay 1993, *Southcorp Wines*	£ 8.80	B
Graham Beck Brut Blanc de Blanc 1991, *Graham Beck*	£ 9.00	B
Cremant d'Alsace Cuvée Prestige NV, *René Mure*	£ 9.10	B
Gratien & Meyer Cuvée Flamme NV, *Gratien & Meyer*	£ 9.20	B
Lindauer Special Reserve NV, *Montana Wines Ltd.*	£ 9.20	B
Mumm Cuvée Napa Brut NV, *Mumm Napa Valley Winery*	£ 9.20	B
Scharffenberger Brut NV, *Scharffenberger Cellars*	£ 9.50	B
Seppelt Sparkling Shiraz 1993, *Seppelt*	£ 9.50	S
Cuvée du President 1991, *Cave du Sieur d'Arques*	£ 9.80	B
Longridge Brut 1993, *Longridge*	£ 9.90	S
Seaview Edwards & Chaffey Pinot Noir Chardonnay 1992, *Southcorp Wines*	£ 10.00	B

CHAMPAGNE • £15 AND UNDER

Malt House Vintners Champagne Paul Langier Brut NV, *F. Bonnet*	£ 11.00	B
Champagne Paul Herard Demi-Sec NV, *Paul Herard*	£ 11.40	B
Champagne F. Bonnet Brossault Rosé NV, *F. Bonnet*	£ 12.00	B
Champagne Duval Leroy Fleur de Champagne Brut NV, *Duval Leroy Champagne*	£ 12.60	B
Champagne Drappier Cuvée Special Brut 1990, *Michel Drappier*	£ 13.00	B
Malt House Vintners Champagne Paul Langier Rose NV, *F. Bonnet*	£ 13.00	B
Tesco Champagne Brut NV	£ 13.00	B
Champagne Jean Moutardier Carte d'Or Brut NV, *J. Saxby*	£ 13.70	B
Safeway Champagne Albert Etienne Brut Rosé NV, *Albert Etienne*	£ 14.00	B
Tesco Blancs de Blancs Champagne Brut NV,	£ 14.00	B
Champagne Chartogne Taillet Brut NV, *Chartogne Taillet*	£ 14.90	B
Champagne Bauget-Jouëtte Carte Blanche Brut NV, *Bauget-Jouette*	£ 15.00	B
Champagne H Blin et Cie Brut Tradition NV, *H Blin*	£ 15.00	B
Champagne Patrick Arnold Brut Reserve Grand Cru NV, *Patrick Arnold*	£ 15.00	B
Champagne Albert Etienne Brut Millesime 1991, *Lanson Pere Et Fils*	£ 15.00	B

STOCKISTS

Every wine in this guide has at least one stockist code beside its entry, identifying where the wine can be sourced. The list below translates the code into the company name, with a telephone number for you to make enquiries direct.

Where the stockists are stated as WIDELY AVAILABLE there are more than 10 outlets who stock this wine. In these cases you should be able to find your wine in most good wine retailers.

Every effort has been made to list all the stockists with their relevant wines. Should you encounter any problems with finding a wine listed in this guide, then please write to: The International WINE Challenge, Publishing House, 652 Victoria Road, South Ruislip, Middlesex, HA4 0SX.

3D	3D Wines	01205 820745
A	Asda Stores Ltd	0113 2418545
A&A	A&A Wines	01483 274666
A&N	Army & Navy	0171 8341234
ABB	Abbey Cellars	01460 77966
ABY	Anthony Byrne Wine Agencies	01487 814555
AD	Andrew Darwin	01544 230534
ADN	Adnams Wine Merchants	01502 727 222
ALD	Allders International	01703 644599
ALE	Alexander Wines	0141 8820039
ALI	Alivini Company Ltd	0181 880 2525
ALL	Alliance Wine Company Ltd	01505 506060
ALZ	Allez Vins!	0385 264445
AMA	Amathus Wines Ltd	0181 8863787
AMW	Amey's Wines	01787 377144
AP	Arthur Purchase	01243 783144
AR	Arthur Rackham	01483 458 700
ARL	Auriol Wines	01252 843190
AUC	The Australian Wine Club	0800 8562004
AV	Averys of Bristol	01275 811 100
AWS	Albion Wine Shippers	0171 404 4554
B&B	Bottle & Basket	0181 3417018
BAB	Bablake Wines	01203 228272
BAL	Ballantynes of Cowbridge	01446 774840
BBO	Barrels & Bottles	0114 2769666
BBR	Berry Bros & Rudd	0171 396 9600
BBU	Bruce Burlington	01268 562224
BBV	Breaky Bottom Vineyard	01273 476 427
BC	Booker Belmont Wholesale Ltd. (formerly Cash & Carry)	01933 371 000
BCL	Best Cellars	01364 652546
BCW	Brian Coad Fine Wines	01752 896545
BD	Direct Wines (Windsor) Ltd	01734 481711
BDT	Benedict's	01983 529596
BEL	Bentalls	0181 5461001

BEN	Bennetts	01386 840392
BFW	Bellefrance Wines Ltd	0171 706 3462
BI	Bibendum Wine Ltd	0171 722 5577
BIL	Billecart-Salmon (UK) Ltd	
		01932 840515
BKI	Barber Kingsland	0161 775 8431
BKT	Bucktrout	01481 724444
BKW	Berkeley Wines (Cheshire)	
		01925 444555
BLS	Balls Bros	0171 739 6466
BNK	Bottleneck (Broadstairs)	01843 861095
BOL	Bacchus of Olney	01234 711140
BOO	Booths of Stockport	0161 4323309
BSN	Benson Fine Wines	0181 673 4439
BTH	Booths of Preston	01772 251701
BU	Bottoms Up	01707 328244
BUD	International Brands Ltd	01892 723 096
BUT	The Butlers Wine Cellar	01273 698724
BWC	Berkmann Wine Cellars	
		0171 609 4711
C&B	Corney & Barrow	0171 2514051
C&D	C & D Wines Limited	0181 650 9095
C&H	Cairns & Hickey	0113 2673746
C&W	Carley & Webb Limited	
CAG	Castiglione Wine Marchants	
		01344 24849
CAN	Canandaigua Wine Co.	0181 296 1868
CAP	Cape Province Wines	01784 451860
CAR	C A Rookes	01789 297777
CC	Chiswick Cellars	0181 9947989
CCC	Cave Cru Classé Ltd	0171 378 8579
CCL	Cockburn & Co	0181 8740142/3
CDE	Cote d'Or	0181 9980144
CDM	Caves de la Madeleine	0171 736 6145
CDO	Chapel Wines Limited	01580 763033
CDT	Cellars Direct	0171 378 1109
CEB	Croque-en-Bouche	01684 565612
CEL	Cellar 5	01925 444555
CEN	Centurion Vintners	01453 763223
CER	Cellar 28	01484 717 914

CES	Cellar Select Limited/Winefinds	
		01722 716100
CFN	Carringtons Fine Wines	0161 446 2546
CFT	The Clifton Cellars	0117 9730287
CHF	Chippendale Fine Wines	01943 850633
CHH	Charles Hennings	01798 872485
CKB	Cockburn & Campbell	0181 875 7007
CLA	Classic Wines and Spirits Ltd	
		01244 288444
CLD	Caledonian Wines	01228 43172
CLR	Castle Growers Limited	01633 250515
CMI	Charles Mitchell Wines Ltd	
		0161 7751626
CNL	Connolly's	0121 2369269
COC	Corks of Cotham	0117 9731620
COE	Coe of Ilford	0181 551 4966
COK	Corkscrew Wines	01228 43033
CPW	Christopher Piper Wines Ltd	
		01404 814139
CRM	Craven's Wine Merchants	
		0171 723 0252
CRS	Cooperative Retail Services	
		01706 713000
CST	The County Stores (Somerset) Ltd	
		01823 272235
CTH	Charterhouse Wine Company	
		01775 630680
CTL	Continental Wine & Food	
		01484 538333
CVR	Celtic Vintner	01633 430055
CWI	A Case of Wine	01558 650671
CWS	CWS Limited	0161 827 5353
D	Davisons	0181 6813222
D&D	D&D Wines Limited	01565 650954
D&F	D&F Wine Shippers Ltd	0181 838 4399
DAV	Dartmouth Vintners	01803 832602
DBS	Denbies Wine Estate	01306 876616
DBY	D Byrne & Co	01200 423152
DIO	Dionysus	0181 8742739
DIR	Direct Wine Shipments	01232 238700

DLA	Daniel Lambert Wine Agenices	01222 666128
E&B	E&B Wines	01732 355 988
EBA	Ben Ellis Wines	01737 842160
EDC	Edencroft	01270 625 302
ELV	El Vino Company Ltd	0171 353 5384
ENO	Enotria Winecellars Ltd	0181 961 4411
EOO	Everton's of Ombersley	01905 620282
EOR	Ellis of Richmond	0181 9434033
EP	Eldridge Pope	01305 258347
ES	Edward Sheldon	01608 661409
ETV	Eton Vintners	01753 790188
EUR	Europa Foods Limited	0181 8451255
EWC	English Wine Centre	01323 870164
EWD	Euro World Wines	0141 649 4544
F&M	Fortnum and Mason	0171 734 8040
FBG	FBG Wine Agencies	0171 978 5300
FEN	Fenwick Limited	0191 2325100
FLM	Ferrers le Mesurier	01832 732660
FLW	For the Love of Wine	01359 270377
FNZ	Fine Wines of New Zealand	0171 482 0093
FRI	Friarwood	0171 736 2628
FRT	Freetraders Group plc	01275 891 400
FSW	Frank Stainton Wines	01539 731886
FTH	Forth Wines Limited	01577 863668
FUL	Fuller Smith & Turner	0181 996 2000
FVM	FVM International Limited	01453 860881
FW	FWW Wines (UK) Ltd	0181 7868161
G&G	Godwin & Godwin	01225 337081
G&M	Gordon & Macphail	01343 545111
GAG	Grape and Grain	0181 426 1562
GC	Graingers Ltd.	0114 2730235
GDS	Garrards Wine Merchants	01900 823592
GGW	The Great Gaddesden Wine Co. Ltd	01582 840001
GHL	George Hill of Loughborough	01509 21277

GI	Grape Ideas	01865 722137
GLO	Global Wines	0121 429 1662
GLY	Gallery Wines	01504 48762
GNW	Great Northern Wine Co	0113 2461200
GON	Gauntleys	01159 110555
GRA	Geoffrey Roberts Agencies	01275 890740
GRH	Greenhouse Wine Company	
GRO	Grog Blossom	0171 7947808
GRT	Great Western Wine Company Ltd	01225 446009
GS	Gerrard Seel Limited	01925 819695
GWC	Greek Wine Centre Ltd	01743 364636
H&B	Hedges & Butler	0171 734 4444
H&D	Hicks & Don	01258 456040
H&W	Hall & Woodhouse Ltd	01258 452141
HAC	Hailsham Cellars	01323 441 212
HAD	Hadleigh Wine Cellars	01473 280275
HAE	Halewood International Ltd	0151 480 8800
HAL	Hall & Batson	01603 415115
HAM	Hampden Wine Co	01844 201641
HAR	Harrods	0171 7301234
HBJ	Heyman, Barwell Jones Ltd	01473 232322
HCK	Pierre Henck Wines	01902 751022
HHC	Haynes Hanson & Clark	0171 259 0102
HLM	The Haslemere Cellar	01428 645081
HLV	Halves	01588 673040
HN	Harvey Nichols	0171 2355000
HOF	House of Fraser Group	0141 2213474
HOL	Holland Park Wine Co	0171 2219614
HOT	House of Townend	01482 326891
HOU	Hoults Wine Merchants	01484 510700
HRV	Harrison Vintners	0171 236 7716
HSV	Hidden Spring Vineyard	01435 812640
HVW	Helen Verdcourt Wines	01628 25577
HW	Hedley Wright & Co Ltd	01279 506512
HWL	Howells of Bristol	01454 294085

ICL	Italian Continental Food & Wine	07628 770110
IRI	Irish Bonding Company	01232 790909
IRV	Irvine Robertson	0131 553 3521
ISW	Isis Wines	01628 771199
IVY	Ivy Wines	01243 377883
IWS	International Wine Services	01494 681857
J&B	Justerini & Brooks	0171 493 8721
JAG	J A Glass	01592 651850
JAK	James Aitken & Son	01382 221197
JBV	Julian Bidwell Vintner	0181 874 9388
JCB	J C Broadbent	01534 23356
JCK	J C Karn	01242 513265
JEF	John E Fells	01442 870900
JEH	J E Hogg	0131 5564025
JHL	J H Logan	0131 6672855
JMC	James E McCabe	01762 333102
JN	James Nicholson Wine Merchant	01396 830091
JOV	Jolly Vintner	01884 255644
JS	Sainsbury Supermarkets Ltd	0171 921 6000
JSS	John Stephenson & Sons	01282 698827
JUS	Just-in-Case	01489 892969
K&B	King & Barnes Ltd	01403 270470
KM	Kendal Milne	0161 8323414
KWI	Kwik Save Stores Ltd	01745 887 111
L&S	Laymont & Shaw Ltd	01872 270545
L&W	Lay & Wheeler Ltd	01206 764446
LAU	Lauriston Wines Ltd	01372 459270
LAW	Chalié, Richards & Company Ltd	01403 250500
LAY	Laytons Wine Merchants Ltd	0171 388 4567
LEA	Lea & Sandeman	0171 3764767
LEF	Le Fleming Wines	01582 760125
LES	Leos (CRS)	0161 832 8152
LIB	Liberty Wines	0171 7205350
LLT	Lloyd Taylor Wines	01738 840494

LLV	Lakeland Vintners	01539 821999
LLY	Luciana C Lynch	01428 606619
LNR	Le Nez Rouge	0171 609 4711
LU	Luigi's Deli	0171 3527739
LUC	Luckins Wines	01371 872839
LV	La Vigneronne	0171 5896113
M&C	Moet & Chandon (London) Ltd	0171 235 9411
M&S	Marks and Spencer plc	0171 935 4422
M&V	Morris & Verdin	0171 357 8866
MAK	Makro Self Service	0161 707 1585
MAY	F & E May Ltd	0171 405 6249
MCD	Marne & Champagne Diffusions "MCD" Ltd	01344 483 200
MCK	Matthew Clark Taunton Ltd	01275 890 283
MCL	McLeod's	01507 601094
MFS	Martinez Fine Wine	01422 320022
MHV	Booker Belmont Wholesale Ltd	01933 371 363
MHW	Mill Hill Wines	01482 29443
MJW	Michael Jobling Wines	0191 2615298
MK	McKinley Vintners	0171 928 7300
MM	Michael Menzel Wines	0114 2683557
MOR	Moreno Wine Importers	0171 723 6897
MRF	Mark Reynier Fine Wines	0171 589 2020
MRN	Morrison Supermarkets	01924 875234
MRS	Morrisons	01924 870000
MSA	Mersea Vineyard	01733 270 318
MTB	Martyn T Barker UK	01279 414808
MTL	Mitchells Wine Merchants	01246 2740311
MTR	Montrachet	0171 928 1990
MWI	Maidenhead Wines	01491 413311
MWW	Majestic Wine Warehouses Ltd	01923 816999
MYS	Mayor Sworder	0181 686 1155
MZ	Mentzendorff & Co Ltd	0171 415 3200

N&P	Nickolls & Perks	01396 830091
NAD	Nadder Wine Co	01722 325418
NBV	Nutbourne Manor Vineyards	
		0171 627 3800
NEI	R & I Neish Limited	01779 472 721
NG	The South African Wine Centre	
		0171 2241994
NI	The Nobody Inn	01647 252394
NIC	Nicolas UK Limited	0171 436 9338
NRW	Noble Rot Wine Warehouses Ltd	
		01527 575606
NY	Noel Young Wines	01223 844744
NYE	Nyetimber Vineyard	01798 813989
OD	Oddbins	0181 944 4400
ODF	Oddbins Fine Wine	0181 944 4411
OWL	O W Loeb	0171 928 7750
P	Parfrements	01203 503646
P&R	Peckham & Rye	0141 3344312
PAG	Pagendam	01937 844711
PAL	Pallant Wines	01903 882288
PAR	Partridges	0171 730 7104
PAT	Patriarche Père et Fils	0171 381 4016
PAV	The Pavilion Wine Co.	0171 628 8224
PCC	Price Cost Co	01708 860 981
PEA	Peake Wine Assocs	0171 7335657
PEC	Pechiney UK Limited	01753 522 800
PES	Penshurst Vineyard	01892 870255
PF	Percy Fox & Co	01279 626 801
PG	Page & Sons	01843 591214
PHI	Philglas & Swiggot	0171 9244494
PIM	Pimlico Dozen Ltd	0171 834 3647
PLA	Playford Ros Ltd	01845 526777
PLB	Private Liquor Brands	01342 318282
PLE	Peter Lehmann Wines (UK) Ltd	
		01227 731353
PMA	Perry Mill Associates	01256 880611
PNA	Phillips Newman	01322 627581
PO	Peter Osborne	01491 612311
POR	Portland Wine Company (Manchester)	
		0161 9628752

PRS	Prestige Wines	01294 602409
PS	Penn Street	01494 715376
PTR	Peter Green	0131 2295925
PV	Prestige Vintners	01264 335586
QR	Quellyn Roberts Wine Merchants	
		01244 310455
R	R S Wines	0117 9631780
RAC	Rackham's Dept Store	0121 2363333
RAE	Raeburn Fine Wine & Foods	
		0131 3431159
RAM	Ramsbottom Victualler	01706 825065
RAV	Ravensbourne Wine	0181 6929655
RBA	Rodrigues Bartholomew	0385 940786
RBS	Roberson Wine Merchants	
		0171 371 2121
RD	Reid Wines	01761 452645
REM	Remy & Associates (UK) Ltd	
		01753 752600
RES	La Reserve	0171 589 2020
RGW	The Rogers Wine Co.	01473 748464
ROB	T M Robertson	0131 229 4522
ROD	Rodney Densem Wines	01270 623665
ROZ	Rozès UK	0181 7422391
RS	Richard Speirs Wines	01483 37605
RSS	Raisin Social Limited	0181 673 3040
RTW	The Rose Tree Wine Co.	01242 583732
RVA	Randalls (Jersey)	01534 887788
S	S Wines	0171 351 1990
S&D	Saltmarsh & Druce	01993 703721
SAF	Safeway Stores plc	0181 756 2924
SAN	Sandiway Wine Co	01606 882101
SAW	South African Wine Imports	
		01509 815656
SB	Sainsbury Brothers	01225 460981
SCA	Scatchard	0151 2366468
SCK	Seckford Wines	01473 626681
SEA	Seagram UK Limited	0181 250 1018
SEB	Sebastopol Wines	01235 850471
SEL	Selfridges Limited	0171 318 3730
SHA	Shawsgate Vineyard	01728 724060

SHG	Wine Shop on the Green	
		01437 766864
SHJ	S H Jones	01295 251179
SIJ	Simpkin & James Ltd	01162 623132
SKW	Stokes Fine Wines Ltd	0181 944 5979
SLM	Salamis & Co Limited	0171 609 1133
SMF	Somerfield Stores Ltd	0117 935 9359
SOA	South African Wine Centre	
		0171 224 1994
SOB	Stones of Belgravia	0171 235 1612
SOH	Soho Wine Supply	0171 436 9736
SOM	Sommelier Wine Co	01481 721677
SPR	Spar Landmark Ltd	0181 863 5511
SSM	Stewarts Supermarkets	01232 704434
STE	Stephane Auriol Wines	01252 843190
STT	Santat Wines	01483 450494
SV	Smedley Vintners	01462 768 214
SWI	Sherston Wine Co (Malmesbury)	
		01666 840644
SWS	Stratfords Wine Shippers and Merchants Ltd	01628 810606
T&T	Thierry's Wine Services	01794 507100
T&W	T&W Wines	01842 765646
TAN	Tanners Wines Ltd	01743 232400
TBW	Talbot Wines	0121 744 5775
TGW	Good Wine Company (London)	
		0181 858 5577
TH	Thresher	01707 328244
THC	Haselmere Cellar	01428 645081
THP	Thos. Peatling	01284 755 948
TMW	Moffat Wine Shop	01683 220554
TO	Tesco Stores Limited	01992 658190
TP	Terry Platt Wines	01492 592971
TPA	Thomas Panton	01666 503088
TRO	Trout Wines	01264 781472
TVH	The Vintage House	0171 437 2592
TW	Thames Wine Sellers Ltd	
		0171 928 8253
TWB	The Wine Bank	01892 514343
U	Unwins Limited	01322 272711

UNC	Uncorked	0171 6385998
UWM	United Wine Merchants	01232 231231
V	The Vintner	01932 351585
V&C	Valvona & Crolla	0131 5566066
VAU	Vaux Breweries	0191 5676277
VD	Vins Direct	01534 482322
VDV	Vin du Van Wine Merchants	
		01233 758727
VEC	Vin Ecosse	01368 864800
VER	Vinceremos Wines	0113 257 7545
VEX	Vinexports Limited	01886 812555
VHW	Victor Hugo Wines	01534 32225
VIL	Village Wines	01322 558772
VIN	Vinum	0181 840 4070
VIW	Vintage Wines	0115 9476565
VLW	Villeneuve Wines	01721 722500
VNO	Vinoceros Imports Ltd	01209 314 711
VR	Vintage Roots	01734 401222
VW	Victoria Wines	01483 715066
VWC	Victoria Wine Cellars	01483 715066
W	Waitrose Limited	01344 824694
W&V	Wine and The Vine	01923 210394
WA	William Addison	01952 670200
WAC	Waters of Coventry Ltd	01926 888 889
WAV	Waverley Vintners Ltd	01738 629621
WAW	Waterloo Wine Co	0171 403 7967
WBE	Wine Bin Ends	01223 568 991
WCK	Wickham	01237 473292
WCR	Greenalls Wine Cellars Ltd	
		01925 444555
WCS	The Wine Cellar (Sanderstead)	
		0181 657 6936
WE	Wine Emporium/Cockburns	
		0131 3461113
WER	Wine Cellar (Douglas)	01624 611793
WES	Wessex Wines	01308 427177
WF	Wine Finds	01584 875582
WFL	Winefare Ltd	01483 458700
WIL	Willoughby's of Manchester	
		0161 8346850

WIM	Wimbledon Wine Cellar	0181 5409979	WSA	Wineshare Limited	01306 742 164
WIN	The Winery	0171 2866475	WSC	Wine Schoppen Ltd	0114 255 3301
WKV	Wyken Vineyards	01359 250240	WSG	Walter S Siegel Ltd	01256 701101
WMK	Winemark	01232 746274	WSO	The Wine Society Ltd	01438 741177
WNS	Winos	0161 6529396	WST	Western Wines Ltd	01746 789 411
WOI	Wines of Interest Ltd	01473 215752	WTL	Whittalls Wines	01922 36161
WON	Weavers of Nottingham	0115 9580922	WTR	The Wine Treasury Ltd	0171 793 9999
WOO	Wooldings Vineyard and Winery		WTS	T B Watson (Dumfries)	01387 720505
		01256 895 200	WW	Wine World	01923 264718
WR	Wine Rack	01707 328244	WWI	Woodhouse Wines	01258 452141
WRI	Wrightson Wines	01325 374134	WWS	Windermere Wine Stores	01966 26891
WRK	Wine Raks	01224 311460	XXBJC	Bodegas Julian Chivite	
WRT	Winerite Limited	0113 283 7654			00 34 48 811 000
WRW	The Wright Wine Co	01756 700886	YWL	Yates Brothers Ltd	01204 391777

TROPHY WINNERS

– WHITE –

CHARDONNAY TROPHY
Morton Estate Black Label Reserve 1995

SAUVIGNON BLANC TROPHY
Villa Maria Wairau Valley Reserve 1996

AROMATIC TROPHY
Stonecroft Gewürztraminer 1996

GERMAN WHITE & RIESLING TROPHY
Grans Fassian Piesporter Goldtröpfchen Riesling 1992

– RED –

BORDEAUX & CABERNET/MERLOT TROPHY
Jacaranda Ridge Cabernet 1991

BURGUNDY & PINOT NOIR TROPHY
Tarrawarra Estate Pinot Noir 1995

RHONE & SHIRAZ/GRENACHE TROPHY
Maglieri Mclaren Vale Shiraz 1995

SPICY RED TROPHY
Jacana Pinotage Reserve 1995

FRENCH REGIONAL RED TROPHY
Château de Pibarnon 1993

ITALIAN RED TROPHY
Umani Ronchi Pelago 1994

TROPHY WINNERS

– SPARKLING –

ROSÉ CHAMPAGNE & SPARKLING WINE TROPHY
Champagne le Brun de Neuville Non Vintage Rosé

SPARKLING WINE TROPHY
Champagne Charles Heidsieck Blanc des Millenaires 1985

– DESSERT & FORTIFIED –

DESSERT WINE TROPHY
Domaine Zind-Humbrecht Pinot d'Alsace 1995

FORTIFIED MUSCAT TROPHY
McWilliam's Liqueur Muscat Show Series

PORT TROPHY
Quinta do Noval Colheita 1937

SHERRY TROPHY
Sandeman's Royal Coregidor Rare Rich Oloroso

– OVERALL WINNERS –

WHITE WINE TROPHY
Grans Fassian Piesporter Riesling 1992

RED WINE TROPHY
Umani Ronchi Pelago 1994

FORTIFIED TROPHY
Sandeman's Royal Coregidor Rare Rich Oloroso

Adega Coop Comenda Santiago Regional 1995 — 206
Adriano Ramos-Pinto LBV Port 1989 — 214
Agapito Jumilla Reserva 1993 — 250
Agontano 1994 — 156
Agramont Tempranillo 1995 — 250
Alastro Planeta 1995 — 162
Albacoro Verdejo Chardonnay 1996 — 258
Albariño Condes de Albarei "Carballo Galego" 1995 — 260
Albariño Condes de Albarei "Classico" Joven 1996 — 259
Albariño Pazo de Barrantes 1995 — 260
Aldeanueva Azabache Rioja Crianza 1994 — 257
Alfonso González Byass — 264
Allan Scott Chardonnay 1995 — 171
Allan Scott Winery Sauvignon Blanc 1996 — 178
Allandale Wines Chardonnay 1996 — 50
Aloxe-Corton 1994, Philippe Le Hardi — 105
Aloxe-Corton 1995, Philippe Le Hardi — 105
Alteserre 1995, Bava — 163
Alvarinho 1996, Moncao — 208
Amarone Brigalda Classico 1991 — 158
Amarone Classico 1990, Zenato — 158
Amarone Classico 1993, Tedeschi — 158
Amarone Classico a Sorte 1993 — 157
Amarone Classico Capitel Monte Olmi 1993 — 160
Amarone Classico della Valpolicella 1991, Allegrini — 159
Amarone Classico della Valpolicella 1993, Amandorlato Corteforte — 159
Amarone della Valpolicella 1993 — 159
Amethystos Fumé 1996 — 267
Amethystos Red 1995 — 267
Amethytos Rosé 1996 — 267
Anagalis 1994 — 152
Añares Reserva 1990 — 252
Anchor Bay Rose NV — 268
Andes Peaks Merlot 1996, Viña Santa Emiliana — 235
Andes Peaks Sauvignon Blanc 1996 — 244
André Simon Châteauneuf-du-Pape 1994 — 138
André Simon Nuits-St-Georges 1994 — 105
Angas Brut NV — 66

Angove's Classic Reserve Cabernet Sauvignon 1995 — 19
Apostoles Gonzalez Byass — 265
Ararimu Cabernet Sauvignon 1994, Matua Valley Wines — 166
Ararimu Chardonnay 1993, Matua Valley Wines — 174
Ararimu Chardonnay 1994, Matua Valley Wines — 174
Argyle Brut 1993 — 199
Arneis Roero 1995 — 162
Arthus Côtes de Castillon 1994 — 97
Asda Muscadet 1996 — 131
Ata Rangi Pinot Noir 1995 — 167
Au Bon Climat Chardonnay 1995 — 195
Azure Bay Sauvignon Blanc Semillon 1996 — 179
Babich Gisborne Unwooded Chardonnay 1996 — 172
Backsberg Cabernet Sauvignon 1994 — 224
Backsberg Chardonnay 1995 — 229
Backsberg Klein Babylonstoren 1994 — 225
Backsberg Merlot 1995 — 222
Backsberg Pinotage 1995 — 222
Baileys 1920 Block Shiraz 1994 — 36
Balbi Vineyard Syrah Malbec 1996 — 231
Barbadillo Solear Manzanilla Pasada — 264
Barbaresco 1994, Marina Macarino — 149
Barbera d'Alba 1995, Prunotto — 148
Barbera d'Alba "Vignasse del Pozzo" 1994 — 149
Barbera d'Alba Vignota 1995, Conterno Fantino — 148
Barbera d'Asti Alasia 1994 — 148
Barbera d'Asti Superiore 1994, Bava — 149
Barbera Passum 1991 — 149
Barco Reale 1996 — 151
Bardolino Chiaretto Classico La Sorte 1996 — 155
Barolo 1993, Aurelio Settimo — 149
Barolo 1993, Fontanafredda — 149
Barolo 1993, Terre del Barolo — 148
Barolo Conteisa Cerequio 1989 — 150
Barolo Riserva 1990, Villa Lanata — 149
Barolo Vigneti Rocche 1993, Aurelio Settimo — 149
Baron de Chirel Reserva 1991 — 255
Barwang Cabernet Sauvignon 1994 — 25
Basedow Bush Vine Grenache 1996 — 43

Basedow Shiraz 1995   33
Bâtard Montrachet Grand Cru 1994,
  Jean Noel Gagnard   110
Bay View Cabernet Sauvignon
  Pinotage 1995   223
Bazzard Estate Reserve Pinot Noir 1996   167
Beaucanon Cabernet Sauvignon 1988   184
Beaucanon Chardonnay 1995   194
Beaujolais Villages 1996,
  Barton & Guester   94
Beaune 1995, Cottin Frères   104
Beaune 1er Cru Les Avaux 1995   105
Beaune Cent Vignes 1er Cru 1995,
  Domaine René Monnier   105
Beaune Clos du Roi 1er Cru 1995,
  Château Philippe Le Hardi   104
Beaune Les Epenottes 1er Cru 1991   106
Beaune Les Epenottes 1er Cru
  Domaine Parent 1994   105
Bellefontaine Merlot 1996   123
Bellingham Sauvignon Blanc 1996   227
Belondrade Lurton 1994   261
Bendigo Cabernet Sauvignon 1995   22
Beringer Cabernet Sauvignon 1994   185
Beringer Chardonnay 1995   194
Beringer Howell Mountain Merlot 1993   187
Beringer Private Reserve
  Chardonnay 1995   196
Beringer Zinfandel 1994   190
Bernkasteler Badstube
  Riesling Kabinett 1994   146
Berry's LBV Port 1990   214
Berry's Quality Australian
  Sparkling Wine NV   68
Berry's St Julien NV, Château Lagrange   98
Berry's Vintage Port 1980   216
Berry's William Pickering Port   216
Best's Great Western
  Cabernet Sauvignon 1993   24
Best's Great Western
  Cabernet Sauvignon 1994   25
Best's Great Western Chardonnay 1996   55
Best's Great Western Dolcetto 1994   44
Best's Great Western Pinot Meunier 1993   47
Best's Great Western Riesling 1995   58
Best's Great Western Shiraz 1994   36
Best's Victoria Shiraz 1996   32
Bethany Pressings Grenache 1995   43
Bethany Pressings Grenache 1996   43
Bethany Shiraz 1995   38

Betsek Tokaji Aszu 5 Puttonyos 1990   83
Blaauwklippen Shiraz 1995   224
Blandy's 10 Year Old Malmsey   210
Blandy's 5 Year Old Bual   209
Blandy's 5 Year Old Sercial   209
Blandy's 5 Year Old Verdelho   209
Blaufränkisch 1993   72
Blue Label Aszu 5 Puttonyos 1991   83
Blue Label Aszu 5 Puttonyos 1993   83
Bobbie Burns Rutherglen Shiraz 1995   35
Bodegas Berberana Gran Reserva 1987   254
Bonoval Cava Gran Reserva Brut 1991   261
Bordeaux Cave Bel Air 1995   96
Bordeaux Superieur 1994   97
Boschendal Chardonnay Reserve 1995   229
Botobolar Shiraz 1994   34
Bottelary Co-op Early Release
  Chenin Blanc 1997   227
Bourgueil Vieilles Vignes 1993,
  Pierre Caslot   129
Bourgueil Vieilles Vignes 1990,
  Domaine Hubert   130
Brancaia 1994   160
Brands Laira Cabernet Merlot 1994   24
Brands Laira Chardonnay 1995   53
Breaky Bottom Müller Thurgau 1992   87
Breaky Bottom Müller Thurgau 1995   87
Breaky Bottom Seyval Blanc
  Oaked Fume 1992   87
Bridgewater Mill Shiraz 1994   32
Bright Brothers Cabernet Malbec 1996   231
Bright Brothers Douro 1996   206
Broke Fordwich Chardonnay 1996   51
Brouilly 1996, Jean-Paul Selles   94
Brouilly 1996, Louis Tete   95
Brown Brothers Family Reserve
  Chardonnay 1994   56
Brown Brothers Family
  Reserve Riesling 1994   59
Brown Brothers King Valley
  Chardonnay 1995   52
Brown Brothers Late Harvest
  Riesling 1995   65
Brown Brothers Liqueur Muscat   70
Brown Brothers Pinot Noir &
  Chardonnay NV   68
Brown Brothers Semillon 1995   61
Brunello di Montalcino 1992, Caprilli   153
Brunello di Montalcino 1992,
  Castello Banfi   152

Brunello di Montalcino
  Castelgiocondo 1992   152
Brunello di Montalcino Riserva 1990   154
Buckley's Wines Malbec 1996   43
Burge Chardonnay Barossa Ranges 1996   52
Buxton Cabernet Merlot 1993   23
BVC Gorchivka Cabernet Sauvignon Estate
  Selection 1993   81
BVC Sliven Cabernet Sauvignon
  Reserve 1991   81
BVC Twin Peaks Cabernet Sauvignon 1991   81
BVC Yantra Valley Cabernet
  Sauvignon Controliran 1992   80
C.J. Pask Cabernet
  Sauvignon Reserve 1995   166
C.J. Pask Chardonnay 1996   171
Cabernet Sauvignon 1994 Wynns   25
Cabernet Sauvignon 1995, Planeta   158
Cabernet Sauvignon Estate Series 1993
  Columbia Crest Vineyards   200
Cabernet Sauvignon VDP 1996,
  Val D'Orbieu   122
Cabreo Riserva 1994   153
Cabrera Amontillado   263
Calem Colheita 1960   219
Calem LBV Port 1992   213
Calem Vintage 1970   219
Caliterra Cabernet Sauvignon 1995   235
Caliterra Reservado
  Cabernet Sauvignon 1995   240
Campbells Old Rutherglen Muscat   70
Campbells Rutherglen Muscat   70
Campillo Crianza 1993   251
Campillo Gran Reserva 1988   256
Campillo Reserva 1990   254
Campo Viejo Gran Reserva 1982   255
Campo Viejo Reserva 1992   251
Canepa Chardonnay 1997   245
Canepa Magnificum
  Cabernet Sauvignon 1993   243
Canoe Ridge Vineyard Chardonnay 1995   201
Canyon Road Chardonnay 1996   192
Cape Mentelle Semillon Sauvignon 1996   61
Capel Vale Chardonnay 1995   53
Capel Vale Merlot 1993   44
Capel Vale Sauvignon Blanc
  Semillon 1996   64
Capel Vale Shiraz 1995   35
Capitel San Rocco Rosso Vdt
  Veronese 1991   156

Carignano Del Sulcis
  Riserva Rocca Rubia 1993   157
Carlyle Liqueur Muscat, Pfeiffer Wines   69
Carmen Grande Vidure
  Cabernet Sauvignon 1995   240
Carmen Merlot Reserve 1995   239
Carmen Reserve
  Cabernet Sauvignon 1995   240
Carmenere Reserve
  Legado De Armida 1996, Santa Ines   238
Carta Vieja Antiguas
  Selection Chardonnay 1996   245
Casa Lapostolle Chardonnay
  Cuvée Alexandra 1996   247
Casa Lapostolle Merlot
  Cuvee Alexandre 1996   242
Casa Lapostolle Sauvignon Blanc 1996   245
Casa Leona Cabernet Sauvignon
  Reserve 1995, Viña Peumo   236
Casa Leona Chardonnay 1996   244
Casa Leona Merlot Reserve 1996,
  Viña Peumo   236
Casablanca Chardonnay Barrel
  Fermented 1995   247
Casablanca Chardonnay Barrel
  Fermented 1996   247
Casablanca Santa Isabel Cabernet 1996   241
Casablanca Santa Isabel
  Chardonnay 1996   246
Casablanca Santa Isabel Merlot 1996   241
Casablanca Santa Isabel
  Sauvignon Blanc 1996   247
Casablanca White Label
  Chardonnay 1996   245
Casablanca White Label
  Sauvignon Blanc 1996   245
Cascade Bordeaux Sauvignon Blanc 1996   101
Castillo De Molina Cabernet Sauvignon
  Reserva 1994, Viña San Pedro   239
Castillo De Molina Cabernet Sauvignon
  Reserva 1995, Viña San Pedro   239
Castillo Labastida Oak-Aged 1996   251
Catarratto Zagara Barrique 1996   161
Cateña Alta Chardonnay 1995,
  Bodegas Esmeralda   234
Cateña Chardonnay 1995,
  Bodegas Esmeralda   233
Cateña Malbec 1995, Bodegas Esmeralda   233
Cathedral Cellars Chardonnay 1996   229
Cave du Haut Poitou Gamay 1996   129

INDEX

Cecchetti Sebastiani
   Cabernet Sauvignon 1993   187
Cepparello 1994   153
Chablis 1995, Bernard Legland   107
Chablis 1èr Cru 1994, Jean Marc Brocard   108
Chablis 1èr Cru Fourchaume
   Château de Maligny 1995   109
Chablis 1èr Cru Mont de Milieu 1992   109
Chablis 1èr Cru Mont de Milieu 1993   108
Chablis 1èr Cru Vau de Vey
   Château de Maligny 1995   108
Chablis Château de Maligny 1995   107
Chablis Côte de Lechet 1èr Cru 1992,
   · Domaine Daniel-Etienne Defaix   109
Chablis Cuvée La Chablisienne 1995   107
Chablis Fourchaume 1èr Cru 1995,
   Domaine des Malandes   109
Chablis Grand Cru Vaudésir 1992,
   Domaine des Malandes   110
Chablis Grand Cru Vaudésir 1993,
   Domaine de la Maladière   109
Chablis Les Vailllons 1èr Cru 1995,
   Domaine Long Depaquit   109
Chablis Vieilles Vignes
   La Chablisienne 1994   108
Chablis Vielles Vignes 1èr Cru Domaine
   Bernard Defaix et Fils 1994   109
Chais Clarendon Chardonnay 1996   53
Chais Cuxac Val d'Orbieu 1996   127
Chambers Old Vine Special Muscat   70
Chambers Rutherglen Muscat   70
Champagne Albert Etienne Brut 1991   112
Champagne Alfred Gratien Brut 1988   118
Champagne Alfred Gratien Brut NV   115
Champagne Bauget-Jouëtte
   Carte Blanche Brut NV   112
Champagne Besserat de Bellefon
   Cuvée des Moines Brut Rosé NV   121
Champagne Billecart-Salmon
   Brut Réserve NV   116
Champagne Billecart-Salmon
   Brut Rosé NV   122
Champagne Bollinger
   Grande Année 1989   119
Champagne Bollinger Special Cuvée NV   118
Champagne Bonnet
   Blanc De Blancs Brut NV   113
Champagne Bonnet Brut 1989   114
Champagne Canard-Duchene
   Charles VII NV   119

Champagne Charles Heidsieck
   Blanc des Millenaires Brut 1985   120
Champagne Charles Heidsieck
   Brut 1990   118
Champagne Charles Heidsieck
   Brut Reserve NV   116
Champagne Chartogne Taillet Brut NV   112
Champagne Chartogne-Taillet
   Brut Rosé NV   121
Champagne Deutz Blanc de Blancs
   Brut 1989   118
Champagne Dom Pérignon
   Prestige Cuvée 1990   120
Champagne Dom Pérignon Rosé
   Prestige Cuvée Brut 1985   122
Champagne Drappier
   Blanc de Blancs Brut 1990   113
Champagne Drappier Brut 1989   116
Champagne Drappier Cuvée
   Special Brut 1990   111
Champagne Drappier Cuvée
   Special Brut NV   112
Champagne Duval Leroy Brut 1990   115
Champagne Duval Leroy
   Fleur de Champagne 1988   113
Champagne Duval Leroy Fleur de
   Champagne Blanc de Blancs Brut 1990   117
Champagne Duval Leroy
   Fleur de Champagne Brut NV   111
Champagne F. Bonnet Brossault Rosé NV   120
Champagne Gauthier 1988   117
Champagne Germain President
   Signature Brut NV   115
Champagne Gosset Brut Excellence NV   117
Champagne H Blin et Cie
   Brut Tradition NV   112
Champagne Henriot Blanc de Blancs
   Brut NV   114
Champagne Henriot Brut 1985   119
Champagne Henriot Brut 1989   115
Champagne Henriot Brut Rosé 1988   121
Champagne Henriot Brut Souverain NV   114
Champagne Jacquart Cuvee
   Mosaique Blanc de Blancs 1990   117
Champagne Jacquert Brut 1990   114
Champagne Jean Moutardier
   Carte d'Or Brut NV   112
Champagne Joseph Perrier Cuvée
   Royale Brut 1989   115
Champagne Lanson Black Label NV   115

Champagne Lanson Brut Rosé NV 121
Champagne Lanson Demi-Sec NV 114
Champagne Lanson Noble Cuvée
Brut 1988 120
Champagne Le Brun de Neuville
Brut Rosé NV 121
Champagne Le Brun de Neuville
Cuvée Brut 1990 114
Champagne Le Brun de Neuville
Cuvée Roi Clovis Brut NV 114
Champagne Moët & Chandon
Brut Impérial 1992 118
Champagne Moët & Chandon
Brut Impérial NV 116
Champagne Moët & Chandon
Brut Impérial Rosé 1990 122
Champagne Mumm Cordon Rouge
Brut 1989 116
Champagne Mumm Cordon Rouge
Brut NV 114
Champagne Nicolas Feuillatte
Blanc de Blancs Brut NV 113
Champagne Nicolas Feuillatte Cuvée
Palmes d'Or Brut 1990 113
Champagne Nicolas Feuillatte Cuvée
Speciale Brut 1989 119
Champagne Nicolas Feuillatte
Demi-Sec NV 113
Champagne Patrick Arnold
Brut Reserve Grand Cru NV 112
Champagne Paul Herard Demi-Sec NV 111
Champagne Perrier-Jouët 1990 118
Champagne Perrier-Jouët Belle
Epoque Brut 1989 120
Champagne Perrier-Jouët Grand Brut NV 116
Champagne Piper Heidsieck Brut 1989 118
Champagne Piper Heidsieck
Cuvée Brut NV 113
Champagne Pol Roger Brut 1990 119
Champagne Pol Roger
White Foil Brut NV 117
Champagne Pommery Brut 1990 117
Champagne Pommery Brut Rosé 1990 121
Champagne Pommery Brut Royal NV 115
Champagne Pommery Cuvée
Louise Pommery Brut 1988 119
Champagne R. Renaudin Réserve
Special Cd 1985 116
Champagne Veuve Clicquot Ponsardin
La Grande Dame Brut 1989 120

Champagne Veuve Clicquot
Ponsardin Réserve 1989 119
Champagne Veuve Clicquot
Ponsardin Rich Reserve 1989 119
Champagne Veuve Clicquot Ponsardin
White Label Demi-Sec NV 117
Champagne Veuve Clicquot Ponsardin
Yellow Label Brut NV 117
Champagne Vilmart Brut NV 115
Chandler's Hill Chardonnay Semillon 1995 48
Chapel Down Wines Epoch Reserve 1995 86
Chapel Hill Cabernet Sauvignon 1993 25
Chapel Hill Shiraz 1995 34
Chapel Hill 'The Vicar' 1994 27
Chapel Hill Unwooded Chardonnay 1996 51
Chardonnay 1995, Planeta 162
Chardonnay 1996, Jermann 163
Chardonnay Ausbruch 1992,
Helmut Lang 78
Chardonnay Ausbruch 1995,
Helmut Lang 74
Chardonnay TBA 1995, Helmut Lang 76
Charlie Melton Shiraz 1995 39
Château Batailley Pauillac
5ième Cru 1993 99
Château Beau-Site Cru Bourgeois 1991 98
Château Beausejour Duffau-Lagarrosse
St Emilion 1èr Grand Cru Classé 1989 100
Château Carsin Cuvée Blanc Sec 1995 102
Château Caville 1995, Alan Vaurigaud 96
Château Clerc Milon Pauillac
5ième Cru 1992 99
Château Combes Canon Bordeaux
Superieur 1995 97
Château Cordeillan Bages Pauillac 1988 100
Château Côtes de Rol
St Emilion Grand Cru 1995 99
Château Coutet Barsac 1èr Cru 1992 103
Château D'Armailhac Pauillac
5ième Cru 1992 99
Château de Calce 1993 125
Château de Chamirey 1995 108
Château de Combebelle 1995 125
Château de Combebelle Comte
Cathare 1994 126
Château de la Chartreuse Sauternes 1994 103
Château de la Grille 1993 130
Château de Lancyre "La Rouvière" 1996 128
Château de Lastours Cuvée
Fûts de Chêne 1991 125

Château de Meyney 1994 St Estèphe Cru
Bourgeois 1994 — 100

Château de Minuty Domaine Farnet 1996 — 143

Château de Pibarnon Bandol 1993 — 135

Château Des Charmes Late
Harvest Riesling 1995 — 202

Château du Seuil Graves Blanc Sec 1995 — 103

Château Ducla Permanence 1995 — 97

Château Flaugergues 1995 — 125

Château Grinou Grande Réserve 1996 — 142

Château Haut Bages Monpelou
Cru Bourgeois 1993 — 98

Château Haut Marbuzet St Estèphe Cru
Bourgeois Excep. 1994 — 100

Château Helene Cuvee Penelope 1993 — 124

Château Julia Chardonnay 1996 — 267

Château l'Evangile Pomerol 1993 — 101

Château La Barde Les Tendoux
Bergerac 1993 — 99

Château La Lagune Haut Medoc
3ième Cru 1993 — 100

Château La Mouliere
Futs de Chéne 1995 — 97

Château Latour Pauillac 1èr Cru 1991 — 101

Château Léoville-Lascases St Julien
2ième Cru 1989 — 101

Château Loubens Ste Croix du Mont
Grand Cru 1990 — 103

Château Magnol Cru Bourgeois
Médoc 1993 — 98

Château Magnol Cru Bourgeois
Médoc 1994 — 98

Château Malescot-St-Exupéray Margaux
3ième Cru 1993 — 99

Château Mansenoble Cabernet
Sauvignon 1995 — 97

Château Mine L'Etane 1995 — 125

Château Paloumey Haut Medoc
Cru Bourgeois 1994 — 98

Château Pichon Longueville Comtesse-de-
Lalande Pauillac 2ième Cru 1990 — 101

Château Pierrousselle 1996 — 101

Château Potensac Medoc Cru
Bourgeois 1990 — 100

Château Ramage La Batisse Haut
Medoc Cru Bourgeois 1993 — 99

Château Reynella Basket
Pressed Shiraz 1994 — 36

Château Reynella
Cabernet Sauvignon 1994 — 26

Château Reynella
Cabernet Sauvignon 1995 — 25

Château Reynella Cabernet Merlot 1995 — 23

Château Reynella Chardonnay 1995 — 53

Château Reynella Chardonnay 1996 — 54

Château Reynella Shiraz 1995 — 35

Château Roquebrum Prestige
St Chinian 1995, — 125

Château Roquebrun St Chinian 1994 — 124

Château Saint Galier St Emilion
Grand Cru 1995 — 96

Chateau Ste Michelle
Cabernet Sauvignon 1994 — 200

Chateau Ste Michelle Chardonnay 1995 — 201

Chateau Ste Michelle Cold Creek
Vineyard Chardonnay 1995 — 201

Chateau Ste Michelle
Cold Creek Vineyard Merlot 1994 — 200

Chateau Ste Michelle Merlot 1994 — 200

Chateau Tahbilk
Cabernet Sauvignon 1992 — 21

Chateau Tahbilk Chardonnay 1995 — 50

Chateau Tahbilk Marsanne 1995 — 63

Château Timberlay Cuvée Préstige 1996 — 102

Château Trotteville St Emilion
Grand Cru Classé 1990 — 100

Château Val Joanis Les Griottes 1993 — 137

Château Villespassans 1995 — 123

Châteauneuf-du-Pape 1994,
Château de Nerthe — 140

Châteauneuf-du-Pape 1995,
Domaine de la Janesse — 140

Châteauneuf-du-Pape Chaupin 1995 — 140

Châteauneuf-du-Pape Clos
Saint Michel 1995 — 138

Châteauneuf-du-Pape
Domaine du Pegau 1994 — 140

Châteauneuf-du-Pape
Domaine Font de Michelle 1995 — 139

Châteauneuf-du-Pape
Domaine La Roquette 1993 — 139

Châteauneuf-du-Pape Laurus 1995 — 139

Chateldon Reserve 'Juan Tetas' 1993 — 252

Chatsfield Mount Barker Shiraz 1994 — 36

Chénas Château du Loron 1996 — 95

Chestnut Grove Verdelho 1996 — 63

Chianti Classico 1994, Barardenga — 152

Chianti Classico 1994, Casa Emma — 151

Chianti Classico 1994,
Castello di Fonterutoli — 151

Chianti Classico 1994,
Fattoria Isole e Olene 151

Chianti Classico Barrique 1994,
Fior di Selva 152

Chianti Classico Montesodi 1993 153

Chianti Classico Mormoreto 1994 153

Chianti Classico Riserva 1982,
Badia a Coltibuono 153

Chianti Classico Riserva 1993,
Badia a Coltibuono 152

Chianti Classico Riserva 1993,
Castello di Brolio 151

Chianti Classico Riserva 1993,
Gestioni Piccini 150

Chianti Classico Riserva
Ducale 'Oro' 1990 152

Chianti Classico Riserva
Rocca di Castagnoli 1991 151

Chianti Classico Ser Lapo Riserva 1994 152

Chianti Classico Villa Cafaggio 1995 150

Chianti Classico Castello
di Nipozzano Riserva 1994 150

Chianti Rufina 1994, Fattoria Selvapiana 151

Chinon Jeunes Vignes 1996,
Charles Joyuet 130

Chinon Varennes du Grand Clos 1995 130

Chiroubles 1996, George Duboeuf 94

Chivite Coleccion 125 Gran Reserva 1990 254

Churchill's Vintage Port 1985 219

Churchill's Vintage Port 1991 218

Ciro Classico Riserva Duca San Felice 1991 156

Claret Calvet 1996, J. Calvet 96

Claret Calvet NV, Calvet 96

Clos D'Iere Cuvée I 1992 135

Clos D'Iere Cuvée I 1993 135

Clos de L'Obac Tinto de Guarda 1994 257

Clos du Bois Marlstone 1993 186

Clos Du Bois Sonoma County
Chardonnay 1995 194

Clos du Bois Sonoma
County Merlot 1994 186

Clos du Val Cabernet Sauvignon
Stags Leap District 1992 186

Clos du Val Reserve
Cabernet Sauvignon 1992 188

Clos Malverne Pinotage 1996 223

Co-op Australian Cabernet Sauvignon 1995 19

Co-op Fino Sherry 262

Co-op Vintage Character Port 212

Cockburn's Anno LBV Port 1992 213

Cockburn's Special Reserve NV Port 212

Codorniu Napa Brut NV 198

Coldstream Hills Briaston Cabernet Merlot
Cabernet Franc 1995 44

Coldstream Hills Cabernet Sauvignon 1994 27

Coldstream Hills Chardonnay 1996 55

Coldstream Hills Grenache Shiraz 1995 45

Coldstream Hills Pinot Noir 1996 46

Coldstream Hills Reserve Chardonnay 1996 57

Coldstream Hills Reserve Pinot Noir 1996 47

Collards Marlborough
Sauvignon Blanc 1996 178

Collards Rothesay Chardonnay 1995 173

Columbia Crest Cabernet
Sauvignon 1994 200

Columbia Crest Chardonnay
Estate Series 1995 201

Commandaria St. John 266

Concerto di Fonterutoli 1994 160

Conde de Valdemar Crianza 1994 252

Conde de Valdemar Gran Reserva 1990 255

Condrieu 1995, Guigal 141

Condrieu La Cote 1996 141

Condrieu Les Chaillets
Vieilles Vignes 1996 141

Condrieu Lys de Volan 1995 141

Cooks Sauvignon Blanc 1996 175

Coopers Creek Sauvignon Blanc 1996 176

Copertino 1992 154

Copertino Riserva 1994 155

Corban's Private Bin Cabernet
Merlot 1995 165

Corban's Private Bin Gisborne
Chardonnay 1995 171

Corley Select Reserve Chardonnay 1994 196

Cornas 1994, Mark Chapouter 140

Correas Cabernet Sauvignon 1996,
Bodega Correas 232

Cosme Palacio y Hermanos Tinto 1995 252

Cossart Gordon 10 Yr Old Verdelho 210

Cossart Gordon 15 Year Old Malmsey 210

Cossart Gordon 5 Year Old Sercial 209

Cossart Gordon 5 Yr Old Malmsey 210

Côte de Beaune 1995,
Maison Joseph Drouhin 105

Côte Rotie 1993, Guigal 140

Côte Rotie Côteaux des Bassenon 1994 140

Côtes de Castillon 1993,
Château de Belcier 97

Côtes du Rhône 1995, Domaine Brusset 136

Côtes du Rhône Cuvée Prestige
Vielles Vignes 1995 137

Côtes du Rhône Villages 1991,
J. Vidal-Fleury 138

Côtes du Rhône Villages Beaurenard
Rasteau 1995 136

Côtes du Rhône Villages Cairanne 1995 137

Côtes du Rhône Villages Cairanne 1996
Domaine Richard 137

Côtes du Rhône Villages Cairanne 1996
Domaine Richard Ebrescade 139

Côtes du Rhône Villages Cairanne
Cuvée Prestige 1995 137

Côtes du Rhône Villages Domaine
de la Berthete 1995 136

Côtes du Rhône Villages Domaine
de la Grande Bellane Valreas 1996 136

Coto de Imaz Gran Reserva 1987 253

Cottage Block Chardonnay 1995,
Corban's Wines 174

Cova da Ursa Chardonnay Vinho
Regional 1995 208

Cranswick Estate Autumn Gold Botrytis
Semillon 1994 65

Cranswick Estate Botrytis Semillon 1995 66

Cranswick Estate Shiraz 1995 30

Crémant d'Alsace Cuvée Prestige NV 93

Crichton Hall Chardonnay 1994 195

Croser 1993 68

Croser 1994 68

Crozes Hermitage 1995, Jean-Paul Selles 136

Curtis Chardonnay 1995 195

Cuvée du President 1991, Cave du Sieur
d'Aques 144

Cyril Henschke Cabernet Sauvignon 1993 29

D'Arenberg Ironstone Pressings 1995 37

D'Arenberg Noble Riesling 1996 65

D'Arenberg 'The Dead Arm' 1995 40

D'Arenberg The High Trellis
Cabernet 1995 21

D'Arenberg The Old Vine Shiraz 1995 32

D'Arenberg The Olive Grove
Chardonnay 1996 49

D'Arenberg The Otherside
Chardonnay 1996 58

D'Arry's Original 1995 43

Daniel Le Brun Brut 1991 181

Daniel Le Brun Brut NV 180

David Wynn Patriach Shiraz 1994 36

De Bortoli Cabernet Merlot 1992 26

De Bortoli Liqueur Muscat 70

De Bortoli Noble One Botrytis
Semillon 1993 66

De Bortoli Yarra Valley Pinot Noir 1995 46

Deakin Estate Brut NV 66

Deakin Estate Sauvignon Blanc 1996 62

Deakin Estate Shiraz 1996 30

Deen De Bortoli Vat 9
Cabernet Sauvignon 1995 20

Delaforce His Eminence's Choice
Tawny Port 215

Delegat's Hawkes Bay Chardonnay 1996 168

Delegat's Proprietors Reserve
Cabernet Merlot 1995 165

Delegat's Proprietors Reserve
Chardonnay 1995 169

Denbies Special Late Harvested 1995 88

Dennis Chardonnay 1996 52

Dennis Shiraz 1994 34

Diemersdal Merlot 1996 222

Disznoko Tokaji Aszu 4 Puttonyos 1992 82

Disznoko Tokaji Aszu 5 Puttonyos 1992 83

Disznoko Tokaji Aszu 6 Puttonyos 1992 83

Dlc Chardonnay Terret,
Chevalière Réserve VDP 1996 128

Dlc La Chevalière Cuvée
Première VDP 1995 129

Dlc Sauvignon, Chevalière
Réserve VDP 1996 128

Dolcetto d'Alba "Priavino" 1995 148

Dom Ramos Manzanilla 263

Domaine Boyar Czar Simeon Cabernet
Sauvignon Special Reserve 1990 81

Domaine Boyar Iambol
Cabernet Sauvignon 1996 80

Domaine Boyar Lovico Rossina
Cabernet Merlot Country Wine NV 80

Domaine Carneros Brut NV 198

Domaine Cigogne 1996 269

Domaine Collin
Blanquette de Limoux NV 144

Domaine de Chatenoy 1996 133

Domaine de Farelles 1996 127

Domaine de la Baume Philippe de Baudin
Chardonnay Viognier 1995 128

Domaine de la Baume Philippe de Baudin
Sauvignon Blanc 1996 128

Domaine de la Commandèrie de
St Jean VDP 1996 123

Domaine de la Pousse d'Or 1er Cru 1992 106

Domaine de la Pousse d'Or 1èr Cru 1993	106
Domaine de Maubet 1996	142
Domaine de Tariquet Cuvée Bois 1994	142
Domaine de Villemajou 1994	126
Domaine du Carroir 1996	133
Domaine du Grand Mayne 1996	142
Domaine du Rivage Merlot Cuxac VDP 1996	124
Domaine La Tour Boisee Cuvée Marie Claude 1994	125
Domaine Le Devois 1995, Les Vignerons	123
Domaine Oriental Cabernet Sauvignon 1996, Agricola Salve	235
Domaine Oriental Merlot Clos Centenaire 1996, Agricola Salve	238
Domaine Saint Antonin Faugeres 1995	126
Domaine Salices Sauvignon VDP 1996	127
Domaine St.Jean de Villecroze Cabernet Sauvignon 1992	126
Domaine Terres Blanches Cuvée Aurelia 1990	135
Domaine Tiffan's Villanyi Cabernet Sauvignon Barrique 1995	81
Don Maximiano Cabernet Sauvignon Reserva 1994	243
Don Maximiano Cabernet Sauvignon Reserva 1995	243
Don Maximiano Cabernet Sauvignon Reserva 1993, Errazuriz Estates	242
Dona Elena NV	204
Dos Cortados Sherry Palo Cortado	265
Double Century Oloroso Sherry	263
Douro Red 1995 Quinta do Crasto	207
Douro Red 1996 Quinta do Crasto	207
Douro Reserva 1994 Quinta do Crasto	207
Douro Reserva 1995 Quinta do Crasto	207
Douro Tinto Sociedade Dos Vinhos 1995	205
Dow's 10 Yr Old Tawny Port	215
Dow's 20 Yr Old Tawny Port	218
Dow's Fine Ruby Port NV	211
Dow's Quinta do Bomfim Single Quinta Vintage Port 1984	217
Dow's Trademark Reserve NV Port	213
Dr. Abbott's Shiraz 1996	124
Dry Creek Chenin Blanc 1996	197
Dry Creek Fumé Blanc 1996	197
Duas Quintas Reserva 1994	208
Dunleavy Te Motu 1994, Waiheke Vineyards	166
Dunnewood Barrel Select Cabernet Sauvignon 1994	183
Dunnewood Dry Silk Cabernet Sauvignon 1993	184
Dunnewood Zinfandel 1994	189
Duque de Bracanga 20 Yr Old Tawny Port A.A.Ferreira	218
Duque De Viseu Sogrape 1992	207
Durney Vineyards Cabernet Sauvignon 1992	186
E&E Black Pepper Shiraz 1994	41
E&E Sparkling Shiraz NV	69
Ebenezer Cabernet Merlot Cabernet Franc 1993	45
Ebenezer Cabernet Merlot Cabernet Franc 1994	46
Ebenezer Chardonnay 1994	55
Ebenezer Chardonnay 1996	54
Ebenezer Shiraz 1993	38
Ebenezer Shiraz 1994	37
Echeverria Chardonnay Reserva 1996	246
Echeverria Family Reserva Cabernet Sauvignon 1994	243
Echeverria Merlot Reserva 1995	240
Eileen Hardy Chardonnay 1995	57
Eileen Hardy Shiraz 1994	41
Eileen Hardy Shiraz 1995	41
El Meson NV	250
El Portico Rioja 1994	251
Elderton Semillon 1994	61
Elderton Shiraz 1994	38
Elderton Shiraz 1994	38
Elspeth Cabernet Merlot 1995, Mills Reef Winery	166
Elston Hawkes Bay Chardonnay 1996,	174
Enate Barrel-Fermented Chardonnay 1995	260
Enate Crianza 1994	253
Erdener Prälat Riesling Auslese 1996	147
Errazuriz Cabernet Sauvignon Reserve 1995	240
Errazuriz Estates Cabernet Sauvignon 1996	237
Errazuriz Estates Cabernet Sauvignon Reserva 1994	241
Errazuriz Estates Merlot Reserva 1996	243
Errazuriz Estates Reserve Chardonnay 1996	246

Errazuriz Estates Syrah Reserva 1996 243
Errazuriz Estates 'Wild Ferment'
   Chardonnay 1996 247
Esk Valley Hawkes Bay Chardonnay 1996 170
Estola Gran Reserva Do 1985 253
Etchart Cabernet Sauvignon 1995,
   Arnaldo Etchart 232
Eventum 1992 253
Fairview Cabernet Sauvignon 1995 223
Fairview Shiraz 1995 223
Faustino I Gran Reserva 1988 255
Fetzer Barrel Select Pinot Noir 1994 188
Fetzer Bonterra Organic
   Cabernet Sauvignon 1994 184
Fetzer Bonterra Organic
   Chardonnay 1995 193
Fetzer Eagle Peak Merlot 1995 183
Fetzer Reserve Cabernet Sauvignon 1994 184
Fetzer Santa Barabra Pinot Noir 1994 188
Fetzer Valley Oaks
   Cabernet Sauvignon 1994 183
Firestone Chardonnay 1995 193
Firestone Vineyards
   Prosperity Merlot NV 239
Fiuza Chardonnay Vinho Regional 1996 208
Fleurie Château du Fleurie Loron 1996 95
Fleurie Domaine Vert-Pré 1996 95
Flors di Uis 1995 163
Folonvie Cabernet Merlot 1996 141
Fonseca Bin 27 Port 213
Fonseca Guimarens Port 1984 216
Fonseca Guimarens Port 1986 216
Fonseca LBV 1992 215
Fonseca LBV Port 1991 214
Fontanario de Pegoes White 1996 208
Fontestella 1995 162
Foral Douro Reserva 1995 205
Foral Douro Reserva 1996 205
Forrest Estate Sauvignon Blanc 1996 177
Fortant de France Grenache
   Rouge VDP 1996 123
Four Rivers Cabernet Sauvignon 1995,
   Viña Gracia 235
Frascati Superiore Vigneto
   Santa Teresa 1996 161
Freemark Abbey Cabernet
   Merlot Bosche 1991 187
Freemark Abbey Cabernet Sauvignon 1993 185
Freemark Abbey Cabernet Sauvignon
   Sycamore 1991 187

Freinsheimer Riesling Halbstrocken
   Spätlese 1994 146
Gaillac Blanc 1996, BRL Hardy 142
Galeria Cabernet Sauvngnon 1995 207
Galet Vineyards Syrah
   Reserve VDP 1996 124
Gallo Northern Sonoma Estate
   Cabernet Sauvignon 1992 187
Gallo Northern Sonoma Estate
   Chardonnay 1994 196
Gallo Sonoma County
   Cabernet Sauvignon 1992 184
Gallo Sonoma County
   Chardonnay 1993 193
Gallo Sonoma Frei Ranch
   Cabernet Sauvignon 1993 186
Gallo Sonoma Frei Ranch Zinfandel 1994 190
Gallo Sonoma Laguna Ranch
   Chardonnay 1995 193
Gallo Sonoma Stefani Ranch
   Chardonnay 1994 194
Gallo Sonoma Stefani Ranch
   Chardonnay 1995 195
Gallo Sonoma Three
   Vineyard Merlot 1993 185
Gallo Turning Leaf Cabernet
   Sauvignon 1994 183
Gandia Castillo de Liria Moscatel NV 258
Gato Negro 1995, Viña San Pedro 235
Gemini Merlot VDP 1996, Yves Pages 123
Gemini Sauvignon Blanc 1996 102
Geoff Merrill Chardonnay 1994 55
Gevrey-Chambertin aux Combottes
   1èr Cru 1995 106
Gewurztraminer SGN 1994, Domaine
   Mittnacht-Klack 92
Gewurztraminer 1994,Domaine Schoffit 91
Gewurztraminer 1994,Pfaffenheim 92
Gewürztraminer BA 1994, Helmut Lang 74
Gewurztraminer Clos Windsbuhl 1995 91
Gewurztraminer Cuvée Alexandre 1994 90
Gewurztraminer Cuvée Karine
   Veille Vignes Res.1993 90
Gewurztraminer Grand Cru Altenberg
   Vendage Tardive 1989 92
Gewürztraminer Grand Cru Brand 1994 89
Gewürztraminer
   Grand Cru Eichberg 1994 91
Gewürztraminer Heimbourg 1994 91
Gewurztraminer Heimbourg 1995 91

INDEX

Gewurztraminer Herrenweg
  Turkheim 1995   92
Gewürztraminer TBA 1995, Helmut Lang   73
Gewürztraminer TBA 1995, Opitz   79
Gewürztraminer Winzerheim 1995   90
Geyser Peak Marietta Cellars Shiraz 1994   191
Geyser Peak Sonoma
  Cabernet Sauvignon 1994   185
Giesen Estate Chardonnay 1996   170
Giesen Estate Chardonnay Reserve 1995   174
Giesen Wine Estate
  Sauvignon Blanc 1996   177
Gigondas 1994, Etienne Guigal   138
Gigondas 1995, Domaine de Front-Sane   138
Gigondas Domaine des Espiers 1995   138
Gigondas Domaine Raspail-ay 1993   139
Gigondas Domaine Raspail-ay 1994   139
Gigondas Domaine Ste Lucie 1995   136
Gigondas Le Grand Montirail 1995   138
Glazebrook Noble Harvest
  Riesling 1996   180
Golan Chardonnay 1994   268
Goldwater Chardonnay 1993,
  Goldwater Estate   171
Goldwater Dog Point
  Sauvignon Blanc 1996   178
Gosling Creek Chardonnay 1996   48
Goundrey Cabernet Merlot 1995   22
Goundrey Reserve Chardonnay 1995   55
Goundrey Reserve Shiraz 1995   37
Goundrey Unwooded Chardonnay 1995   52
Graacher Domprobst Riesling
  Spätlese 1994   146
Graffigna Shiraz Cabernet 1995   231
Graham Beck Brut Blanc de Blanc 1991   230
Graham's 20 Yr Old Tawny Port   217
Graham's LBV 1991 Port   214
Graham's Malvedos Vintage Port 1984   217
Graham's Six Grapes
  Vintage Character Port   215
Gran Lurton Cabernet Reserve 1995,
  J & F Lurton   232
Gran Sangre de Toro Reserva 1993   252
Grant Burge Cabernet Sauvignon 1995   23
Grant Burge Meshach Shiraz 1993   41
Gratien & Meyer Cuvée Flamme NV   134
Graves 1994, Château du Seuil   98
Grechetto dell'Umbria 1996   161
Green Point 1994 Domaine Chandon   68
Green Point Blanc de Blancs 1993   68

Green Point Chardonnay 1995   54
Green Point Pinot Noir 1995   46
Green Point Rosé 1993   68
Green's Hill Riesling 1995   59
Groot Constantia Gouverneurs
  Reserve 1994   226
Grove Mill Sauvignon Blanc 1996   176
Grove Mill Sauvignon Blanc Reserve 1996   178
Grüner Veltliner BA 1991, Helmut Lang   73
Grüner Veltliner TBA 1995, Helmut Lang   75
Guelbenzu Crianza 1994   252
Guelbenzu Evo Crianza 1993   255
Hacienda San Carlos
  Cabernet Sauvignon 1996,   238
Hamilton Ridge Shiraz 1995   31
Hamilton Russell Chardonnay 1996   229
Hardy's Bankside Shiraz 1995   31
Hardy's Coonawarra
  Cabernet Sauvignon 1994   24
Hardy's Padthaway Chardonnay 1995   51
Hardy's Sparkling Pinot Noir
  Chardonnay NV   67
Harveys Bristol Cream   264
Hatzimichalis Cabernet Sauvignon 1995   267
Hatzimichalis Kapnias 1994   267
Hatzimichalis Merlot 1995   268
Hautes Côtes de Nuits 1995,
  Denis Philibert   104
Hautes Côtes de Nuits Les Mouchottes
  Tête de Cuvée 1995   104
Hautes Côtes de Nuits Prestige du
  Val de Vergy 1995   104
Hedges Cabernet Merlot 1994   200
Heggies Vineyard Botrytis Riesling 1996   65
Heggies Vineyard Merlot 1993   45
Heggies Vineyard Riesling 1992   58
Heggies Vineyard Viognier 1996   64
Henriques & Henriques 10 Year
  Old Malmsey   210
Henriques & Henriques 15 Year
  Old Malmsey   210
Henriques & Henriques 15 Year
  Old Verdelho   210
Henriques & Henriques NV   209
Heredad Cava Brut Reserva NV
  Segura Viudas   262
Herencia Lasanta Crianza 1994   253
Hermanos Lurton Tempranillo
  Crianza Vino de Mesa 1994   249
Hermitage 1995, Domaine Fayolle   140

Hermitage Les Bessards 1994 — 139
Heysen Shiraz 1994 — 36
Hidden Spring Gothic Dry Table Wine 1995 — 87
Highfield Estate Chardonnay 1995 — 169
Highfield Estate Sauvignon Blanc 1996 — 178
Highland Heritage Chardonnay 1995 — 50
Hill Smith Estate Chardonnay 1995 — 51
Hill Smith Estate Sauvignon Blanc 1996 — 63
Hillstowe Udy's Hill Chardonnay 1994 — 51
Hollick Coonawarra 1993 — 45
Houghton's HWB 1996 — 62
Hugh Ryman Jacana Pinotage 1995 — 223
Hugh Ryman Jacana Pinotage Reserve 1995 — 225
Huntaway Chardonnay 1995, Corban's Wines — 172
Hunter's Chardonnay 1994, — 173
Hunter's Chardonnay 1996 — 173
Hunter's Riesling 1996 — 180
Hunter's Sauvignon Blanc 1996 — 179
Idlerock Merlot Reserve 1996 — 84
Idlerock Pinot Noir Reserve 1996 — 84
Il Pordere Dell 'Olivos' Tocai Friulano 1995 — 197
Indian Wells Vineyards Merlot 1994 — 200
Inglewood Show Reserve Cabernet Sauvignon 1995 — 24
Inglewood Show Reserve Chardonnay 1995 — 54
Inglewood Show Reserve Shiraz 1995 — 36
Inniskillin Icewine 1995 — 202
Ironstone Cabernet Shiraz 1995 — 20
Ironstone Semillon Chardonnay 1996 — 60
J.I Wolf Wachenheimer Gerumpel Riesling Spälese 1996 — 146
J.Lohr Cypress Chardonnay 1994 — 193
J.Lohr Riverstone Chardonnay 1995 — 194
J M Gremillet Chardonnay Brut 1991 — 113
J.P. Barrel Selection Vinho Regional 1991 — 204
Jacaranda Ridge Cabernet Sauvignon 1989 — 29
Jacaranda Ridge Cabernet Sauvignon 1991 — 29
Jackson Estate Chardonnay 1996, — 171
Jackson Estate Sauvignon Blanc 1996 — 177
Jackson Brut 1993 — 181
Jacob's Creek Semillon Chardonnay 1996 — 59
Jade Mountain La Provincale Reserve 1995 — 191

Jade Mountain Mourvédre Reserve 1995 — 192
James Halliday Chardonnay 1995 — 53
James Herrick Cuvée Simone 1995 — 124
Jamieson's Run Red 1995 — 44
Jarrah Ridge Dry White 1996 — 62
Jean Leon Cabernet Sauvignon Reserva 1990 — 256
Jekel Gravelstone Chardonnay 1995 — 193
Jim Barry McCrae Wood Shiraz 1994 — 39
Jim Barry The Armagh Shiraz 1994 — 41
John Riddoch Cabernet Sauvignon 1994 — 30
Jose Neiva 1995 — 205
Judd Estate Chardonnay 1996, Matua Valley Wines — 172
Julius Riesling 1995 — 59
Jurançon Sec Chant des Vignes 1996, Domaine Cauhapé — 143
Kaituna Hills Chardonnay 1996, Averill Estate — 168
Kanarie Creek Cabernet Shiraz NV — 19
Katnook Estate Chardonnay 1995 — 56
Katnook Estate Coonawarra Cabernet Sauvignon 1995 — 27
Katnook Estate Merlot 1995 — 46
Katnook Estate Sauvignon Blanc 1996 — 64
Kautz Ironstone Library Collection Meritage 1992 — 186
Kendall Jackson Grande Reserve Chardonnay 1995 — 196
Kendall Jackson Vintner's Reserve Chardonnay 1995 — 195
Kendall Jackson Vintner's Reserve Pinot Noir 1995 — 189
Kendall-Jackson Grande Reserve Cabernet Sauvignon 1994 — 187
Kendall-Jackson Vintner's Reserve Cabernet Sauvignon 1994 — 185
Kenwood Sauvignon Blanc 1995 — 197
Kenwood Yulupa Cabernet Sauvignon 1992 — 184
Kenwood Yulupa Chardonnay 1995 — 194
Kenwood Zinfandel 1994 — 190
Keyneton Estate 1994 — 28
Keystone Grenache Shiraz 1996 — 42
Kim Crawford Marlborough Chardonnay 1996 — 169
Kim Crawford Marlborough Unoaked Chardonnay 1996 — 169
Kim Crawford Tietjen Gisborne Chardonnay 1996 — 174

Kingston Estate
   Cabernet Sauvignon 1994   20
Kingston Estate Chardonnay 1996   48
Kingston Estate Jarrah Ridge
   Shiraz Mataro 1995   30
Kingston Print Shiraz Mataro 1996   30
Kirchheimer Schwarzerde BA 1994   147
Klawervlei Estate Pinotage 1995   224
Klein Constantia Estate
   Chardonnay 1996   229
Koberner Weisenberg Riesling BA 1995   147
Krondorf Show Reserve
   Cabernet Sauvignon 1994   22
Krondorf Show Reserve
   Chardonnay 1996   54
KWV Cathedral Cellar
   Cabernet Sauvignon 1994   224
KWV Cathedral Cellar Triptych 1993   224
KWV Merlot 1993   222
Kym Milne Rosenview
   Cabernet Sauvignon 1996   221
L A Cetto Cabernet Sauvignon 1994   182
L A Cetto Nebbiolo 1993   268
'L' de la Louvière 1994,
   Château La Louviere   98
L' Excellence de
   Château Capendu 1995   125
L'Hereu Cava Brut NV   261
La Concha Gonzalez Byass   264
La Cotte Sparkling Demi Sec 1996   230
La Cotte Sparkling Sauvignon
   Blanc Brut 1996   230
La Domeque Tête de Cuvée
   Vieilles Vignes 1996   128
La Graveliére 1995, Joseph Mellot   132
La Motte Shiraz 1994   224
La Palma Cabernet Merlot Reserve 1996,
   Vina La Rosa   235
La Palma Cabernet Sauvignon 1996,
   Viña La Rola   234
La Palma Cabernet Sauvignon Reserve
   1996, Vina La Rosa   241
La Palma Chardonnay 1996   244
La Palma Chardonnay Reserve 1996   246
La Palma Merlot 1996, Viña La Rosa
   Cachapoal   234
La Palma Merlot 1996, Viña La Rosa
   Rapel   234
La Palma Reserve Merlot Reserve 1996,
   Viña La Rosa   241

La Val Albariño 1995   260
Lagar de Cervera Albariño 1996   260
Lagoalva De Cima 1992   206
Lagunilla Gran Reserva 1987   257
Lakeside Oaked Chardonnay 1996   82
Lamberhurst Millennium
   Sauvignon Blanc 1996   102
Langue Garde Rouge 1993   135
Laperouse VDP d'Oc Blanc 1995   127
Las Torres Merlot 1996   251
Laurel Glen Reds 1994   182
Lawson's Dry Hills
   Sauvignon Blanc 1996   177
Lawson's Shiraz 1992   39
Lawson's Shiraz 1993   39
Le Montaillant Chardonnay 1995   131
Le Volte 1995   151
Leacocks Fine Rich Madeira NV   209
Leasingham Classic Clare
   Cabernet Sauvignon 1994   28
Leasingham Classic Clare
   Cabernet Sauvignon 1995   28
Leasingham Classic Clare Shiraz 1994   40
Leasingham Classic Clare Shiraz 1995   40
Leasingham Domaine
   Cabernet Malbec 1995   21
Leasingham Domaine Chardonnay 1995   52
Leasingham Domaine Shiraz 1995   33
Lello Reserva Sociedade
   Dos Vinhos 1995   205
Les Arbousiers
   Cabernet Sauvignon 1995   123
Les Deux Anées 1995   134
Lindauer Special Reserve NV   180
Lindemans Bin 65 Chardonnay 1996   48
Lindemans Cawarra Unoaked
   Chardonnay 1996   48
Lindemans Coonawarra Pyrus 1993   46
Lindemans Hunter Valley Shiraz 1991   35
Lindemans Limestone Ridge
   Shiraz Cabernet 1993   39
Lindemans Padthaway Chardonnay 1996   52
Lindemans St Geroge
   Cabernet Sauvignon 1993   27
Linden Estate Hawkes Bay
   Chardonnay Reserve 1995   174
Lirac Domaine de la Mordorée 1996   137
Little's Chardonnay 1995   53
Little's Shiraz 1992   35
Longridge Brut 1993   230

Longridge Hawkes Bay
   Sauvignon Blanc 1995 — 175
Luis Pato 1995 — 207
Luis Pato Tinto 1995 — 206
Lustau Old East India Solera — 265
Lustau Puerto Fino Solera Reserva — 265
M. G. Vallejo Chardonnay 1994 — 192
Mâcon Solutré 1996, Maison Auvigne — 107
Madfish Bay Unwooded
   Chardonnay 1996 — 53
Maglieri Cabernet Sauvignon 1995 — 22
Maglieri Mclaren Vale
   Cabernet Merlot 1993 — 21
Maglieri Mclaren Vale Semillon 1995 — 60
Maglieri McLaren Vale Shiraz 1994 — 33
Maglieri McLaren Vale Shiraz 1995 — 34
Malbec Oak Reserve 1994, La Agricola — 232
Malt House Vintners
   Beaujolais Villages 1995 — 93
Malt House Vintners Bergerac Dry 1996 — 142
Malt House Vintners Carta Vieja
   Chilean Merlot 1996 — 234
Malt House Vintners Chablis
   Beauroy Premier Cru 1995 — 108
Malt House Vintners
   Champagne Paul Langier Brut NV — 111
Malt House Vintners Champagne
   Paul Langier Brut Rosé NV — 121
Malt House Vintners Chianti 1996 — 150
Malt House Vintners
   Côtes du Roussillon NV — 122
Malt House Vintners Domaine
   Charpenay Beaujolais Villages 1996 — 93
Malt House Vintners Fleurie 1996 — 94
Malt House Vintners Gran
   Capataz Equilaz Amontillado — 262
Malt House Vintners Gran
   Troya Cava Brut NV — 261
Malt House Vintners Mainzer
   Donnherr Spätlese 1995 — 145
Malt House Vintners Nuits-St-Georges
   Henri La Fontaine 1994 — 105
Malt House Vintners Pouilly Fuissé
   Henri La Fontaine 1995 — 108
Malt House Vintners
   Regimental LBV Port 1990 — 212
Malt House Vintners
   Scenic Ridge Australian White — 62
Malt House Vintners
   Tohani Romanian Merlot 1995 — 84

Malvasia del Lazio Terre dei Grifi 1996 — 161
Manso de Velasco 1995 — 243
Manzanilla La Goya — 264
Marienberg Cabernet Sauvignon 1993 — 20
Marienberg Semillon Chardonnay 1994 — 60
Marienberg Shiraz 1993 — 31
Marimar Torres Chardonnay 1994 — 196
Marimar Torres Pinot Noir 1994 — 189
Marqués de Alella Chardonnay 1994 — 259
Marqués de Alella Chardonnay 1995 — 260
Marqués de Caceres Reserva 1992 — 251
Marqués de Grinon Cabernet
   Sauvignon Viño de Mesa 1995 — 256
Marqués de Grinon Durius Collecion
   Personal Viño de Mesa 1994 — 250
Marqués de Grinon
   Rioja 1995 — 251
Marqués de Grinon
   Rioja Reserva 1990 — 254
Marqués de Grinon
   Syrah Viño de Mesa 1995 — 254
Marqués de Murrieta
   Tinto Reserva 1992 — 254
Marqués de Riscal Reserva 1993 — 253
Marqués de Riscal Rueda 1996 — 258
Marqués de Riscal Sauvignon 1996 — 259
Marrugat Cava Gran Reserva Brut NV — 261
Martinborough Vineyards
   Chardonnay 1995 — 173
Martinborough Vineyards
   Pinot Noir 1995 — 167
Martinborough Vineyards
   Reserve Pinot Noir 1995, — 167
Martinez Bujanda Cabernet
   Sauvignon Gran Reserva 1990 — 257
Martinez Bujanda Garnacha
   Reserva 1990 — 256
Matra Mountain Oaked
   Chardonnay 1996 — 82
Matua Valley Dartmoor Smith
   Cabernet Sauvignon 1995 — 166
Matua Valley Dartmoor Smith
   Merlot 1995 — 168
Matua Valley Hawkes Bay
   Sauvignon Blanc 1996 — 176
Matua Valley
   Unoaked Chardonnay 1996 — 169
Matusalem Gonzaléz Byass — 265
Mauro 1994 — 256
Mavrodaphne Of Patras — 266

Mavrodaphne Patraiki Reserve 1993 267
Maximin Grünhaus
  Riesling Kabinett 1995 146
McGuigan Brothers Personal
  Reserve Botrytis Semillon 1995 66
McGuigan Brothers Personal
  Reserve Cabernet Sauvignon 1995 28
McGuigan Brothers Personal
  Reserve Chardonnay 1996 57
McGuigan Brothers Personal
  Reserve Shiraz 1995 38
McGuigan Brothers Shareholders
  Chardonnay 1994 50
McWilliam's Liqueur Muscat 71
Megas Oenos White 1996 266
Merlot 1995, Planeta 158
Merlot Gran Tarapaca Reserve 1995,
  Viña Tarapaca 237
Meursault 1993, Domaine
  Château de Meursault 110
Meursault 'les Chevalieres' 1995,
  Domaine René Monnier 110
Mick Morris Rutherglen Liqueur Muscat 69
Miguel Torres Waltraud 1996 260
Milenio Reserva 1992 255
Mills Reef Reserve Riesling 1995 179
Minervois Domaine de Buadelle 1996 124
Miranda Grey Series
  Cabernet Sauvignon 1994 24
Miranda Grey Series Cabernets 1995 26
Mission Hill Chardonnay 1995 202
Mission Hill Pinot Blanc Reserve 1994 202
Mitchelton Victoria Reserve
  Chardonnay 1994 52
Moculta Shiraz 1995 32
Monbazillac
  Domaine du Haut Rauly 1994 143
Mont Gras Vineyards Reserva
  Cabernet Merlot 1996 240
Mont Gras Vineyards Reserva
  Cabernet Sauvignon 1996 240
Montana Brancott Estate
  Sauvignon Blanc 1996 179
Montana Church Road
  Cabernet Merlot 1996 165
Montana Church Road Chardonnay 1995 170
Montana Church Road Reserve
  Cabernet Merlot 1994 165
Montana Church Road Reserve
  Chardonnay 1995 172

Montana Church Road Reserve
  Merlot 1994, 166
Montana Marlborough Riesling 1996 179
Montana Marlborough
  Sauvignon Blanc 1996 175
Montana Patutahi Estate
  Gewurztraminer 1995 180
Montana Reserve Chardonnay 1996 170
Montana Reserve Sauvignon Blanc 1996 176
Monte Cheval Vranac 1993 84
Monte Cheval Vranac 1993 269
Monte De Terruge Alentejo 1995 206
Montepulciano d' Abruzzo 1995,
  Umani Ronchi 154
Montepulciano d'Abruzzo Barrique
  Chiero di Luna 1995 155
Montepulciano
  d'Abruzzo "Pelago" 1994 159
Montes Alpha Cabernet Sauvignon
  1994, Discover Wines 242
Montes Alpha
  Chardonnay Reserve 1995 247
Montes Alpha Merlot 1995,
  Discover Wines 242
Montes Cabernet Sauvignon Oak
  Aged 1994, Discover Wines 237
Monteviña Barbera 1994 191
Monteviña Cabernet Sauvignon 1993 183
Monteviña Chardonnay 1994 192
Montgras Reserve Merlot 1996 241
Montrose Cabernet Sauvignon 1994 20
Montrose Chardonnay 1995 49
Móreson Unwooded Chardonnay 1995 228
Morey-St-Denis Clos des Lambrays
  Grand Cru 1989 107
Morgon 1995, George Duboeuf 95
Morgon 1996,Château de Pizay 94
Morgon Domaine Jambon 1996 94
Morris Cabernet Sauvignon 1994 22
Morris Durif 1994 45
Morton Estate Black Label
  Cabernet Merlot Reserve 1995 166
Morton Estate Black Label
  Chardonnay Reserve 1995 173
Morton Estate Hawkes Bay
  White Label Chardonnay 1996 171
Morton Estate Hawkes Bay
  White Label Sauvignon Blanc 1996 176
Morton Estate Marlborough
  White Label Chardonnay 1996 170

Moscato d'Asti Cru Cardinale Lanata 1996 162
Moulin A Vent 1995, George Duboeuf 95
Moulin-a-Vent 1995, Domaine Jacky Janodet 95
Mount Edelstone Shiraz 1994 41
Mount Eden Chardonnay 1995 193
Mount Eden Zinfandel 1995 190
Mount Helen Cabernet Merlot 1995 25
Mount Helen Chardonnay 1996 54
Mount Hurtle Chardonnay 1995 51
Mount Hurtle Shiraz 1994 33
Mount Langi Ghiran Shiraz 1995 39
Mount Pleasant Elizabeth Semillon 1992 61
Mountadam Riesling 1995 59
Mountadam "The Red" 1994 28
Moyston Unoaked Chardonnay 1996 48
Mumm Cuvée Napa
  Blanc De Blancs NV 198
Mumm Cuvée Napa Brut NV 198
Murfatlar Chardonnay 1996 85
Muscadet de Sèvre et Maine Domaine
  de Basse-Ville Sur Lie 1996 131
Muscadet de Sèvre et Maine Domaine
  de L'Ecu Sur Lie 1996 131
Muscat d'Alsace Reserve
  Personelle Sigelle 1995 90
Muscat de Rivesaltes Chapoutier 1995 129
Muscat No.5 Zwischen
  den Seen TBA 1995, Kracher 75
Muscat Sec Val d'Orbieu VDP 1996 128
Nagyrede Winery Pinot Grigio 1996 81
Nanya Estate Malbec Ruby
  Cabernet 1996 42
Napa Valley Cabernet Sauvignon 1992,
  William Hill 184
Napa Valley Cabernet Sauvignon
  Reserve 1993 186
Nautilus Estate Sauvignon Blanc 1996 177
Navajas Reserva 1990 252
Navajas Reserva 1990 253
Neethlingshof Shiraz 1993 224
Neil Ellis Sauvignon Blanc 1996 228
Neil Joubert Cabernet Sauvignon 1996 221
Nero d'Avola Zagara di Sicilia 1996 154
Nexus 1994 156
Nine Popes 1995 46
Ninth Island Chardonnay 1996 51
No.11 Muskat TBA 1995, Kracher 76
Nobilo Marlborough Sauvignon Blanc 1996 176
Nöe Gonzalez Byass 265
Noilly Prat Dry 129

Norman's Chais Clarendon Shiraz 1995 37
Norton Barbera 1995, Bodega Norton 232
Norton Cabernet Sauvignon 1996,
  Bodega Norton 232
Norton Malbec 1994, Bodega Norton 233
Nouvelle Vague Chardonnay
  No.13 TBA 1995, Kracher 78
Nouvelle Vague Chardonnay
  Welschriesling No.7 TBA 1995 76
Nouvelle Vague Scheurebe
  No.14 TBA 1995, Kracher 78
Nouvelle Vague Traminer
  No.8 TBA 1995, Kracher 77
Noval 10 Yr Old Tawny Port 215
Nuits St Georges Clos de l'Arlot
  1èr Cru 1994, Domaine de l'Arlot 110
Nuits-St-Georges 1995, Cottin Frères 104
Nuits-St-Georges 1èr Cru, 1993,
  Domaine de l'Arlot 106
Nuits-St-Georges Aux Boudots
  1èr Cru 1990, Meo-Camuzet 107
Nuits-St-Georges Clos de l'Arlot 1994,
  Domaine de L'Arlot 106
Nuits-St-Georges Forets St Georges
  1èr Cru 1994, Domaine de L'Arlot 106
Nutbourne Vineyards Schonburger 1992 86
Nyetimber Premier Cuvée 1992 88
Nyulaszo 5 Puttonyos
  1st Growth 1700 1991 84
Nyulaszo 6 Puttonyos
  1st Growth 1700 1993 83
Oakville District Cabernet Sauvignon 1993 187
Old Vine Muscadelle 70
Omaka Springs Estate Riesling 1996 180
Omaka Springs Estate
  Sauvignon Blanc 1996 175
Opitz Goldackerl TBA 1995 77
Opitz One TBA 1994 79
Opus One 1993 188
Ormond Estate Chardonnay 1994,
  Montana Wines 172
Ornellaia 1993 154
Orvieto Classico Salviano 1996 162
Oxford Landing Chardonnay 1996 48
Oyster Bay Marlborough
  Chardonnay 1996 169
Oyster Bay Marlborough
  Sauvignon Blanc 1996 176
Pago de Carraovejas 1995 255
Palacio de la Vega Merlot Crianza 1994 252

INDEX

Palacio de Leon 1994	249
Palha Canas 1996	206
Palliser Estate Martinborough Pinot Noir Pinot Noir 1995	167
Palliser Estate Martinborough Sauvignon Blanc 1996	178
Palliser Martinborough Chardonnay 1995	172
Pando Fino Sherry	264
Pedro Grand Chardonnay 1996	247
Pedro Ximénez	265
Pedroncelli Cabernet Sauvignon 1993	183
Pedroncelli Cabernet Sauvignon 1994	183
Pedroncelli Zinfandel 1994	190
Pelavet 1995	156
Penfolds Barossa Valley Old Vine Semillon 1996	61
Penfolds Barossa Valley Old Vine Shiraz Grenache Mourvedre 1994	45
Penfolds Barossa Valley Semillon Chardonnay 1996	60
Penfolds Barrel Fermented Semillon 1994	60
Penfolds Bin 28 Kalimna Shiraz 1994	34
Penfolds Bin 389 Shiraz Cabernet 1994	38
Penfolds Bin 407 Cabernet Sauvignon 1994	23
Penfolds Bin 707 Cabernet Sauvignon 1994	30
Penfolds Clare Valley Cabernet Shiraz 1995	21
Penfolds Koonunga Hill Shiraz Cabernet 1995	31
Penfolds St Henri 1993	40
Penfolds The Valleys Chardonnay 1996	49
Penley Estate Cabernet Sauvignon 1993	28
Penley Estate Cabernet Sauvignon 1994	29
Penley Estate Shiraz Cabernet 1994	38
Pepper Tree Shiraz Reserve 1996	35
Pepperwood Grove Cabernet Franc 1995	191
Pergola 1996	249
Pesquera Reserva 1993	256
Petaluma Chardonnay 1993	56
Petaluma Chardonnay 1994	57
Petaluma Chardonnay 1995	56
Petaluma Coonawarra 1994	28
Petaluma Riesling 1995	59
Petaluma Riesling 1996	59
Peter Lehmann Barossa Valley Grenache 1996	42
Peter Lehmann Cabernet Sauvignon 1995	21
Peter Lehmann Clancy's Red 1995	44
Peter Lehmann Clancy's White 1996	61
Peter Lehmann Mentor 1991	47
Peter Lehmann Shiraz 1995	31
Peter Lehmann Stonewell Shiraz 1992	40
Pewsey Vale Riesling 1996	58
Philipponnat Clos des Goisses Brut 1986	120
Philipponnat Grand Blanc Chardonnay Brut 1988	118
Philipponnat Le Reflet Brut NV	116
Pierro Cabernets 1994	29
Piesporter Goldtropfchen Riesling 1992	145
Pillitteri Chardonnay Barrel Aged 1995	202
Pinot Bianco 1996, Jermann	163
Pinot Blanc 1996,Cave Ingersheim	89
Pinot Blanc Ausbruch 1991, Helmut Lang	78
Pinot Blanc QW 1995	72
Pinot Blanc Rotenberg 1995	89
Pinot Blanc TBA 1990, Helmut Lang	77
Pinot Blanc TBA 1993, Helmut Lang	78
Pinot d'Alsace 1995, Domaine Zind-Humbrecht	92
Pinot Grigio Isonzo 'Dessimis' 1995	164
Pinot Gris Ausbruch 1992, Helmut Lang	74
Pinot Gris Clos Jebsal 1994	93
Pinot Gris Clos Winsbuhl 1995	91
Pinot Gris Heimbourg 1995	91
Pinot Gris Heimbourg 1994	92
Pinot Gris Oaked Reserve 1996, Nagyrede Winery	82
Pinot Gris TBA,Opitz	78
Pinot Gris Vieilles Vignes 1995	91
Pinot Noir TBA 1995, Helmut Lang	77
Pioneers Raisined Muscat Bin 168 1996	65
Pipers Brook Chardonnay 1995	56
Pipers Brook Pinot Noir 1995	46
Plaisir de Merle Cabernet Sauvignon 1995	226
Plaisir De Merle Chardonnay 1996	229
Plaisir de Merle Merlot 1995	226
Plantagenet Cabernet Sauvignon 1994	26
Plantagenet Mount Barker Chardonnay 1996	55
Poliziano Elegia 1994	153
Porfyros 1996	266
Porto Feist Colheita Port 1987	219
Porto Feist LBV Port 1990	215
Pouilly Fuissé 1994, Domaine Corsin	
Pouilly Fuissé Vieilles Vignes 1994, Domaine Manciat Poncet	108
Pouilly Fumé 1996, Henri Bourgeois	133

Pouilly Fumé Château de Tracy 1995 134
Pouilly Fumé Domaine Dagueneau 1996 133
Pouilly Fumé Les Griottines 1996 132
Preece Chardonnay 1996 49
Preece Sauvignon Blanc 1996 63
Prima de Martino Cabernet Sauvignon
  Reserve 1995, de Martino 237
Primitivo del Salento
  Cantele le Trulle 1996 154
Prosecco Spumante 1996, La Marca 164
Puligny-Montrachet Sous Le Puits
  1èr Cru 1994 110
Quady Starboard Vintage 1989 199
Quinta da Ervamoira Vintage Port 1994 216
Quinta de Azevedo 1996 208
Quinta de Lagoalva 1994 206
Quinta do Bom-Retiro 20 Yr Old
  Tawny Port 219
Quinta do Crasto Vintage Port 1994 217
Quinta do Infantado Organic Vintage
  Character Port 216
Quinta do La Rosa
  Finest Reserve NV Port 213
Quinta do La Rosa LBV Port 1992 214
Quinta do Noval 20 Yr Old Port
  Quinta Do Noval 218
Quinta do Noval Colheita Port 1937 220
Quinta do Noval Colheita Port 1976 214
Quinta do Noval Colheita Port 1981 212
Quinta do Noval Colheita Port 1982 213
Quinta do Noval Colheita Port 1984 211
Quinta do Noval LBV Port 1990 212
Quinta do Noval Over 40 Yr Old Port 219
Quinta do Noval Vintage Port 1966 220
Quinta do Porto 10 Yr Old Tawny Port 215
Quinta do Sagrado Ruby Port NV 211
Quinta do Sagrado
  Vintage Character NV 211
Quinta do Vargellas Vintage Port 1984 217
Quinta Dos Bons Ares 1994 208
Qupé Bien Nacido Syrah Reserve 1994 191
Railroad Red 1996 222
Raimat Chardonnay 1996 259
Raimat Merlot 1991 251
Ramada 1995 204
Ramos-Pinto 30 Yr Old Tawny Port 219
Ramos-Pinto LBV Port 1992 213
Ramos-Pinto Quinta Da Urtiga NV Port 213
Ramos-Pinto Vintage Port 1982 218
Ramos-Pinto Vintage Port 1983 218

Ramos-Pinto Vintage Port 1994 218
Rapsani Tsantalis 1993 267
Ravenswood Cabernet Sauvignon 1993 29
Recioto Classico della Valpolicella 1993 159
Recioto Classico Domini Veneti 1995 158
Recioto Classico
  Monte Fontana Doc 1993 160
Redwood Trail
  Cabernet Sauvignon 1994 182
Redwood Trail Pinot Noir 1995 188
Regiano NV 157
Regnie 1995, Gilles Ducroux 94
Remonte Chardonnay 1996 258
Renaissance Cabernet Sauvignon 1994 185
Renaissance Cabernet Sauvignon
  Reserve 1993 185
Renaissance Chardonnay Reserve 1994 195
Renaissance Select Late Harvest
  Sauvignon Blanc 1994 198
Renwick Estate Chardonnay 1994,
  Montana Wines 172
Reuilly 1996,Claudre Lafond 132
Reuilly Blanc 1996,
  Henri Beurdin & Fils 132
Reuilly Rouge 1996, Claude Lafond 129
Ribeirinho 1995 206
Richmond Grove Verdelho 1995 62
Riddoch Chardonnay 1996 49
Riddoch Sauvignon Blanc 1996 63
Riddoch Shiraz 1995 32
Ridge Geyserville 1995 192
Ridge Lytton Springs 1994 192
Ridge Monte Bello 1993 188
Riesling Clos Hauseren 1995 90
Riesling Clos St Theobald
  Grand Cru 1995 90
Riesling Clos St Theobald
  Grand Cru SGN 1994 93
Riesling Trocken 1995, Grans Fassian 145
Riesling Wineck-Schlossberg
  Grand Cru 1995 90
Rioja Gran Reserva 904 1987 257
River Route Pinot Grigio 1996 85
Rivers Meet Merlot Cabernet 1996 96
Robert Mondavi Cabernet
  Sauvignon Reserve 1994 188
Robert Mondavi Carneros
  Chardonnay 1994 196
Robert Mondavi
  Carneros Pinot Noir 1994 189

Robert Mondavi Pinot Noir
Reserve 1994 — 189
Rochioli Sauvignon Blanc 1996 — 197
Roederer Estate Quartet NV — 199
Roger Jorgensen Red Wellington 1994 — 226
Rooiberg Pinotage 1994 — 221
Rosemount Estate Balmoral Syrah 1994 — 41
Rosemount Estate
Cabernet Sauvignon 1995 — 21
Rosemount Estate Orange
Cabernet Sauvignon 1993 — 27
Rosemount Estate
Orange Chardonnay 1995 — 56
Rosemount Estate
Semillon Chardonnay 1996 — 60
Rosemount Estate Show Reserve
Chardonnay 1995 — 54
Rosemount Estate Show Reserve
Cabernet Sauvignon 1994 — 26
Rosso del Salento
Duca di Aragona 1991 — 157
Rothbury Hunter Valley
Reserve Shiraz 1994 — 37
Rothbury Hunter Valley Verdelho 1995 — 63
Rouge Homme
Cabernet Sauvignon 1993 — 24
Roux Laithwaite S5 VDP NV — 137
Rowan Brook Cabernet Merlot 1995,
Vinicola Las Taquas — 236
Rowan Brook Cabernet Sauvignon 1994,
Vinicola Las Taquas — 237
Rozes LBV Port 1992 — 211
Rozes Vintage Port 1994 — 217
Rozzano 1995 — 155
Rubesco Rosso di Torgiano Riserva 1987 — 158
Rüdesheimer Magdalenenkreuz
Riesling Kabinett 1996 — 146
Rueda White 1996 — 258
Rust en Vrede Merlot 1996 — 223
Rymill Cabernet Sauvignon 1994 — 23
Sacred Hill Semillon Chardonnay 1996 — 60
Safeway Amontillado — 263
Safeway Australian Oaked
Cabernet Sauvignon 1996 — 20
Safeway Cava Brut NV — 261
Safeway Champagne Albert Etienne
Brut Rosé NV — 121
Safeway Chianti 1995 — 150
Safeway Chianti Classico 1995 — 150
Safeway Cotes De Luberon Rouge 1995 — 135

Safeway Fino — 263
Safeway Smith Woodhouse
LBV Port 1991 — 212
Safeway Soave 1996 — 160
Safeway Young Vatted
Cabernet Sauvignon 1996 — 80
Safeway Young Vatted Merlot 1996 — 80
Sahateni Vineyards Barrel Matured Merlot
Special Reserve 1994 — 84
Sainsbury's La Mancha
Tempranillo 1996 — 249
Saint Joseph 1990, Georges Duboeuf — 137
Salice Salentino 1994, Vallone — 155
Salice Salentino Cantele Le Trulle 1996 — 161
Salice Salentino Riserva 1993, Francesco
Candido — 155
Salisbury Estate Grenache 1996 — 42
Saltram Classic Chardonnay 1996 — 49
Saltram Classic Shiraz 1996 — 31
Sämling 88 Ausbruch 1989, Helmut Lang — 77
Sämling 88 Ausbruch 1991, Helmut Lang — 74
Sämling 88 Ausbruch 1993, Helmut Lang — 74
Sämling 88 Ausbruch 1995, Helmut Lang — 73
Sämling 88 BA 1991, Helmut Lang — 73
Sämling 88 BA 1994, Helmut Lang — 73
Sämling 88 TBA 1991, Helmut Lang — 76
Sämling 88 TBA 1994, Helmut Lang — 75
Sämling 88 TBA 1995, Helmut Lang — 75
Sämling 88 TBA 1995,
Weinbau Nekowitsch — 73
Sämling 88 Welschriesling Eiswein 1990,
Helmut Lang — 78
Sancerre 1996, Henri Bourgeois — 133
Sancerre Blanc Grand Cuvée
Comte Lafond 1993 — 134
Sancerre Blanc Les Roches 1996 — 133
Sancerre Château Favray 1996 — 132
Sancerre Domaine du Carrou 1996 — 132
Sancerre La Clemence
Domaine Pinard 1996 — 133
Sancerre Les Baronnes
Bonnes Bouches 1996 — 133
Sancerre Les Caillottes 1995 — 134
Sancerre Rouge 1995, Domaine Vacheron — 130
Sancerre Rouge 1995, Serge Laloue — 130
Sancerre Rouge Belles Dames 1995,
Domaine Vacheron — 130
Sandalford Winery Shiraz 1995 — 37
Sandeman 20 Yr Old Tawny Port — 218
Sandeman LBV Port 1991 — 214

Sandeman Royal Corregidor
 Rare Rich Oloroso   265
Sandeman Vintage Port 1994   211
Sanford Chardonnay 1995   195
Sanford Pinot Noir 1995   189
Santa Carolina Cabernet
 Sauvignon Reserva 1994   237
Santa Carolina Cabernet
 Sauvignon Reserva de Familia 1993   242
Santa Carolina Chardonnay
 Gran Reserva 1996   247
Santa Carolina Chardonnay
 Reserva 1996   245
Santa Carolina Chardonnay
 Reserva de Familia 1996   248
Santa Carolina Merlot
 Gran Reserva 1995   241
Santa Carolina Merlot Reserva 1996   238
Santa Carolina Tierra Del Rey 1996,
 Santa Carolina   234
Santa Digna Cabernet Sauvignon 1995,
 Miguel Torres   237
Santa Digna Cabernet
 Sauvignon Rosé 1996   248
Santa Ines Legado De Armida Merlot
 Reserve 1996   238
Santa Julia Alamos Ridge Malbec 1994,
 Bodegas Esmeralda   232
Santa Julia Cabernet Sauvignon
 Oak Reserve 1994, La Agricola   232
Santara Cabernet Merlot 1995   250
Santara Carbonell Cabernet
 Sauvignon 1995   253
Santenay 1995, Antoine de Peyrache   104
Sanz Rueda Superior 1996   259
Sarget de Château Gruaud-Larose
 St Julien 1993   99
Saumur Château de Montgueret 1996   131
Saussignac Château Grinou 1995   143
Saussignac Cuvée Marie Jeanne 1994   143
Sauternes Baron Philippe de
 Rothschild 1991   103
Sauternes Cuvée Aristide 1989   103
Sauvignon Bianco Isonzo 'Vieris' 1995   163
Sauvignon Blanc 1996, BRL Hardy   131
Sauvignon Blanc 1996, J Calvet   102
Sauvignon Blanc De Martino 1997   244
Sauvignon Gris 1996, Yvon Mau   102
Savagnin Fruitière
 Vinicole d'Arbois 1990   89

Saxenberg Cabernet Sauvignon
 Private Collection 1992   227
Saxenburg Cabernet Merlot 1996   222
Saxenburg Chardonnay 1996   228
Saxenburg Merlot
 Private Collection 1994   226
Saxenburg Sauvignon Blanc 1996   228
Scharffenberger Brut NV   198
Scheurebe No.4 Zwischen
 Den Seen TBA 1995, Kracher   77
Scheurebe No.6 Zwischen
 den Seen TBA 1995, Kracher   75
Scheurebe No3 Zwischen
 den Seen TBA 1995   76
Schilfwein Tradition 1994   76
Schilfwein Tradition 1995   76
Schloss Johannisberger Auslese 1995   147
Schloss Johannisberger Kabinett 1995   145
Schloss Johannisberger Spätlese 1993   147
Schloss Johannisberger Spätlese 1995   146
Schramsberg Blanc De Blancs 1991   199
Schramsberg Blanc De Noirs 1988   199
Schramsberg "J. Schram" 1989   199
Seaview Brut Rosé NV   66
Seaview Edwards & Chaffey Pinot Noir
 Chardonnay 1992   67
Seaview Edwards & Chaffey Pinot Noir
 Chardonnay 1993   67
Seaview Pinot Noir Chardonnay 1994   67
Sebastiani Chardonnay 1995   192
Sebastiani Sonoma Cask
 Chardonnay 1994   194
Seghesio Vitigno Toscano
 Sangiovese 1995   191
Seghesio Zinfandel 1994   189
Selak's Founder's Reserve Chardonnay,
 Matador Estate 1994   170
Selection Salvaterre Syrah 1995   124
Sella del Boscone Chardonnay 1994   163
Senorio de Nava Reserva 1990   254
Seppelt Chalambar Shiraz 1994   34
Seppelt Great Western Brut Rosé NV   66
Seppelt Pinot Noir Chardonnay 1991   67
Seppelt Rutherglen Show Muscat Dp 63   70
Seppelt Sparkling Shiraz 1993   67
Seppeltsfield Show Palomino Dp117   69
Sfursat 5 Stelle 1995   159
Shadnach Cabernet Sauvignon 1993   29
Shaw & Smith Reserve Chardonnay 1994   56
Shaw & Smith Sauvignon Blanc 1996   64

Shaw & Smith Unoaked Chardonnay 1996	54
Shawsgate Bacchus 1994	87
Shawsgate Bacchus 1996	87
Shingle Peak Sauvignon Blanc 1996	176
Shottesbrooke Cabernet Merlot Malbec 1994	45
Simonsig Cabernet Sauvignon 1993	225
Simonsig Shiraz 1994	225
Simonsvlei Shiraz Reserve 1996	221
Skillogalee Shiraz 1995	38
Skylark Hill Chardonnay VDP 1996	126
Smith Woodhouse Traditional LBV Port 1984	216
Soave Classico Colombara 1996	160
Soave Classico Pra 1996	162
Soave Classico Superiore 1995	162
Sogrape Reserva Douro 1992	207
Solagüen Reserva 1989	254
Soljans Chardonnay 1996, Tony Sowan	170
Soltero Rosso Vino da Tavola 1993	154
Somerfield Amontillado Sherry	262
Somerfield Chardonnay Brut NV	143
Somerfield Chilean Chardonnay 1996	244
Somerfield Crémant de Bourgogne 1991	111
Somerfield Douro Red Do 1994	205
Somerfield Fine Old Amontillado Sherry	262
Somerfield Merlot VDP NV	127
Somerfield Navigator Vintage Character	211
Somini Veneti Recioto Spumante 1995	164
Sonoma Cask Merlot 1994	184
Sorevi Sparkling Chardonnay NV	144
Southbrook Cabernet Franc 1995	201
Southbrook Canadian Cassis NV	203
Southbrook Canadian Framboise NV	203
Southbrook Lailey Cabernet Sauvignon 1995	201
Spar Chilean Merlot 1996	234
Spar Hungarian Country Danube White NV	82
Special Cuvée Sauvignon Blanc 1996	228
St Emilion 1994, Baron Philippe de Rothschild	97
St. Hallett Barossa Shiraz	33
St. Hallett Blackwell Shiraz 1994	37
St. Hallett Cabernet Merlot 1995	23
St. Hallett Chardonnay 1996	50
St. Hallett Faith Shiraz 1995	33
St. Hallett Grenache 1996	44
St. Hallett Old Block Shiraz 1993	39
St. Hallett Poacher's Blend 1996	62
St. Hallett Riesling 1995	58
St Hilary Chardonnay 1994	50
St Hilary Chardonnay 1995	53
St Hilary Chardonnay 1996	51
St Joseph 1994, Jean-Paul Selles	136
St. Joseph 1995, Cave de Tain	138
St Joseph Bernard Gripa 1995	139
St Michael Beaujolais 1996	94
St Mont d'Andre Daguin 1996	127
St Ursula Riesling Auslese 1993	147
Stanton & Killeen Rutherglen Muscat	69
Stellenzicht Cabernet Sauvignon 1994	223
Stellenzicht Chardonnay 1996	228
Stellenzicht Shiraz 1994	225
Stockmans Bridge Cabernet Shiraz 1995	19
Stoneleigh Marlborough Chardonnay 1995, Corban's Wines	168
Stoneleigh Marlborough Sauvignon Blanc 1996	175
Stonestreet Cabernet Sauvignon 1994	186
Stonestreet Chardonnay 1995	196
Stonier's Chardonnay 1995	55
Stonier's Pinot Noir 1996	45
Stonier's Reserve Cabernet Sauvignon 1993	27
Stonier's Reserve Chardonnay 1994	57
Stonier's Reserve Pinot Noir 1994	47
Stonyfell Metala Shiraz Cabernet 1994	32
Stonyfell Metala Shiraz Cabernet 1995	34
Stratmer Vineyards Who Cares Red 1995	42
Sutter Home Cabernet Sauvignon 1994	182
Sutter Home Reserve Zinfandel 1991	190
Table Bay Early Release Chenin Blanc 1997	227
Tanners Mariscal Manzanilla	264
Tanners Sauvignon Blanc VDP 1995	127
Tarrawarra Estate Chardonnay 1995	57
Tarrawarra Estate Pinot Noir 1994	47
Tatachilla Cabernet Sauvignon 1995	21
Tatachilla Merlot 1995	43
Tatachilla Partners Cabernet Sauvignon Shiraz 1996	20
Taylor's 10 Yr Old Tawny Port	216
Taylor's 20 Yr Old Tawny Port	219
Taylor's First Estate Reserve	212
Taylor's LBV Port 1991	214
Taylor's Quinta do Vargellas Vintage Port 1986	217

INDEX

Te Kairanga Pinot Noir 1995 — 167
Te Kairanga Reserve Chardonnay 1996 — 173
Te Kairanga Reserve Pinot Noir
Reserve 1996 — 167
Te Kairanga Sauvignon Blanc 1996 — 177
Te Mata Estate Cabernet Merlot 1995 — 166
Tenterden Estate Dry NV — 86
Teroldego Rotaliano 1995 — 156
Terra Rosa 1995 — 183
Terre Brune 1993 — 159
Terre di Tufi 1996 — 163
Terret VDP 1996 — 126
Terroir Club Chardonnay VDP 1996 — 126
Terroir Club Sauvignon VDP 1996 — 127
Tesco Australian Shiraz Cabernet — 30
Tesco Beyers Truter Pinotage NV — 222
Tesco Blancs de Blancs Champagne NV — 112
Tesco Cabernet Sauvignon Reserve 1996 — 123
Tesco Champagne Brut NV — 111
Tesco Coonawarra Cabernet Sauvignon — 20
Tesco Finest Amontillado — 263
Tesco Muscadet Sur Lie 1996 — 131
Tesco New Zealand Chardonnay — 168
Tesco Paarl Cabernet Sauvignon — 221
Tesco Premium Shiraz 1995 — 224
Tesco Schloss-Böckelheim
Kupfergrube Riesling — 145
Tesco Shiraz 1995 — 32
Tesco Superior Manzanilla — 262
Tesco Superior Oloroso Seco — 262
Tesco Superior Palo Cortado — 263
The Gyöngyös Estate Barrel
Fermented Chardonnay 1996 — 82
The Gyöngyös Estate Chardonnay 1996 — 82
The Millton Vineyard Barrel Fermented
Chardonnay 1996 — 170
The Millton Vineyard
Riesling Opou 1996 — 180
The Willows Shiraz 1994 — 32
Thistle Hill Cabernet Sauvignon 1992 — 23
Thomas Hardy Cabernet Sauvignon 1993 — 29
Thomas Mitchell Cabernet Shiraz
Cabernet Franc 1995 — 42
Thomas Mitchell Marsanne 1996 — 63
Thornton Holmes Mersea 1995 — 87
Tim Adams Shiraz 1995 — 35
Tim Adams 'The Aberfeldy' 1995 — 40
Tim Adams 'The Fergus' 1996 — 44
Tim Knappstein Cabernet Merlot 1994 — 22
Tim Knappstein Cabernet Merlot 1995 — 22

Tim Knappstein Chardonnay 1995 — 52
Tim Knappstein Sauvignon Blanc
Semillon 1996 — 62
Tim Knappstein "The Franc" 1995 — 43
Tio Pepe — 264
Tisdall Mount Ida Shiraz 1995 — 35
Tokaji 6 Puttonyos Aszu 1981 — 83
Tokaji Aszu 5 Puttonyos 1993 — 83
Tokay Pinot Gris SGN 1992, Domaine
Mittnacht-Klack — 92
Tokay Pinot Gris Vieilles Vignes 1995 — 90
Topolos Piner Heights Zinfandel 1995 — 190
Torre del Falco Murgia Rosso 1995 — 155
Torre Demontalbo 1996 — 250
Torreon de Paredes
Cabernet Sauvignon Reserve 1989, — 238
Torreon de Paredes
Sauvignon Blanc 1996 — 244
Torres Gran Viña Sol 1996 — 259
Torres Mas La Plana 1990 — 257
Torres Mas La Plana 1994 — 257
Torres Milmanda 1995 — 261
Torres Sangre de Toro 1995 — 250
Toso Syrah 1995, Pascual Toso — 231
Touriga Nacional Douro Red 1995 — 208
Trapiche Cabernet Sauvignon
Oak Cask 1993, — 233
Trentham Estate Merlot 1995 — 43
Trentham Estate Noble Taminga 1995 — 65
Tres Candidas Pedro Ximénez — 263
Triere Cabernet Sauvignon 1994 — 182
Trio Chardonnay 1996 — 245
Tunnel Hill Chardonnay 1995 — 56
Tunnel Hill Pinot Noir 1996 — 44
Twin Islands Sauvignon Blanc 1996 — 175
Twin Islands Unwooded Chardonnay
1996, Negociants New Zealand — 169
Two Rivers Sauvignon Semillon 1996 — 102
Tyrrell's Old Winery Chardonnay
Reserve 1996 — 49
Tyrrell's Vat 1 Semillon Reserve 1992 — 61
Tyrrell's Vat 47 Chardonnay Reserve 1996 — 57
Uiterwyk Pinotage 1994 — 226
Undurraga Cabernet Sauvignon
Reserva 1995, Viña Undurraga — 239
Undurraga Gewürztraminer 1996 — 244
Vacqueyras Cuvée de Marquis
de Fonseguille 1995 — 136
Valdivieso Caballo
Loco Numero Uno NV — 242

Valdivieso Caballo Loco NV 243
Valdivieso Cabernet
    Franc Reserve 1995 242
Valdivieso Cabernet Sauvignon 1996 235
Valdivieso Cabernet Sauvignon
    Reserva 1995 240
Valdivieso Merlot 1996, 235
Valdivieso Merlot Reserva 1995 241
Valduero Reserva 1991 256
Valentin Bianchi Malbec Reserve 1991 233
Valpolicella Classico La Grola 1993 157
Valpolicella Classico Palazzo
    della Torre 1993 157
Valpolicella Classico Superiore
    Corteforte 1993 156
Valtellina Sfurzat 1991 158
Valtellina Superiore
    Riserva Grumello 1989 157
Valtellina Superiore
    Riserva Inferno 1989 157
Vasse Felix Cabernet Merlot 1995 24
Vasse Felix Semillon Sauvignon Blanc
    Chardonnay 1996 64
Vavasour Awatere Sauvignon Blanc 1996 178
Vavasour Single
    Vineyard Chardonnay 1996 174
Veenwouden Classic 1996 226
Veenwouden Merlot 1994 227
Vega Sindoa Barrel-Fermented
    Chardonnay 1996 258
Verdicchio Classico Villa Bianchi 1996 161
Verdicchio dei Castelli di Jesi
    Classico San Sisto 1993 161
Vergelegen Cabernet Sauvignon 1995 223
Vergelegen Chardonnay Reserve 1995 229
Vergelegen Sauvignon Blanc 1995 228
Veuve Clicquot Ponsardin Reserve
    Brut Rosé 1989 122
Victoria Reserve
    Cabernet Sauvignon 1994 26
Victoria Reserve Marsanne 1994 64
Vidal Estates Cabernet Merlot 1995 165
Vidal Hawkes Bay Chardonnay 1996,
    Elsie Montgomery 169
Vidal Hawkes Bay Reserve Chardonnay
    1995, Elsie Montgomery 173
Vidal Hawkes Bay Reserve Chardonnay
    1996, Elsie Montgomery 173
Vidal Hawkes Bay Sauvignon Blanc 1996 175
Vieux Château Certan Pomerol 1993 100

Vigna Pedale Castel del Monte 1994 156
Vigneti di Caramia Chardonnay
    Cantele Le Trulle 1996 161
Vila Regia Sogrape 1995 205
Villa Maria Private Bin
    Lightly Oaked Chardonnay 1996 168
Villa Maria Private Bin Riesling 1996 179
Villa Montes Malbec 1996,
    Discover Wines 237
Villa Mount Eden
    Cabernet Sauvignon 1994 185
Villard Reserve Chardonnay 1996 246
Villarta Tempranillo
    Viño de la Tierra 1996 249
Villiera Cru Monro 1995 225
Villiera Merlot 1996 225
Vin de Pays Blanc 1996,
    Jacques Veritier 142
Vin Sec du Château Coutet 1993 103
Viña Arana Reserva 1989 255
Viña Ardanza Reserva 1989 256
Vina Bisquertt Vineyards Merlot 1995,
    Bisquertt Vineyards 236
Vina Calera Sauvignon Blanc 1996 258
Viña Carta Antiguas Selection Cabernet
    Sauvignon 1995 236
Viña Gracia Cabernet Premium 1994 236
Viña Gracia Cabernet Sauvignon 1996 238
Viña Porta Cabernet Sauvignon 1996 239
Viña Porta Cabernet Sauvignon
    Reserva 1995 239
Viña Porta Casa Porta Cabernet
    Sauvignon 1996, Viña Porta 242
Viña Tarapaca Chardonnay 1996 246
Vinal Cayen Chardonnay 1995,
    Bodegas Chandon 233
Vinfruco Oak Village
    Pinotage Merlot 1996 222
Vinho Regional Estemadura Red 1994 204
Vini Santo 1990, Ca'Vit 164
Vinnae Jermann 1996 163
Viognier 1996, Georges Duboeuf 141
Vionta Albariño Reserva 1995 260
Visconde de Ayala Rioja Reserva 1990 250
Viu Manent Cabernet Sauvignon
    Reserve 1993 236
Viu Manent Cabernet Sauvignon
    Reserve 1994, 236
Volnay Clos de la Rougeotte
    1èr Cru 1992 106

Vosne-Romanée Aux Brulees
1èr Cru 1993, Meo-Camuzet 107

Voss Vineyards Sauvignon Blanc 1996 197

Waipara Springs Chardonnay 1995,
Mark & Michelle Rattray 172

Waipara Springs Riesling 1996 179

Waipara West Chardonnay 1995,
Tutton Sienko Hill 171

Waipara West Sauvignon Blanc 1996 177

Wairau River Chardonnay 1994,
Wairau River Wines 171

Wairau River Sauvignon Blanc 1996 177

Waitrose Bordeaux
Sauvignon Blanc 1996 101

Waitrose Mönchhof Zeltinger
Himmelreich QBA 1988 145

Waitrose Pouilly Fumé 1996 132

Waitrose Puligny-Montrachet
1er Cru 1994 110

Wakefield Estate Chardonnay 1995 50

Wakefield Estate Clare Crouchen
Chardonnay 1995 63

Wakefield Estates Riesling 1992 58

Warburn Estate Show
Reserve Shiraz 1996 34

Warre's Quinta da Cavadinha
Vintage Port 1986 217

Warre's Sir William
10 Yr Old Tawny Port 215

Warre's Warrior Finest
Reserve NV Port 212

Water Wheel Vineyards Shiraz 1995 33

Weinert Malbec 1991,
Bodega Y Cavas de Weinert 233

Weingut Kollwentz-Römerhof
Chardonnay von Leithagebirge 1995 72

Weingut Sonnhof Jurtschitsch Grüner
Veltliner Loiserberg 1995 72

Welmoed Chardonnay 1996 228

Welschriesling Ausbruch 1989,
Helmut Lang 75

Welschriesling Ausbruch 1991,
Helmut Lang 74

Welschriesling No.15 Zwischen
den Seen TBA 1995 78

Welschriesling No1 Zwischen
den Seen TBA 1995, Kracher 74

Welschriesling TBA 1994, Helmut Lang 75

Welschriesling TBA 1994, Opitz 79

Welschriesling TBA 1995, Helmut Lang 76

Welschriesling TBA 1995,
Johan Muzenrieder 74

Wente Estate Grown Chardonnay 1995 193

Wente Murrieta's Well Vendimia 1992 187

Wente Riva Ranch Chardonnay 1995 194

William Hill Chardonnay Reserve 1995 195

Wolf Blass Barrel- Fermented
Chardonnay 1996 49

Wolf Blass President's Selection
Cabernet Sauvignon 1994 26

Wolf Blass President's Selection
Chardonnay 1996 55

Wolf Blass President's Selection
Shiraz 1994 36

Wolf Blass Silver Label Reisling 1995 58

Wooldings Vineyard
Quality Sparkling 1994 88

Wyken Sonata 1994 86

Wyndham Estate Bin 777 Semillon
Chardonnay 1996 60

Wynns Chardonnay 1996 50

Wynns Coonawarra Estate Shiraz 1995 31

Wynns Michael Shiraz 1994 41

Xanadu Cabernet Sauvignon 1995 28

Xanadu Chardonnay 1996 57

Yaldara Julians Shiraz 1995 37

Yaldara Old Whitmore Vineyard
Grenache 1996 42

Yaldara Reserve Old Tawny,
Yaldara Wines 69

Yaldara Reserve Shiraz 1996 31

Yaldara The Farms Merlot 1996 47

Yaldara The Farms
Merlot Cabernet 1992 47

Yalumba Cuvée "D" 1994 68

Yalumba Cuvée One Pinot Noir
Chardonnay NV 67

Yalumba Cuvée Two Sparkling
Cabernet NV 67

Yalumba Family Reserve Botrytis
Semillon 1996 65

Yalumba Museum Show Reserve
Rutherglen Muscat 69

Yalumba Reserve Viognier 1996 64

Yalumba "The Menzies" 1993 22

Yalumba 'The Octavius' 1993 40

Yalumba "The Signature" 1993 25

Yarra Valley Shiraz 1994 39

Yvecourt Premium 1995 96

ACKNOWLEDGMENTS

If the International WINE Challenge is the haystack, this guide is the needle. It's taken a while to find it, but here it is, containing the essence of the world's largest wine tasting. Mind you, there was an awful lot of hay - for example, the 6,500 wines tasted generated over 50,000 hand-written tasting notes! We would like to thank the team behind the guide for their dedication and good humour, and wish them well as they return to the 'real world'. By name they are;

• **for their proof reading** - Ann McLain of The New Zealand Wine Guild, Jane Hunt MW of Wines of South Africa, Caroline Park of The Australian Wine Bureau, Jordanis Petridis of the Greek Wine Centre, Michela Pain of the Bulgarian Wine Guild, Venla Freeman of the Wine Institute of California, José Leitao of D&F Wine Shippers, Veronica Chambers of Moreno Wine Shippers and Sarah Murphy of Boutinot Prince.

• **from the International WINE Challenge** - to the team for performing so well under pressure and particularly to the computer boffins and the hand-writing decipherers - we hope your integration back into society is painless. Thanks, also, to all the tasters who gave their time and expertise to help us.

• **from WINE magazine** - Robert Joseph, Charles Metcalfe, Sarah Chapple, Lorna Crosbie-Smith, Alan Scott, Marcin Miller and Damian Riley Smith.

• **for subbing and database management** - special thanks go to the core team of Tom Forrest, Dominic Kelly, Clare 'Mo' de Mowbray, Annelie Grobbelaar and Philip Davis, without whose sweat and tears this Guide would still be no more than a mere twinkle in the eye.

Finally, thanks go to **editor** Chris Mitchell and **sub-editor** James Gabbani for dragging the team through the last few weeks. P.S. Weekends are for play, not work (well, not all the time!).

HOW YOU CAN HELP US

If you have any ideas about how we can improve the format of the
WINE Magazine Pocket Wine Buyer's Guide then please write to us at
652 Victoria Road, South Ruislip, Middlesex, HA4 0SX.

The type of subjects we would particularly like to hear about are:

• **Do you prefer to have countries sub-divided by region or grape variety?**
• **Do you find the £5 and Under guides useful?**
• **Would food and wine pairing suggestions be useful?**
• **How else might you like to see the wines sorted or divided?**
• **What other information regarding wines and stockists would be of interest?**
• **Would you prefer the Guide to be ring-bound or loose leafed?**